P9-AFX-556

BINDING AND FILTERING

Binding and Filtering

Edited by Frank Heny

The MIT Press
Cambridge, Massachusetts
London, England

© 1981 by
F.W. Heny

All rights reserved. No part of this book may be reproduced in any form or by any
means, electronic or mechanical, including photocopying, recording, or by any information storage and retrieval system, without permission in writing from the
publisher.

ISBN 0-262-08117-2

Printed and bound in Great Britain
by Billing and Sons Limited
Guildford, London, Oxford, Worcester

Contents

P158
B56
1981

Preface

This volume started out as a collection of papers from the GLOW Colloquium on Local Processes held at the University of Amsterdam, 7–9 April 1978; not a proceedings, exactly, since a number of the participants had already decided to publish their contributions elsewhere, but a collection of at least some of the others.

Editorial work on the volume brought me to a realisation of the far-reaching implications of the approach to linguistic analysis underlying Chomsky's 'On Binding'. It constitutes a radical break with his previous work, of a very exciting and promising kind. Since the bases of the new theory seemed far from transparent, and rather hard to derive from the papers that had been written within that framework, I felt it worthwhile to try to introduce the collection with an account of what I took to be the really striking new properties of this framework. I hoped also that a reasonably detailed introduction would make the papers accessible to a significantly wider audience. Other commitments and accidents intervened persistently and the book has been inordinately delayed. The introduction, too, insisted on growing beyond all reasonable bounds. That will be justified if it makes the collection more accessible, or the bases of the Binding framework a little clearer.

Whatever the negative effects of the delay, it has undoubtedly had some positive effects. On the way through the editorial process, the papers by Harlow and Reuland were picked up, and several of the original contributions were fundamentally changed, some as a result of modifications that have been made to the Binding framework itself. As a result, the book includes widely different perspectives. Although all but the last two papers in the volume (which are more concerned with filters) explicitly take some syntactic framework related to 'On Binding' as their basis, each takes off in a different direction, and from a different point in time. That is as it should be, for the theory itself has undergone many changes during the last two years, and precisely where it will all end up is still unclear in detail.

The paper which started it all, Chomsky's 'On Binding', (OB) was added at a very late stage, but it is highly appropriate that this paper should be reprinted here. I am grateful to Noam Chomsky for agreeing to this, and to the MIT Press for permission to use it. The paper appears here essentially unchanged from the original version in *Linguistic Inquiry* 11, 1 (Winter, 1980).

Of the other papers, several were completed during the writing of OB. That by George and Kornfilt is one of these. Because of its early date it does not in fact adopt the OB theory explicitly but a theory more akin to Chomsky's 'On *Wh*-Movement'. Rizzi's paper appears here in essentials unchanged from the version he read in April 1978. Reuland's paper was written largely in 1979, independently of the changes which were then being made to the theory during the Pisa workshop; it reflects many of the same concerns as those which motivated those changes. Kayne's paper was originally written for the GLOW conference but was later quite substantially altered to take account of the 'Pisa' changes. Harlow's paper is even later. It began in a version which just predated Pisa, but as published here was re-written so that it falls squarely within that later framework. Thus these papers present a chronological picture of the development of the Binding framework from just before it really began right up to almost the present time.

The paper by Maling and Zaenen, like Rizzi's, is published almost as it was given at the conference. It reflects strongly the interest at that time in the role of filters in the Extended Standard Theory, an interest which is now probably better represented in 'lexical' grammar than in the further direct developments of OB itself. Muysken's paper, too, addresses issues which have not yet become central in the OB framework — though it has been considerably re-written since it was given at the conference.

I should like to thank Jet van Everdingen and Hennie Zondervan-Kimsma for help with typing and other related chores, and also those of the authors who have waited long and (fairly) patiently for their work to appear.

Frank Heny

Introduction*

1. The Theoretical Background

The Grammatical Transformation, as defined in Chomsky (1955), embodies a number of implicit theoretical claims. Each classical transformation consists of two parts: the Structural Description (SD) and the Structural Change (SC). The first, which determines the set of trees to which the transformation applies, does so by means of a linear factorisation of tree structure. The second, which defines the nature of the change effected by the rule, does this by specifying for each element of the factorisation constituting the SD of the rule what changes, if any, need to be made under transformation. Described in this way, the formalism can be rather naturally viewed as making the following implicit claims: the structural characterisation of the set of input trees by the SD represents a significant unit; the complex of operations defining the SC represents a significant unit; and since the latter is crucially derived from the former, the relation between SD and SC is also significant.

An example might help to clarify at least some of this. One very common version of the English Passive rule was roughly as follows:

(1)	SD	NP	AUX	V	NP
		1	2	3	4
	SC	4	2+be+en	3	by+1

Since the elements NP-AUX-V-NP in that order were used to define the input to the rule, it is *prima facie* reasonable to suppose that this sequence itself was thereby represented as significant. Likewise the complex of operations which make up the change (the whole complex operation in which the fourth element moves to the first position, with the insertion of the two elements after the second term of the SD and so on) seems to be represented as a single significant

1

unit. And finally, since this complex change was specifically linked by the theory to the sequence represented in the SD, i.e. NP-AUX-V-NP, then it is not in fact just the movement of *any* fourth term to the position occupied by the first (etc.) that is assigned significance by this representation; it is the movement of the fourth term to the first position when both are noun phrases — and all the other conditions are satisfied. This must count as a significant theoretical unit.

We are of course free to assume that certain aspects of the representation lack significance. Perhaps we *must* assume that *some* do. But we *cannot* assume that *all* do; for the purpose of adopting a theoretical framework is to be able to make systematic claims about what is significant. So we must assume, until told specifically that this is not so, that the explicit representation of a relationship amounts to an implicit claim that this relationship is significant. We do not incorporate the notion Grammatical Transformation into a theory, requiring that analyses be made in terms of these theoretically-defined objects, without thereby implying that there is something significant about the kinds of relationship that this kind of rule is especially suited to capturing.

But just what is it in the transformation that is significant? What properties of the SD, for example, characterise (1) as 'natural'? The theory did not tell us. It incorporated no claims to the effect that certain sequences were more 'natural', others 'impossible'; and did not even define which sequences counted as 'the same'. Would a Grammatical Transformation with the SD NP-AUX-V-Adj count as 'the same' as (1)? Presumably not. But what if an optional adverb node were permitted between the second and third terms of (1)? Some changes seem more relevant than others, and yet no well motivated way of distinguishing them emerges from a theory based on rules like (1). Such problems can be profitably rephrased in terms of language acquisition. Would a learner 'expect' to find the English Passive rule in a language, while not 'expecting' a rule just the same in all respects but with the fourth term of the SD 'Adj'? If not, what might determine, within the theory, that such a rule would be less natural? Viewed as a sequence of nodes, NP-AUX-V-Adj has no obvious properties which might be used to distinguish it from the SD of (1). There are in fact no obvious leads in this direction, which will permit us to analyse Grammatical Transformations so as to distinguish between them on the basis of smaller analytical units. If the Passive rule is really to be defined as in (1), it is one of the smallest meaningful units on the transformational level. Any attempt to extract significant sub-transformational elements simply ends up in confusion and questions of the sort we have been trying to frame cannot be asked coherently. The Passive is essentially an un-analysable whole. The SC is meaningless without the SD, the latter without (some of — but which of?) its parts.

If that is true, then it is not surprising that attempts to ask questions about the cross-linguistic significance of transformations made little headway while the classical transformation formed the core of grammatical theory.[1] During the late 1960s it is true that various assumptions began to be made which had the effect of excluding certain otherwise possible SDs or SCs. In particular the idea that cyclical transformations must be structure preserving began to enjoy widespread acceptance,[2] and this alone was enough to prevent the fourth term of rule (1) from having the value 'Adj'. It also meant that the only possible movement that could occur in (1) would involve the first and fourth terms. But while this began to narrow the possibilities, it made no contribution to the deeper problem. The basic meaningful elements of the theory (those which captured the significant relationships) remained the Grammatical Transformations, rules directly reflecting the apparent properties of traditionally recognised 'grammatical constructions'. As long as this remained so, no amount of restriction could yield the analytical tools required to ask meaningful questions about those trans-formations on a deeper level. These complex transformations being the minimal significant units on the transformational level, one could expect no general answers. And the theory remained com-mitted to the claim that specific structural relations between sentence pairs (relations like the Active-Passive relation) were the only, or at least most, significant properties that characterise natural language. There was no fruitful way of asking why that should be so, and seeking more fundamental properties of language.

During the last eight years there has been a radical change.[3] The full significance of this has not yet been realised, even by those working within the new framework. Many linguists still notice only that in the work of Chomsky and of others following his lead there apparently has been a proliferation of levels, abstract elements, over-generation, filters and so on, accompanied by a significant reduction, it seems, in the number of transformations; as if a series of minor, and perhaps dubious, changes had been made, in a basically unchanged framework. This illusion has perhaps been fostered in part by the name which has sometimes been given to work in the new framework. At least until very recently, it was common for proponents of the theory to refer to it as the (Revised) Extended Standard Theory — as if it were no more than a revision of the theory of Aspects (Chomsky, 1965). There have indeed been a series of minor changes, with the theory of Aspects as the starting point, and no clear dividing line. But, I want to argue here, what has emerged is a totally new theory. The kinds of claims it can make about what is significant in natural language differ fundamentally from the kinds of claims that could be made in the theory of Aspects. And (though this remains contentious) the newer claims seem in principle a good deal more interesting and fruitful than the older ones. They seem, on reflection, more plausible, too.

The foundations of the new approach, which I shall call the Binding theory, thereby emphasising what all the different versions seem to have in common, are still comparatively little understood. In introducing a collection of papers, all of which have some affinity to the Binding theory and most of which accept some version as their basis, it seems worth trying to explore the specific methodological bases of the theory itself. Whatever the temporary empirical fruitfulness of the theory, it will ultimately be the conceptual framework that will have to provide a basis for further expansion and (to the extent that that is ever possible) validation of this approach. To explore this aspect of the theory, even to try and lay out as clearly as possible what seem to be its principal characteristics, I shall be forced to assign theoretical significance explicitly to parts of the apparatus. In doing so I shall certainly make decisions which are at variance with the original intentions of the authors of those ideas; more important I shall undoubtedly often be proved wrong. It is important that what follows be seen simply as one possible interpretation of these developments. Hopefully, it will encourage further reflection on the significance of what is happening in 'transformational' grammar.

2. Binding

The most obvious characteristic of the analyses offered here is that they make scarcely any use at all of complex rules like the Passive transformation given in (1). Even when they depend on operations that effect changes in constituent structure comparable to that effected by an 'elementary transformation' in Chomsky (1955) — by moving constituents, deleting them etc. — the syntactic transformations employed in these papers are not at all comparable to the Grammatical Transformations of the older transformational frameworks. Most crucially, these new rules simply do not include any component comparable in complexity to the detailed tree factorisations (SDs) which formed the basis of each such Grammatical Transformation — like the Passive. Hence, even though the operations which are assumed in the new theory, most notably movement, may seem to have just the same effect as elementary transformations on trees to which they are applied, nevertheless they differ fundamentally in significance from the Grammatical Transformations. There are, in fact, no direct counterparts of the latter. There are no rules of significance which can map a set of *structurally identified* trees onto another set. So there are no rules which implicitly represent the claim that a structural relationship of that sort is linguistically significant.

It would be a serious conceptual error to regard this change as just a reduction in the complexity of the transformations — in particular in the complexity of the conditions required to ensure proper application. It would be equally mistaken to suggest that since these rules presuppose various output conditions if they are to work effectively, the theory as a whole is simply a notational variant of the older one. For the primitives, which are used to express linguistically-significant generalisations, have changed so fundamentally that it seems unlikely that any of the more important claims made by either theory is also made by the other — or indeed *could* be made by the other. Instead of seeking generalisations about linguistic structure expressible as complex relations between entire subtrees, this theory seeks, as we shall see, very different generalisations. It would, as a result, be very hard to represent the active-passive relation as a distinct relation between two 'sentence-types' in this theory. Whereas that sort of claim lay at the very heart of the classical theory of transformational grammar. The orientation towards a direct representation of traditional 'grammatical constructions' has quite disappeared.

It is time to consider, more positively, what kinds of generalisation are now possible candidates for representation, and the mechanisms which are available in the Binding framework. The really significant component now consists of a set of well-formedness conditions. It is these, and not the rules, that have the sort of richness and complexity which makes it possible to express claims about what is linguistically significant. Naturally, this theory must have enough power to correctly describe the same kinds of data as the earlier one; it simply selects quite different ways of generalising about that data. Very crudely, the complex transformations have been replaced by simple, unanalysable and unconstrained rules applying to deep structures, and by two sets of filtering devices applying to the output: the conditions already mentioned, and the filters proper. Leaving the filters until later, we turn to the conditions.

Most of these, probably all, have the effect of limiting the domain within which an interpretive dependency may, or must, exist unresolved. If we understand 'anaphor' in a rather wide sense, then they set principled limits upon where an anaphor may or must find an antecedent. Given that, then we might expect that unlike the earlier transformations, the conditions will make reference not to linear sequences of terms but rather to different kinds of boundaries. And that is in general the case. Of course, they also make reference to different kinds of anaphors, or as we shall call them henceforth *dependent terms*. (It will be convenient to reserve the term 'anaphor' for a sub-type of dependent term.) Naturally we should expect of a theory, in which such constructs as these formed the basic significant counters, that it would offer fundamentally different analyses of the data from one based upon the classical transformations. Again, this is in fact the case. Consider the following examples:

(2) a.   The children said that <u>they</u> were happy.
     b.   The children punched <u>each other</u>.
     c.   The children tried ____ to swim.
     d.   The children seemed ____ to be happy.
     e.   Who did the children see ____ .
     f.   The children were happier than their parents were ____ .

Each of these sentences contains a dependent term of some sort, underlined in (2). Sometimes this term is just a 'gap', sometimes it is a lexical item of a special sort, which must or may become linked to an antecedent upon which it is in some way dependent for its full interpretation. Given a theory based upon classical transformations and committed to expressing significant generalisations by means of these constructs, there is no special reason to expect this group of sentences to possess any interesting properties in common. Nor should the dependent terms in them display any interesting shared properties.

In fact, the classical theory, at least in the earlier versions, derived each of these sentences by the application of a distinct, unrelated complex transformation. Most versions of transformational grammar would have derived (2a–f) by the application of Pronominalisation, *Each*-movement, Equi, Raising, *Wh* Movement, and Comparative Deletion respectively. Such analyses would naturally lead us to look for interesting generalisations, if any, in common factors in the SD or SC of these rules. Looking further afield, we might expect cross-linguistic generalisations to be represented by some kind of similarities in the SDs or SCs of these distinct rules in a number of languages. No special significance could be attached by such a theory to the fact that the surface forms of all these sentences contains a lexical or null dependent term. The trouble (looking back now with the benefit of hindsight) is that none of the 'expected' kinds of cross-linguistic generalisation ever emerged from the grammars of different languages, no interesting common properties can be isolated when the transformations are examined.

In contrast, a single set of conditions affecting the resolution of dependencies might well be expected to establish some quite specific relations between the elements underlined in (2). And that is exactly what the theory of Binding has set out to do. Just what kinds of constraints might need to be imposed upon such terms? Restricting attention to the pronoun *they* in (2a) and the reciprocal, *each other*, in (2b), let us see what kinds of observation might be relevant. We observe, first, that the dependent term is never 'higher' in structure than its antecedent. Thus neither can be interpreted as dependent on *the children* in

(3)   Mary told $\begin{Bmatrix} them \\ each\ other \end{Bmatrix}$ that the children were happy.

When a dependent term is in subject position, this requirement that the antecedent be at least as high means that any acceptable antecedent will have to be in the next S up, for the subject is the 'highest' NP in an S, being directly dominated by it. So we would expect that neither dependent term can take *the children* as antecedent in the following:

(4)   Mary said that $\begin{Bmatrix} they \\ each\ other \end{Bmatrix}$ liked the children.

While already suggesting that *they* and *each other* possess interesting properties in common, these examples are also enough to demonstrate effectively that they are not quite alike with respect to how they resolve dependency. In neither of the above examples can the dependent term find an antecedent within the sentence in question. Thus far, *they/them* and *each other* are alike; where they differ is that while *they/them* can be understood in a non-dependent sense, *each other* cannot function at all without an antecedent. There are, of course, many other ways in which these two kinds of element function in very different ways, some of which we discuss directly.

What is striking is not, in fact, that they behave alike — for they don't — but that despite fundamental differences they exhibit interesting, persistent co-variance. When we interchange these two terms in (2a) and (2b) (where both had dependent readings) we find further evidence for this co-variance; for then neither term has a dependent reading:

(2′) a. *The children said that *each other* were happy.
 b. The children punched *them*.

What determines whether or not a dependent reading is possible? From these and many other similar examples, we might postulate that *they* is able to assume a dependent reading only when a potential antecedent occurs in a higher sentence — and that *each other* is barred from occurring with an antecedent in such environments. Such an analysis is supported by the following:

(5) a. The children said that Mary helped $\begin{Bmatrix} each\ other \\ them \end{Bmatrix}$.

 b. The children wanted Mary to help $\begin{Bmatrix} each\ other \\ them \end{Bmatrix}$.

Thus, we might suppose that the dependency of *each other* must be resolved within a minimal clause, while that of *they* must not — the antecedent being in either event 'higher' than the term dependent on it.

However, there are examples which are hard to reconcile with this simple analysis:

(6) The children wanted $\left[_{\bar{S}} \begin{Bmatrix} them \\ each\ other \end{Bmatrix} \text{to be happy} \right]$.

Despite the fact that the potentially dependent phrases are (at least arguably) in the lower clause, being its subject, *each other* can be dependent on *the children* while *them* cannot. We might therefore suggest, on the basis of (6), that the subject of an infinitive simply acts as if it were part of the higher clause. But that is still somewhat over-simplified:

(7)   The children tried $\left[_\text{S} \underline{\quad\quad} \text{to hit} \begin{Bmatrix} them \\ each\ other \end{Bmatrix}\right]$.

Assuming that the infinitive here is not just a VP, then the subject of the lower sentence is itself dependent, a gap of some kind, marked by '_____', which is dependent on the subject of the higher clause, *the children*. Without an account of whether gaps like this behave like *them* or *each other* we cannot yet say whether this supports the hypothesis that the subject of an infinitive is in effect part of the higher clause; but the following facts show clearly that it is not. While *each other* can be dependent on the gap, and hence indirectly on *the children*, the pronoun *they* cannot be dependent on *the children*. In order to acquire a reading in which it were read as if dependent on *the children* it would in fact have to be dependent on the gap — which is in its own clause. Hence, the dependency of *them* would in effect have been resolved within a minimal clause, contrary to the postulated restrictions. Thus the behaviour of both *them* and *each other* in (7) is perfectly regular, provided the subject of an infinitive is in general in the lower clause — as one might expect. Examples like (8) confirm the general correctness of this supposition: since *the children* can be the antecedent of *each other* and not of *them*.

(8)   Mary wanted $\left[_\text{S} \text{the children to like} \begin{Bmatrix} them \\ each\ other \end{Bmatrix}\right]$.

To sum up, the very general hypothesis that while *each other* must find an antecedent higher in its own clause while *they* may not be read so as to be dependent on an antecedent in its own clause runs into difficulties with examples like (6), where the subject of an infinitive appears to act as if in the higher clause although, as examples like (7) and (8) show, it cannot be analysed in general as part of that clause.

That the subject of an infinitive will have to be assigned a special

status by any theory attempting to account for such phenomena is
shown by other facts. 'Gaps' like those in (10c) and (7) can occur
only in that position:

(9) a. *John tried Bill to punch _____ .
     b. *John hopes that _____ punches Bill.

No examples like (9) are found. Likewise, the 'gap' left by movement
must be in the subject of an infinitive if the moved phrase has gone to
a higher sentence.

(10) a. John seems [s _____ to like Mary].
      b. *Mary seems [s John to like _____].
      c. *John seems [s that _____ likes Mary].

Neither movement from the object of an infinitive (10b) nor from the
subject of a tensed S (10c) yields an acceptable output.

  If (as suggested in regard to the examples of (2)) the gaps
associated with verbs like *try* and those resulting from movement are
treated as dependent terms, and more specifically if they are treated
as like *each other* rather than like *them*, then the acceptability of the
gap in (7) but not in (9a,b), and the acceptability of the gap in (10a)
but not in (10b) or (10c) will turn out to be just the same
phenomenon as the acceptability of (6): the dependency in question
must be resolved within a minimal clause — and the subject of an
infinitive acts *for certain purposes* (as in (6), (7) and (10a)) as if it
were in the higher clause. A theory seeking general restrictions on
the domains within which dependencies must be resolved will have
to account for this special status of the subjects of infinitives, while
giving due weight to the behaviour of *them* and *each other* in
sentences like (7) and (8), where the infinitive subject seems part of
its own clause.

  The Binding conditions, which form the heart of the new
framework, are intended to capture the necessary restrictions on the
resolution of dependency, reflecting the special status of infinitive
subjects. The structural properties of sentences need to provide a
basis for the definition of these Binding conditions rather than (as
was previously the case) forming the basis for appropriate Structural
Descriptions defining the input to Grammatical Transformations.
The most significant relation between constituents, which underlies
the Binding conditions — and other derivative notions — is that of

c-command. A node α *c*-commands another, β, if β is dominated by the first branching node dominating α and α does not contain β. If α *c*-commands β, then β is in the *domain* of α.

We must assume that the phrase structure rules assign to sentences an appropriate underlying structure, and that (whatever occurs between the initial trees and that level on which the conditions are applicable) sufficient hierarchical structure remains at the stage where conditions apply to permit the appropriate structural relations to hold at that level. In addition, it is necessary to assume that at some point in the derivation, Case is assigned to certain NPs. This is not itself directly a structural relation between nodes but is a property of the NP in question which is assigned in part on the basis of its structural relations to other nodes. Saving the details for later, we need only assume that the subject of a Tensed-S (but not an infinitive) has Nominative Case at the relevant level, to permit a general formulation of the *Binding Conditions* along the following lines:

(11) a. *Command:* a dependent term must be in the domain of its antecedent.
b. *Nominative Island Constraint:* A Nominative anaphor cannot be free in $\bar{S}$.
c. *Opacity:* An anaphor in the domain of the subject of a phrase cannot be free in that phrase.

We are explicitly making a distinction in (11) between 'dependent terms' in general and 'anaphors'. Both *they* and *each other* are dependent terms; only *each other* is an anaphor. Thus only (11a) applies to pronouns like *they*.

Command prevents any dependent term from acquiring an antecedent lower than itself. The Nominative Island Constraint (NIC) prevents *each other* from occurring as subject of a Tensed-S, thus ruling out (2'a), and together with Command, (4). Opacity prevents *each other* in (5a,b) from 'waiting' until the higher S makes *the children* available as antecedent. The effect of NIC and Opacity together is that virtually all anaphors must find an antecedent in their own minimal clause, but since neither applies to the subject of an infinitive, the appropriate NP being neither Nominative nor in the domain of a subject in its own $\bar{S}$, nothing forces *each other* to find an antecedent in (6), until the next $\bar{S}$. Hence, it may take *the children* as antecedent. In the same way, if the 'missing' subject of the lower sentence in (7) or (10) is treated as an anaphor, then this dependency, too, may remain unresolved until the higher S, since the anaphor, being subject of an infinitive, is neither a nominative anaphor nor in the domain of a subject. Once again, a noun phrase in the higher sentence may serve as antecedent — but this time as antecedent of a 'gap'. The Binding conditions, in the very rough form given above, provide quite a general account of the properties of anaphors.

While the Binding conditions thus account rather systematically for the domains in which the dependency of anaphors must be resolved, they do not, in the form given in (11), apply immediately to pronouns. Neither NIC, nor Opacity (which together are sometimes called the 'Opacity Conditions') applies to pronouns. They cannot be easily made to do so. Pronouns are in fact *only* able to take as antecedent a phrase which if they were anaphors would be excluded by the Opacity conditions from their possible antecedents. (Hence the complementary behaviour between anaphors and pronouns already observed.) In more recent work in the Binding framework, a satisfactory general way has been found of capturing this obviously significant relationship between pronouns and anaphors, as we shall see. Postponing discussion of the details and assuming that the Binding conditions in some form permit a general account which extends perfectly naturally to pronouns, let us return to more general matters.

We set out to compare the newer framework with that of classical transformational grammar in some form. It was suggested that this newer account was in some way preferable *in principle* to the older account. One way in which that seems to be the case might be presented as follows. Aside from any empirical superiority of the Binding theory, it brings together a number of phenomena which involve dependent phrases, and does so by treating as a natural class all those elements which depend for their interpretation on some phrase elsewhere in structure. Formerly, the structural relationships expressible by Grammatical Transformations were the basic, significant elements. What we have isolated here as systematic constraints on the resolution of dependency simply resulted in the older theory from the interaction of rules designed to capture structural relations having nothing intrinsically to do with dependency. Given only that a theory has the effect of isolating a class of elements and predicting, as an automatic consequence of the structure of that theory, considerable underlying systematicity in their behaviour, and that this predicted systematicity is indeed observed, then this would already constitute *prima facie* grounds for taking that theory seriously.

There are in fact more positive grounds for thinking that the specific class distinguished by the Binding theory has some real significance. Hence, aside from any interesting empirical generalisations which emerge from this approach, there seem to be some quite general considerations which may provide independent motivation for a theory in which conditions like those outlined in (11) play a prominent role. This possible motivation has received rather little attention in the literature, so I will summarise what seem to me to be the main lines of the argument.

The basis of this is the well-known principle of *compositionality*, which goes back, at least, to Frege.[4] One way of stating this principle is that the meaning of the whole is a function of the meaning of its parts. While this remains rather vague, it will do for the present. The idea is that in any approach to semantics, meaning must be built up systematically, the contribution of each component being fixed, and the meaning of each intermediate structural unit being composed out of the meaning of its parts and serving as the input (as a single, unanalysed unit) to the formation of the meaning of whatever is the 'whole' on the next level up. In artificial languages, like those constructed purely on the basis of categorial grammars, or the fragments of English for which Montague gave categorial grammars,[5] this compositionality is automatically built into the syntax — and hence into the semantics. The structural units are formed by rules which in most cases are paired with semantic rules having the effect of applying the meaning of one syntactically combined 'part' as a function to the meaning of the other(s) — to yield the meaning of the 'whole'. If this occurs at each stage, of course, then the meaning cannot but be compositional in every respect. However, it is far from obvious how this principle is to be applied in general to natural languages.

The basic problem is that one simply does not start out with an analysis of the language into given 'parts' and 'wholes' and the meanings associated with what seem from one point of view like independent parts act as if they depend on each other. To return, for example, to the kinds of sentences we have been discussing, we do not know in advance at what stage the meaning of *each other*, or a reflexive, or a 'gap' must be treated as a 'part' that must be combined with other parts to form a 'whole'. If we could wait until the level of the very top sentence in each case, before combining *each other* with other elements, it would only form a 'part' of that sentence, and any antecedent in that sentence would obviously be available for combining with it. At the other extreme, if the VP is a significant structural unit, which counts as a 'whole' which has to be semantically composed before becoming in turn a part of the sentence in which it occurs, then there will be no obvious way of giving a strictly compositional semantics of a sentence like *The children* [*punched each other*]. The meaning of the anaphor *each other* will have been combined with that of *punched* to form a semantic unit corresponding to the VP *punched each other* before the antecedent of *each other* becomes available. Thus the VP seems to be automatically ruled out, as the level at which *each other* must lose its semantic identity, and form a part of an unanalysed whole; if this phrase, and other anaphors, are really semantically dependent in some way on their antecedents, then they must obviously remain semantically available until the stage at which their antecedents appear. Could it be the case, however, that the interpretation of the elements of a natural language is simply delayed until, if necessary, the very top sentence level? That is, does the other extreme make any theoretical sense? That seems most unlikely. Apart from anything else, there is every reason to believe that embedded sentences and phrases have some kind of meaning of their own. If so, they must represent intermediate semantic units, suggesting that there must be intermediate levels at which meanings are composed. In any case, since there is no principled limit to the length of a sentence, we should have to suppose that the semantic rules were capable of combining unlimited numbers of elements at a single stroke to form sentential meanings. It seems clear that this alternative simply could not be made to work. Again, there must be some intermediate stage at which *each other* is semantically composed with the other available parts to form a complex, unanalysed whole.

And that is where the Binding conditions come in. Opacity and NIC, even in the very rough form outlined above, can easily be interpreted as setting bounds upon the domains within which anaphoric elements may persist with unresolved dependencies.[6] NIC requires that any anaphoric dependency originating in a position assigned Nominative Case, such as the subject of a Tensed-S, be resolved before the next S̄ boundary (thus in effect prohibiting Nominative terms from being anaphoric). Opacity requires resolution of all other anaphoric dependencies before the next NP or S̄ boundary. With the one important exception of the subject of an infinitive, all anaphoric dependencies will have been resolved before the next S̄ (or, if one intervenes, NP). In other words, every S̄ and NP, with certain specific exceptions, is a fully composed semantic unit. At any higher point in structure, no part of that unit is analysable as a distinct sub-part of a higher level whole.

As a general rule, it is probably inadvisable to offer plausibility arguments in favour of one theory or grammatical model as opposed to another; they should obviously be treated with some caution. Nevertheless, it seems worth remarking upon the potential significance of this interpretation of the Binding conditions within a theory of language learning. The task of a language learner would be markedly simpler if he or she were to approach unanalysed language data with explicit, narrowly variable bounds on the domains within which non-resolved dependencies, and hence not strictly compositional interpretation, were permitted. It is by no means unreasonable to suppose that a set of conditions defining these bounds might form the core of the universally available cognitive apparatus with which the language learner approaches unanalysed language data. In fact, it would be difficult to imagine a more useful tool, in the circumstances since it would provide an immediate clue to the semantically-relevant units. Whereas the theory based upon Grammatical Transformations implicitly made the claim that the analytical parameters determining the learner's task involved structural relations between sentences (such as that represented in (1) above), the Binding framework claims in effect that language learning is guided by a set of highly restrictive conditions defining the bounds of non-compositional interpretation. It is likely that the availability of a highly restrictive framework of this sort, within which the boundaries of semantic 'wholes' are immediately determined, would greatly facilitate learning.

Let us turn from such speculative matters to the Binding theory itself again, and to the apparent non-compositionality of such dependent terms as anaphors, which the Opacity conditions restrict. It was noticed earlier that if the VP phrase in a sentence like *The children punched each other* were to be treated as a structural unit by the semantic rules (whatever those turn out to be) then the anaphor would cease to be available as a dependent above the VP level since it would cease to be a semantically-independent unit once the VP had been treated as a 'whole'. Opacity requires only that *each other* not be still dependent at the S̄ boundary. The condition does not determine what we do with the VP. Some provision must be made to permit the anaphor and antecedent to be related. One of three possibilities must be chosen: (1) the VP is not treated as a semantically relevant 'whole', the constituents there being carried on up to sentence level, or (2) some way is developed of permitting the semantics to 'look down' into an already composed VP-level semantic unit, or (3) the VP is interpreted in such a way that when the subject *the children* is added on at the next level up, it is able to interact appropriately with the VP as a whole so as to yield the same effect as if it 'looked down'. Lest this seem too mysterious, we should compare this last alternative with the use of variables to solve a comparable problem of compositionality in formal languages.

A formula containing only free variables, like $Px \& Qx$ may at any later stage, have a quantifier added to bind the variables, yielding for example $Vx (Px \& Qx)$. When this is interpreted, we seem perhaps to be proceeding without due regard to the requirement of compositional interpretation: does not the quantifier have to 'dip down' inside the smaller expression in order to access the variable — or whatever corresponds to that variable — if it is to bind it at every point *inside* the expression? That is precisely what is *not* going on. The variables allow us to construct a meaning for the entire unquantified expression such that it interacts appropriately as a unit with the quantifier. It is not necessary to de-compose the meaning of the open sentence in order to add the quantifier, precisely because the meaning of that open sentence as a unit is such that the meanings corresponding to the positions occupied by the variable are appropriately distinguished at the level of that open sentence (and every higher structural level). In this way, the variables are always available for binding, without any de-composition of existing units. It is in this way, too, that lambda-operators binding variables in an expression permit what appear superficially to be non-compositional analyses.

For many reasons, it seems likely that if dependent terms have to be semantically available at a higher structural level than that on which they superficially appear, then either semantic composition must somehow be delayed until an appropriate antecedent appears, or else dependent expressions are incorporated into the intermediate structural units by means of variables. In other words we can safely ignore the possibility that existing, fully composed units must later be de-composed. Practically, what this means is that either there will have to be a mechanism for delaying the composition of the elements of a VP (as in *The children punched each other*) or of the whole lower infinitive S (as in *The children wanted each other to be happy*) until an appropriate higher level is reached: or something like variables will have to be employed in the interpretation of anaphors.

This is not the place to explore these two alternatives in detail. What is important is to notice how the Opacity conditions could become relevant. Under an account in which variables were used, those conditions would have the effect of requiring that an appropriate quantifier be found *before the relevant $\bar{S}$ were passed*, while under the alternative in which composition is delayed, the conditions would simply insist on proper compositional interpretation, while having the effect of removing the VP (or, when an infinitive sentence has an anaphoric subject, the $\bar{S}$ itself) so that the relevant compositional unit was the next one up. In either event, the effect of the conditions is such that the power added to a formal language by the incorporation of variables is severely limited. In the predicate calculus, an unlimited number of distinct variables are available and these can all be bound by quantifiers an unlimited distance away. Even if some kind of variable-like mechanism is necessary for the proper interpretation of anaphors, the resulting variable will always be locally bound. In terms of language learning, what this means is that the learner approaches the data knowing that anaphors are not like free variables waiting to be bound at an unlimited distance away. It also suggests that any device with the full power of quantification theory, like the standard predicate calculus, may not provide the most appropriate model for the semantic analysis of these expressions, since it will be far more powerful than is required. But that aspect of the matter can be left unexplored on this occasion.

Given an account of the Binding conditions which attributes such significance to them, can we extend it to the other dependent terms like pronouns, the traces of moved phrases, and so on, which have so far been left out? Although the Opacity conditions of (11) do not immediately apply to pronouns, an appropriate extension would have the effect of preventing the resolution of a pronoun dependency until the next level up, where the relevant levels are those required by the account of anaphors just given. One effect of this is that pronouns will never be able to take as antecedent a phrase which could be antecedent of an anaphor occurring in the same position. Obviously this will contribute further to reducing the problem faced by the learner, restricting the ways in which there can be interaction between elements that are problematic from the point of view of strictly compositional semantics. Once again, this probably means that the full power of quantification theory is not required in order to yield a satisfactory account of the pronouns — for like the anaphors they can relate only to antecedents in a restricted way rather than being, like the variables of quantification theory, available for binding at any point by any quantifier-like operator. It is an interesting open question precisely what device would introduce the requisite power without adding more than is needed. Whatever that turns out to be, it is clear that the Opacity conditions have the effect of significantly reducing the options open for the resolution of dependency, and in turn most likely reducing the power necessary in the semantics, and hence the task of the learner.

We have not yet discussed the interaction of *Wh* Movement with the Binding conditions, and will postpone a detailed discussion till the next section. Some brief remarks along the lines of those above might however not be out of place. Suppose that *Wh* Movement leaves a *Wh*-brace, which is a dependent term, at the left boundary of every S̄. Then this might be seen as guaranteeing an unbroken chain of structures, each of the form '*wh*-trace + *S̄-with-a-gap*'. Once again, we might suppose that a fully compositional account could be given of each S̄ such that the full power of quantification theory need not be invoked.

While these suggestions for a semantic underpinning of aspects of the Binding theory are necessarily brief and quite speculative, they are, I hope, enough to suggest strongly that it would be natural for the syntactic framework with which a learner approaches his or her task to incorporate devices severely limiting the freedom of dependent elements.

3. The OB Framework

Chomsky's 'On Binding', which is reprinted as the first paper of this collection, lays the foundation for the theory of Binding. It provides the first detailed statement of the new approach, after a long period in which various attempts were being made to modify the classical *Aspects* framework to cope adequately with problems that had emerged. The most notable addition had probably been the indexed 'traces' which the classical movement rules were now assumed to leave behind, making possible the assumption that semantic interpretation could be carried out on surface structures.[7] Prior to the development of the OB framework itself the theory could be properly regarded as no more than an extended and modified form of the standard Aspects framework. The developments that have taken place since OB on the other hand, must be regarded as extensions and modifications not of Aspects but of the Binding framework — which as has already been pointed out, differs (in all its variations) more fundamentally from Aspects, even in the trace-enriched versions, than Aspects did from Syntactic Structures. Whatever modifications have been and are being made to OB, the basic framework remains in crucial ways constant. In the other papers in this book, many modifications to the basic theory will be encountered. The essentials of OB remain at the heart of all these versions of the theory, and it is necessary to describe them briefly in order to place the Binding conditions in their proper context.

Three distinct sets of well-formedness conditions make up the principal components of the OB framework. Each applies on a different level. At deep structure, the appropriate sub-categorial restrictions associated with lexical items form the first of those sets of well-formedness conditions. In this, the model differs little from the classical transformational one, but the sub-categorial requirements of the head of a phrase may be met equally well by empty or lexically filled phrases.

The other two sets of well-formedness conditions are the Filters and the Conditions on binding etc. like those discussed earlier. Each set of conditions applies at the extremity of one branch of the grammar. The Filters apply at 'superficial' or surface structure, while the Binding conditions apply at what has been called Logical Form (LF). The three branches of the grammar meet in a level at which Case is assigned. This level is called 'surface' structure in OB, but it is much more abstract than the classical surface structure. This level has sometimes been called S-structure. Linking S-structure to the levels at which the well-formedness conditions apply, are a number of different kinds of rules, which have the effect that the well-formedness conditions and the Case-assigning rules apply to structures differing somewhat in properties. The principal components of the grammar may be represented thus:

(12)

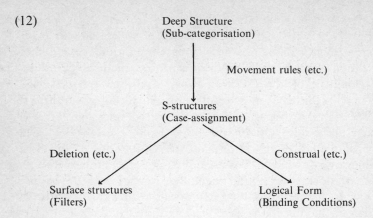

3.1 Deep Structure and Movement

The principal structural properties of the language are determined at deep structure. The most significant difference between these deep structures and classical ones has already been mentioned: lexical material need not be present in order for sub-categorial requirements to be met. This is achieved in part by making the PS rules optionally applicable. An unexpanded and hence lexically unfilled NP, for example, in object position, will not block insertion of a transitive verb like *hit*, for the fact that the NP is empty is not recognised by sub-categorial frames:

(13)   John hit [$_{NP}$ e]

Mapping these (potentially only part-filled) deep structures onto the S-structures of (12) are the rules which are called 'transformations' but which, as remarked in section 2 above are not comparable with the Grammatical Transformations of the classical theory, since they incorporate neither SD nor SC and hence cannot be interpreted as defining structurally related sets of trees. The only one of these rules which has received extended treatment is a general rule of movement. This lacks both specific Structural Description and defined Structural Change. Any constituent, α, may be moved by this rule to any position of type 'α' which is empty. The contents of the moved node appear in the new position, and are indexed with the node α in the original position, now empty. Where α is NP for example, '*Move α*', is a rule of substitution. The moved NP may occupy any previously empty NP. There is another mode of application in which the moved node is adjoined to COMP; in that case the moved node dominates a *wh* element, and the rule is '*Move Wh*'. The formulation of the rule *Move* α itself does not guarantee that there will be just these two distinct modes of application — that movement of a quantifier to an empty verbal position will be rejected. The rule itself may apply quite freely, yielding undesirable results; but then principles independent of the rule will evaluate the output and may result in rejection. What principles are to be invoked in particular in order to guarantee that there are just the two modes of application given above will not be discussed here. They do not appear to have been fully developed in the theory at this point, which, if true, may be properly regarded as a weakness. At all events, we shall simply assume that *Move NP* is restricted by some principle(s) so that in its output NPs occupy NP positions, while *Move Wh* is restricted in effect to adjunction to COMP. Of course even when we assume these very general restrictions, the rules could yield many undesirable forms; it is one of the principle tasks of the conditions on LF, as we shall see, to reject many of those undesirable outputs.

Most instances of substitutional application of movement affect NPs. They permit an NP entered at one point in deep structure (where it satisfies sub-categorial filters) to occur in S-structure at some other NP position. Hence, *Move NP* permits an NP to be assigned a Case which it would not have acquired in its deep structure position. It is by the application of *Move NP* to a deep structure object that the NP in question can appear in subject position in S-structure; likewise, application of the rule to the subject of an infinitive below *seem* places the relevant NP in the subject of the higher S by the time S-structure is reached. In both instances, we must, of course, assume that the subject position occupied by the lexical NP in S-structure was originally empty. Relevant derivations might be as indicated in the following:

(14) a. [$_{NP}$ e] was punched [$_{NP}$ John]
      b. [$_{NP_i}$ John] was punched [$_{NP_i}$ e]

(15) a. [$_{NP}$ e] seems [$_S$[$_{NP}$ John] to be happy]
      b. [$_{NP_i}$ John] seems [$_S$[$_{NP_i}$ e] to be happy]

Given the assumption that the rule *Move NP* itself is quite unconstrained and optional, we could of course just as well find the un-modified (a) forms at S-structure. Likewise, the filled NPs could have been moved to any other available empty NP positions anywhere in the whole tree structure under consideration. Thus, the movement rule itself is not of sufficient richness to capture any significant generalisations, to ensure that the (b) structures are obtained, or to rule out any other inappropriate structures that might result.

If we assume that the original NP position in (14b) and (15b) is in some relevant way dependent upon the moved NP with which it is now indexed, it is natural that this empty position will fall under constraints on dependent terms. And given that it is the level LF, where movement has already applied, that is relevant for interpretation, then it is likely that the rules of interpretation will need to relate the 'higher' superficial, lexically filled subjects of (14b) and (15b) to their original positions — with which they are now indexed. That being the case, it is perfectly consistent to regard these indexed gaps as anaphors. They will fall under the Binding conditions already roughly outlined in (11), and these will automatically rule out many sentences derived by the application of *Move NP* such as the following:

(16)   a. $[_{NP_i}$ John] seems $[_S$ that $[_{NP_i}$ e] is happy]
       b. $[_{NP_i}$ John] seems $[_S$ that Bill was seen $[_{NP_i}$ e]]

The NIC could rule out the first, Opacity the second. If so, then it is these conditions on LF, rather than properties of distinct rules of Passive and Raising that account for any significant features of (14b) and (15b). The function of movement in the grammar as a whole is simply that it provides a mechanism permitting a discrepancy between deep structures and all other levels, allowing NPs etc. to meet sub-categorial requirements at positions where they do not appear at the surface — but where, in principle, the conditions on LF can place further constraints on their traces.

3.2 S-structure and Surface Structure

By the application of movement rules to the deep structure trees, various constituents may appear in new positions, as in (14) and (15). NPs will in particular, appear either in other possible NP positions or within a COMP structure. Before these resulting forms are mapped onto LF and surface structure, Case is assigned in S-structure to all NPs bearing an appropriate relationship to some potential Case assigner. In general, an NP governed by a verb or

Tense or a preposition will acquire Case. An NP is governed by an element if it is c-commanded by that element and no major category intervenes — is 'minimally' *c*-commanded by it. The Case assigned varies. The object of a verb is standardly assigned Objective case. In OB, the objects of non-passivisable verbs, and prepositions, are Oblique. (This is to prevent movement of NPs from these positions, except by *Wh* Movement; since there are other ways of blocking this movement proposed in more recent work, the differences between Objective and Oblique case will not be pursued here.) The subject of a Tensed S, being governed by Tense, will be assigned Nominative, while the subject of an infinitive, not being governed at all (since it is not *c*-commanded within its own S by any relevant element) is assigned no Case at all. As we shall see, there are certain instances in which Case is exceptionally assigned to other NPs.

Aside from those instances where special Case is assigned, and the possible assignment of Oblique case in deep structure, there is one very general exception to the principles as they have been outlined so far. *Wh*-moved NPs, having been moved to COMP prior to S-structure, would never acquire Case at that level, for they would never be governed. However, in OB it is proposed that a mechanism be built into the movement rule itself, which effectively marks both the moved *Wh*-NP and its trace with the case that that phrase would have acquired at S-structure. Notice that if there were no movement rule (or just *Wh* Movement with this power of assigning Case itself) and if the surface subjects of (14b) and (15b) were also their deep subjects, then all Case could be assigned in deep structure. In most instances, Case is assigned by that element, verb or preposition or Tense, which requires that the Case-assigned NP be present in deep structure, that is, the element sub-categorised for it. The effect of movement is to permit the deviations from this norm implied by such examples as (14) and (15); and it is because of such cases that a distinct level of S-structure is required.

In this framework, the assignment of Case has far more than just morphological significance. We have already seen how the NIC of (11), which operates on LF, needs to make reference to Nominative. Besides this, Case assignment is essential for the proper application of a constraint which, in OB, is included among the Filters. It is for this reason that Case must be assigned in the framework of (12) at some level prior to the separation of the left and right branches leading respectively to surface structure and LF. The filter which depends in this way on Case assignment can be stated thus:

(17)   *N where N has no Case.

The effect is to reject any sentence containing a lexical NP which has not been marked for Case, and this in turn means that the only NP which can occur in a position where Case will not be assigned is an empty NP. It may have been empty at every level; and it may have become empty by the application of *Move NP*.

The one position that is standardly not assigned Case is the subject of an infinitive, as we observed. As a result, this position cannot, in general, contain lexical material. If it did, then filter (17) would apply. Hence it is filter (17), together with the structural properties of infinitives and the principles of Case assignment which together combine to force the application of movement to the lower subject in (15a) to yield (15b). The same principles determine that rather than (18a), we get (18b):

(18)   a.   *John tried [$_S$ Bill to leave]
       b.   John tried [$_S$[$_{NP}$ e] to leave]

Notice how the subject of an infinitive is therefore special in two distinct ways in the original OB framework: it is a position from which, uniquely, an anaphor may be related to an antecedent in a higher S, and it is assigned no Case, thus preventing it, in the standard case, from dominating lexical material by the time S-structure is reached. Both these special properties are necessary, if examples like (15b) are to be generated as well as those like (18b), where the empty NP is an anaphor falling under the Opacity conditions while the (a) counterpart of each is, at the same time to be rejected.

There are of course, cases where infinitives seem to permit lexical NPs. Those embedded below verbs like *believe* actually require them:

(19)   a.   *John believes [$_S$[$_{NP}$ *e*] to be happy]
       b.   John believes [$_S$ them to be happy]

Such subjects do not occur in the Nominative, but in the Objective. To account for these exceptional features of infinitives embedded below *believe*, OB incorporates a special Exceptional Case Marking rule triggered by this verb and some others but not, for example, by *seem*, as should be clear from the discussion immediately above of example (15) which assigns Objective to the lower subject.

The effect of the Case filter (17) of OB has since been extended. For example, it has been proposed, and is quite widely assumed now, that it is this filter which ensures that the object of a passive is moved out of its original position. In other words, the explanation of the obligatory movement occurring in (15) is now extended to (14). The basis of this extension is as follows. Passive participles are, as has long been recognised, akin to adjectives in many respects. When adjectives select NP arguments, they do not assign Case to them. At least this is supposed to be why prepositions must occur in the object position of adjectival counterparts of verbs. (Comparé: *John fears Bill/John is afraid of Bill.*) If passive participles likewise fail to assign Case themselves but do not trigger whatever mechanism is responsible for the appearance of the prepositions with true adjectives, then the only way to avoid application of the Case filter is to move the original, lexical object away from that position, to the formerly empty subject. Hence, when a non-Case-assigning verbal form occurs, like the Passive participle, then any lexical NP in object position must be moved away to escape filter (17).

The status of the Case filter in OB is in fact not entirely unproblematical. It replaces a more complex, structural filter proposed by Chomsky and Lasnik (1977), in what was in effect the last major attempt to modify the structurally-based classical framework. That filter rejected structures of the form *[s NP to VP]. Because of the assumption that Filters recognise only lexical material, passing over empty nodes, the Chomsky and Lasnik filter only rejected those instances of *NP to VP* containing a lexical NP. Given the assumption in question, it was natural to suppose that it was a filter that was responsible for the facts. However, there is less reason to attribute the phenomenon to the effect of a filter in the new framework; aside from anything else, the filter, as formulated in (17) above would never apply to empty NPs since it is framed in terms of the lexical node 'N', which need not appear in empty NPs. Hence, it could in principle apply on the other branch of (12), at LF.

This assumption has been made rather generally, in fact, in further developments of the OB model. On the face of it, that is quite reasonable. The assignment of Case is closely dependent on government relations between a phrasal head and its arguments, and these relations are in turn closely connected with the logical properties of heads of phrases of different kinds. Hence it makes sense for Caseless NPs to be treated as in some sense ill-formed on that level where logical well-formedness is at issue: LF. In OB itself, it is largely the resolution of dependencies between anaphors or pronouns and their heads which is controlled at LF, but with the more recent extensions to the system of government, it is very natural to add to this level, well-formedness conditions on argument structure (in effect on dependencies between heads and their arguments). Whether (17) should properly be regarded as a Filter in the sense of (12), or a condition on LF, it is in principle a good deal more interesting in its implications than the *NP to VP* filter it replaces. As we have seen it may be this same Case filter that forces Raising and Passive (in the old terms), and excludes lexical material from infinitives embedded below verbs like *try*. Thus, this account acquires some independent explanatory power.

In this respect, (17) differs considerably from the filters proposed in earlier work. Since both the Binding conditions and the Filters in the OB framework are sometimes discussed in terms which would be appropriate for those earlier filters but are totally inappropriate to either the Filters or the Binding conditions, it is worth emphasising just how different the role of filters was in the earlier theory. One sometimes finds the claim made, even by those working within the Binding theory, that it leads to serious 'over-generation' or 'mis-generation', but that this is rectified by an appropriate interaction between the output of the rules and various filters, conditions on LF, etc. Even if in one sense true, this is very misleading. It is the theory as a whole that defines the sentences of the language. Not just the PS rules. Not just the PS rules plus transformations. The main source of interesting generalisations in the OB framework is in fact the very well-formedness conditions on the output of the right-hand branch of (12) which probably include the Case 'filter'. Whereas it made methodological and intuitive sense to think of the classical transformational grammar as capturing the interesting generalisations in the PS and transformational components, with output conditions correcting 'over-' or 'mis-generation', this conception of the situation totally misses the point of the output well-formedness conditions in OB.

That having been said there remains the interesting question is how far Filters on the left branch of (12) do serve a central explanatory purpose in the new framework. As already pointed out, the Case filter seems in fact to belong more properly among the conditions on LF, and there are few clear cases of Filters left. Most of those filters proposed by Chomsky and Lasnik (1977), for example the *that*-trace filter, the filter on doubly filled COMP nodes, the one just discussed, and even the filter which was used to rule out adjacent *for + to* have been at least provisionally replaced by devices operating at other levels, especially as the OB theory has developed. It may be that the Filters on the left branch are indeed to be regarded as devices capable of correcting minor 'mis-generation' — either reflecting real, superficial corrective devices available in the grammar or simply *ad hoc* measures signalling the linguist's analytical failure. They clearly play a rather minor role in the theory.

At the same time, it is important to recognise that the subcategorisation well-formedness conditions at deep structure, the Case assignment principles at S-structure, together with the Case filter, and the Binding conditions at LF are all in effect simply complex filters of different sorts. The model outlined in (12) consists of a set of independent filters at different levels, with the rules linking each level able to modify (generally rather trivially) the structures undergoing filtering at each level.

Finally, notice that the distinction made in (12) between S-structure and surface structure is necessitated not so much by the fact that the input required for the Filters differs significantly from that required for Case assignment and the rules of Construal, as by the fact that there are superficial forms found in language which do not contain the information needed by the Construal rules. Thus, it is not the Filters, but the Deletion and Stylistic rules which require the left branch. The relevant assumption underlying the model given in (12) is that a sentence like *John will not see Mary but Sam will* has the additional material *see Mary* at S-structure and hence at LF. The postulation of deletion rules on this branch certainly opened the way to postulating that in some cases material deleted on the left branch could otherwise have interfered with the proper operation of Filters. In this way, for example, *wh*-phrases could be freely deleted in COMP, thus escaping a Filter, even though they would be necessary in LF. So, the S-structure *the man who$_i$ that John saw t$_i$* could yield both a well-formed LF *containing* the *wh*-phrase, and a well-formed surface structure *lacking* it. But I think we must see these as minor by-products of the interaction of deletion and filtering. They have become less and less a vital part of the OB framework. The Deletion and Stylistic rules are independent of the Filters; but even they have received less attention in more recent developments. Phenomena like 'VP-deletion' can, as Chomsky remarks in OB itself, be analysed without recourse to deletion rules, and this component is not central to the framework.

3.3 Conditions on Logical Form

It is clear that LF constitutes, along with deep structure and the principles of Case assignment, the heart of the theory. The main conditions proposed in OB have already been outlined in sufficient detail. It remains only to show how they interact with the rules of movement, especially *Wh* Movement, and with the rules of Construal, which separate LF from S-structure.

Movement is, as we have seen, quite free. However, the traces left behind by movement are responsive to an additional condition on LF, Subjacency, which has the effect of limiting most *Wh* Movement extending beyond a single $\bar{S}$ structure to successive-cyclic COMP-to-COMP movement. The basic idea of Subjacency is familiar enough, as is the way in which it blocked *Wh* Movement from *wh*-islands, complex NPs, etc. in the later versions of the structure-based framework such as that of Chomsky (1977). Re-framed as a condition on LF, it is simply a requirement that co-indexed traces not be separated from each other or from the co-indexed, moved phrase by more than a single relevant boundary. Which boundaries count as 'relevant' may, it is supposed, vary from language to language. It is supposed in OB that the relevant boundaries for English are both S and $\bar{S}$, as well as NP.

Simple movement from argument position to COMP is then no problem: a single S boundary separates the trace and the moved phrase:

(20) $[_{\bar{S}}[_{COMP} \text{Wh-NP}_i] [_S \dots [_{NP_i} e]$

Moving the *Wh*-NP from this COMP to the next higher one, which is the basic operation involved in successive cyclic *Wh* Movement, would appear to yield structures which would violate Subjacency, since it crosses the boundary of the $\bar{S}$ shown above and also the next S boundary up:

(21) $[_{\bar{S}}[_{COMP} \text{who}_i] [_S \text{ does John believe } [_{\bar{S}}[_{COMP} [_{NP_i} e] \text{ that}] [_S \dots$
       $\uparrow\_\_\_\_\_ 2 _____ 1 \_\_\_\_\_|$

The suggestion in OB, modified somewhat in more recent work, but essentially still maintained, is that verbs like the English *believe* have the property of allowing the $\bar{S}$ node dominating their complements to be ignored for Subjacency. Assuming some such account of COMP-to-COMP movement, the assumption that the output of *Wh*

Movement is subject to Subjacency permits blocking of movement from *wh*-islands and complex NPs, since the relevant traces would be separated by at least two S, S̄ or NP boundaries.

Leaving aside further discussion of the details of Subjacency, the following question now arises: assuming that the application leaves behind empty (indexed) nodes, which depend in some way for their interpretation on a phrase appearing elsewhere (the *wh*-phrase) it might be expected that these traces would count as dependent terms of some sort, and would thus fall under the Binding conditions at LF, as well as Subjacency. Yet they appear to ignore them. A trace of *Wh* Movement can be the subject of a Tensed S, or occur in the domain of the subject of a sentence:

(22)　a.　Who$_i$ does Sam believe [$_S$ t$_i$ saw Bill]
　　　　b.　Who$_i$ does Sam believe [$_S$ Bill saw t$_i$]

Moreover (though this will not be shown here in detail), these traces behave quite unlike pronouns. Hence it seems that they act like neither of the hitherto distinguished kinds of dependent term.

Nevertheless, it is supposed in OB that these traces are indeed anaphors subject to the Opacity conditions. What prevents this from being directly observed is the trace of the *wh*-phrase which survives (though it is not shown in (22)) in the COMP of the lower S̄. See, for example, the structure shown in (21). This trace can serve as the antecedent of a co-indexed trace *anywhere* in the lower S, ensuring that such a trace will never be free in its S̄; and the higher trace itself, being in COMP, will not be in the domain of the subject, hence will not be subject to Opacity. Whether it is marked Nominative will depend on precisely how the special Case assignment effected by *Wh* Movement works. As long as the trace in COMP is not marked for Nominative, however, as we may assume, then it will not be subject to the NIC either. Hence this trace in COMP is what ensures that *Wh* Movement is not obviously subject to the Opacity conditions.

While this account may still turn out to be basically correct, there are facts, briefly referred to in OB, which have tended to lead to a reinterpretation of the traces of *Wh* Movement under which they are explicitly analysed as not subject to the Binding conditions. One kind of evidence for the need to interpret *wh*-traces as non-anaphors is provided by languages which, like Italian, permit *Wh* Movement out of certain *wh*-islands. In Italian, the counterpart of (23) can be grammatical:

(23)   Wh-NP$_i$ [$_{\bar{S}}$ Sam wondered [$_{\bar{S}}$ who$_j$ [$_S$ t$_j$ saw t$_i$]]]

Such movement could be permitted if in Italian only $\bar{S}$ is a bounding node for Subjacency. Then the Wh-NP$_i$ is separated from its trace by only a single 'relevant' node, the $\bar{S}$. The problem is that while this will provide an account of the difference between Italian and English with respect to *Wh* Movement, it cannot do so if *wh*-traces are subject to the Opacity conditions. For there is no trace within the lower $\bar{S}$ of (23) to serve as the antecedent of t$_i$.

Within the general Binding framework, there are two properties that set off the *wh*-traces from other null phrases: they are assumed to be mapped onto phrases containing variables in LF, and they alone are marked for Case. Descriptively there is no problem in distinguishing them, therefore, and exempting them from the conditions. Whether this is a fully motivated step is a question which will be taken up briefly in the next section.

We turn now to the interaction of the rules of Construal with the Binding conditions. As a matter of fact, one of those rules has already by implication come under discussion: the rule of *Wh* Interpretation, which is responsible for mapping sentences containing *wh*-phrases onto structures in which those phrases are treated as quantifiers binding variables in the original NP position from which they were moved. Other similar rules have been proposed, including one for mapping certain expressions containing overt quantifier phrases and pronouns onto structures in which variables occur in the position of the pronouns, variables bound by the counterparts of the quantifiers. A similar possibility for '*there*-insertion' expressions is touched on in OB. Such rules of 'interpretation' are clearly intended to convert S-structures into forms more transparent for semantic purposes. Where expressions containing variables result, these will (at least in the versions of the OB theory discussed briefly in the next section) be exempted in principle from the Binding conditions — though Subjacency will be relevant if movement has occurred on the path between deep and S-structure.

The other major class of construal rules deals with instances of Control. The empty infinitive subject below verbs like *try, persuade, promise* will have to be brought into the proper relationship of dependency with the relevant phrase in the higher S. Also, the infinitive subject in relatives like *the man PRO to speak to*, or expressions like *John asked who PRO to speak to* will have to be assigned an antecedent where appropriate, or arbitrary reference where that is possible. The resulting expressions are clearly subject to the Binding conditions, as we would expect.

4. Further Developments in Binding and Government

The major components of the OB theory have now been presented in sufficient detail to provide a reasonably clear picture of how the theory operates, and where the explanatory power of this model is principally concentrated: in the Binding conditions, interacting with deep structures and the principles of Case assignment. Each is rich enough to embody quite specific claims about language, and in interaction they account for a large number of interesting generalisations. As is clear from the papers which follow and from the many other publications that are in preparation or have already appeared within the general framework, these generalisations can be profitably investigated across languages of many different types, yielding interesting insights into significant regularities. That this is so provides significant empirical support for the framework.

Largely as a result of the considerable degree of success which has attended attempts to apply this framework to such a wide variety of languages, it also became clear, quite rapidly, that there are many details requiring modification. The need to make the bounding node for Subjacency variable rather than fixed has already been mentioned, together with some of the quite far-reaching consequences for the status of *wh*-traces that seem to result from this seemingly minor change. Yet however far-reaching the consequences of such a change, they remain in some sense changes in detail. They certainly do not affect the central claims of the theory. All the changes that have been proposed seem to fall into that category. Most of the other papers in this volume adopt one or another version of the Binding framework. Because the theory is undergoing such rapid development, on the basis of very different empirical work, the assumptions made in some of the papers run quite contrary to those made in others. It is impossible to give a single account of the developments that are taking place. However, the changes proposed during the Pisa lectures [8] which took place during the preparation of this volume, and during the (re-)writing of the majority of the papers, have been sufficiently influential on the further development of research and are sufficiently significant to warrant brief description before the other contributions themselves are dealt with.

It has been repeatedly emphasised, in the account above of the OB framework, that it is the constraints on LF which are at the heart of the theory. If so, it is important to try and *define in general terms the kinds of conditions which can be placed on LF*. Interesting as it is to find that useful generalisations about natural language can be made on this level, it cannot be left at that. Without a general account of what can and more important what cannot constitute such a constraint, the OB model could turn out to be as powerful and unconstrained in principle as the unconstrained version of classical transformational grammar. In the theory presented in OB itself there was actually very little generality in the Binding conditions, and no obvious way of projecting from them to develop a general notion of what can constitute such a condition. Moreover the relationship between the conditions and the independent Case principles was quite undefined. One would be hard pressed, given a proposed addition, to decide whether it qualified in principle or not. In contrast, even the rejected classical theory had the methodological advantage that the basic device, the Grammatical Transformation was sufficiently richly defined to permit the exclusion of many putative candidates. Indeed it was obviously this characteristic of the theory that has permitted it to be rejected on the basis of empirical evidence.

There is actually still no general account of conditions on LF, or indeed even of LF, which is sufficiently well-defined to permit a principled investigation of putative constraints. But the changes which have been proposed in the conditions do help to unify them, and to relate the Binding conditions in turn to the Case principles. The revised Binding theory has been formulated along the following lines:

(24)   a. If NP is lexical or a bound variable, then it is free.
        b. If NP is pronominal, it is free in its governing category.
        c. If NP is an anaphor, it is bound in its governing category.

The pivotal concept here is that of government, which playcd a minor role in Case assignment in OB. A node *governs* an NP if it minimally c-commands it, without the intervention of any major category boundary. The *governing category* of an NP is the minimal NP or S (*not* S̄) within which it is governed. Only lexical categories and certain co-indexed nodes are potential governors. So it follows that an NP can fail to have a governing category: when it is not minimally governed by some potential governor. In general the subject of an infinitive will not have a governing category. Most of the other terms in (24) can be given an obvious interpretation, or the one they have in the original OB framework, but 'free' needs some further explanation, as it is used in (24). It has a very specific meaning. A term is bound if it is *c*-commanded by a co-indexed *argument*. Otherwise it is free. Binding by a quantifier such as a *wh*-phrase in COMP is not relevant to this special sense of 'bound'..

Notice how in (24) the notions of government and binding interact to define the domains in which dependencies, including those resulting from *Wh* Movement and similar rules may, must and must not be resolved — at the same time restricting the possible antecedents. First, neither lexical NPs nor variables may be co-indexed with a *c*-commanding argument. This has the interesting effect that it excludes movement of a 'quantifier-type' phrase like *Wh-NP* to any NP position, thus forcing COMP-to-COMP movement which formerly had to be stipulated. Then the pronominals, pronouns and PRO, are prevented by (b) from being co-indexed with any argument within their governing category. For pronouns, this has the effect of ruling out antecedents in most of those positions in which in the earlier version anaphors would have been forced to seek an antecedent. In other words, the effect is precisely what was necessary but hard to capture naturally by means of (11): as we observed (24b) directly reflects the complementarity of anaphors and pronouns with respect to their antecedents. Assuming that the pronoun has a governing category, as will generally be the case, this will prevent it from being co-indexed with another NP in that category. It is this which generally forces pronouns to find their antecedents outside the S.

PRO is more complex since it is not merely pronominal but also an anaphor. Hence if it had a governing category it would have to be both bound and free in it — a contradiction. Therefore PRO can only occur in a position where it acquires no governing category. As already noted, that is the subject of an infinitive, and even then only when that subject is not in the complement sentence of a verb like *believe*. For such verbs are able, exceptionally, to govern the infinitive subject. (The governing category is then the S of the matrix verb.)

Given these assumptions, the main effects of both NIC and Opacity can be derived directly from (c), which is now not merely parallel in form in an interesting way to the comparable condition, (b), for pronominals, but is distinctly simpler than in the earlier version. The effect is as follows. In a Tensed S. Tense governs the subject. Otherwise the V or a preposition governs all NPs except for the subjects of infinitives which are not complements of a verb like *believe*. Except for those special cases, then, the governing category will generally be the minimal S, and the anaphor will have to be co-indexed with some argument position within that domain. It remains only to recall the effects of the Case filter, which is still operative, though, as was remarked earlier, it may now apply within LF itself. Because of this, lexical NPs, including those that are pronominal or anaphoric, will have to have acquired Case; and to do so, they must have a governing category (for Case is assigned, as always, by a governor). Hence they are properly excluded from standard infinitive subjects.

Aside from any gain in simplicity in the conditions themselves, and from any increase in empirical effectiveness, these constraints now form a coherent framework in which sub-categorisation (which in the standard cases defines government relations) interacts with other minor components to determine (through the Binding Theory (24)) the domains which are relevant for the resolution of anaphoric and pronominal dependencies. In this way, the deep structure sub-categorial properties of lexical items and morphemes like Tense restrict the (non-)compositionality of the language. If this is in fact true in a non-trivial way, it is, of course, a very interesting fact about natural language.

5. Extensions and Modifications to OB

The other papers in this volume all explore problems closely related to those that arise naturally within the OB framework. They will be discussed briefly in this Introduction mainly with reference to that framework, even where they are not explicitly developing it.

Chapter 2, by George and Kornfilt, argues that for Turkish the distinction between finite and non-finite is not the presence or absence of Tense, but the presence or absence of Agreement marking. So the counterpart of the NIC could not be made to depend on Nominative marking based, in turn, upon the presence of Tense. Because this paper essentially pre-dates OB, George and Kornfilt present their argument not in terms of conditions on LF but in the older framework, where what is relevant is the Tensed-S Constraint. However, they suggest in a note that there may be reasons for preferring a restatement in the later framework. Since all their examples are relevant for the NIC, this would appear to present no serious difficulties and I shall not pursue the question further. They argue, for Turkish, that in both NPs and Ss, it is the presence of Agreement that prevents the application of the relevant rules, or in the OB framework, that induces the applicability of the NIC. Since the discussion is not framed in terms of the NIC, they do not of course consider whether this is through the assignment of Nominative Case by the Agreement morphemes. But they do explicitly reject the idea that it is Agreement itself which has cross-linguistic significance. Rather, they suggest that the relevant parameter of cross-linguistic significance for distinguishing finite from non-finite constructions (and hence, the applicability of the NIC or Tensed-S Constraint) may involve quite abstract considerations, for example whether in the phrase in question the highest specifier of the head is aparadigmatic. Whether this turns out to be the relevant parameter must, of course, await further research. What is significant is that any attempt to constrain the set of possible constraints on LF along the lines programmatically suggested in the previous section would clearly have to take such questions into account.

The third paper by Rizzi is also concerned with extending the validity of the NIC or its equivalent to a language differing significantly from English. It is also like theirs in having been completed quite some time ago. In fact it reflects a very early stage in the development of the OB theory. Rizzi points out that a certain Italian infinitive construction displays a number of interesting irregularities. Under certain assumptions, these can be explained if the subject of these infinitives obeys the NIC — as predicted by the fact that in the rather marked cases where what appears to be the same construction takes a lexical subject, this is Nominative. The facts are as follows. A lexical subject of infinitives below a certain class of Italian verbs is normally ungrammatical. This is parallel to the situation with the English *try* and is predicted by the Case filter. However, when *Move-Wh* has applied, apparently to the same basic construction, moving the subject away, grammaticality results. On the other hand *Move-NP* applied to these same subjects (to yield passives of the higher verb, or clitic movement to that verb) does not yield a grammatical output.

Crucial in the explanation which Rizzi proposes, is the fact, already remarked upon, that under certain marked circumstances, overt lexical subjects can appear with infinitives, and that when this happens they are Nominative, and occur to the right of the infinitive verb. That the trace of *wh*-moved NPs can survive in these structures while the trace of *Move NP* cannot would be accounted for if both were assigned Nominative — by whatever rule accounts for the special Nominative marking of subjects to the right of the infinitive. For they would then both be subject to the NIC, counting as Nominative anaphors; and the *wh*-trace (but not an ordinary trace) would be bound within its $\bar{S}$ by the trace of movement in COMP, thus:

(25)   a.   Wh-NP$_i$ [$_S$ ... V ... [$_{\bar{S}}$[COMP t$_i$] [$_S$ V$_{inf}$ t$_i$
        b.   NP$_i$ ... V ... [$_{\bar{S}}$[COMP ...] [$_S$ V$_{inf}$ t$_i$

(Since only $\bar{S}$ appears to be relevant to Subjacency in Italian, as noted earlier, (25b) will not be rejected by that condition.) Whereas in (25a) the Nominative trace is bound within its $\bar{S}$ by the trace in COMP, this is not so in (25b). This explanation relies, of course, on the observation in OB, and remarked on above, that the presence of the trace in COMP effectively removes *wh*-traces from the class of anaphors.

In that respect, Rizzi's analysis here is quite consistent with the suggested developments of the Binding theory discussed in section 4 above. In other ways, too, his proposals are similar to developments mentioned there and elsewhere. One point, though, where his analysis differs radically from more recent work is in his assignment of Case. To account for the ungrammaticality of infinitives like (25b) he applied NIC to the trace left by *Move NP*. This involves no change from OB. However, the subject of an *ordinary* infinitive extracted by NP movement (i.e. a structure like (25b) but with the trace to the left of the verb) would fail to be rejected, even though it lacked Case. The trace, not being Nominative, would escape the NIC. Not being lexical, it would escape the Case filter. Hence a structure like (25b) but with trace to the left of V$_{inf}$ should be acceptable: the trace is not Nominative (lacking all Case), is not in the domain of a subject, and is not, in the OB theory, rejected by the Case filter. As noted already, subjacency, in Italian, would also fail to reject such cases. Rizzi's proposal is that the Case filter apply to *all* NPs. At first blush, this proposal seems to run into difficulty. It could lead to the rejection of PRO infinitive subjects, along with those that are traces. If the filter rejects *any* Caseless NP, and if infinitive subjects are standardly Caseless, then it will reject PRO infinitive subjects. And it was by virtue of the fact that the filter (whether in LF or at the surface) ignored PRO that empty subjects were permitted in infinitives, where lexical ones were not.

The idea of preventing *Move-NP* from removing the subjects of standard infinitives by extending the domain of the Case filter to all NPs, lexical or otherwise, runs counter to the developments outlined in the previous section, since within most developments of the Binding framework, it is crucial that *wh*-traces be the only non-lexical NP marked for Case. Or, at least that distinction has been incorporated centrally in the revisions to the theory which have been widely adopted, providing the basis upon which *wh*-traces and lexical NPs are treated alike in (24a). But the fact remains that some account is needed of why *Move-NP* cannot apply to remove the subjects of standard Italian infinitives. (In English, if S and S̄ are both bounding nodes for Subjacency then *Move-NP* will only be able to apply when the effect of one of these nodes is removed, as when the infinitive occurs with a verb like *seem*; but that is not going to help avoid such movement in Italian, if, as seems likely, only S counts for Subjacency.) The proposed extension of the filter would provide a means for making this distinction, as long as the filter applied, as in OB, at the surface, not LF. In that case, a PRO deletion rule assumed to operate between S-structure and the surface in the original OB proposals, would automatically remove PRO but not traces. Unbound Caseless traces alone would be rejected.

The position remains therefore somewhat unsettled. If, as assumed in the original OB framework, and most other developments of it, Case is not acquired by the trace of *Move-NP*, then some other means must be found for distinguishing plain traces from PRO in such contexts so as to block the trace of *Move-NP* in standard infinitives. One possibility might be the 'thematic relations' which assume some significance in very recent work in the framework;[9] but there is no space to do justice to these ideas here.

Whatever the outcome of further developments in regard to this aspect of Rizzi's analysis, there is another aspect in which his proposals are entirely compatible with (and perhaps the source of) an important modification to the Binding theory which has not yet been explicitly mentioned. This concerns the close relationship which he sets up between the trace in COMP and a *wh*-trace in argument position. Rizzi discusses this relationship in terms of Binding: the subject trace in (25a) is bound by the trace in COMP and so escapes the NIC. In the Binding theory of section 4, the trace in COMP, not being itself an argument position, cannot result in an NP in the lower S being 'bound' in the new sense. But it can, and indeed does, *govern* that trace, being co-indexed with it. The significance of this will become clearer as we discuss the contributions of Reuland, Kayne and Harlow, all of which deal with related phenomena.

Reuland's paper, which follows, is built on a similar observation to the one that underlies Rizzi's argument. Dutch, like Italian, contains an infinitive construction in which a Nominative non-null subject appears. The constructions seem to have little else in common, and Reuland makes use of the Dutch data to argue for changes which in many ways are quite different from those proposed by Rizzi. He suggests, as George and Kornfilt did, that the finiteness distinction may depend on an Agreement morpheme rather than Tense. But his proposal is more radical than theirs. He suggests that there is a very close relationship between Agreement and Case assignment. The assignment of Nominative he makes optional. A non-null NP in subject position may acquire Nominative. Then, making use of the fact that Agreement and the subject NP are sister nodes and hence in each other's domains, he adds two conditions to LF. On the one hand, the presence of Nominative requires that it be governed by an appropriate Agreement morpheme; on the other hand, the presence of an Agreement morpheme requires that it be governed by Nominative. Thus agreement, like Case in OB, is removed by this proposal from the class of purely morphological phenomena.

A verb exhibiting agreement, a finite verb, must standardly have a Nominative subject. At the same time, since only non-null NPs acquire Case, PRO is excluded from finite subjects because the Agreement would then fail to be governed by Nominative. Given this analysis, PRO will be excluded from subjects of finite sentences not by virtue of the NIC, but by virtue of the fact that the Agreement morpheme is then not governed in the required manner. So in the end agreement is handled in effect by an extension of the NIC of the OB framework. The Agreement morpheme is treated as a kind of anaphor, for it is linked to the NP in subject position with which it agrees, and being in the domain of that subject it has to be not bound, in the OB sense, but governed by the Nominative case on the phrase with which it agrees. To evaluate the theoretical significance of such a proposal, we require, of course, some constraints upon what may and may not constitute possible conditions on LF.

Aside from the methodological interest which this proposal derives from the attempt to motivate this rather radical but not implausible extension to the conditions, it has, if Reuland is correct, some interesting empirical consequences. He argues that it can be used to account for the '*that*-trace' filter phenomena in English and, with a little extension, for the phenomena associated with 'subject-pronoun deletion' in languages like Czech, where the subject of a sentence may apparently be empty. In such languages, he claims, Agreement is not an anaphor but a pronoun. Both in the analysis of the Agreement element as a kind of anaphor, and in the use which he puts this to in dealing with empty subjects and the '*that*-trace' phenomena, Reuland's proposal comes quite close in detail to independent developments along the same lines which have been made by Chomsky, Kayne and others. In particular, his account of the '*that*-trace' cases, of the ungrammaticality of English sentences like *Who does John believe that t left*, is very close to those proposals in which the NIC ceases to appear as an independent element. Such sentences might seem to provide a reason for retaining the NIC and have it apply to *wh*-traces. This is of course suggested by the fact that objects can be freely moved from such sentences: *Who does John believe that Bill saw t*. However, as is well known, 'deletion' of the complementiser in the ungrammatical cases restores grammaticality: *Who does John believe t left*. In earlier work, such as Chomsky and Lasnik (1977), these facts were accounted for on a rather *ad hoc* basis, using the *that*-trace filter.

The newer Binding theory, as represented in part by the conditions given in (24) is able to give a more principled account of these facts, along with a number of others. The necessary addition is the Empty Category Principle (ECP). An empty category, which includes all traces but not PRO (since the latter is assumed to incorporate typical pronominal features of number and gender), must be lexically governed. The essentials of the account of *that*-trace phenomena by means of the ECP are as follows: whereas the complementiser prevents lexical government of the trace, deletion of *that* permits the bridge verb *believe* to govern the trace. There is an alternative account: the trace in COMP, as a co-indexed phrase, is able to govern the one in subject position. (Recall Rizzi's use of a similar idea.) This follows from the fact that the traces are co-indexed and the definition of lexical governors includes, for independent reasons, co-indexed terms. Reuland's account comes quite close to this second version.

His analysis differs of course significantly from any based on the ECP, since it sets up generalisations which are distinct from those underlying the ECP accounts. Nevertheless like those accounts, his attributes the *that*-trace effect to the fact that the complementiser, when present, prevents a necessary relationship of government from being established.

Kayne begins his paper by showing how there are empirical advantages in formulating the Binding conditions as conditions on LF rather than constraints on rules. In particular, he shows how the very dubious rule of Equi, still assumed in OB, can be avoided when the conditions are so interpreted. The main burden of the chapter, however, is an argument, which recalls that of Rizzi discussed earlier, that the traces of NP movement and other cases of *Move α* not involving quantifier-like elements must be distinguished from the traces linked to quantifiers. His analyses are of French constructions.

Specifically, he shows that although the application of L-Tous to the object of an infinitive can result in a grammatical sentence, clitics cannot be moved out of this position. L-Tous moves a quantifier; clitics are not quantifiers. We have already seen how in much of the work based on OB it is assumed that *wh*-traces are immune to the Binding conditions. In the version of the Binding theory outlined in (24) this is represented by classifying variables along with 'lexical' NPs (not including *each other* etc., of course), and requiring that these be 'free'. The assumption is that some rule of construal will map *wh*-traces onto variables at that level. (Of course, the distinction in question does not require that the output of this construal rule be precisely equivalent to logical 'variables'; all that is necessary is that the traces linked to 'quantifier-like' elements including *tous* and the *wh*-phrases be distinguished in LF from other dependent terms.) Given some such assumption, then it is natural for the trace of clitic movement to obey the Binding conditions but the trace of L-Tous not to do so.

There is an interesting complication, of a sort that should by now be predictable. Even the *wh*-trace is ungrammatical when it is in *subject* position. And there, of course, the empty category, the trace, comes under the ECP — for subject position, as we observed with reference to Reuland's paper, is not normally lexically governed. Hence the fact that even a *wh*-trace is rejected in that position. However, there is a way out. The element **qui** can be substituted for the complementiser **que**. And the *wh*-trace can then be rescued. This is of course reminiscent of the *that*-trace facts, and is obviously to be analysed in a somewhat analogous fashion. The details differ. Kayne supposes that the element **qui** itself is co-indexed with the trace, hence providing the necessary lexical governor.

Harlow's starting point in his analysis of relative clauses in Welsh and Irish is this same ECP. He also makes crucial use of another aspect of the newer versions of the Binding theory: the integration of the Agreement element into the central core of the system of binding and government. In essence this is very similar to the independent proposals by Reuland outlined above, to treat the Agreement morpheme as an anaphor, or, in a language like Czech — or Italian — as a pronoun not requiring a Nominative governor. The details of the account developed by Chomsky along with the Binding theory of (24) differ, of course, from Reuland's account in terms of anaphors and pronouns, since Chomsky uses the definitions of binding and government assumed in (24).

In that account, assumed by Harlow, the Agreement element (AG) is capable of being indexed (with the subject) in those languages which permit empty subjects, and a transformational rule of PRO-drop is postulated. If a language has an indexed AG, then this AG will govern the empty subject, preventing the ECP from rejecting such sentences to which the transformation has applied. (It must be a transformation, since were it to apply on the left branch of (12) its output would not be available to the ECP at LF. Like all the new transformations, it is quite general and unconstrained.)

Welsh allows empty subjects and hence must index AG. It also has a class of prepositions and possessives agreeing with their objects and 'possessed' NPs respectively. If this agreement is AG, too, we would expect it to be indexed, just as it is when on the verb, hence permitting pronoun objects etc. to drop. This expectation is fulfilled. In addition, Harlow shows how the assumption that the agreeing element is a species of AG permits an explanatory account of a very complex set of interrelationships between apparently optional and obligatory applications of a (putative) rule, Relative Deletion, in both Welsh and Irish. A simple, unconstrained rule of deletion can be applied obligatorily — up to the point where the result would violate the ECP. Many cases of what had been assumed to be resumptive pronouns in earlier analyses of these languages, resulting from the optional non-application of the deletion rule, turn out to be simply the AG component of verbs, prepositions, etc.

One particularly interesting result of the analysis is worth special attention. Welsh appears to have an element in COMP which, like the French **qui** discussed by Kayne, is able to lexically govern empty categories, rescuing them from the effect of the ECP. It would seem that the VSO structure, which, Harlow argues, characterises Welsh, prevents the verb from lexically governing even empty *objects* to which the relative deletion has applied. Yet, because of the VSO structure, the co-indexed element in COMP is able to rescue these as well. Moreover, he argues, this element is a base generated pro-nominal in COMP, and this, he is able to show, could account for the fact that it occurs obligatorily in the highest COMP of direct relatives — and not at all in indirect relatives.

It is interesting that Harlow assumes throughout this paper that the basic relativisation rule responsible for the structures he is dealing with is an unbounded deletion rule. Such a rule would be excluded in principle from most versions of the OB framework. But (see his note 23) it is not clear that the analysis depends crucially upon assuming such a rule.

6. Filters

It was remarked earlier that the Filters applying on surface struc-tures in the model of OB have to a large extent been abandoned as a source of real explanation in the Binding theory itself. It was pointed out at the same time that the deep structure sub-categorisation frames, and the conditions on LF were both in effect simply a species of positive filter. Largely independent of the OB framework itself, and in fact virtually pre-dating it, but interacting with it at certain points, the paper by Maling and Zaenen, sets out to explore the possible explanatory value of an account of Germanic word-order which is based entirely on the unconstrained application of a number of movement rules combined with positive filters. The latter are associated with speech acts like 'Statement', 'Question'.

While their syntactic framework is not totally incompatible with a Binding theory, they explicitly set out to question the validity of some of the assumptions which seem to be regarded as fundamental to most versions of the OB framework. For example, they argue that for a number of Germanic languages Topicalisation and *Wh* Movement cannot be regarded as resulting from differential appli-cations of *Move-Wh* but are separate rules. Likewise, they claim that the facts force a separate treatment of Left Dislocation and

Topicalisation. It remains an open question whether there would be any essential problem in incorporating such distinct rules, if they are in fact necessary, into a model based upon Binding conditions. Of course it was not their goal to answer such questions. Of perhaps even more direct relevance to further developments of the Binding framework is the question how far positive filters associated in some way with speech acts could be insightfully incorporated into a framework of that sort. It would of course do injustice to the paper to suggest that the authors' own interest in the explanatory power of such filters is dependent on whether they can be incorporated into some such framework. The proposal can stand perfectly well on its own; but given the relative lack of constraint on the components of the Binding theory it is very relevant to consider whether the addition of such devices as those proposed by Maling and Zaenen could contribute to the explanatory power of the theory or would merely weaken it.

Muysken's paper, the last in the volume, is also in part an exploration of a more extended system of filtering than has been actively adopted in the OB framework. Unlike all the others, this paper deals primarily with morphology: the borderline between syntax and morphology, and possible criteria for distinguishing these components — using data from Quechua. In further developments of the OB framework, it seems certain that the relationship between syntax and morphology will assume critical importance, at least from time to time. The AG element, which is so crucial to the analyses given by Harlow (and in fact by Reuland, though he does not frame his explicitly in terms of AG), is a bound morpheme. Yet, at least in many versions of the theory, it is assumed to enter into structural relations like *c*-command, which form the basis of government, in just the same way as the elements of the syntax with which it interacts. Of course, the crucial interactions are on the level LF; but at the very least it is necessary that the morphological and syntactic elements be mutually related in structural terms at least rich enough to enable rules of construal (?) to yield appropriate structures on that level. Given the morphological richness of languages like Quechua this may well turn out to be a far from trivial task for such languages — or it may turn out to permit only a trivial solution, in which none of the morphological structure is relevant.

For example, Muysken argues that, contrary to assumptions which have been made in much recent work, there is no principled distinction between derivational and inflectional morphology.

Moreover, while c-command and Subjacency possess significance in the morphology they do so not as independent principles, but derivatively, because of characteristics inherent in morphological rules. It is difficult to know what to make of such facts, until the interaction of the syntax and morphology is explored systematically within, for example, the OB framework. Clearly it is possible that conditions on LF and structurally defined domains controlling them may treat syntax and morphology as a single network; or, equally, the morphological structures may turn out to be irrelevant. The question then arises, of course, whether structurally determined relations in the syntax are of any greater significance for the determination of the domains relevant to the conditions on LF. But this is not the place to pursue such questions any further.

Notes

* For helpful comments on an earlier draft I should like to thank Noam Chomsky, Stephen Harlow, Richie Kayne, Jacklin Kornfilt and Luigi Rizzi.

1. The only really serious attempt I know of is Bach (1965).
2. In particular work developing out of Emonds (1970). I ignore here the possible relevance of root and minor movement rules.
3. See for example Chomsky (1973), Chomsky (1977), and the other contributions to (and many references in) Culicover, Wasow and Akmajian (1977).
4. See for example Frege (1879).
5. Montague (1974).
6. Chomsky in 'On Binding' and elsewhere suggests an analogy between the effect of the Tense morpheme or the subject in preventing anaphoric dependency beyond certain structures and the 'Opacity' induced for example by verbs of propositional attitude. There does seem to be a very close relationship between the 'Opacity' conditions of OB and the principle of compositionality. And there may well be some relationship between 'Opacity' in Chomsky's sense and 'Opacity' in the sense used by Quine (1960). However, the problems with Quantifying in, which Chomsky seems to have in mind in suggesting this metaphor, are complex. The phenomena associated with the term 'Opacity' by both logicians and a good number of linguists cannot be handled in any natural way by a simple ban on quantifying into intensional contexts (such as propositional attitudes). See the introduction and various papers in Heny (1981) for relevant discussion. In any case, the phenomena that Chomsky is dealing with in terms of 'Opacity' rarely, if ever, have to do with free variables in the logicians' sense. There is no way that I can see of developing the metaphor so that it has deep consequences for linguistic theory. A descriptively more adequate term for the conditions might be *constraints on domains of compositionality*.
7. Again, see note 3 above.
8. For further details see Chomsky (1979a), (1979b).
9. See Chomsky (1980).

References

Bach, Emmon (1965), 'On Some Recurrent Types of Transformations' in C. W. Kreidler (ed.), *Sixteenth Annual Round Table Meeting on Linguistics and Language Studies*, Georgetown University, South Carolina

Chomsky, Noam (1955), *The Logical Structure of Linguistic Theory*, Plenum Books, NY

———— (1965), *Aspects of the Theory of Syntax*, MIT Press, Cambridge, Massachusetts

———— (1973), 'Conditions on Transformations' in S. Anderson and P. Kiparsky (eds.), *Festschrift for Morris Halle*, Holt, Rinehart and Winston, NY

———— (1977), 'On *WH*-movement' in P. Culicover, T. Wasow and A. Akmajian (eds.) (1977)

———— (1979), 'Principles and Parameters in Syntactic Theory' to appear in D. Lightfoot and N. Hornstein (eds.), *Explanation in Linguistics*, Longmans, London

———— (1980), 'On the Representation of Form and Function', unpublished paper

———— (1981), *Lectives on Government and Binding*, Foris Publications, Dordrecht

Chomsky, Noam and Howard Lasnik (1977), 'Filters and Control', *Linguistic Inquiry* 8, 425–504

Culicover, P., T. Wasow and A. Akmajian (eds.) (1977), *Formal Syntax*, Academic Press, NY

Emonds, Joseph (1970), 'Root and Structure Preserving Transformations', unpublished doctoral dissertation, Massachusetts Institute of Technology

Frege, Gottlob (1879), *Begriffschrift*, translated edition in J. van Heijenoort (ed.), *Frege and Gödel*, Harvard University Press, Cambridge, Massachusetts, 1970

Heny, Frank (ed.) (1981), *Ambiguities in Intensional Contexts*, Reidel, Dordrecht

Montague, Richard (1974), *Formal Philosophy*, Yale University Press, New Haven

Quine, Willard V. O. (1960), *Word and Object*, MIT Press, Cambridge, Massachusetts

1   On Binding*

Noam Chomsky

The earliest work in transformational generative grammar aimed to develop a concept of 'Grammatical Transformation' rich enough to overcome, in a unified way, a variety of problems that arose in the attempt to develop a satisfactory theory of sentence structure and an associated account of meaning and use for natural language. While the goal, from the outset, was what has sometimes been called 'explanatory adequacy', the devices proposed were of so rich and varied a nature as to leave this goal fairly inaccessible. Since that time, research has advanced both in range and in depth. Many new phenomena have been studied, and there has been some progress, I believe, towards a more principled theory of grammar with far more restricted descriptive devices and some abstract principles that are, on the one hand, rather natural for a system of mental computation, and on the other, genuinely explanatory in that they interact to ground and unify a number of properties of rule systems that have been discovered. As proposals have successively been put forth towards a theory of this nature, a variety of problems have arisen, as should be expected. In some cases, they have been overcome by more far-reaching descriptive study or modifications of theory, or shown to be illusory, though many remain.

The idiosyncratic properties of particular languages, which must be learned as language is acquired, set the limit that linguistic theory aims to approach. A person learning English requires empirical evidence to establish that *each other* is a reciprocal phrase, linked to some antecedent. The particular grammar of English must state this fact. It is an open question whether it need state any other facts about reciprocals. It is possible that all other conditions on the position of the reciprocal and the choice of its antecedent are determined by universal grammar, which we may assume to be given as a part of biological endowment. Similarly, the grammar of English must state that a rule of contraction optionally applies to the verb *want* followed by *to*, but it may be that the range of application of this rule is otherwise determined by properties of universal grammar.

The task for linguistic theory is to discover the true nature of the biological endowment that specifies the general structure of the language faculty. It is a good research strategy to try to design a linguistic theory that permits a close approach to the absolute limit set by obvious idiosyncrasies; for example, a linguistic theory that permits the particular grammar of English to stipulate only that *each other* is a reciprocal phrase, that *want + to* undergoes optional contraction, etc. Such a strategy may overshoot the mark by underestimating the idiosyncrasy of particular languages. Investigation of a variety of languages offers a corrective; in principle, there are others, but limitations on human experimentation make them difficult to pursue. But it must be kept in mind that superficial study of a language is rarely informative, and becomes less so as linguistic theory begins to achieve a degree of deductive structure and abstractness. It has often been found in the better-studied languages that apparent idiosyncrasies or exceptions to proposed general principles disappear upon deeper investigation. Furthermore, linguistic principles of any real significance generally deal with properties of rule systems, not observed phenomena, and can thus be confirmed or refuted only indirectly through the construction of grammars, a task that goes well beyond even substantial accumulation and organisation of observations.

If some remarkable flash of insight were suddenly to yield the absolutely true theory of universal grammar (or English, etc.), there is no doubt that it would at once be 'refuted' by innumerable observations from a wide range of languages. One reason is that we have little *a priori* insight into the demarcation of relevant facts — that is, into the question of which phenomena bear specifically on the structure of the language faculty in its initial or mature state as distinct from other faculties of mind or external factors that interact with grammar (in the broadest sense) to produce the data directly presented to the investigator. For another reason, the particular data may be misconstrued in the context of inadequate grammars.

In short, linguistics would perhaps profit by taking to heart a familiar lesson of the natural sciences. Apparent counter-examples and unexplained phenomena should be carefully noted, but it is often rational to put them aside pending further study when principles of a certain degree of explanatory power are at stake. How to make such judgments is not at all obvious; there are no clear criteria for doing so. But as the subject progresses there will come a time — perhaps it has already come — when such moves are quite reasonable. Just as in the sciences that are incomparably more advanced, we can expect with confidence that any theory that will be conceived in the foreseeable future will at best account for some subdomain of phenomena, for reasons that will be unexplained pending further insights. It is a near certainty that any theoretical framework for particular or universal grammar that can be advanced today, or for a long time to come, will be wrong at least in part, or perhaps entirely misdirected. This is true of any effort that goes beyond taxonomy. But this contingency of rational inquiry should be no more disturbing in the study of language than it is in the natural sciences.

In this paper I will assume the general framework of the Extended Standard Theory of generative grammar, and more specifically the version of this theory developed in Chomsky (1975; 1977a; 1977b), Fiengo (1977), Chomsky and Lasnik (1977; henceforth C&L), Lasnik and Kupin (1977), and related work. It is part of a continuing effort to devise a general theory of grammar that will approach the limit set by the idiosyncratic facts of English and a few other fairly well-studied languages. I want to consider a number of problems that have arisen in this framework and some possible solutions to them.

I will assume here that universal grammar provides a highly restricted system of 'core grammar', which represents in effect the 'unmarked case'. Fixing the parameters of core grammar and adding more marked constructions that make use of richer descriptive resources, the language learner develops a full grammar representing grammatical competence. I will assume that core grammar has roughly the following structure:

(1) 1. Base rules
    2. Transformational rules
    3a. Deletion rules   3b. Construal rules
    4a. Filters   4b. Interpretive rules
    5a. Phonology and stylistic   5b. Conditions on
        rules   binding

Base rules fall under some version of X-bar theory. Apart from minor movement rules in the sense of Emonds (1976), transformational rules are restricted to the single rule: Move α, where α is a category. For concreteness, assume the lexicon to be part of the base, with its specific properties.

The rule systems 1 and 2 of (1) constitute the syntax of core grammar. Rules of the syntax are optional and unordered (apart from the ordering in (1)). I will refer to the structures they generate as 'surface structures', though they differ from surface structures as postulated in other variants of generative grammar, being considerably more abstract.

The rules 3a–5a associate phonetic representations to surface structures, the rules 3b–5b, representations in 'logical form' (LF). Empirical considerations enter into the choice of the system of phonetic representation and LF. See the references cited for some discussion.

Assuming the notation of labelled bracketing, we stipulate the following base convention: if the category α is not expanded in a derivation, then apply the rule (2), where e is the identity element:

(2)　$\alpha \to [_\alpha\ e]$

For (3) we use the notation PRO:

(3)　$[_{NP}\ e]$

Movement of the category α is assumed to 'leave behind' the category $[_\alpha\ e]$, in accordance with trace theory. This assumption was implicit in earlier versions of transformational grammar, and becomes explicit when compounding of elementary transformations is forbidden, as discussed in the cited references. Assume that α and its trace are co-indexed, by convention. Thus, the basic transformational rule 'Move α' converts a labelled bracketing of the form (4a) to (4b):

(4)　a.　$\varphi[_\alpha\ \beta]\psi$
　　　b.　$\varphi'[_{\alpha_i}\ e]\psi'$, where (i) $\varphi = \varphi'$ and $\psi' = \psi([_{\alpha_i}\ \beta]/e)$
　　　　　　 or (ii) $\psi = \psi'$ and $\varphi' = \varphi([_{\alpha_i}\ \beta]/e)$
　　　　　 where $\chi(\gamma/\delta)$ results by substitution of γ for δ in χ and
　　　　　 $[_\gamma \ldots]$ is not distinguished from $[_\gamma[_\gamma \ldots]]$

If α in (4a) is already indexed as α_j by an earlier movement rule, then take $i = j$ in (4b); otherwise, let i be a new index previously unused in the derivation.

Further conditions will determine the possibilities for $\chi(\gamma/e)$ (substitution, adjunction, the position to which movement takes place). I assume further that movement rules are subject to the principle of Subjacency and some version of the A-over-A Principle, but I will not pursue these or other related technical questions here.

If we assume that LF has basic properties of some variant of predicate calculus in familiar notations, then NPs must appear in 'argument position' in LF (cf. references cited and Freidin (1978)). It follows that NP Movement must be structure-preserving in the sense of Emonds (1976) if well-formed representations in LF are to be generated, unless there is some rule of interpretation that converts the surface structure into an appropriate representation in LF. Suppose, for example, that the syntax of *there*-insertion is as in Milsark (1974) and that there is a rule of *There* Interpretation among the rules 4b of (1) that assigns to a surface structure of the form (5) a representation such as (6) in LF.[1]

(5) $[_{\bar{S}}[_{NP_i}$ there] is $NP_i...]$ (There is a book on the table.)

(6) (there is $NP_i)_x$ $[_{\bar{S}}[_{NP_i}$ $x]...]$ ((there is a book)$_x$ $[_S$ x on the table])

The rule giving (6) from (5) may be related to the quantifier rule given in May (1977); we may think of (6) as having the sense of (7), where NP_i specifies the type of the variable x:

(7) $(\exists x, x$ an $NP_i)$ $[_{\bar{S}}[_{NP}$ $x]...]$

Then LF has the proper form, even if the rule of NP Movement which (followed by the rule $NP \rightarrow there$) gives the surface structure (5) is not structure-preserving. Cf. Chomsky (1977a, Ch. 2).

Apart from NP Movement, I assume that all instances of the rule 'Move α' are adjunctions, governed perhaps by a 'landing site' theory of the sort developed in Baltin (1978), which requires movement to the end of an appropriately determined category. Assuming that *Wh* Movement is adjunction to COMP, the output will be of the form (9) if the rule is applied to (8):

(8) $[_{\bar{S}}[_{COMP} \pm WH]$ $[_S... [_\alpha$ *wh*-phrase$]...]]$

(9) $[_{\bar{S}}[_{COMP}[_{\alpha_i}$ *wh*-phrase$]$ $[_{COMP} \pm WH]]$ $[_S... [_{\alpha_i}$ $e]...]]$

Double adjunction will be impossible because of the *c*-command requirement for bound anaphora (see below). Hence, repeated *Wh* Movement to COMP is excluded.[2] In a structure such as (9), a rule of *Wh* Interpretation will apply, assigning the status of a quantifier to the *wh*-phrase in COMP and the status of a variable bound by this quantifier to an appropriately selected element within the position of $[_{\alpha_i} e]$, the trace of *Wh* Movement. Cf. Chomsky (1977b) for details.[3] For the proper application of this rule, it is necessary to identify the trace left by *Wh* Movement by an appropriate notational convention. Suppose we assume that movement from S to COMP, by convention, assigns the feature [+COMP] to the trace along with the normal index assigned by the movement rule. We return to the notational question below. Then the trace $[_{\alpha_{[i, +COMP]}} e]$ will be subject to the *Wh* Interpretation rule involving the *wh*-phrase α_i. Movement of *wh*-phrases to COMP may be related to their quantifier-like character, hence a property of LF analogous to the structure-preserving property of NP Movement.

Note that it need not be stipulated, as in C&L, that the position of the *wh*-phrase is to the left of the complementiser when both appear; this follows from the theory of adjunction rules.

Turning next to the rules 3a, 4a, ..., which give ultimately phonetic representation, I will assume[4] that rules of deletion are of restricted variety:

(10) a. free deletion in some domain; e.g. the rule of free deletion in COMP of C&L;
      b. deletion of specific items; e.g. *self*-deletion under EQUI;
      c. deletion of specific categories; e.g. subject deletion as in Spanish;
      d. deletion under identity, which is either governed by Subjacency (e.g. *John went more often to Paris than (*I think) Bill to London*[5]) or is free of all rule conditions (e.g. *John has some friends and I believe your claim that Bill has some ____ too, I don't think that Bill will win but I know a woman who does ____*).[6]

Deletion is governed by a principle of recoverability, the exact nature of which is a nontrivial matter, discussed in the references cited and elsewhere.[7]

We assume that LF cannot contain 'free variables' — i.e. $[_\alpha e]$ — unless α is co-indexed with a *c*-commanding category (and is thus 'bound') or is NP indexed as arbitrary in reference; see below. Suppose we carry this requirement over to the phonetic interpretive component by a convention that $[_\alpha e]$ is automatically deleted unless α is indexed. It follows, in particular, that if α is deleted and β exhaustively dominates α, then β is also deleted. This convention has certain empirical consequences. It follows that PRO and the position of EQUI will not block optional contraction rules, though trace will, an assumption that seems warranted. The same convention enters into a proposed explanation for an interesting generalisation due to Perlmutter concerning subject deletion. Cf. C&L, Chomsky and Lasnik (1978), for discussion.

I will assume that filters have the basic properties discussed in C&L, where it is argued that all aspects of obligatoriness of syntactic rules, contextual dependencies, and ordering fall in a natural way under local surface filters concerned primarily with COMP, something that evidently need not be the case in principle and is therefore interesting, if true.

With these background assumptions, I would like to turn now to the system of rules 3b, 4b, ... that ultimately give representations in LF.

Consider first the 'rules of construal'. These relate anaphors to antecedents. I will assume that the device employed is again co-indexing, where we may think of an index as one of the features constituting the complex symbol for a category, in the sense of Chomsky (1965). A typical and particularly interesting example is the structure (11), which appears in such sentences as (12):

(11) [$_{COMP}$ *wh*-phrase + WH] [$_S$ PRO to V ... t ...] (*t* the trace of the *wh*-phrase)

(12) a. It is unclear who to visit.
      b. John asked Bill who to visit.
      c. John told Bill who to visit.

In C&L and elsewhere, the structure (11) and others like it are called 'structures of obligatory control'. I would like to consider this notion more carefully, pursuing an approach to the phenomenon illustrated in (12) that was suggested in a rather cryptic remark in footnote 30 of C&L.

Some general properties of the structure (11) are familiar and call for explanation in any adequate theory. For example, in (12a) PRO is arbitrary in interpretation, whereas in (12b) it is controlled by *John* and in (12c) by *Bill*. To survey the relevant properties more systematically, consider the structures (13a–c):[8]

(13) a. ... [$_\alpha$ who [$_\beta$ NP visited t]] (*It is unclear who Bill visited.*)

b. ... [$_\alpha$ who [$_\beta$ t visited NP]] (*It is unclear who visited Bill.*)
c. ... [$_\alpha$ who [$_\beta$ NP$_1$ to visit NP$_2$]] (*It is unclear who to visit.*)

In (13), *t* is the trace of *who* and ... may be as in (12).

It is clear, in the first place, that *Wh* Movement takes place in α in each case. Therefore, $\alpha = \bar{S}$ and $\beta = S$. We would not, for example, want to take $\beta = VP$ (with NP$_1$ missing) in case (13c), since *Wh* Movement is an $\bar{S}$-rule and we would like to avoid complicating the base by allowing the expansion of $\bar{S}$ to COMP + VP in contexts where we must also expand $\bar{S}$ to COMP + S in the normal way for the case of (13a), then further stipulating that in COMP + VP, VP must be an infinitive.

In cases (13a) and (13b), NP $\neq$ PRO; that is, construal is impossible. For example, we cannot have such sentences as *John asked Bill who visited*, meaning that John asked Bill which person he, John, visited or which person visited him, John; even though *ask* assigns control by its subject (*John*, in this case), as we see from (12b).

In case (13c), NP$_2$ cannot be PRO with NP$_1$ = trace. Thus, *It is unclear who to visit* cannot mean that it is unclear who is to visit some unspecified person.

In case (13c), NP$_1$ must be PRO; that is, control is obligatory. There is no such sentence as *It is unclear who Bill to visit* meaning that it is unclear which person Bill is to visit, nor can NP$_2$ be missing, even though *visit* can be intransitive.

These are the elementary properties of indirect questions. They might be described in various ways. I will return to a more explicit account directly. In effect, the Specified Subject Condition (henceforth, SSC) and the Propositional Island Condition (henceforth, PIC; alternatively, the 'Tensed-S Condition') of the references cited imply most of these properties. To put it differently, some version of the SSC and PIC is independently motivated by these properties of indirect questions, and is therefore available elsewhere in grammar to serve a truly explanatory function.

The only property of indirect questions that does not fall under the SSC and PIC is the last one mentioned: the fact that control is obligatory in the case of an infinitive. This property was expressed in C&L by designating (11) as a structure of obligatory control, obviously an unsatisfactory stipulation. It was further assumed there (though not discussed clearly) that this property follows from an independently motivated filter (namely, *NP-to-VP); I return to this matter directly.

Assuming some appropriate version of the SSC, the PIC, and a filter requiring control, we can then assign control properly in the case of indirect questions by the simplest rule possible, namely: Co-index. We interpret this as meaning that an arbitrary occurrence of PRO in the embedded structure of (13) is co-indexed with some NP in ... or assigned the index *arb* indicating arbitrary reference if there is no lexical NP in ...[9] General principles ensure that the NP-PRO relation must have PRO *c*-commanded (in the sense of Reinhart (1976)) by its antecedent. See note 27. Therefore, the only meaningful application of the rule Co-index will select NP in the matrix clause and an embedded PRO. If Co-index does not apply and the embedded clause contains PRO, then we end up with a 'free variable' in LF; an improper representation, not a sentence but an open sentence. If the embedded PRO is not in subject position or is in a finite clause, the sentence will be excluded by the SSC or PIC. All cases are therefore covered, if we can formulate the SSC and PIC properly. Application of Co-index is governed by lexical properties of the verb in ...; these determine whether control is assigned by the subject of the matrix verb or an NP in its complement.[10] This seems the optimal solution. It is contingent on a proper account of the SSC, the PIC, and the principle of obligatory control.

Consider next structures of the form (14), the other familiar case of control:

(14) a. John promised (persuaded) Bill [$_\alpha$ that NP$_1$ would (should) visit NP$_2$]
   b. John promised (persuaded) Bill [$_\alpha$ to visit NP]
   c. John tried [$_\alpha$ to visit NP]
   d. it is time [$_\alpha$ to visit NP]

The general properties of these constructions are exactly those of the indirect questions of (13). If we take $\alpha = \bar{S}$ in (14) or, more exactly, assume that (14b)–(14d) have the embedded structure of (15), then we already have the mechanisms to account for the required representations in LF, with no new rules of interpretation needed:

(15) [$_S$ COMP [$_S$ NP$_1$ to visit NP$_2$]]

To account for (14), we apply the rule Co-index, invoking the SSC and PIC to guarantee that only the subject of the infinitive is open to control. We still have the problem of explaining why these infinitives are 'structures of obligatory control'.

Notice that this approach maximises the uniformity of the lexicon and base system, just as in the case of the analogous indirect questions. It is clear that the base rules permit structures of the form V–S̄ (*promise that* ...) and V–NP–S̄ (*promise Bill that* ..., *persuade Bill that* ...). Verbs that take one or the other structure typically allow infinitives in place of S̄ (*promise to* ..., *promise Bill to* ..., *persuade Bill to* ...). In accordance with the assumptions of X-bar theory, we expect to find the same behaviour typically with other lexical categories (*his promise (to Bill) that* ..., *his promise (to Bill) to* ...),[11] though we find throughout the kind of variability that is characteristic of contextual restrictions in the lexicon.[12] We may therefore maintain what seems the simplest base theory: clauses can be finite or infinitive (*I'd prefer that he leave, I'd prefer for him to leave, I persuaded him that* ..., *I persuaded him to* ..., **I persuaded that* ..., **I persuaded to* ..., etc.), and there is no non-clausal source for infinitives.[13] The same is true of the [+WH] analogues, as in (13).

Assuming that we can fill in the gaps cited, we can then give the basic construal rule in the simplest possible form: Co-index. Consider now a second construal rule: namely, the rule that assigns an antecedent to *each other*. Clearly the simplest possible formulation of this rule would be (16):

(16)   *Each other* is a reciprocal phrase.

No grammar of English can say less than this; within an adequate general theory, the grammar of English should say no more than this. That is, (16) should be the only idiosyncratic fact that the language learner must determine from the linguistic environment. Assuming that the notion 'reciprocal' falls into its natural place within universal grammar, it will follow from (16) that *each other* must have an antecedent, in fact, a plural antecedent. We can think of the rule (16) as co-indexing *each other* and some NP that c-commands it; conventions will be required to ensure that this co-indexing is consistent with others. If *each other* is within a tensed clause or the VP of an infinitive, then the PIC or the SSC will exclude the sentence. It seems, then, that the grammar of English can be reduced to (16), for the core cases of reciprocals. In a similar way, we can deal with other cases of 'bound anaphora', including reflexives. Essentially the same analysis carries over to disjoint reference. If we assume the NP-trace relation to be simply a case of bound anaphora, then the general properties of movement rules also follow. Cf. references cited.

In this way, we considerably reduce the complexity of the required rules, approaching the potential limits. And we also have a highly unified theory, with a few abstract principles governing a wide range of phenomena.

Let us now turn to the Specified Subject and Propositional Island Conditions. The preceding discussion suggests that these be regarded as conditions on anaphora, alongside of the Command Condition, rather than as conditions on rule application. In the basic cases, the Command Condition asserts that an antecedent must c-command its anaphor, where β is said to *c-command* α if β does not contain α (and therefore $\beta \neq \alpha$) and α is dominated by the first branching category dominating β; then α is in the *domain* of β. This requirement may be regarded as a general property of co-indexing rules. What about the PIC and SSC?

Let us assume, for the moment, that the basic expansion of $\bar{S}$ and S is (17a), as in Emonds (1976), so that Tense c-commands both the subject and the predicate of S; and let us assume further that NP is the subject of $\bar{S}$ in (17a) and of NP in (17b):

(17) a. $[_{\bar{S}} \text{ COMP } [_{S} \text{ NP Tense VP}]]$
      b. $[_{NP'} \text{ NP } \bar{N}]^{14}$

Thus, we understand 'subject of α' to refer to the least embedded or most prominent NP in α ($\bar{S}$ or NP), in a configurational language such as English, and we understand 'tense of α' to refer to the occurrence of Tense that is, correspondingly, least embedded in α.
Consider now a structure of the form (18):

(18) ... $[_{\beta} \dots \alpha \dots] \dots$

We can formulate the SSC and PIC as in (19):

(19) If α is an anaphor in the domain of the tense or the subject of β, β minimal,^{15} then α cannot be free in β, $\beta = $ NP or $\bar{S}$.

We return to the notion 'anaphor' below. Lexical NPs are not anaphors; PRO, trace, and reciprocal are anaphors; on pronouns, see the appendix.

We say that an anaphor α is *bound* in β if there is a category c-commanding it and co-indexed with it in β; otherwise, α is *free* in β. Note that by this definition, NP_{arb} (i.e. PRO with arbitrary reference) is always free. When we say, still loosely, that a well-formed representation in LF cannot contain a 'free variable', we mean, in the case of [$_{NP}$ e], that it must either have the index *arb* or be bound in LF. This loose usage should not be confused with the technical sense of 'free' just defined. See the appendix.

The condition (19) suggests the familiar phenomenon of Opacity.[16] Thus the domain of modal operators or verbs of propositional attitude is opaque in the sense that a variable within such a domain cannot be bound outside it (under the opaque or *de dicto* interpretation); existential generalisation cannot apply when the quantifier is outside of the domain, nor can substitution of identicals apply; expressions within the domain are non-referential, or at least do not have their normal primary reference in the Fregean sense. For example, from (20) we cannot derive (21):

(20)   John believes that the devil is persecuting him.
(21)   There is something (viz., the devil) that John believes is persecuting him.

While (20) may be true, (21) is presumably false, literally understood.

Given the analogy, we will henceforth refer to (19) or subsequent modifications as the 'Opacity Condition'. In effect, Tense and Subject are 'operators' that make certain domains opaque.

It can easily be seen that this formulation covers the standard cases, as a few examples will illustrate.

Consider (22a–g), where *t* in each case is the trace of the *wh*-phrase:

(22)   a.   it is unclear [$_S$ who PRO to visit t]
       b.   it is unclear [$_S$ who t to visit PRO]
       c.   John asked Bill [$_S$ who PRO to visit t]
       d.   John asked Bill [$_S$ who t to visit PRO]
       e.   they told me [$_S$ what PRO to give each other t]
       f.   I told them [$_S$ what PRO to give each other t]
       g.   they saw [$_{NP}$ John's pictures of each other]

In (22a–f), *t* is co-indexed with the *wh*-phrase and is thus bound in S̄. Therefore, the Opacity Condition does not apply to the trace. In case (22a), PRO is open to arbitrary interpretation, since it is not in the domain of Tense or Subject in the embedded S̄; cf. note 15.

Therefore, (22a) is grammatical, meaning that it is unclear who some unspecified person is to visit. In case (22b), PRO is in the domain of Subject (namely, the trace of *who*), and therefore cannot be free in S̄ in accord with the Opacity Condition; (22b) is not a well-formed structure. The sentence *It is unclear who to visit* cannot mean that it is unclear who is to visit some unspecified person. In case (22c), lexical properties of the verb *ask* make *John* the antecedent (controller) of PRO, which is not subject to the Opacity Condition, so that the sentence means that John asked Bill who John is to visit. Case (22d) is ruled out by Opacity; *John asked Bill who to visit* does not mean that John asked Bill who is to visit John.

Cases (22e) and (22f) are a step more complex. The reciprocal phrase *each other* requires an antecedent, which can only be PRO, by the Opacity Condition. Therefore, PRO and *each other* must be co-indexed for the structure to be well-formed. Lexical properties of *tell* require *me* be the antecedent in (22e), co-indexed with PRO and *each other*, and that *them* be the antecedent in (22f), co-indexed with PRO and *each other*. Since the reciprocal requires a plural antecedent, (22e) is uninterpretable and (22f) means that I told them what they are to give each other, where *they* and *them* are coreferential and the common antecedent of *each other*.

In case (22g), Opacity prevents any interpretation, since *each other* is in the domain of the Subject *John* and is free in the domain NP, though bound by *they*, outside this domain.

Other familiar cases of Control. Reciprocal, Bound Anaphora, and Disjoint Reference fall into place in the same terms.[17] Since Opacity governs trace, the familiar properties of movement rules also follow; movement can be regarded as free, but the resulting structure is ill-formed if the trace is free in an opaque domain. Freidin has shown that the standard arguments for (strict) cyclicity of rule application are without force, in that Opacity and reasonable conditions on argument position in LF have the same consequences (Freidin (1978)). Thus in effect it appears that the principle of (strict) cyclic application of rules follows, where it is relevant, without the need to stipulate it.

The Opacity Condition as given here differs in several important respects from earlier formulations of the PIC and SSC. First, it is given as a condition on LF (or at least, some late stage of interpretation within the rules 3b, 4b, ... of (1)), rather than as a condition on some collection of rules of grammar, including transformations, Control, Bound Anaphora, etc. Second, the Opacity

Condition is not given as a 'constraint on variables' relating two positions involved in some rule, but rather as a condition on the anaphor. This is a significant change, since it allows us to incorporate without specific mention the case of Arbitrary (uncontrolled) Reference, as in (22a,b). It is evident that Arbitrary Reference has essentially the same properties as Bound Anaphora, but earlier formulations did not cover it, since there are no two positions involved in the rule; there is no constraint on variables, in the familiar sense due originally to Ross (1967). This fact raised a problem for earlier formulations, now overcome in a natural way. Third, it is now unnecessary to introduce the notion 'specified' in the analogue to the SSC. In (22f), the reciprocal phrase is co-indexed with PRO, and is therefore not free in $\bar{S}$. This simplification overcomes a problem for the SSC noted by Lasnik. Consider the sentence (23):

(23)   which men did Tom think that Bill believed t saw each other

Here *t* is the trace of *which men*, but if the Reciprocal rule associates *which men* and *each other*, it should be blocked by the SSC, since the specified subject *Bill* intervenes. We now co-index *each other* and the trace *t*, so that it is not free in any opaque context. Note that it was improper in any event to relate the quantifier phrase *which men* to the reciprocal *each other*, which requires a 'referring expression' as its antecedent; cf. the discussion of crossover in Chomsky (1975, 99f.) and Chomsky (1977a, 199ff.). Taken as a condition on LF, the Opacity Condition avoids these problems.

Let us continue now to analyse the Opacity Condition further. Note that there is a certain redundancy in this condition, illustrated by (24), the Tensed-S counterpart to (22e):

(24)   they told me [$_{\bar{S}}$ what I gave each other]

The structure (24) is blocked by the PIC, since *each other* is free in the domain of Tense, but also by the SSC, since it is free in the domain of the subject *I*. It has often proven a useful strategy to try to eliminate redundancies of this sort. We might do so in the present case by restricting the PIC to the subject of a tensed clause. Note that the subject of a tensed clause is unique in another respect; namely, it is assigned nominative Case by a special rule, though the phonetic effects, in English, are seen only with pronouns. Let us assume that there is a general principle of Case Assignment (25) and a general condition (26):[18]

(25) The subject of a tensed clause is assigned nominative Case.

(26) A nominative anaphor in S cannot be free in $\bar{\text{S}}$ containing S.[19]

I will refer to (26) as the 'Nominative Island Condition' (NIC). It will be reconsidered in a more general setting below. It follows from (26) that the trace of *Wh* Movement to COMP can be nominative, but no other trace and no other anaphor (PRO, reciprocal, etc.) can be. We can now revise the Opacity Condition as (27), incorporating only the former SSC:

(27) If α is in the domain of the subject of β, β minimal, then α cannot be free in β.[20]

Let us compare these alternative formulations of the binding conditions. At the metatheoretic level, (26)–(27) has the advantage that it overcomes a redundancy and has the disadvantage that (26) contains a reference to S, for the reasons of note 19, an undesirable complication that will be eliminated below. At the empirical level the two theories of binding differ slightly. Consider such sentences as (28), noted by Jean-Roger Vergnaud [21] which pose a problem for the PIC (hence (19)):

(28) they expected [s that pictures of each other (each other's pictures) would be on sale]

Sentence (28) should be blocked by the PIC, exactly as (29) is:

(29) they expected [s that each other would be there]

Evidently, the status of (28) and (29) is very different. In earlier work based on the PIC, I adopted Vergnaud's suggestion that the PIC be constrained by Subjacency. But now we have a much simpler explanation for the status of these sentences. The reciprocal phrase in (29) is nominative, but in (28) it is not. Thus, the NIC makes the correct prediction. Note that the position of *each other* in (28) is not subject to movement: we cannot derive either (30a) or (30b) from an analogue of (28), where t is the trace of *the men, which men*:

(30) a. the men were expected that pictures of *t* would be on
           sale
      b. which men did they expect that pictures of *t* would be on
           sale

The sentences of (30) are not blocked by the NIC or Opacity; rather,
presumably, by Subjacency, a property of movement rules but not of
such interpretive rules as the rule of construal assigning an antecedent to a reciprocal phrase.[22]
   Luigi Rizzi has observed that in certain infinitival constructions in
Italian in which the subject appears in the nominative Case to the
right of its verb, reflexivisation is blocked. This fact too follows from
the NIC, but not from the PIC.
   I will assume tentatively that (27) is the Opacity rule, and that the
NIC replaces the PIC. Note that it is no longer crucial whether the
analysis of S is as in (17a).
   The COMP position of a tensed sentence has been described as an
'escape hatch' for movement, a fact stipulated in earlier formulations. Under the theory of binding given in (19), no such
stipulation is required. Thus, consider the structures (31) and (32):

(31)   who do they think [$_{\bar{S}}$[$_{COMP}$ t^1] [Bill will see t^2]]
(32)   who do they believe [$_{\bar{S}}$ t to be incompetent]

Both cases are legitimate. Thus in effect we have two 'escape
hatches', as Freidin (1978) notes: the COMP position and the
subject of an infinitive. Nothing further has to be said about the
latter case. Consider (31). Here t^2 is not free in $\bar{S}$ and t^1, while free in
$\bar{S}$, is not in the domain of its subject or tense, hence not in an opaque
domain. Thus, no condition blocks (31). Under the alternative
theory, the NIC gives the same result but, as noted, with a residue of
the stipulation because of the reference to S still to be eliminated. Cf.
note 19.
   Koster (1978a,b) suggests that bounded *Wh* Movement is 'the
unmarked case' and that 'bridge conditions' (in the sense of
Erteschik (1973)) that permit (31) while blocking its counterparts
with *murmur*, *whisper*, etc., in place of *think*, must be specifically
stipulated. Suppose this to be so. Then such languages as Russian,
which do not appear to permit 'unbounded' (i.e. successive-cyclic)
Wh Movement, would reflect the unmarked case. We cannot appeal
to Opacity or to the NIC to express this fact. Presumably, then, it

must be attributed to Subjacency. There is evidence that for English, at least, S is a bounding node for Subjacency.[23] Suppose that $\bar{S}$ is also a bounding node (perhaps universally). Then *Wh* Movement is always 'local' (bounded). The bridge conditions would in effect state that with certain matrix verbs, $\bar{S}$ does not count as a bounding node for Subjacency, a marked property of these verbs.

Both the NIC and the Opacity Condition stipulate that certain anaphors cannot be free in some circumstances. One might imagine that languages vary as to what elements count as 'anaphors' for the binding conditions. Perhaps $[_\alpha\, e]$ (i.e. PRO and trace) fall under the binding conditions universally, and more 'lexicalised' items less freely. There is evidence that the items naturally translated as 'reflexive' in Japanese and Korean do not fall under these conditions, and in fact may be governed by conditions that do not belong to sentence-grammar at all: cf. Kim (1976) and Oshima (1977). Assuming that the binding conditions apply at the level of LF, the trace of *Wh* Movement will be 'partially lexicalised' in that it will have been expanded into a phrase with a true variable by the *Wh* Interpretation rule mentioned earlier (and perhaps also assigned Case; see below. Rizzi (forthcoming) presents evidence that in Italian the trace of *Wh* Movement is not governed by the Opacity Condition, though *Wh* Movement is governed by Subjacency, leading to an interesting configuration of data quite different from English. In fact, Rizzi proposes that Italian differs from English as well in that S is not a bounding node for Subjacency. Given S as a bounding node for Subjacency, there seems to be no empirical effect to the assumption that the trace of *Wh* Movement is an anaphor for Opacity, so that we might assume English to be like Italian in this respect, differing only in the bounding nodes for Subjacency (bounding by S suffices for the *Wh*-Island Condition in English).

The correct theory of core grammar should be expected to have the property that slight changes in the parameters would lead to complex effects on generated structures. These are the kinds of properties that one should search for as theories of core grammar gain a certain degree of deductive structure.

Consider such sentences as (33a,b):

(33) a. They expect there to be pictures of each other in the exhibition.
  b. They expect that there will be pictures of each other in the exhibition.

While judgments are variable and uncertain, these examples seem to have roughly the status of (28), and certainly do not seem at all as unacceptable as comparable examples such as (34):

(34) a. *They$_i$* expect the galleries to exhibit pictures of *each other$_i$*.
      b. *They$_i$* expect that the galleries will exhibit pictures of *each other$_i$*.

Under earlier formulations of the PIC and SSC, (34) and (33) were on a par as violations of these conditions. But now that we are regarding the NIC and Opacity as conditions on LF, this is no longer the case. The sentences of (34) remain in violation of Opacity. But under the analysis of *there*-constructions proposed above (cf. (5)–(7)), the sentences (33a,b) will appear as something like (35) in LF, so that the binding conditions no longer apply:

(35) they expect [(there be pictures of each other)$_x$ [$_S$[$_{NP}$ x] in the exhibition]]

While serious questions arise as to just how such structures should be more closely analysed, there is no longer any reason to expect that their status will be comparable to that of (34a,b), so far as the antecedent-anaphor relation is concerned.

Note that the notion 'subject' in the Opacity rule is a syntactic, not a semantic, notion, even though it appears at the level of LF. Consider, for example, the sentences (36a,b):

(36) a. They expect the books to be given to each other (to them).
      b. They expected John to appear to each other (to them) to be qualified for the job.

The phrases *the books* in (36a) and *John* in (36b) are not 'subjects' of *be given*, *appear* in any semantically significant sense of the notion 'subject' (if there is one), but yet they invoke Opacity, blocking Reciprocal Interpretation and the rule of Disjoint Reference. Furthermore, no overt subject need appear to invoke Opacity, as we can see from the *wh*-questions corresponding to (36):

(37) a. what books did they expect t to be given to each other (to them)

   b. who did they expect t to appear to each other (to them)
       to be qualified for the job

In (37) too the rules of Reciprocal Interpretation and Disjoint
Reference are blocked in the domain of the trace of the *wh*-phrase.
In general, it is the abstract syntactic subject that invokes Opacity,
where 'syntactic subject' is a formal, configurational notion in
English. The subject that induces Opacity may have any semantic
relation — or no semantic relation — to the elements within its
domain. There is, furthermore, no reason to postulate a semantic
rule of 'subject-predicate interpretation' as proposed in Chomsky
(1977a, 177) and elsewhere on the basis of examples that can be
better analysed along different lines.

   The Opacity Condition applies after all rules that assign control
or antecedents. It is therefore reasonable to suppose that it applies at
the level of LF, the system of representations determined by the rules
3b, 4b, ... of (1), the rules referred to as SI-1 in Chomsky (1975;
1977a). If so, the Opacity Condition provides some insight into the
syntax of LF. It suggests that LF should have the form of a syntactic
phrase marker, a position often advanced but certainly not logically
necessary. There is other evidence that the syntax of LF involves
quantifiers and variables in familiar notation — again, there is no
logical necessity for this (cf. Chomsky (1975, Ch. 3; 1977a, Ch. 4)).
The investigation of empirical conditions on the syntax of LF may
prove an important part of the study of grammar.

   It is interesting that we find data suggestive of opacity conditions
in structures lacking a syntactic subject at surface structure, as noted
by Joan Bresnan and David Duncan. Consider, for example, the
following examples:

   (38) a. They regard me as very much like each other (them).
         b. I impress them as very much like each other (them).

There seems to be no syntactic motivation for assigning anything
beyond the obvious surface structure to such sentences. But in
(38a,b) the rules of Reciprocal Interpretation and Disjoint
Reference are blocked, as if there were a subject invoking Opacity. If
subject and object were inverted in (38a,b), neither rule would be
blocked. Such observations might tempt us to develop some semantic analogue to the Opacity Condition, but this is a dubious move,
since as we have already seen the condition relates to the syntax, not

the semantics, of LF. Since the properties of (38a,b) are so similar to those that fall under the syntactic notion of opacity, it seems natural to extend the Opacity Condition directly to them. This is straight-forward, if we assume that at the level of LF these sentences are represented as in (39):

(39) a. they regard me as [ₛ PRO be very much like each other (them)]
      b. I impress them as [ₛ PRO be very much like each other (them)]

The verbs *regard* and *impress* have essentially the control properties of *persuade* and *promise*, respectively; *regard* assigns object control and *impress*, subject control. Thus, PRO is co-indexed with *I*, *me* in (39a) and (39b), not with *they*, *them*. In each case, PRO is the antecedent of the anaphor *each other (them)*; it serves as the semantic antecedent for *each other* and is disjoint in reference from *them*. It follows that *each other* cannot appear in either case because its antecedent is singular, being controlled by *I*, *me*; and *them* in the embedded clause need not be disjoint in reference from the plural pronoun of the matrix clause, because it is 'free' in the domain of a subject (namely, PRO). The situation is reversed if matrix subject and object are inverted.

In short, the Opacity Condition applies without modification if we assume that among the rules of interpretation 3b, 4b, ... of (1) there are 'structure-building' rules that assign to (38a,b) representations such as (39a,b) in LF. This fact provides positive, though indirect, evidence for such rules. In other respects too the structures of (39) seem appropriate for LF — though again, not logically necessary. Thus, considerations of opacity again provides evidence concerning the syntax of LF.

Structure-building rules that associate (39a,b) as the represen-tations of (38a,b) in LF are reminiscent of earlier work that relied on transformational rules for lexical decomposition; for example, the analysis of causatives suggested in Chomsky (1965, 189), or the elaboration of lexical decomposition by transformation guided by a principle that paraphrases should have the same or similar under-lying structure — that is, that transformations map semantic representations onto surface structures.[24] Apart from numerous technical problems, this approach suffered from a serious flaw: since the rules in question were in general quite arbitrary and varied, in accordance with the arbitrariness and variability of lexical structure, there was no reason at all why their 'output' should constitute a class of structures with the simple, regular properties that follow from the assumption of base-generation, as is invariably the case. The point is discussed in detail in Chomsky (1972; 1974) and elsewhere. But similar considerations do not apply if the rules of interpretation operate in the manner suggested here. The syntactic structures fall into a restricted and systematic class of patterns because they are derived by a narrow class of transformational rules from base-generated underlying structures. The representations in LF are 'propositional' because that is the character of the syntax of LF. Abandoning any general effort at lexical decomposition, it is unlikely that the structure-building rules of interpretation go beyond narrow limits, though this remains to be investigated.

Summarising so far, the Opacity Condition (27) and the NIC (26), applying at the level of LF, suffice to account for basic properties of control, several types of anaphora, and movement rules. We have still not dealt with one property of control, however: namely, the fact that the subject of an infinitive not only may be open to control (as the Opacity Condition states) but in many structures must be controlled. Let us turn now to an examination of this property.

Consider again such structures as (40):

(40) ... [$_S$ *wh*-phrase [$_S$ NP to VP]] ... (*I asked whom to visit.*)

This is a structure of obligatory control: the embedded NP must be PRO, subject to a rule of construal. Within the framework of C&L, the obligatory control property of (40) followed from the filter (41), which was independently motivated:

(41) *[$_\alpha$ NP to VP], unless α is adjacent to and in the domain of Verb or *for* ([−N])

By convention, NP in filters was taken to be 'lexical', i.e. containing lexical material or trace. In the immediate domain of a *wh*-phrase, as in (40), the filter requires that NP=PRO.

Although the filter (41) is quite general and leads to some desirable consequences, particularly with regard to infinitival relatives, still it raises certain problems. In the first place, it is unclear why PRO should be excepted; that is, why filters should be restricted to 'lexical' NP. Second, the 'unless clause' seems curious: why should the context [−N] ⎯⎯⎯ (that is, following verb or preposition) play such a central role, and why the requirement of adjacency and command? Furthermore, the filter seems in a certain sense redundant: it in effect recapitulates the basic content of the PIC and SSC (NIC and Opacity), in that it explicitly stipulates a property of subjects of infinitives.

In addition to these metatheoretic questions, there are some other problems. In order to deal with such examples as (42), where trace appears as subject of an infinitive, it was necessary to assign the feature [−N] to the ϕ-complementiser:

(42)   John is certain [ϕ t to win] (*t* the trace of *John*)

This assumption was entirely *ad hoc*; worse, it was essentially for this reason that we were unable, in C&L, to improve the analysis of the complementiser system by eliminating the ϕ-complementiser in favor of [COMP *e*], that is, nonapplication of an optional rule for analysing COMP. In our system, all rules of syntax are optional: therefore, a null complementiser is predicted. There is indeed a phonetically null complementiser, but we were unable to admit it and were compelled, rather, to exclude [COMP *e*] by convention while introducing a zero-complementiser which, furthermore, had an *ad hoc* feature. This seems an indication that something is amiss.

A further technical problem in our analysis, noted by Vergnaud, is that our reliance on the A-over-A Condition required further clarification. Thus, in the case of (43), we relied on this condition to ensure that α_2 and not α_3 would be submitted to the filter (41), but our formulation of this condition would in fact have submitted only α_1 to the filter:

(43)   I believed [$_{\alpha_1}$ him to have found [$_{\alpha_2}$ a man [$_{\alpha_3}$ t to do the job]]] (*t* the trace of the deleted *wh*-phrase of α_3)

The result is unintended, and leads to certain problems. Further technical difficulties arise with reference to indirect questions in such examples as (44) and (45):

(44)   a.   What to do is unclear.
         b.   I told him what to do.

(45)   *I know who t to see Bill (*t* the trace of *who*)

In (44), the phrase *what to do* is represented as (46):

(46) [s[COMP what + WH] [s PRO to do t]] (*t* the trace of *what*)

The phrase (46) is in fact of the form NP-*to*-VP, with NP = *what*, and in (44) is not in the context excluded from the filter (41) under the 'unless-condition'. Yet (46) is not assigned * by the filter (41) in the contexts of (44). And in (45) the embedded clause, though again of the form NP-*to*-VP, with NP = *who*, must be assigned * by (41), although it is in the context covered by the 'unless-condition' of (41). Both of these problems can be overcome by assuming + WH to be a terminal symbol, which blocks application of the filter; but this seems a questionable move.

These problems do not demonstrate that the approach taken was incorrect, but they do raise serious doubts about it and suggest that it might be worthwhile to explore some alternatives. I would now like to turn to one alternative that seems promising.

Consider first the case of infinitival relatives. As shown in detail in C&L, these constructions, with their curious properties, fall under the filter (41), which was independently motivated, with no new rules required at all. Thus we have a genuine explanation for the properties of infinitival relatives. Evidently, this fact argues strongly in favour of (41), despite its problems. It is not easy to improve on an analysis that requires no special rules at all; we can argue against it only if a different and more principled approach suffices to explain the properties of these constructions.

There are two basic cases to be considered: the first, (47), with relativisation of a phrase in the VP; the second, (48), with relativisation of the subject:

(47) a. a man [s[COMP whom for] [NP to give the book to t]]
      b. a man [s[COMP to-whom for] [NP to give the book t]]

(48) a man [s[COMP who for] [t to fix the sink]]

In all cases, at least one of the elements of COMP must delete. If *for* deletes in (47a), we derive (49); if *whom* deletes, we derive (50); if both delete, we derive (51):

(49) a man whom NP to give the book to
(50) a man for NP to give the book to
(51) a man NP to give the book to

The corresponding examples derived from (47b) are (52)–(54):

(52)   a man to whom NP to give the book
(53)   a man for NP to give the book
(54)   a man NP to give the book

The corresponding examples derived from (48 are (55)–(57):

(55)   a man who to fix the sink
(56)   a man for to fix the sink
(57)   a man to fix the sink

The examples (49)–(57) are the basic ones to be considered. Of these, we can at once exclude (53) and (54), since these involve an unrecoverable deletion of *to whom*.[25]

Consider the remaining examples. In (49), no choice of NP gives a grammatical sentence. In (50), choice of a lexical NP gives a grammatical sentence (e.g. *a man for you to give the book to*). Examples (51) and (52) are grammatical only if NP is missing or empty (*a man to give the book to, a man to whom to give the book*). Example (57) is grammatical while (55) and (56) are not, in the dialect under consideration here. These are the basic facts that must be explained, without reliance on (41), which accounts for them directly, as shown in C&L.

An alternative approach to these facts is suggested by the analysis in C&L of such structures as (58):

(58)   I asked the man who you had visited.

Note that (58) may have either the structure (59) (an indirect question) or (60) (a relative clause):

(59)   I asked [NP the man] [s who you had visited]
(60)   I asked [NP the man who you had visited]

The ambiguity of (58) is resolved by stress; *who* is stressed in (59) but not in (60). Correspondingly, *who* cannot be deleted in (59) but may be deleted in (60). In C&L, we suggested that a proper formulation of the condition of recoverability of deletion should account for these facts. In (59), *who* has semantic content: it corresponds to a quantifier, under natural rules of interpretation, as in Chomsky (1977a,b). In (60), it is devoid of semantic content. In this case, stress corresponds to semantic content and immunity to deletion. While it remains to develop the technical details, I think that this is the right approach. Let us consider an extension of it to the infinitival relatives.

Suppose that we stipulate that the rule of free deletion in COMP is obligatory in the context (61):

(61) ——— infinitive complement

We now understand 'obligatory deletion' to mean: delete wherever possible, that is, except where deletion is unrecoverable. (Recall that the rule of free deletion in COMP of C&L does not apply to *whom* in PP, for principled reasons.) Consider the effect of this assumption on (47)–(48).

In case (47a), *whom* must delete; similarly, *who* must delete in (48). In (47b), *to whom* cannot delete. In (47a), *for* may or may not delete and NP may or may not be lexically realised; thus, there are four possible outcomes. In (47b), *for* must delete (since *to whom* does not) and NP may or may not be lexically realised; thus, there are two possible outcomes. There are also two outcomes from (48), since *for* may or may not delete. The result of application of deletion in COMP is therefore (62)–(64):

(62) a. a man to give the book to   (from (47a))
     b. a man for you to give the book to   (from (47a))
     c. a man to whom to give the book   (from (47b))
     d. a man to fix the sink   (from (48))
(63) a. a man to whom you to give the book (from (47b))
     b. a man you to give the book to   (from (47a))
(64) a. a man for to give the book to   (from (47a))
     b. a man for to fix the sink   (from (48))

The examples of (62) are the sole grammatical outputs. To exclude (64a,b), we may appeal to the **for–to* filter of C&L. An alternative would be to restate (61) as (65), extending the obligatory deletion rule to all elements in COMP:[26]

(65) ——— to + VP

The **for–to* filter is now in effect incorporated in the deletion rule.

Dialects would then differ as to whether *for* falls under the obligatory part of the rule, or only the *wh*-phrase in COMP. This alternative has ramifications that I will not consider here. The result of this discussion is as follows. If we assume deletion in COMP to be free, but obligatory before infinitives, and if we interpret 'obligatory' to mean 'delete wherever possible, subject to recoverability', then all examples of infinitival relatives are accounted for except the ungrammatical cases of (63). The principle relied on to account for indirect questions (cf. (59)–(60)) is now extended to infinitival relatives generally. The only cases that 'survive deletion' are those in which deletion is unrecoverable. This seems to be a plausible and principled account of infinitival relatives, assuming that we can somehow account for the examples of (63).

We will see directly that there is an alternative to the *NP-*to*-VP filter that accounts for all of the cases covered by that filter, avoiding the problems noted, and which also accounts for (63), though not for the cases of infinitival relatives that fall under the principle just discussed. That is, this alternative approach, along with the rule of obligatory deletion, accounts for exactly the class of cases covered by the *NP-*to*-VP filter (41), with no redundancy and without the problems of (41).

Recall that rules of deletion, under the analysis of (1), are part of the system of rules that associates surface structures and phonetic representation. As noted in C&L, this is a reasonable assumption, since it captures the fact that deleted elements figure in the determination of LF. But although we have argued that the syntactic component of core grammar consists of rules that are optional and unordered, this is plainly not true of the interpretive components. Thus, rules of phonology are obligatory (up to free variation), as are filters. It does not seem unnatural, then, that deletion rules should be in part obligatory. We might, nevertheless, ask why this obligatory character is present. Perhaps an answer is possible along the 'functional' grounds explored in C&L, where it is noted that the rules governing infinitival relatives, whatever they may be, have the property of radically reducing free variation, permitting exactly one output (or in one case, two outputs) from a set of four or eight generated surface structures. In the framework considered here, this is a consequence of the obligatory proviso of (61) or (65), which is perhaps motivated by this fact.

The analysis just suggested is similar to one proposed for French relatives in Kayne (1975). It might perhaps be extended to other structures. Consider the distribution of English cleft constructions:

(66) a. It is John to whom I gave the book.
      b. It is John (who, that) I gave the book to.
      c. *It is to John to whom I gave the book.
      d. It is to John that I gave the book.
      e. *It is to John (who, that) I gave the book to.

Case (66a) indicates that *Wh* Movement is involved in at least one type of cleft formation; cf. Chomsky (1977b). Case (66b) then follows in the normal way, as in relatives, except that this is one of several constructions where at least some element must appear in COMP — as, for example, in *the idea *(that) John might leave*; cf. C&L. Whatever the further structure of clefts may be, they would seem at least to have the form (67):

(67) it is α $\bar{S}$, where $\alpha = $ NP or PP

But cases (66c) and (66d) are problematic. As (66d) indicates, *to John* may appear in the position of α in (67); as (66a) indicates, *to whom* may appear in the COMP position of the embedded $\bar{S}$. If we assume that α is base-generated in place, then (66c) will be formed, though it is ungrammatical. Furthermore, (66d) seems to involve deletion of *to whom*, generally impossible as we have seen, on grounds of recoverability.

Suppose that we were to say that deletion of the *wh*-phrase is obligatory, subject to the requirement that COMP $\neq$ null, where 'obligatory deletion' is understood as above. Evidently, some relationship is established between α and the complement of $\bar{S}$ in (67). Suppose that this relationship suffices to make deletion 'recoverable' in case (66c). Then deletion is obligatory, giving (66d) as the obligatory variant of (66c), overcoming both problems.

It seems unnatural to try to extend a principle of recoverability to case (66e), which remains unexplained. But there is a simpler reason why (66e) should be excluded, namely, the antecedent *John* does not *c*-command the phrase *who* to which it is connected by the rule of interpretation associating α with the COMP of the embedded sentence.[27]

Such an approach to (66) raises a number of problems, among them the fact that it makes deletion contingent upon construal, something that is not impossible but is still a complication, given the analysis of the structure of grammar in (1). We might avoid this consequence by denying the assumption that α is base-generated. It seems that the rule of relativisation developed in Vergnaud (1974), involving raising of the content of the *wh*-phrase in COMP to the head NP position of the relative, might be extended to the present case, thus co-indexing α and the *wh*-position in the COMP of the embedded $\bar{S}$ by a transformational rule. Now the facts of (66) follow without any assumption of obligatory deletion and without consideration of *c*-command if Vergnaud's rule can be extended to this case.

Returning to the main theme, it remains to account for the deviance of (63) and for the other cases that fall under the *NP-*to*-VP filter (41). I would like to explore an approach to these questions suggested by Jean-Roger Vergnaud.

Among the problems connected with the *NP-*to*-VP filter is the idiosyncratic character of the 'unless condition', which specifies the domain of verbs and prepositions. This seems a strange context for non-application of the filter. However, this configuration is natural elsewhere in grammar, namely, in the context of Case Assignment. See note 18. Suppose we think of Case as an abstract marking associated with certain constructions, a property that rarely has phonetic effects in English but must be assigned to every lexical NP. Roughly, the properties of Case Assignment are as follows. The subject of a tensed clause is assigned nominative Case, the object of a preposition is assigned oblique Case, and the object of a verb is assigned objective Case. But the subject of an infinitive is not ordinarily assigned Case at all, assuming Case Assignment to be a 'local' phenomenon internal to major categories and, in particular, clause-bound.

Evidently, verbs with infinitival complements fall into two categories in English with regard to control: non-control verbs such as *believe*[28] and control verbs such as *try*, *persuade*, and *promise*. Suppose we assume the (partially idiosyncratic) property in question to be that non-control verbs are permitted to govern objective Case across a clause boundary. If, finally, we assume as a general principle that all lexical NPs must have Case, then it will follow that infinitives with lexical subjects will be excluded except as complements of non-control verbs. While this analysis is not equivalent to the *NP-*to*-VP filter, it does cover many of the cases that fall under it, although not those accounted for in terms of the obligatory deletion rule for infinitival constructions. Furthermore, this approach seems to avoid the problems connected with the filter. This is the essential idea. Let us now try to work it out in more detail, aiming at maximum generality.

Suppose that Case Assignment follows these general principles:

(68) a. NP is oblique when governed by P and certain marked verbs;
   b. NP is objective when governed by V;
   c. NP is nominative when governed by Tense.

The notion 'government' will no doubt be related to grammatical relations. In a configurational language such as English, we can specify it in terms of c-command, perhaps as follows:

(69) α is *governed* by β if α is c-commanded by β and no major category or major category boundary appears between α and β.[29]

Assuming (68c) and (69), we must again adopt the analysis (17a): S = NP Tense VP.

We must next determine at what point in derivations Case is assigned and to which NPs, and what the exact meaning of a rule of Case Assignment is. Assuming Case to be assigned to NP under (68), let us suppose further that the feature 'percolates' to the head noun and its determiner and modifiers, in the sense of Dougherty (1969). The feature will have a phonetic effect, in English, only in the case of pronouns and *wh*-phrases, with some dialectal variation that we will not consider. We require further that lexical NPs must have Case, let us say, by the filter (70):

(70) *N, where N has no Case

Suppose that we take oblique Case to be assigned in the base, determined in part by lexical properties of the governing category. Note that Case will then be carried along under movement rules.

Assignment of nominative Case enters into the Nominative Island Condition (NIC; cf. (26)), which figures in the LF-interpretation component of the grammar (3b, 4b, ... of (1)).[30] Furthermore, it must follow NP Movement. But if (70) is to be satisfied generally, non-oblique Case must be assigned to *who-whom* prior to *Wh* Movement; there is a phonetic reflex of this requirement in dialects that distinguish *who* and *whom* in questions and relatives. We can satisfy these requirements by extending the analysis of movement to COMP presented above. Let us now interpret the rule 'Move α' as follows in the case of movement from S to COMP, incorporating earlier conventions:

(71) a. Assign the index [+COMP];
      b. Assign Case under (68);
      c. Adjoin α to COMP (co-indexing, by convention).

Under this convention, non-oblique Case too will be carried along under a movement rule from S to COMP. We will reconsider (71) below.

Finally, let us assume that (68) applies by convention at surface structure, assigning Case to any properly governed NP. Note that these conventions require no ordering of syntactic rules.

There are other constructions to be considered if (70) is to apply properly. We might extend (68b) to the direct object of a dative construction by assuming that verb + indirect object constitutes a 'small VP', replacing V in (68b) by V^i (V with *i* bars). If relative clauses are of the form [$_{NP}$ NP' S̄], then NP' must be assigned the Case of NP, let us say, by extension of the 'Case percolation' device. The same would be required for NPs of the form [$_{NP}$ NP PP]. The subject of gerunds might be assigned Case on the assumption that the possessive element that c-commands it governs Case Assignment as an addendum to (68). Questions of appropriate analysis, which I will not consider here, arise as we attempt to extend the approach to other constructions, for example, predicate nominals or objective subjects of gerunds.

To summarise, an NP has Case when (a) it is properly governed under (68); (b) it is in COMP and its trace is properly governed under (68); (c) it is oblique and it or its trace is properly governed under (68a). An NP with lexical head must have Case, under (70). We may tentatively assume that none of this discussion falls within the particular grammar of English, but rather follows from principles of universal grammar.

Note that these conventions permit an NP subject to be nominative while its trace is governed by V, but they do not permit an NP subject to be nominative or objective (i.e. non-oblique) while its trace is governed by P. If we interpret conflict of Case Assignment rules as assigning *, it then follows that there can be no preposition stranding under NP Movement, though there can be under *Wh* Movement. Furthermore, pseudo-passives are possible only if there has been reanalysis of a [verb ... P] construction as a verb, in the base, so that the NP following P is objective rather than oblique, in such constructions as (72):

(72) a. ... laugh at NP
     b. ... take advantage of NP

These properties of preposition stranding and pseudo-passive, in any event a marked phenomenon, seem quite general; cf. Van Riemsdijk (1978b). That reanalysis is involved in pseudo-passives is also a well-motivated assumption; cf. van Riemsdijk (1978b) and Anderson (1977). The conclusions of Anderson (1977) on NP movement in nominal constructions also fall naturally into this framework. It seems reasonable to assume that re-analysis takes place in the base, among other idiom rules, which generally apply to base structures.

Let us now turn to a comparison of this approach with the *NP-to*-VP filter (41). Note that the exclusion of PRO, stipulated for (41), now requires no special comment. Since PRO does not contain lexical N, it will simply not be subject to the filter (70) or will be deleted by the convention discussed below (10). The 'unless condition' has been replaced by principles that assign Case in the domain of verbs and prepositions, under proper government. The principles (68) and (70) do single out the subject of an infinitive, but indirectly, without the explicit redundancy of the *NP-to*-VP filter, and on principled grounds, if (68) and (70) prove to be of some generality. Hence, the three general problems noted in connection with (41) are resolved.

Before turning to the more technical problems raised concerning (41), let us see how the Case Assignment theory deals with the question with which we began, namely, the requirement that the embedded NP in (40), repeated here as (73), must be PRO:

(73) ... [s *wh*-phrase [s NP to VP]] ... (*I asked whom to visit.*)

The embedded NP, if lexical, must be assigned Case, which is impossible by (68). Thus, unless this NP is PRO, the construction will be blocked by (70). For the same reason, the subject of an indirect question cannot be the 'questioned' item, as in (74):

(74)   *I wonder [s who [s t to read the book]] (*t* the trace of *who*)

In the structure (74), which if grammatical should have the perfectly sensible interpretation *I wonder who is to read the book*, no Case has been assigned to *who*, so that * is assigned by (70).

We noted above that the *Wh*-Island Condition follows from Subjacency, apart from the case of the subject of the embedded *wh*-complement, as in (75a) and perhaps (75c):

(75)   a.   *they wondered [what [each other to tell Bill t]]
       b.   *who [s is it unclear [s t [s t to tell Bill]]]
       c.   *who [s is it unclear [s what [s t to do]]]

In case (75a), *each other* is not assigned Case and is blocked by (70); thus, (75a) does not mean that they each wondered what the others are to tell Bill. Case (75b) might arise from successive cyclic movement, with *t* the trace of *who*. But again, no Case is assigned to *who*. The same is true of (75c), with *t* the trace of *who*, though in this case Subjacency would also be violated.[31] Thus the *Wh*-Island Condition follows, in full.

Let us turn now to the technical problems raised in connection with filter (41). The first of these had to do with the case of raising, as in (76), where *t* is the trace of *John*:

(76)   a.   John is certain [t to win] (=(42))
       b.   John seems [t to be a nice fellow]

In (76), *John* is assigned nominative Case by (68c). Thus, the filter (70) does not apply and (76a,b) are grammatical. Compare the analogous case of *Wh* Movement, as in (77a,b), where *t* is the trace of *who*:

(77)   a.   *who is it certain [t to win]
       b.   *who does it seem [t to be a nice fellow]

Here no Case is assigned to *who*, so the sentences are ungrammatical under (70).

In C&L, to accommodate (76) it was necessary to assign the feature [−N] to the ϕ-complementiser, one of the defects of the NP-*to*-VP filter (41) noted above. Now this is unnecessary. What is more, we can dispense with the ϕ-complementiser entirely, adopting the optimal analysis of COMP, with [comp *e*] as the null COMP when the optional rule expanding COMP is not applied.

The further technical problems discussed in connection with (43) and (44)–(46) do not arise. We can now complete our alternative analysis of infinitival relatives. Recall that all cases of this construction were accounted for in a rather natural way in terms of a rule of obligatory deletion, with the exception of (63a,b), repeated here as (78a,b):

(78) a. *a man to whom you to give the book
     b. *a man you to give the book to

The Case Assignment theory accounts for these examples directly: the subject *you* of the embedded clause is not assigned Case, so that * is assigned by (70).

We have so far been considering infinitival complements to verbs with the subject PRO, which we take to be 'the unmarked case'. But in English, as in some other languages, there are certain constructions with lexical subjects for infinitives. A special marked rule is therefore required to accommodate them.

We have been taking Case Assignment to be clause-bound in the unmarked case, as seems natural. Cf. (68). Suppose that certain verbs are assigned a marked feature, call it F, which permits Case to be assigned across clause boundary. In English, for example, the verb *believe* with infinitival complement will be marked [+F], so that Case will be assigned to the embedded subject NP in (79) by (68b):

(79) I believe [s̄[s NP to be a fool]]

NP in such structures as (79) may be lexical or it may be trace, as in (80):

(80) a. I believe [John to be a fool]
     b. John is believed [t to be a fool]
     c. who do you believe [t to be a fool]

In (80a), *John* is assigned objective Case by (68b); in (80b), it is assigned nominative Case by (68c). In (80c), *who* is assigned objective Case by (68b) under the interpretation of 'Move α' given in (71).

It appears to be an idiosyncratic property of *believe* that it has the feature [+F]. Thus, the corresponding verb in French (or German) is a control verb, so that we have (81):

(81) a. *je crois [PRO avoir vu cet homme]
          (*I believe [PRO to have seen that man]*)
      b. *je crois [Jean avoir vu cet homme]
          (*I believe [John to have seen that man]*)

Note that if marked cases of lexical subjects of infinitives are described in these terms, then there will never be such structures as (82):

(82) a. NP V NP [Tom to VP]
          (cf. *John persuaded Bill [PRO to win]*)
      b. NP V PP [Tom to VP]
          (cf. *John appealed to Bill [PRO to win]*)
      c. NP V [*wh*-phrase [Tom to VP]]
          (cf. *John asked [what [PRO to do]]*)

Similarly, since adjectives do not assign Case under (68), there is no analogue to the feature F for adjectives. Thus, we have adjectives of control, raising adjectives, and adjectives with *for*- and *that*-complementisers, as in (83), but no adjectives that take infinitive complements with lexical subjects and empty COMP, as in (84), analogous to (80):

(83) a. John was lucky [PRO to win]
      b. John is certain [t to win]
      c. John is eager [for Tom to win]³²
      d. John is sorry [that Tom won]
(84) a. John is ADJ [Tom to VP] (cf. (83a))
      b. it is ADJ (for NP) [Tom to VP] (cf. *it is pleasant (for us)* [*for Tom to do the hard work*])
      c. John is ADJ of NP [Tom to VP] (cf. *John is proud of Bill for having won*)³³
      d. it is ADJ of NP [Tom to VP] (cf. *it was nice of John* [*to have done that*])

We have been attempting to maintain throughout what seems to be the minimal theory of embedded clauses: namely, they can be finite or infinitival; all rules analysing some category (in particular,

COMP and NP) are optional. It follows then that the underlying structures for (82) and (84) will be generated in the base (but see note 33), but will be blocked by the filter (70), invariably, with no possibility for the kind of marked exception that we find in the adjacent complement to a verb.

Clearly some lexical feature, which is at least in part idiosyncratic, must distinguish English *believe* from French **croire** 'believe' and from standard English *try*, and must distinguish the latter from the dialectal variants that permit infinitives with lexical subject as complements of *try* (cf. C&L). We have been assuming that in the unmarked case, verbs that take bare (i.e. null COMP) infinitive complements are verbs of control. Considering other languages and earlier stages of English, it appears that *for*-infinitivals too constitute a marked category. Let us assume, then, that embedded clauses may freely be tensed or infinitival, and that in the unmarked case tensed clauses take *that* (or an equivalent; cf. C&L) while infinitival complements of verbs do not expand COMP — they have [$_{COMP}$ *e*]. In the unmarked case, verbs with infinitival complements are 'control verbs'; they have the redundantly determined feature [+Control]. Non-control verbs — that is, those with the feature [−Control] — constitute the marked case; these are the verbs that we have designated [+F]. For the moment, then, we may take [+F] to be another notation for [−Control]. Among the noncontrol verbs there are two categories: those that take *for*-COMP and those that take null COMP, like control verbs. As Lasnik and Bresnan have observed, these categories are at least in part associated with semantic features: *want*-type versus *believe*-type verbs. The feature [+F] permits Case Assignment across the clause boundary of the infinitival complement, a marked property.[34]

The marked *for*-infinitive construction has the form (85) in the base:

(85)   [$_{\bar{S}}$[$_{COMP}$ for] [$_S$ NP to VP]]

Only [+F] verbs take such complements as (85), though of course (85) appears quite freely in other contexts. To accommodate these constructions within the present framework, we must assume that *for* assigns Case to NP in (85) (presumably, oblique Case by rule (68a)) and that when it does so it is undeletable. Under these assumptions, the examples discussed in C&L will follow. It has been observed that the *for*-complementiser shares some of the properties of the homophonous preposition; thus, there is a correspondence between derived nominals that take *for*-NP complements and *for*-S̄ complements (*desire for food, desire for Bill to leave*, etc.). Again following a suggestion of Vergnaud's, let us assume that in the base, the complementiser *for* may or may not be assigned the feature [+P] (that is, assigned to the category Preposition). If it is assigned this feature, it is undeletable under the recoverability condition.[35] If *for* is not assigned [+P], it will not assign Case and may delete, and in the complement to a [+F] verb such as *want*, the subject of the infinitive will be assigned objective Case by the governing [+F] verb; there are dialectal differences regarding deletion of *for* in these contexts. On these assumptions, we obtain the basic results of C&L. Other possible approaches come to mind, but it is difficult to evaluate alternatives, given the rarity of the construction.

Certain other marked properties of the verbal system might be accommodated with special additional rules. We have taken [+F] to be the same as [−Control]. Suppose that we distinguish these features, adopting the redundancy rules (86a,b), which in effect identify them, in the unmarked case:

(86) a. If [+Control] then [−F].
      b. If [−Control] then [+F].

Case (86a) may be exceptionless, though this is not a logical necessity. Its effect is to establish partial complementary distribution between PRO and lexical NP; see note 38. An exception to (86b) would be a noncontrol verb that does not assign Case and thus does not permit a lexical subject in an infinitive complement. Such a verb cannot take an infinitive complement with PRO or lexical subject, but it can take an infinitive complement with a raised (NP-moved) subject. We thus have the situation illustrated by (87a–c):

(87) a. *I said (alleged) John to be a fool.
      b. *I said (alleged) PRO to be a fool.
      c.   John is said (alleged) t to be a fool. (*t* the trace of *John*)

In (87a), *John* receives no Case since the matrix verb is [−F]. In (87b), PRO is uncontrolled since the verb is [−Control]. But in (87c), *John* receives nominative Case, so that the sentence is grammatical. Note that *Wh* Movement from the embedded position is impossible, as in (88a), though (88b) is grammatical:

(88) a. *who [is it said (alleged) [t to be a fool]]
      b. who [t is said (alleged) [t to be a fool]]

In case (88a), *Wh* Movement assigns no Case to *who*, but in case (88b), Case is assigned by the nominative construction of the trace of *who*.[36] Such exceptional verbs as *say*, *allege*, and so forth, can therefore be marked [−F] but not as verbs of control.

Note that normal raising verbs such as *seem* can simply be given the unmarked specification [−F]. By virtue of their inherent argument structure, they cannot take lexical subjects (they are in effect monadic predicates, taking a propositional argument), and a matrix PRO subject cannot appear uncontrolled in LF, so that raising is obligatory.

There is a curious and somewhat marginal phenomenon in French that may be related to these considerations.[37] While **croire** '*believe*' is a verb of control, sentences with trace instead of **PRO** in the position of the embedded subject of an infinitive seem to be more or less acceptable. Thus we have the situation of (89a–d):

(89) a. je crois [PRO avoir vu cet homme] (=(81a))
      b. *je crois [Jean avoir vu cet homme] (=(81b))
      c. ?qui crois-tu [t avoir vu cet homme]
          ('who think-you [t to have seen that man]')
      d. ?il le croit [t avoir vu cet homme]
          ('he him thinks [t to have seen that man]')

One might express these facts by stipulating that while **croire** as distinct from *believe* does not have the marked feature [+F], it marginally permits Case Assignment across clause boundary to a null NP, in violation of (86a). It may be that the marginal constructions (89c–d) are taken as somehow analogous to (89a).

Turning once again to the notion of control, recall that verbs of control impose either subject control, as in (90a–c), or complement control, as in (91a–d):[38]

(90) a. John tried [PRO to win]
      b. John promised (Bill) [PRO to win]
      c. John asked (Bill) [what [PRO to do t]]
(91) a. John persuaded Bill [PRO to leave]
      b. John told Bill [what [PRO to do t]]
      c. John appealed to Bill [PRO to leave]
      d. it was sad for us [for [PRO to leave]]

Arbitrary control (i.e. the index *arb*) is assigned to PRO in such constructions as (92a–e):

(92) a. it is unclear [what [PRO to do t]]
      b. it is time [for [PRO to leave]]
      c. it is sad [for [PRO to leave]]
      d. it is a nuisance [for [PRO to have to leave]]
      e. John was asked t [what [PRO to do t]]

I will assume that the basic principle of control is the 'Minimal Distance Principle' of Rosenbaum (1967). That is, a verb with a complement assigns complement control and a verb lacking a complement assigns subject control. But certain verbs (e.g. *promise* or *ask* with an indirect question complement; cf. Chomsky (1977a, Chapter 3)) are marked in the lexicon with the feature [+SC] indicating 'assigns subject control'. Other verbs (e.g. *want, believe*) are lexically marked [−Control], therefore [+F] (redundantly, for verbs such as *want* with *for*-complement). The notion 'complement' must be properly defined to include direct objects and the NP of certain prepositional phrases, NPs that are 'thematically related' to the verb in an appropriate sense. Cf. notes 10 and 27.

Consider now the theory of control for the context (93):

(93) ... V ... [$_\bar{S}$ COMP ... [$_{NP}$ *e*] ...]
      where V = [−F] and V and $\bar{S}$ *c*-command one another
(94) NP is a *controller* for V in (93) if
      a. NP is an indexed NP properly related to V;
      b. if V = [+SC] then NP is the subject of V.

The notion 'properly related', still to be clarified, includes subjects, direct objects, and certain complements. We assume that Control applies in the course of a systematic indexing procedure for NPs to which we return in the appendix. Assume the procedure to be 'top-to-bottom', in the sense that an index is assigned to an NP only if all NPs *c*-commanding or dominating it have been indexed. NPs not yet indexed by a movement rule will be indexed by this procedure; the procedure assigns but does not change indices. A controller, then, can be a lexical NP, trace, or PRO already assigned an index by Control, as in *it is sad for us [PRO to try [PRO to win]]*, where the subject of *try* controls the doubly-embedded PRO.

The rule of Control for the context (93) can be given as (95):

(95) In (93),
- a. if COMP ≠ null and V has no controller, then [NP e] is assigned *arb*;
- b. [NP e] is assigned the index of the nearest controller.

A controller c-commanded by S̄ of (93) is 'nearer' to [NP e] than one not c-commanded by S̄; see the appendix for an extension to other cases. Case (95b) thus assigns to [NP e] the index of an appropriate NP in the complement of V = [−SC] if there is such a complement, and otherwise the index of the subject of V.

Assume the order (a), (b) as given in (95). We continue to assume that (95) is an index-assigning and not an index-changing rule, like other rules of indexing, so that if *arb* is assigned by case (a), then case (b) is inapplicable; [NP e] must be without index for (95) to apply. Like other rules of the interpretive component, rule (95) is obligatory. In the context (93), the rule of Control (95) must apply or the construction is assigned *.

As noted earlier, conventions are required to ensure that co-indexing under (95b) is consistent with other indexing rules. The Control rule must be extended to other constructions that we have not considered; for example, if there is no V as in (93), then (95a) applies without regard to the (vacuous) condition on V, as in *for PRO to leave would be a mistake*.

The Opacity Principle and the NIC ensure that only subjects of nontensed categories S̄ and NP will be anaphors under the rule of Control; and the principles of Case Assignment guarantee that lexical NP will not appear in place of PRO in (92a,e), though it may in (92b,c,d). Cf. note 38. It is also necessary to ensure that [NP e] in (95) not be contained in another NP within S̄ (e.g. *it is a nuisance (for us) for pictures of PRO to be on sale*). We will simply stipulate this requirement, leaving it unexplained.[39]

Consider now the examples (90)–(92). All are of the form (93), so that (95a) must apply if its condition is met and (95b) must apply if (95a) has not applied. In the examples of (90) and (91), the condition of (95a) is never met. Therefore, rule (95b) applies, assigning subject control in (90) and complement control in (91). In case (92a), the condition of (95a) is met: COMP = *what* ≠ null and V lacks a controller, *it* being nonlexical. Therefore, (95a) applies, assigning *arb* to PRO. The same is true of (92b,c,d), where COMP = *for*. Case (92e) is more complex. The verb *ask* is assigned [+SC] in the lexicon in this construction. COMP = *what* ≠ null and *ask* lacks a controller, *John* being the subject of the copula, not of *ask*; and *ask* is the only verb *c*-commanded by $\bar{S}$ of (93). Therefore, the condition of rule (95a) is satisfied and the rule applies, assigning *arb*. Consider next the examples of (96), where *t* is the trace of *John*:

(96) a. *John was tried [t to VP]
      b. *John was promised [t to VP]
      c. *John was promised t [PRO to VP]
      d. John was persuaded t [PRO to VP]
      e. John was believed [t to VP]

Examples (96a)–(96d) fall under (93), so the Control rule (95) is applicable and must apply. Since COMP=null in each case, rule (95a) is inapplicable. In cases (96a,b,c), the verb V of (93) is a verb of subject control; but as in (92e) the verb lacks a subject. Therefore, the Control rule cannot apply and the construction is assigned * by virtue of nonapplication of an obligatory rule.

Case (96d) is straightforward: *persuade* is a verb of complement control and the trace *t*, in object position, assigns control properly under (95b). Given that *believe* is lexically marked [+F], case (96e) does not fall under (93). Therefore, the Control rule (95) is inapplicable and (96e) is grammatical.

We can therefore accommodate in a natural way the well-known resistance of verbs of subject control to passivisation;[40] there is no subject under passive, and hence no way for control to be assigned. Note that it would be incorrect to say that verbs of subject control do not passivise, as we can see from (92e), contrary to what is stated in Chomsky (1977a, 14). Rather, such verbs do not passivise unless arbitrary control is assigned in the complement. That is, the operative principle seems to be that the Control rule (95) is obligatory where applicable, as is generally the case with interpretive rules.

Consider next such forms as (97a,b):

(97) a. *I believe [PRO to VP]
      b. *I want (very much) [for [PRO to VP]]⁴¹

Neither example falls under (93), since the verbs are [+F]. Therefore, the Control rule does not apply and PRO is left without an index; the representation in LF is not well-formed, containing a 'free variable'.

Notice that if a verb of the *want*-category appears as V of (98), the constructions are more or less acceptable if NP is lexical but not if NP = PRO:

(98)   it is V + en [for [NP to VP]]

Thus we have (99a–c):

(99)   a.   It is preferred that John arrive a few minutes late.
       b.   It is preferred for John to arrive a few minutes late.
       c.   *It is preferred to arrive a few minutes late.

The constructions are marginal and judgments uncertain but this conclusion seems to me correct. It follows from the status of *prefer* as [−Control], so that the Control rule (95) is inapplicable, leaving a 'free' PRO in (99c).

Consider examples (100a–c), where *t* is the trace of *John*:

(100)   a.   John was asked [what [t to do]]
        b.   John asked [what [t to do]]
        c.   John told Bill [what [t to do]]

All of these examples correspond to well-formed sentences, but with unwanted derivations. In each case, the sentence is derived by NP Movement of *John* from the subject position of the embedded clause to the subject position of the matrix sentence. The embedded clause in each case is of the form (93) so that the Control rule (95) must apply (rule (95a) in case (100a); rule (95b) in cases (100b,c)). But the requirement that the Control rule (95) be an index-assigning rule prevents application of (95), so that * is assigned. Note that the derivations also violate Subjacency. (See note 23.)

The empirical effect, apart from preventing obviously unwanted derivations, is that idiom chunks do not appear in the subject position of such constructions as *NP asked (NP) what to VP*, *NP promised (NP) to VP*, etc. The latter property might, alternatively, be stipulated in terms of the argument structure of verbs of subject control, but this seems a questionable move, since clearly we want to say quite generally that the subject position is not obligatorily filled in semantic representation, as in agentless passives. The general property of verbs that we hope to capture in the theory of LF is that one argument position must be filled (object, for transitive verbs;

subject, for intransitive verbs — in effect, an 'ergative' requirement, extended in an obvious way for verbs that take other obligatory complements). If the analysis presented here is tenable, then no more than this is required.

To conclude this discussion, let us return to the inelegance of formulation in the NIC discussed earlier, namely the reference to S in (26), repeated here as (101):

(101)   A nominative anaphor in S cannot be free in $\bar{S}$ containing S.

The reference to S was required on the assumption that in (102), t^1 and t^2 are nominative; cf. note 19:

(102)   who did they think $[_{\bar{S}}[_{COMP} t^1] [_S t^2$ would win]]

If t^1 is not nominative in (102), then (101) can be simplified to (103), which should be its proper form:

(103)   A nominative anaphor cannot be free in $\bar{S}$.

With the formulation (103), the metatheoretic disadvantages of the NIC as compared with the PIC disappear, while the empirical advantages of the NIC remain.

The relevant rule of Case Assignment is (71), repeated here as (104), which gives conventions for the rule 'Move α' in the case of movement from S to COMP:

(104)   a.   Assign the index [+COMP];
         b.   Assign Case under (68);
         c.   Adjoin α to COMP, co-indexing.

Recall that assignment of the feature [+COMP] in step (a) was simply a device to facilitate the rule of *Wh* Interpretation.

Under a strict interpretation of the system developed above, when some category α is moved by a transformational rule,[42] all features of the category (including Case) are moved, and no feature (even Case) is left behind as part of the trace. Thus in fact there is no reason to suppose that t^1 is nominative in (102), and hence no reason not to accept (103) as the NIC. There is, however, reason to suppose that t^2 in (102) does retain the case assigned under (104b); namely, on this assumption, the NIC will apply to block the sentence (105):

(105)   who$_1$ [$_S$ did you wonder [$_{\bar S}$ what$_2$ [$_S$ t$_1$ saw t$_2$]]]

It is not entirely clear what weight to give to this consideration, since (105) is also blocked by Subjacency. But compare (105) with (106):

(106)   what$_1$ [$_S$ did you wonder [$_{\bar S}$ who$_2$ [$_S$ t$_2$ saw t$_1$]]]

Most speakers find (106) considerably better than (105). But if a violation of Subjacency is what faults (105), then the judgments should be similar, since (106) violates Subjacency (as well as, perhaps, Opacity).[43] Similarly, consider the examples of (107):

(107)   a.   what$_1$ [$_S$ do you know [$_{\bar S}$ how$_2$ [$_S$ PRO to do t$_1$ t$_2$]]]
        b.   what$_1$ [$_S$ did you wonder [$_{\bar S}$[how well]$_2$ [$_S$ he did t$_1$ t$_2$]]]
        c.   who$_1$ [$_S$ did you wonder [$_{\bar S}$[how well]$_2$ [$_S$ t$_1$ did his job t$_2$]]]

For reasons not relevant here, (107a) is grammatical. Again, (107b,c) differ in acceptability for many speakers, with case (107b) being more acceptable than the completely unacceptable case (107c). Assuming that (105) and (107c) violate the NIC, we can describe (though not explain) the difference of judgment by taking the NIC to be an 'inviolable' constraint, as compared with Subjacency (and Opacity, if relevant), which is, for some reason, 'weaker' in these constructions (that is, with the trace of a *wh*-phrase as anaphor). There is then some reason to suppose that t_1 in (105) and (107c), and t^2 in (102), retain their Case under *Wh* Movement.[44]

It is not unreasonable that this should be so. Recall that the position of movement to COMP is 'semi-lexicalised' in the sense that the rule of *Wh* Interpretation inserts a variable in that position, a fact with interesting consequences as noted in Chomsky (1975; 1977a). So far, Case has been restricted in well-formed structures to lexical NPs. If we consider the position of a bound variable in LF to be 'lexical', then Case should be extended to this position as well. On this assumption, let us replace the convention (104) by (108), for the case of movement of α from S to COMP:

(108)   a.   Assign Case under (68);
        b.   Adjoin α to COMP, co-indexing, with the assigned Case as part of the index.

We can now dispense with (104a) and the feature [+COMP]. The position of movement to COMP will be identified for the rule of *Wh* Interpretation by the fact that this is the only instance of [$_{NP}$ *e*] indexed with Case in a well-formed LF.[45]

Summarising, we take the general structure of core grammar to be as in (1). The base rules include the lexicon, in which such marked features as F and SC are assigned. The transformational part of the syntax consists of the rule 'Move α' and the Case Assignment rule (68); the convention (108) applies in the special case of movement from S to COMP. The phonetic interpretation component includes deletion rules such as free deletion in COMP, obligatory before infinitive complement (cf. (61)); and filters, such as (70), which requires Case on N. The LF-interpretive component includes lexically-determined structure-building rules to give such forms as (39); the Control rule (95); the Reciprocal rule (16); rules interpreting quantifiers such as the *There* Interpretation rule (5)–(6) and the *Wh* Interpretation rule; and the binding conditions NIC (104) and Opacity (27).

Appendix

As noted in the text, some technical details must be added to incorporate the rule of Disjoint Reference under the binding conditions. I will sketch the outlines of a more general theory of indexing within which such an account can be given.

Suppose we continue to associate non-negative integers with NPs as their indices, now reserving the integer 1 for arbitrary reference, what was called *arb* above. Assume that each movement rule assigns indices as described above; cf. (4). This convention gives a partial indexing in surface structure, with no conflict of indices. Turning to the interpretive component, let us assume that indexing applies to the full sentence 'from top to bottom' to assign indices to the remaining NPs; an index is assigned to NP only when all NPs that *c*-command or dominate it have been indexed.

Indexing is assigned in part by rules of construal; Control in the case of [$_{NP}$ *e*], Reciprocal in the case of *each other*, and Bound Anaphora in the case of pronouns in certain idioms (e.g. *John lost his way, John blew his cool, John hurt himself*). The last rule, which I will not discuss here, is very similar to the Reciprocal rule; see references cited earlier and Helke (1971) for the basic idea. We will refer to the items indexed by rules of construal as *anaphors*. It remains to assign indices to nonanaphors: lexical NP and pronouns apart from the bound idioms.

Take the index of each nonanaphor to be a pair (r, A), where r is the *referential index* and A the *anaphoric index*. The referential index is an integer, the anaphoric index a set of integers. Proceeding still from top to bottom, suppose we reach the nonanaphoric NP α. If α has already been assigned the index i by a movement rule, take i to be its referential index; otherwise assign it some new referential index $i \geq 2$. Take the anaphoric index A of α to be $\{a_1, \ldots, a_n\}$, where a_j is the referential index of some NP c-commanding α (A maximal). Omitting null anaphoric indices, we will now have such representations as (109):

(109)   John$_2$ told Bill$_{(3, \{2\})}$ about him$_{(4, \{2,3\})}$

We will interpret the anaphoric index $A = \{a_1, \ldots, a_n\}$ of α to mean that α is disjoint in reference from each NP with referential index a_i. Thus, *him* in (109) is disjoint in reference from *John* and *Bill*, and if *John* were to replace *him* (or *Bill*) in (109), the two occurrences of *John* would be disjoint in reference. Of course, 'disjoint reference' in this context has to do with intended reference; actual reference is outside the scope of grammar. On coreference of lexical and pronominal NPs, see Lasnik (1976).

The rules of Control, Reciprocal, and Bound Anaphora make reference to the referential index of the c-commanding NP. Applying these rules and the rule of index-assignment for nonanaphors systematically from 'top to bottom', we fully index the sentence under consideration. It remains to add details and clarification,[46] but this will suffice as a general framework.

Turning now to the binding conditions, we may think of them as deleting certain indices from the anaphoric index of a pronoun, thus in effect blocking certain cases of disjoint reference and permitting reference to be free. The binding rules hold of anaphors and pronouns, not lexical NPs; thus, pronouns are like lexical NPs in the manner of their indexing, and like anaphors in that they fall under binding conditions. It follows, then, that disjoint reference will hold between *John* and the embedded subject in (110a) whether the latter is lexical or a pronoun, but in (110b) only if it is a lexical NP:

(110)   a.   John expected [NP to win] (NP = *John* or *him*)
        b.   John expected [that NP would win] (NP = *John* or *him*)

To unify the discussion of anaphors and pronouns for the binding conditions, let us call i the *designated index* of α, α an anaphor or pronoun, if i is the anaphoric index in the case of a pronoun or the referential index in the case of an anaphor. Thus, if the index of α is (r,A), the designated index is A; and if the index of α is r, the designated index is r. We can now generalise the technical notion 'free' defined above:

(111)   Suppose that α has the designated index j and i is an integer such that $i=j$ or $i \in j$. Then α is *free*(i) in β if there is no γ in β with index i that c-commands α.

The index i is necessarily referential; the case $i=j$ is the case of an anaphor, and the case $i \in j$ the case of a pronoun. We can now restate the binding conditions as rules that modify the designated index, as follows:

(112)   Suppose that α has the designated index j and is free(i) in β
(β = NP or $\bar{\mathrm{S}}$)
where (a) α is nominative
or (b) α is in the domain of the subject of β, β minimal.
Then $j \rightarrow 0$ if j is an integer, and $j \rightarrow (j-\{i\})$ if j is a set.

Case (a) of (112) is the NIC and case (b) is Opacity. When α is an anaphor and is nominative or in an opaque domain, and is free(i) in NP or $\bar{\mathrm{S}}$, then i must be its referential index and it is changed to 0. When α is a pronoun and is nominative or in an opaque domain, and is free(i) in NP or $\bar{\mathrm{S}}$, then i is removed from its anaphoric index. Note that if α is a nominative pronoun, then rule (112) deletes all indices from its anaphoric index, leaving the latter null; and if α is a pronoun in an opaque domain, then (112) deletes from its anaphoric index the referential indices of all NPs outside of this domain, so that α is not necessarily disjoint in reference from any such NP. For example, consider (113):

(113)   John$_2$ told Bill$_{(3,\{2\})}$ [$_{\bar{\mathrm{S}}}$ PRO$_3$ to visit him]

In (113), *John* (with null anaphoric index omitted) and *Bill* have been indexed by the assignment rule for nonanaphors, and PRO has been indexed by the rule of Control. Turning next to *him*, as a nonanaphor it is assigned the index (4, $\{2,3\}$). Since *him* is free(2) in $\bar{\mathrm{S}}$ but not free(3) in $\bar{\mathrm{S}}$ and is in the domain of the subject of $\bar{\mathrm{S}}$, *him* undergoes rule (112), which removes 2 from its anaphoric index, leaving *him* with the index $(4, \{3\})$. Thus, *him* in (113) is understood as disjoint in reference from PRO (hence *Bill*) but not necessarily disjoint in reference from *John*.

Suppose we define the notation $[j-i]$ as follows:

(114) $[j-i]=(j-i)$ if j is an integer and $(j-\{i\})$ if j is a set.

Then we can restate (112) as follows:

(115) Suppose that α has the designated index j and is free(i) in β ($\beta =$ NP or $\bar{\text{S}}$),
      where (a) α is nominative
      or (b) α is in the domain of the subject of β, β minimal.
    Then $j \rightarrow [j-i]$.

It remains only to add that NP_0 is not permitted in LF, where 0 is the referential index. This is the case of an inadmissible free variable, an anaphor that is not properly bound.

With this somewhat more systematic account of indexing, we can return to some possible generalisations of the rule of Control. Consider examples (116a–c), of a type studied in Faraci (1974) and Lasnik and Fiengo (1974):

(116)   a. John bought the dog [$_\alpha$ to play with Mary]
      b. John bought the dog [$_\alpha$ for Mary to play with]
      c. John bought the dog [$_\alpha$ to play with]

In keeping with the general point of view so far, we take $\alpha = \bar{\text{S}}$ throughout, with α of the form (117):

(117) [$_{\bar{\text{S}}}$ for [NP_1 to play with NP_2]]

In (116a), $NP_1 =$ PRO; in (116b), $NP_2 =$ PRO; in (116c), $NP_1 = NP_2 =$ PRO.

These structures resemble infinitival relatives but differ from them in some respects. For one thing, α is a constituent of VP[47] rather than a relative clause with the head *the dog*. For another, there is no corresponding form such as *with which to play*, etc., for α of (116).

Where NP = PRO in these cases, the rule of Control must apply or the sentence is not well formed. But NP_2 of (117) is in an opaque domain. NP_2 can be subject to a rule of Control, consistent with Opacity, only if it is moved by the rule 'Move α' to the COMP position of (117). Then both NP_2 and NP_1 are in a position to which the rule of Control is applicable with proper binding. Suppose, then, that the special feature of these 'purposive' constructions is that the Control rule (95) is modified to allow PRO to appear in COMP of (93).[48] If this approach is adopted, then underlying (116b,c) we have (118):

(118)   [$_{\bar{S}}$ PRO_2 for [NP_1 to play with t_2]]

Consider now the application of the rule of Control. In case (116a), with $\alpha = (117)$ and $NP_1 = PRO$, the rule of Control applies under the Minimal Distance Principle to assign to PRO the index of *the dog*. In case (116b), with $\alpha = (118)$, the rule of Control again assigns *the dog* as controller of PRO (this time, PRO_2). Thus, both (116a,b) are properly assigned control. Note that *for* is undeletable in (116b), under the principles of the theory of Case Assignment.

Consider next (116c), with $\alpha = (118)$ and $NP_1 = PRO$. Here, the rule of Control must apply twice — the maximum possible number of applications, since there are exactly two positions in which an anaphor can be controlled with proper binding, namely, COMP and subject. Assuming still our 'top-to-bottom' procedures of indexing, the first instance of PRO that we reach in (118) is PRO_2. By the Minimal Distance Principle, this is assigned the index of *the dog*. We turn next to $PRO_1 = NP_1$ of (118). Evidently, in this case we want the controller to be taken as *John*, not *the dog*. This requires a simple modification of the theory of control so far developed. Suppose that we add to the definition (94) of 'controller for V' the clause (119):

(119)   The index of NP is not bound in $\bar{S}$.

That is, once a controller has assigned control, it is no longer a controller. With this proviso, double control is properly assigned in (116c).

The fact that there are only two possible positions of control in the embedded phrase α of (116) is an important consequence of the theory developed earlier. Note that there is no reason why this should be so if in fact the analysis simply deleted or interpreted some unfilled position in α. We can easily find cases with three possible controllers in the matrix sentence and three possible positions of control in the embedded structure, e.g. (120):

(120)   John bought Bill the dog [＿＿＿ to give ＿＿＿ to ＿＿＿]

Any of the three matrix NPs can be a controller, as in the examples
to which we turn directly. Any of the positions of ＿＿＿ can be
controlled, as in (121):

(121)   a.   John bought the dog [＿＿＿ to give companionship to
             Mary]
        b.   John bought the dog [for Bill to give ＿＿＿ to Mary]
        c.   John bought the dog [for Bill to give bones to ＿＿＿]

Furthermore, there are two possibilities for double control: (122)
but not (123):

(122)   a.   John bought the dog [＿＿＿ to give ＿＿＿ to Mary]
        b.   John bought the dog [＿＿＿ to give bones to ＿＿＿]
(123)   John bought the dog [for Bill to give ＿＿＿ to ＿＿＿]

Finally, in (122) the arrangement of control is exactly as predicted
on the assumption that there has been movement from VP to
COMP; movement of subject to COMP is precluded in these cases,
since the remaining PRO in VP is in an opaque domain. Thus, the
arrangement of possible forms and interpretations of these forms is
exactly as predicted by the Opacity Condition, which allows only
COMP and subject as positions of possible control.
   Consider next the following slightly more complicated cases:

(124)   a.   John bought Bill the dog [$_\alpha$ to play with]
        b.   John bought the dog for Bill [$_\alpha$ to play with]

Again, (118) underlies α. The 'minimal distance' condition of (95)
takes *Bill* and *the dog* in (124) to be 'nearer' to α than *John*, but does
not differentiate *Bill* and *the dog* with respect to 'nearness to α'.
Suppose that we extend the definition to (125):

(125)   In (93), a controller c-commanded by $\bar{S}$ is nearer to [$_{NP}$ e]
        than one not c-commanded by $\bar{S}$, and a controller im-
        mediately c-commanded by $\bar{S}$ is nearer to [$_{NP}$ e] than one
        not immediately c-commanded by $\bar{S}$.

By the first case of (125), *the dog* and *Bill* in (124) are nearer to the embedded PRO than *John* (as before), and by the second case of (125) *the dog* in (124b) is nearer to the embedded PRO than *Bill*, which is within PP. Suppose that we take the structure of (124a) to be (126):

(126)   John [$_{VP}$[$_{\bar{V}}$ bought Bill] [$_{NP}$ the dog] α]

Then in (124a) as well as (124b), *the dog* is nearer to embedded PRO than *Bill*. It follows that *the dog* will be taken as the controller for PRO$_2$ of (118) in (124), and that *Bill* will be taken as the controller of PRO$_1$ (cf. note 47). In short, *John bought the dog to play with* (=(116c)) means that John bought the dog so that he (John) would play with the dog, whereas both cases of (124) mean that John bought Bill the dog so that Bill would play with the dog, as required.

Along these lines, a fair number of structures can be accommodated within the framework already developed.

There is a broader context within which these problems should be considered. Under a variety of conditions, reflexive constructions are excluded in LF. The rule of Disjoint Reference has such an effect. The same is true of the condition (119), which prevents a single NP from serving as controller for two occurrences of PRO. Or consider the structure (127):

(127)   *who [t³ decided [$_S$[$_{COMP}$ t²] [Bill will visit t¹]]]

Example (127) might be formed by free application of 'Move α', moving *who* from the position of t^1 to t^2 to t^3 to its final position in the matrix COMP. The rule of interpretation for *wh-* will assign the status of a bound variable to the position of t^1 and t^3, again violating a requirement of irreflexivity. In general, this requirement is relaxed only in the case of a verb of control with a base-generated controller, in the class of constructions we have been considering; in fact, this is what it means for a verb to be a 'verb of control'. Putting the point a bit differently, suppose that the rule of *Wh* Interpretation applies to surface structures in which Case and grammatical relations are assigned. At that point, the irreflexivity requirement seems to hold without exception. The subsequent rules of control provide the only relaxation of this requirement. To assign a precise sense to these remarks it would be necessary to proceed to the mechanisms by which semantic (thematic) relations are assigned in LF, and in particular, the role of trace in that assignment. To construct an appropriate formalism seems not particularly difficult, but it remains to be seen whether this can be done in a way that yields some interesting consequences.

Notes

* This paper was written in January 1978 as a first draft, not intended for publication, and circulated to a few friends and colleagues for comment. I then used some of the material in it as a basis for lectures in a graduate course at MIT in the spring of 1978. As anticipated, a fair number of errors came to light in my own further work, class discussion, and discussion with others who had read the paper, and in a number of cases it was possible to introduce substantial improvements. I had intended to prepare the paper for publication by mid-1978, but other demands intervened and I was unable to do so. Meanwhile, others have referred to the paper in their own work, proposing alternatives, offering criticism, or developing the ideas further. The unavailability of the paper poses a certain problem for these researchers, since they are compelled to make reference to material that their readers will not have seen. In the interest of facilitating ongoing research and communication, I have agreed to allow the paper to be published in its preliminary form, though with natural reluctance. I have introduced only very minor corrections. I hope to be able to prepare an improved and more comprehensive version, taking account of the extremely interesting work based on these or related ideas and other work. The purpose of this note is simply to explain the rather peculiar status of the paper as it now appears in print.

1. On the rule of *There* Interpretation, cf. Milsark (1977) and Dresher and Hornstein (1979). Kayne and Pollock (1978) note that such quasi-idiomatic constructions as *there came to mind a terrible thought, there arose a clamour*, may be formed by the same rule of NP Movement that gives such structures as (5), with a special interpretive rule, which they discuss. The French analogue to such Stylistic Inversion (to which their study is primarily devoted) is particularly interesting, for one reason, because of the possibility of explaining some of its basic properties on the assumption of successive cyclicity of *Wh* Movement.

2. Cf. Huang (1977) for the possibility of marked exceptions.

3. We may assume that a similar rule applies in relatives, giving a *such that* construction in LF containing a bound variable in the same positions in which a bound variable appears under the *Wh* Interpretation rule for questions. See Vergnaud (1974).

4. Following observations by Jan Koster. See also Den Besten (1975), where it is argued, in particular, that deletion rules should follow all other transformations.

5. I will use the notation *(…) to mean that the element in parentheses cannot be omitted, and the notation (*…) to mean that it cannot appear.

6. From Sag (1976). See this study and Williams (1977) for alternative approaches to the phenomenon of 'deletion under identity', which is perhaps to be excluded from sentence-grammar, at least in part.

7. See Peters and Ritchie (1973), Peters (1973), and Lapointe (1977) for some proposals concerning a condition on deletion in cyclic transformational grammars that would guarantee recursiveness of generated languages. The significance of this issue has often been misconstrued. For discussion, see Chomsky (1965, Chapter 1, sec. 9); Chomsky (1977b).

8. I consider here only transitive verbs, but these constructions exhaust the relevant cases.

9. I am putting aside a number of relevant problems. In some cases, PRO can be understood as arbitrary in reference even where there is a lexical NP in ...; for example, *John knows how to solve the problem* might be understood as meaning that John knows how he (John) is to solve the problem or how the problem is to be solved (by anyone). The same is true in nominal constructions: e.g. *John's attitudes about how to solve the problem*. Also relevant are the problems concerning interpretation of gerunds, as in *John's attitude towards watching TV too much*, or the interpretation of derived nominals, as in *John's attitude towards excessive concentration on school work*. Cf. Wasow and Roeper (1972), Horn (1975).

10. See Jackendoff (1972) and Solan (1977).

11. There are well-known exceptions; for example, $*N-NP-\bar{S}$ *(persuasion (of) Bill that (to) ...)*. See Anderson (1977) for discussion of a general principle governing nominalisations that would have this and other desirable consequences.

12. In some English dialects, *try* (cf. (14c)) takes $\bar{S}$. Cf. C&L.

13. See Baltin (1978) for independent arguments to this effect.

14. I ignore here the question of the right number of bars.

15. That is, β is the least (smallest) such domain: if γ has tense or subject and α is in γ, then β is in γ. The qualification is required only for the case of NP_{arb}, to ensure the relevant choice of β in (18), e.g. β_1 and not β_2 in (i), (ii):

(i) $[_{\beta_2}$ it is unclear $[_{\beta_1}$ what PRO to do]]

(ii) $[_{\beta_2}$ their uncertainty as to $[_{\beta_1}$ what PRO to do]]

Cf. note 9. The minimality condition prevents taking β of (18) to be β_2 in these cases. Thus (19) permits PRO to be indexed *arb* in (i) and (ii), even though it is (irrelevantly) in the domain of Tense and Subject (namely, *it*) in (i) and in the domain of Subject (*their*) in (ii).

16. Hence the terminology of note 13, C&L.

17. More must be said about the case of Disjoint Reference. See the appendix.

18. I will follow the practice of capitalising 'Case' when it is used in the technical sense, to avoid confusion with informal use, as in 'the unmarked case', etc.

19. Reference to S will be eliminated under an alternative formulation to be given below. It is necessary here because of such constructions as *who did they think* $[_S[_{COMP} t^1]$ $[_S t^2$ *would win*]], derived by successive-cyclic *Wh* Movement from the subject position of the tensed embedded clause. Assuming for the moment that both t^1 and t^2 are nominative, (26) permits this construction because t^2, though a nominative anaphor, is bound in $\bar{S}$ and t^1, though free in $\bar{S}$, is not in S contained in $\bar{S}$. The qualification has the same effect as 'in the domain of Tense' in (19), which distinguishes t^1 and t^2 appropriately.

20. Note that the minimality requirement is now limited to the former SSC. Cf. note 15.

21. See the discussion of some similar examples, noted by Richard Kayne, in Chomsky (1977a, Chapter 3, 108f.). These problems no longer arise in the present framework.

22. Cf. Koster (1978a,b) for discussion of many problematic cases. Judgments in crucial cases are often unclear, but it seems to me that where they are at all clear, the distinction between movement and interpretive rules holds.

23. Cf. Chomsky (1977b). See van Riemsdijk (1978a,b) for Dutch. Rizzi (forthcoming) gives evidence that for Italian, $\bar{S}$ but not S is a bounding node for subjacency. Perhaps we find here one of the parameters of core grammar. Note that if the approach of the text is taken, then Subjacency will have to be understood as permitting movement across $[_\alpha ... [_\beta$ (or $]_\beta ...]_\alpha)$, where α and β are bounding categories and ... is null, to permit raising in *John seems* $[_S$ $COMP$ $[_S$ t ...]] (t the trace of *John*), etc. On the null COMP in such cases, see below.

24. Some principle of this sort is generally assumed to have been a leading idea for generative semantics, and similar ideas appear frequently in popular and informal

discussion. However, careful work in generative semantics always assumed that surface structures enter into determination of semantic representation, so that it was no more based on the principle in question than work in the extended standard theory. The only fairly close approach to this principle, at least in careful work, is to be found in the standard theory as developed, for example, in Katz (1972). See Chomsky (1972) for discussion.

25. Example (54) might derive from *a man [who for] [NP to give* t *the book]*, in some dialects, but this fact is irrelevant here.

26. We must then assume that an obligatory deletion rule is applicable anywhere in the 'deletion component' of the grammar (namely, 3a of (1)), so that deletion of the *wh*-phrase will follow deletion of *for* or NP (under EQUI). We must also assume the standard framework of transformational grammar, under which the structure with *for* deleted is subject to the structural analysis (..., *wh*-phrase, *to*, ...) of the deletion transformation, since the intervening NP is terminally null. Cf. C&L.

27. This may not be a correct assumption, however. Questions arise about c-command in *to*- and *for*-phrases.

28. In the framework of Chomsky (1955), these verbs have a direct object in the base and become 'complex verbs' by an embedding rule. They are 'raising verbs' in a theory such as that of Postal (1974). For an enlightening discussion of the issues, see Lightfoot (1976).

29. This convention builds in the 'adjacency and *c*-command' condition of the filter (41). Excluded are the structures β [, α and $\beta\gamma\alpha$, where γ is a major category. The notion 'government', like the notion 'grammatical relation', must be defined at a level of abstraction that excludes from consideration parenthetical elements, interpolated adverbs, and the like.

30. Because of the NIC, Case must be assigned to PRO. Suppose we were to stipulate instead that the rule of Case Assignment assigns * to NPs containing no lexical head. Note that this would give the effect of the Opacity Condition and the NIC for the case of control in indirect questions discussed at the outset, but would not generalise to the other cases to which these conditions apply, though one might explore the possibility further.

31. NP Movement from the embedded subject is blocked by the obligatory presence of *it* in such structures as *it is unclear what to do*, **John is unclear what* t *to do* (*t* the trace of *John*), assuming the analysis in C&L, which related obligatory presence of *it* to nonnull COMP. The latter analysis can be a bit improved now that ϕ-complementiser is eliminated. Thus, it was unclear in C&L why ϕ-complementiser should behave differently from *that* or *for*. Note that **John is unclear what* t *to do*, etc., are also blocked by Subjacency if S is assumed to be a bounding node; cf. also note 23. If that analysis proves feasible, then it may be possible to eliminate the rule relating *it* to non-null COMP completely.

32. On constructions with *for*-complementisers, see the discussion in Quirk (1977), which raises questions not dealt with properly here.

33. But even though *proud* and others are adjectives that take 'objects' and propositional complements in their semantic representation, there seem to be no adjectives that take NP+$\bar{\text{S}}$ complements in the base, so (84c) may derive from other conditions.

Note that there is a reason, under the Case Assignment theory, for the fact that 'objects' of adjectives and nouns require *of*, perhaps by a rule of *Of* Insertion (*the destruction of Rome, proud of John*). Otherwise, the 'object' is not assigned Case by (68). We might assume, then, that in a base-generated structure such as [NP *the* [N̄ *destruction Rome*]], either optional *Of* Insertion must apply, assigning oblique Case, or NP Movement must apply to give *Rome's destruction*, with possessive Case assigned. Cf. Anderson (1977).

34. Alternatively, we might say that *for* assigns Case to S in the construction *for*-S

just as it does to NP in *for*-NP, with Case percolating to NP of S just as it does to the head of a relative construction. Thus, reference to F is unnecessary.

35. That is, it is undeletable under the rule of free deletion in COMP. This approach has a range of consequences, some perhaps problematic. Such structures as *who is it illegal t to take part* are blocked as required, since if the embedded *for*-complementiser assigns Case it does not delete (violating the *for–to* filter), while if it deletes it does not assign Case (violating filter (70)). But *a man to fix the sink*, from *a man* [ₛ[*who for*] [ₛ t *to fix the sink*]] is no longer generated, for the same reasons. To account for the latter instance, we must add a special rule which deletes *for* in just this structure, after Case Assignment, or which makes Case Assignment unnecessary. The latter alternative can easily be formulated and is quite natural in other constructions (for example, the class of constructions studied in Chomsky (1977b) in which the *wh*-element is obligatorily deleted), but not in this case. Assuming that we have a special rule deleting *for*, the structure *a man to fix the sink* appears only as a marked construction, distinct from other infinitival relatives. This may not be an unacceptable conclusion. This construction is unique in its severe distributional constraints, as noted in C&L. But the consequence should be noted.

36. Note that (88a) is also blocked by Subjacency. See note 31.

37. These observations are due to Jean-Roger Vergnaud and Jean-Yves Pollock. Luigi Rizzi points out that there are similar phenomena in Italian.

38. In C&L it was assumed that PRO and lexical NP are in complementary distribution. That assumption was crucial to the theory of control developed there, but it plays no role in the present theory. We may therefore drop the assumption. It follows that such structures as *a topic to work on* can now be assumed to have PRO subject in the embedded infinitival relative, and the EQUI analysis proposed in C&L can be dropped, simplifying the theory of infinitival relatives and avoiding a new rule of control. It was also noted in C&L that such structures as *a book to read* share properties of *a book for you to read* but not *a man to fix the sink*, a problem for that analysis but now quite natural. In (91d) and (92b,c,d), lexical NP can appear freely in the position of PRO, which is simply the case of nonapplication of the rule developing NP.

39. For case (95b), the stipulation amounts to the requirement that PRO be subjacent to its controller, if S but not S̄ is taken as a bounding node. Subjacency seems to be a general property of null anaphors: movement rules and control. For case (95a), however, an account along these lines is not available. Perhaps the minimality assumption of (27) extends to this case; cf. note 15.

40. This analysis follows the suggestion of Chomsky (1977a, introduction). As noted there, it extends to a problem cited in Chomsky (1965, 229) with regard to such forms as *I was struck t (by John) as pompous*, *I was impressed t (by his remarks) as unintelligible*. The point is now clear under the analysis of these forms presented above. There are some curious exceptions to this principle. Hust and Brame (1976) and Solan (1977) cite such double-passives as *John was promised to be allowed to leave*, which should be blocked but is not for reasons that are unclear. It seems that some syntactic property is involved, since substitution of a near synonym for the embedded passive changes the grammatical status to the expected *: e.g. *John was promised to get permission to leave*. Cf. George and Kornfilt (1977) for some interesting discussion that might be relevant to this case.

41. Following the discussion in Chomsky (1977a) and C&L, I am assuming that EQUI involves *self*-deletion, not control of PRO. One of the reasons given in C&L, namely, the complementary distribution of PRO and lexical NP, no longer holds in the present framework (cf. note 38), suggesting a reconsideration.

42. We might say 'the transformational rule' in the context of core grammar.

43. The situation is complicated by the fact that (105) also violates the 'Superiority Condition' of Chomsky (1977a, Chapter 3), which blocks *I don't remember what who

saw as compared with *I don't remember who saw what*. But as Kayne has pointed out, this condition seems ambiguous, for example in such sentences as *I don't remember what books which people read*, which is relatively acceptable. But *which people did you wonder what saw* is as bad as (105), indicating that Superiority, whatever its status may be, is not what is causing the problem here. Note that in (106) indexing is nested, though not in (105); such 'index-crossing' has occasionally been suggested as possibly a property assigning *, but it seems difficult to formulate an acceptable version of this proposal for reasons discussed in Chomsky (1977b); cf. also (107a).

44. It should follow that in a language in which the *Wh*-Island Condition does not hold for *Wh* Movement (perhaps for the reasons discussed by Rizzi (1978); cf. text and note 23 above), the analogues of (106) and (107b) should be fully acceptable while the analogues of (105) and (107c) are ungrammatical. In French, for example, this gives the contrast between (i) and (ii) (examples provided by Nathalie von Bockstaele):

(i)   à qui   est- ce que je me demande qu'   est- ce que Jean a donné t
      to whom is   it that I wonder   what is   it that John gave
(ii) *qui est- ce que je me demande qu'   est- ce qu' t a donné à Marie
      who is   it that I wonder   what is   it that gave   to Mary

See Rizzi (1978) for an explanation for the different status of (ii) in Italian.

45. Recall that PRO is assigned nominative Case, invoking the NIC, in *I know what [PRO did* t], etc.; see note 30.

46. For example, suppose that the anaphor *each other* has been moved by transformation and thus assigned an index. But it must then be co-indexed with an antecedent. Since the rules of index assignment are not allowed to change indices, there will be a well-formed LF only if the index assigned to *each other* under movement is the same as the index that has been assigned to the NP taken as its antecedent. We can deal with the problem in various ways; for example, by permitting re-indexing of an anaphor under control (and corresponding re-indexing of any trace of this anaphor). There are several other conventions of this sort required.

47. For (116a) there is a possible structure with α a constituent of S rather than VP, so that the only possible controller for the missing subject is *John*, giving the interpretation *John bought the dog so that he could play with Mary*, more natural in such examples as *John bought the dog to please Mary*. We ignore this possibility here. Note that it is ruled out in (116c), which requires two controllers, but we offer no explanation for the fact that it is also ruled out in (116b).

48. The requirement that NP must be in argument position in LF must also be relaxed to permit NP = PRO in COMP — or perhaps any NP, under certain approaches to NP-fronting that have been proposed in a number of analyses of Germanic languages. Further questions arise in this connection that I will not consider here. Cf. Koster (1978c), Lowenstamm (1977), and Thiersch (1978) for some relevant discussion.

References

Anderson, M. (1977), 'Transformations in Noun Phrases', mimeographed, University of Connecticut, Storrs, Connecticut

Baltin, M. R. (1978), *Toward a Theory of Movement Rules*, Doctoral dissertation, MIT, Cambridge, Massachusetts

Besten, H. den (1975), 'A Note on Designating Lexical Delenda', unpublished mimeographed paper, University of Amsterdam, The Netherlands

Chomsky, N. (1955), *The Logical Structure of Linguistic Theory*, Plenum, New York, 1975

———— (1965), *Aspects of the Theory of Syntax*, MIT Press, Cambridge, Massachusetts

———— (1972), *Studies on Semantics in Generative Grammar*, Mouton, The Hague

———— (1974), *The Amherst Lectures, Documents Linguistiques*, Université de Paris VII

———— (1975), *Reflections on Language*, Pantheon, New York

———— (1977a), *Essays on Form and Interpretation*, American Elsevier, New York

———— (1977b), 'On *Wh*-Movement', in P. Culicover, T. Wasow, and A. Akmajian (eds.) (1977)

Chomsky, N. and H. Lasnik (1977), 'Filters and Control', *Linguistic Inquiry* 8, 425–504

———— (1978), 'A Remark on Contraction', *Linguistic Inquiry* 9, 268–74

Culicover, P., T. Wasow, and A. Akmajian (eds.) (1977), *Formal Syntax*, Academic Press, New York

Dougherty, R. C. (1969), 'An Interpretive Theory of Pronominal Reference', *Foundations of Language* 5, 488–519

Dresher, B. E. and N. Hornstein (1979), 'Trace Theory and NP Movement Rules', *Linguistic Inquiry* 10, 65–82

Emonds, J. E. (1976), *A Transformational Approach to English Syntax*, Academic Press, New York

Erteschik, N. (1973), *On the Nature of Island Constraints*, Doctoral dissertation, MIT, Cambridge, Massachusetts

Faraci, R. (1974), *Aspects of the Grammar of Infinitives and For-Phrases*, Doctoral dissertation, MIT, Cambridge, Massachusetts

Fiengo, R. W. (1977), 'On Trace Theory', *Linguistic Inquiry* 8, 35–62

Freidin, R. (1978), 'Cyclicity and the Theory of Grammar', *Linguistic Inquiry* 9, 519–49

George, L. and J. Kornfilt (1977), 'Infinitival Double Passives in Turkish' in J. Kegl, D. Nash, and A. Zaenen (eds.), *Proceedings of the Seventh Annual Meeting of the North Eastern Linguistic Society*, Cambridge, Massachusetts

Helke, M. (1971), *The Grammar of English Reflexives*, Doctoral dissertation, MIT, Cambridge, Massachusetts

Horn, G. (1975), 'On the Non-Sentential Nature of the Poss-ing Construction', *Linguistic Analysis* 1, 333–88

Huang, P. (1977), *Wh-Fronting and Related Processes*, Doctoral dissertation, University of Connecticut, Storrs, Connecticut

Hust, J. and M. Brame (1976), 'Jackendoff on Interpretive Semantics', *Linguistic Analysis* 2, 243–77

Jackendoff, R. S. (1972), *Semantic Interpretation in Generative Grammar*, MIT Press, Cambridge, Massachusetts

Katz, J. J. (1972), *Semantic Theory*, Harper and Row, New York

Kayne, R. S. (1975), *French Syntax: The Transformational Cycle*, MIT Press, Cambridge, Massachusetts

Kayne, R. S. and J.-Y. Pollock (1978), 'Stylistic Inversion, Successive Cyclicity, and "Move NP"', *Linguistic Inquiry* 9, 595–621

Kim, W. C. (1976), *The Theory of Anaphora in Korean Syntax*, Doctoral dissertation, MIT, Cambridge, Massachusetts

Koster, J. (1978a), *Locality Principles in Syntax*, Foris Publications, Dordrecht, The Netherlands

———— (1978b), 'Conditions, Empty Nodes, and Markedness', *Linguistic Inquiry* 9, 551–93

———— (1978c), 'Why Subject Sentences Don't Exist' in S. J. Keyser (ed.), *Recent Transformational Studies in European Languages*, Linguistic Inquiry Monograph 3, MIT Press, Cambridge, Massachusetts

Lapointe, S. G. (1977), 'Recursiveness and Deletion', *Linguistic Analysis* 3, 227-65
Lasnik, H. (1976), 'Remarks on Coreference', *Linguistic Analysis* 2, 1–22
Lasnik, H. and R. Fiengo (1974), 'Complement Object Deletion', *Linguistic Inquiry* 5, 535–71
Lasnik, H. and J. Kupin (1977), 'A Restrictive Theory of Transformational Grammar', *Theoretical Linguistics* 4, 173–96
Lightfoot, D. (1976), 'Trace Theory and Twice-Moved NPs', *Linguistic Inquiry* 7, 559–82
Lowenstamm, J. (1977), 'Relative Clauses in Yiddish', *Linguistic Analysis* 3, 197–216
May, R. (1977), 'Logical Form and Conditions on Rules' in J. Kegl, D. Nash, and A. Zaenen (eds.), *Proceedings of the Seventh Annual Meeting of the North Eastern Linguistic Society*, Cambridge, Massachusetts
Milsark, G. L. (1974), *Existential Sentences in English*, Doctoral dissertation, MIT, Cambridge, Massachusetts
―――― (1977), 'Toward an Explanation of Certain Peculiarities of the Existential Construction in English', *Linguistic Analysis* 3, 1–30
Oshima, S. (1977), 'Trace Theory and the Ordering of SI-1 Rules', unpublished mimeographed paper, Kochi University, Japan
Peters, P. S. (1973), 'On Restricting Deletion Transformations' in M. Gross, M. Halle, and M.-P. Schützenberger (eds.), *The Formal Analysis of Natural Language*, Mouton, The Hague
Peters, P. S. and R. W. Ritchie (1973), 'On the Generative Power of Transformational Grammars', *Information Sciences* 6, 49–83
Postal, P. (1974), *On Raising*, MIT Press, Cambridge, Massachusetts
Quirk, R. (1977), 'A Tough Object to Trace', *Journal of Linguistics* 13, 99–102
Reinhart, T. (1976), *The Syntactic Domain of Anaphora*, Doctoral dissertation, MIT, Cambridge, Massachusetts
Riemsdijk, H. van (1978a), 'On the Diagnosis of *Wh* Movement' in S. J. Keyser (ed.), *Recent Transformational Studies in European Languages*, Linguistic Inquiry Monograph 3, MIT Press, Cambridge, Massachusetts
―――― (1978b), *A Case Study in Syntactic Markedness: The Binding Nature of Prepositional Phrases*, Foris Publications, Dordrecht, The Netherlands
Rizzi, L. (1978), 'Violations of the Wh Island Constraint in Italian and the Subjacency Condition'
Rosenbaum, P. (1967), *The Grammar of English Predicate Complement Constructions*, MIT Press, Cambridge, Massachusetts
Ross, J. R. (1967), *Constraints on Variables in Syntax*, Doctoral dissertation, MIT, Cambridge, Massachusetts
Sag, I. A. (1976), *Deletion and Logical Form*, Doctoral dissertation, MIT, Cambridge, Massachusetts
Solan, L. (1977), 'On the Interpretation of Missing Complement NPs', unpublished mimeographed paper, University of Massachusetts, Amherst
Thiersch, C. (1978), *Topics in German Syntax*, Doctoral dissertation, MIT, Cambridge, Massachusetts
Vergnaud, J. R. (1974), *French Relative Clauses*, Doctoral dissertation, MIT, Cambridge, Massachusetts
Wasow, T. and T. Roeper (1972), 'On the Subject of Gerunds', *Foundations of Language* 8, 44–61
Williams, E. (1977), 'Discourse and Logical Form', *Linguistic Inquiry* 8, 101–39

This paper was first published in *Linguistic Inquiry*, Vol. 11, No. 1 (Winter 1980), pp. 1–46, and is reprinted here essentially unchanged.

2　Finiteness and Boundedness in Turkish

Leland M. George and Jaklin Kornfilt

0. Introduction

In this paper we consider a variety of Turkish constructions entirely analogous to those that originally motivated the 'Tensed S' and 'Specified Subject' Conditions for English (Chomsky, 1973). We find our constructions subject to just the same constraints as their English analogues except that the presence of Personal Agreement, rather than Tense, is what characterises finite ('opaque') clauses (section 3), that is, subordinate clauses whose Subjects are inaccessible to rules operating in the main clause domain. This of course immediately suggests a generalisation of the Tensed-S Condition on the universal plane to the analogous 'Finite-S' Condition (where 'finite' is appropriately defined — cf. section 4).

A further extension is indicated by the fact that non-finite forms (i.e. non-opaque constructions) are distinguished among certain clause-like constituents ('gerunds') which we show (§1) to be NPs, just as they are distinguished among clauses; that is, the usual Personal Agreement is lacking in these forms. We thus pass from the Finite-S Condition to the Finite Phrase Condition (FPC).

(1)　Finite Phrase Condition:
　　　Let A be a phrase of which $X^\daleth$ is a proper constituent. Then if $X^\daleth$ is finite, no rule operating in the domain A can involve a proper constituent of $X^\daleth$,

where $X^\daleth$ is the 'maximal projection' of X in the bar theory (we assume $\bar{S} = V^\daleth$ — see George (1980) for discussion).

All of the Turkish rules we discuss that obey the FPC also obey a constraint modelled on the Specified Subject Condition, the Subject Accessibility Condition (SAC):

(2) Subject Accessibility Condition:
     Let $X^\neg$ be a proper constituent of A and let B be the Subject of $X^\neg$. Then no rule can involve a proper constituent C of $X^\neg$ unless C = B, or C is contained in B.

Over a wide range of cases, and certainly in all of our examples, the same rules seem to obey the one as obey the other. Nevertheless, we keep the two conditions separate, partly because we feel there may be rules obeying only one of them (e.g. Tough Movement in English), and partly because of certain Turkish examples[1] where violating both of the conditions creates greater unacceptability than violating just one. We will not here be concerned with the circumstances in which a rule (like *Wh*-Movement) may appear to violate these two conditions (see Chomsky (1976) and Rizzi (1978) for some discussion).

Our statement of (1)–(2) as conditions on rules may seem out of place in a volume where other papers reformulate them as 'filters on Logical Form', sensitive to case rather than finiteness (which is supposed to be only indirectly relevant to Opacity, by virtue of governing Case assignment). We preserve the original format mainly to emphasise that our amendments to the older Conditions on Transformations theory are entirely independent of the changes made in 'On Binding' (Chomsky, 1980) (but see note 8 below, and George, 1980, Ch. 4).

1. Differences between Direct Complements and Gerunds

In this section, we show that there are two types of verb-headed complements in Turkish: the purely sentential ('Direct Complements'), and those dominated by NP ('Gerunds'). Some of the following arguments will show only that the two complement types are different; others will demonstrate that the Gerunds are, in fact, NPs.

1.1 Tense

In Turkish root sentences, verbs exhibit a rich variety of suffixes for tense, some of which are demonstrated below:

(3) (biz) viski-yi   iç-**eceğ**-iz
     we   whisky-Acc drink-FUTURE-1pl
                      iç-**iyor**-uz
                         -PRES PROG-1pl
                      iç-**ti**-k
                         -PAST-1pl
     We will drink/are drinking/drank the whisky

Direct complements can exhibit all of these tenses:

(4) herkes   [(biz) viski-yi iç-**eceğ**-iz]
     everybody   drink-FUTURE-1pl
                                      -**iyor**-uz
                                      -PRES PROG-1pl
                                      -**ti**-k
                                      -PAST-1pl
     san-iyor
     believe-Pres Prog
     Everybody believes we will drink/are drinking/drank the whisky

However, Gerunds do not exhibit all of these forms. Instead, certain 'nominalisation' suffixes fill the slot otherwise occupied by the tense markers in the sequence of verbal morphemes, to a certain extent neutralising tense.

There are basically two 'nominalisation' morphemes in Gerunds: **-mA** and **-dIg**.[2] These we symbolise GER in the glosses below. **-mA** forms cannot express tense at all:

(5) Ahmet [(biz-im) viski-yi   ⎧dün   ⎫
            we-Gen   whisky-Acc   ⎨bugün ⎬
                                   ⎩yarin ⎭
                           yesterday/today/tomorrow
     iç-**me**-miz]-i   iste-di
     drink-GER-1pl-Acc wanted
     Ahmet wanted us to drink the whisky yesterday/today/tomorrow

-dIg forms differentiate between future and non-future only:

(6)   Ahmet [(biz-im)   viski-yi $\begin{Bmatrix} \text{dün} \\ \text{bugün} \end{Bmatrix}$ iç-**tiğ**-imiz]-i

$\qquad\qquad\qquad\qquad\quad \begin{Bmatrix} \text{yesterday} \\ \text{today} \end{Bmatrix}$ GER

Ahmet [(biz-im)   viski-yi   yarin   iç-**eceğ**-imiz]-i
$\qquad\qquad\qquad\qquad\quad$ tomorrow   GER Fut

anla-di
understood

Ahmet
understood
$\left\{\begin{matrix} that\ we\ drank\ the\ whisky\ yesterday/ \\ today \\ we\ were\ drinking\ the\ whisky\ yesterday/ \\ today \\ that\ we\ will\ drink\ the\ whisky\ tomorrow \end{matrix}\right\}$

These facts alone are not sufficient to argue that Gerunds are NP rather than S; we might at this point, in fact, mention a similarity between Gerunds in -**dIg** and Direct Complements: both are capable of accepting morphological marking for Future Tense. These same Gerunds diverge from the Direct Complements, however, in that for them non-future tense marking is neutralised. In what follows we shall see that they otherwise behave like lexical NPs.

1.2 Case

Traditional grammars of Turkish recognise five Cases, all of which are exemplified on lexical NPs in the following sentence:

(7)   Ahmet-**∅**   viski-**yi**   dolap-**tan**   çikar-ip
      -NOM   -ACC   closet-ABL   take out-and
      mutfak-**ta**-ki   masa-**ya**   koy-du
      kitchen-LOC-wh(Rel)   table-DAT   put-Past
      Ahmet took the whisky out of the cupboard and put it on the table in the kitchen

From a generative point of view, the Genitive is also a Case in Turkish. Its use with lexical NPs is exemplified below:

viski-**nin**   koku-su
whisky-GEN   smell-3 sg Poss
the smell of the whisky

The relevant point for our purposes is that Gerunds, like lexical

NPs, end with Case markers, showing the full range of possible Cases, including Genitive. In fact, a Gerund in a given context is assigned just the Case that a lexical NP would have in the same context:

Nominative

    (8) a. [ayak-lar-imiz-i   masa-ya   koy-**ma**-miz]-∅
                foot-pl-1pl-Acc table-Dat put-GER-1pl-NOM
                anne-miz-i   üz-dü
                mother-1pl-Acc sadden-Past
                That we put our feet on the table saddened our mother.

Compare:

    (8) b. Ahmet-∅   anne-miz-i   üz-dü
             .-NOM mother-1pl-Acc sadden-Past
           Ahmet saddened our mother.

Accusative

    (9) a. Ahmet [(biz-im) viski-yi iç-**me**-miz]-i
                      we-Gen   -Acc drink-GER-1pl-ACC
                isti-yor
                want-Pres
                Ahmet wants that we drink the whisky.

Compare:

    (9) b. Ahmet bu kitab-ı   isti-yor
                    this book-ACC want-Pres
           Ahmet wants this book.

Dative

    (10) a. anne-miz [ayak-lar-imiz-i masa-ya
              mother-1pl foot-pl-1pl-Acc table-Dat
              koy-**ma**-miz]-**a**   kiz-di
              put-GER-1pl-DAT get angry-Past
              Our mother got angry at our putting our feet on the table.

Compare:

(10) b. anne-miz   Ahmed-e   kɨz-dɨ
mother-1pl   -DAT   get angry-Past
Our mother got angry at Ahmet.

Locative

(11) a. felç-li   sporcu [oğl-un-un   futbol-cu
paralysed athlete   son-his-Gen   soccer-player
ol-**ma**-sin]-**da**   teselli bul-du
be-GER-3sg-LOC   solace find-Past
*The paralysed athlete found solace in his son's being/
becoming a soccer player.*

Compare:

(11) b. felç-li   spor-cu   din-in-**de**
paralysed athlete   religion-his-LOC
teselli bul-du
solace find-Past
The paralysed athlete found solace in his religion.

Ablative

(12) a. anne-miz   [ayak-lar-imɨz-i   masa-ya
mother-1pl   foot-pl-1pl-Acc   table-Dat
koy-**ma**-mɨz]-**dan**   kork-uyor
put-GER-1pl-ABL   afraid-Pres
Our mother is afraid of our putting our feet on the table.

Compare:

(12) b. anne-miz   bu köpek-**ten**   kork-uyor
this dog-ABL   afraid-Pres
Our mother is afraid of this dog.

Genitive

(13) a. [[ayak-lar-imiz-i   masa-ya   koy-**ma**-miz]-**in**
foot-pl-1pl-Acc table-Dat   put-GER-1pl-GEN

anne-miz-i   üz-eceğ-i]   muhakkak
mother-1pl   sadden-GER Fut   certain (is)
  -Acc   -3sg
*That our putting our feet on the table will sadden our
mother is certain.*

The Genitive in Turkish is not governed by verbs (which is probably why it was not recognised as a Case in traditional grammar); it
shows up, rather, in Possessive NP-Compounds and 'Gerunds'. As
will be seen later, this fact will be used as part of a further argument
for our claim that Gerunds are NPs. In example (13a), the Gerund:
Our putting our feet on the table is marked with the Genitive as the
Subject of the higher Gerund NP[*That* NP[...] *will sadden our mother*],
as is the lexical NP *the maid* in the same frame:

(13) b. NP[NP[bu   hizmetçi]-**nin**   anne-miz-i
             this   maid-GEN   mother-our-Acc
         üz-**eceğ**-i]   muhakkak
         sadden-GER Fut   certain (is)
                     -3sg
         NP[*That* NP[*this maid*] *will sadden (upset) our mother*] *is
         certain*[3]

   In contrast to Gerunds, Direct Complements take no Case
marking. In the following example, a Direct Complement shows up
in a frame where the corresponding Gerund has to be marked with
an Accusative suffix. The version with the Direct Complement
cannot be so marked, however:

(14) a. herkes   [(biz) viski-yi
         everybody   we   whisky-Acc
         iç-**ti**-k]   bil-iyor
         drink-PAST-1pl-(no case) believe-Pres
         *herkes   [(biz) viski-yi
         everybody   we   whisky-Acc
         iç-**ti**-{k}]-**i**   bil-iyor
               {ğ}   believe-Pres
         Everybody believes we drank the whisky

Compare:

(14) b. herkes   bu   hikâye-**yi** bil-iyor
         everybody   this story-ACC   know-Pres
         Everybody knows this story.

112   *Finiteness and Boundedness in Turkish*

Here is the corresponding Gerund construction, where Accusative marking is obligatory as in (14b) and in direct contrast to (14a):

(14) c. herkes   [(biz-im)   viski-yi
          everybody   we-Gen   -Acc
          iç-**tiğ**-imiz]-**i**   bil-iyor
          drink-GER-1pl-ACC know-Pres
          *herkes   [(biz-im)   viski-yi
          everybody   we-Gen   -Acc
          iç-**tiğ**-imiz]-∅   bil-iyor
          drink-GER-1pl   know-Pres
          Everybody knows that we drank the whisky.

Thus, by the criterion of Case Marking, Gerunds, but not Direct Complements, pattern just like lexical NPs.

1.3 Possibility of Being Objects of Postpositions

Postpositions normally require NP objects. Because of this fact, it is significant that they can also govern Gerunds (but not Direct Complements). The element **için** ('for') is typical in this regard: **için** with a lexical NP object:

(15) herşey-im-i   PP[NP[**çocuğ-um**] **için**]
      everything-my-Acc   child-my   for
      feda   et-ti-m
      sacrifice do-Past-1sg
      I sacrificed everything for my child.

için with a Possessive NP-Compound:

(16) herşey-im-i PP[NP[**çocuğ-um-un** **geleceğ-i** **için**]
                         child-my-Gen future-his for
      feda et-ti-m
      I sacrificed everything for the future of my child.

için with a Gerund:

(17) herşey-im-i PP[NP[**çocuğ-um-un**   **okul-a**
                         child-my-Gen school-Dat

gid-ebil-me-si]   için]
go-able-GER-his for
feda et-ti-m
I sacrificed everything for my child's being able to go to school.

Note the parallel internal structure of (16) and (17) (cf. also section 1.5, below). As noted, Direct Complements, unlike Gerunds, cannot be Objects of Postpositions. The following example is representative of cases where a Direct Complement is 'trying' to be a Postpositional Object, and the result is ungrammatical:

(18) *herşey-im-i PP[[çocuğ-um   okul-a   gid-ebil-ecek] için]
                          child-my school-Dat go-able-FUT   for
feda et-ti-m
Attempted reading: *I sacrificed everything so that my child would be able to go to school.*

In this instance, too, Gerunds pattern like NPs, as against Direct Complements.

1.4 Focus and Toppling

In Turkish, there are at least two situations in which the normal SOV word order appears to be altered by a movement rule. First, the primary Focus of a Sentence, as marked by superordinate accent, must appear just before the verb:

(19) ??**yazár** viski-yi   iç-ti
        author   -Acc drink-Past

Example (19), which exemplifies the unmarked SOV order, is unacceptable when the subject is the Focus and bears primary sentence stress. The acceptable counterpart to (19) with the stressed subject is given under (20):

(20) viski-yi **yazár** iç-ti
        The author drank the whisky.

Secondly, 'presupposed' constituents may regularly follow the Verb in what Turkish grammarians call '*devrik cümle*', (toppled sentence), with a distinctive fall in pitch marking the passage from the Verb to the postposed phrase. We tentatively propose two transformations, which may be schematised as follows, to generate these marked constructions:

(21)   Focus Movement:
      ... Foc ...   V

(22)   Toppling:
      ... Presupposition ... V

These rules provide a useful test for distinguishing Direct Complements from Gerunds (and, as we will see in section 3, at least one gives evidence for our reformulation of the Tensed-S Condition). To substantiate our theory, therefore, we must eventually provide a more precise statement of the transformations and justify it more carefully. Since none of the reasonable reformulations known to us would affect their diagnostic value, however, we postpone the needed study for now.

The application of Focus Movement and Toppling to lexical NPs is exemplified by the sentences in (22):

(22)   a.   (Unmarked order):
      yazar   viski-yi   çocuğ-a   ver-di
      author   -Acc child-Dat give-Past
      The author gave the whisky to the child.

Focus Movement:

(22)   b.   viski-yi   çocuğ-a   **yazar**   ver-di
           -Acc   -Dat author give-Past

Toppling:

(22)   c.   viski-yi   çocuğ-a   ver-di   **yazar**
           -Acc   -Dat give-Past author

Sentences with Gerunds undergo both rules freely. Thus from the point of view of external distribution Gerunds act just like lexical NPs.

Unmarked order:

(23) a. herkes   [yazar-lar-in   viski-yi
        everybody author-pl-Gen   -Acc
        iç-**tik**-lerin]-i   bil-iyor
        drink-GER-3pl-Acc know-Pres
        Everybody knows that the authors drank the whisky.

Focus Movement:

(23) b. [yazar-lar-in viski-yi iç-**tik**-lerin]-i herkes bil-iyor

Toppling:

(23) c. herkes bil-iyor [yazar-lar-in viski-yi iç-**tik**-lerin]-i

Both rules are blocked when Direct Complements are involved:

Unmarked order:

(24) a. herkes   [yazar-lar   viski-yi   iç-**ti**]
        everybody author-pl   -Acc drink-PAST
        san-iyor
        believe-Pres
        Everybody believes the authors drank the whisky.

Focus Movement:

(24) b. *[yazar-lar viski-yi iç-**ti**]
                              -PAST
        herkes   san-iyor
        everybody

Toppling:

(24) c. *herkes san-iyor [yazar-lar viski-yi iç-**ti**]
                                              -PAST

If we assume that a Direct Complement is simply a clause, but that a Gerund, because of its NP-nature, is not *as a whole* a sentence, the relevant restriction on the output of these word order rules can be formulated in a very simple way:

A bare clause must appear just before the governing V in surface structure.

All the facts in (22) to (24) are then accounted for automatically if Gerunds but not Direct Complements are NPs.

1.5 Internal Morphology

In this section, we show that the internal morphology of Gerunds mirrors exactly that of Possessive NP-Compounds consisting of lexical NPs. Since the latter are unquestionably NPs, we take this fact as a further argument for the NP-nature of those complements we have been calling Gerunds.

The structure of Possessive NP-Compounds is exemplified below:

(25)   yazar-lar-**in**   viski-**si**
           -GEN   -3 POSS
         the authors' whisky

In (26), we give the whole paradigm for this construction. Notice that the Genitive suffix on the 'possessor' changes slightly with the different persons and that the 'possessed'-suffix on the 'possessed'-NP agrees in person and number with the 'possessor':

(26)

	NP$_1$-Gen.	NP$_2$-Possessive Agreement
1sg	ben-im	viski-m
2sg	sen-in	viski-n
3sg	on-un	viski-si
1pl	biz-im	viski-miz
2pl	siz-in	viski-niz
3pl	onlar-in	viski-si
	∅	viski-leri

Exactly the same paradigm is found in NP-Complements:

(27)

	-GEN		-POSS	
Ahmet	[ben-**im**	viski-yi	iç-tiğ-**im**]-i bil-iyor	
			1sg	know-Pres
	[sen-**in**	viski-yi	iç-tiğ-**in**]-i	
			2sg	
	[on-**un**	viski-yi	iç-tiğ-**in**]-i	
			3sg	
	[biz-**im**	viski-yi	iç-tiğ-**imiz**]-i	
			1pl	

$$
\left\{
\begin{array}{l}
\text{[siz-\textbf{in}]} \quad \text{viski-yi} \quad \text{iç-tiğ-\textbf{iniz}]-i} \\
\qquad\qquad\qquad\qquad\quad \text{2pl} \\
\text{[onlar-in} \quad \text{viski-yi} \quad \left\{\begin{array}{l}\text{iç-tiğ-\textbf{in}]-i}\\(\text{iç-tik-\textbf{lerin}]-i})\end{array}\right\} \\
\qquad \emptyset \qquad \text{viski-yi} \quad \text{iç-tik-\textbf{lerin}]-i} \\
\qquad\qquad\qquad\qquad\quad \text{3pl}
\end{array}
\right\}
$$

Ahmet knows that (person) drank the whisky.

These morphological peculiarities are never found in root sentences. The internal structure of Direct Complements, on the other hand, shows no sign of Possessive NP-Compounds; rather, this complement type is structured like root sentences, which suggests that we are right in claiming that these complements are clausal, while Gerunds are not. As argued above, they are NPs.

Here is the complete paradigm for Direct Complements:

(28) Ahmet   [(ben)   viski-yi   iç-ti-**m**]   san-iyor
                                                       -Past-1sg
           [(sen)   viski-yi   iç-ti-**n**]
                                                -2sg
           [(o)   viski-yi   iç-ti-**∅**]
                                                -3sg
           [(biz)   viski-yi   iç-ti-**k**]
                                                -1pl
           [(siz)   viski-yi   iç-ti-**niz**]
                                                -2pl
           [(onlar)   viski-yi   iç-ti-(**ler**)]
                                                -3pl

Ahmet believes (person) drank the whisky

A comparison with root sentences like those in (3) will show that Direct Complements have the same morphological features: no overt case marking on the subject, full-scale tense marking after the verbal stem, verbal agreement markers after tense. The agreement suffixes themselves clearly belong to a different paradigm than that exhibited for NPs in (26) and in (27). It is in fact the same as that for root sentences.

2. A Parallel between Direct Complements and Gerunds

So far we have been labouring to distinguish Direct Complements from Gerunds, so as to show that the former are Sentences and not

NPs, and that the latter are NPs but not Sentences. We now turn to a similarity between the two complement types: both can be finite, and both can be non-finite. For the moment we confine our attention to the morphological consequences of this opposition; in section 3, we will see its effects in terms of 'Opacity' under the Finite Phrase Condition.

Within the grammar of Turkish we may define a finite phrase as one whose Specifier exhibits Subject Agreement, where it is immaterial whether the Agreement marker is taken from the nominal or the verbal paradigm (see section 4 below for a more general definition).

Under this definition, (4) and (5) show that both Gerunds and Direct Complements can be finite — they exhibit the full range of agreement markers (nominal and verbal, respectively).

Now we show the reverse parallel — both types can be non-finite:

Non-Finite Gerund

(29) (ben) [viski-yi   iç-**meğ**-]e
        I   -Acc   drink-GER-(no Agr)-Dat
        razi ol-du-m
        consent-Past-1sg
        I consented to drink the whisky.

Corresponding Finite Gerund

(30) (ben)[kiz-im-in   viski-yi   iç-**me-sin**]-e
        daughter-my-Gen   -Acc   drink-GER-3SG-Dat
        razi ol-du-m
        I consented to my daughter's drinking the whisky.

Non-Finite Direct Complement

(31) Ahmet [biz-i   viski-yi   iç-ti]
                  we-Acc   -Acc   drink-Past-(no Agr)
        san-iyor
        believe-Pres
        Ahmet believes us to have drunk the whisky.

Corresponding Finite Direct Complement

(32) Ahmet [biz viski-yi iç-ti-**k**] san-iyor
                                    -Past-1PL
        Ahmet believes we drank the whisky.

Another type of Non-Finite Direct Complement

(33) (siz) [t bütün viski-yi   bitir-di]
      2pl   whole -Acc   finish-Past-(no Agr)
      gibi görün-üyor-sunuz⁴
      like look-Pres-2pl
      You look like you finished all of the whisky

Corresponding finite Direct Complement

(34) [siz bütün viski-yi bitir-di-**niz**]
                            finish-Past-2PL
      gibi görün-üyor-∅
      like look-Pres-3sg
      It looks like you finished all the whisky.

3. Rules Subject to Opacity

Now we illustrate how our test rules, Reciprocal, Toppling, Passive, Disjoint Reference, Reflexivisation and Control, differentiate finite and non-finite phrases as to accessibility. In each case, we see that while the rule applies into a non-finite Complement it cannot apply into a finite phrase, whether Direct Complement or Gerund.

Reciprocal

Applying into a non-finite Direct Complement:

(35) (biz$_i$) [birbir-imiz$_i$ -i   viski-yi   iç-ti]
       we   each other-our-Acc   -Acc drink-Past-(no Agr)
      san-iyor-uz
      believe-Pres-1pl
      We believe each other to have drunk the whisky.

Trying to apply into a finite Direct Complement:

(36) *(biz$_i$) [birbir-imiz$_i$ viski-yi   iç-ti-**k**]
       we   e.o.-our   -Acc drink-Past-1pl
      san-iyor-uz

believe-Pres-1pl
We believe each other drank the whisky.

Trying to apply into a finite Gerund:

(37) *yazar-lar$_i$ [birbir-lerin$_i$-in viski-yi
      author-pl e.o.-their-Gen   -Acc
      iç-**tik-lerin**]-i   san-iyor-lar
      drink-GER-3PL-Acc believe-Pres-3pl
      The authors believe that each other drank the whisky.

Toppling

Applying into a non-finite Direct Complement:

(38) dinleyici-ler [——— viski-yi   iç-ti]
      auditor-pl   -Acc drink-Past-(no Agr)
      san-iyor-lar   **biz-i**
      believe-Pres-3pl we-Acc
      The auditors believed us to have drunk the whisky.

Trying to apply into a finite Direct Complement:

(39) *dinleyici-ler [——— viski-yi iç-ti-**k**] san-iyor-lar
                                          -1PL
      biz
      we-Nom
      The auditors believed we drank the whisky.

Trying to apply into a finite Gerund:

(40) ?dinleyici-ler [——— viski-yi iç-**tiğ-imiz**]-i san-iyor-lar
                                        -GER-1PL-Acc
      biz-im[5]
      we-Gen
      The auditors believed that we drank the whisky.

Passive (NP-Movement)

Applying into non-finite Direct Complement:

(41) (biz) [t viski-yi   iç-ti]
      we   -Acc drink-Past (no Agr)

san-il-iyor-uz
believe-PASS-Pres-1pl
We are believed to have drunk the whisky.

Trying to apply into a finite Direct Complement:

(42) *(biz) [t viski-yi   iç-ti-k]
      we   -Acc   drink-Past-1PL
      san-il-iyor-uz
      believe-PASS-Pres-1pl   ·
      Attempted reading: *We are believed to have drunk the
                          whisky.*

Disjoint Reference

Applies into non-finite Direct Complement:

(43) *(ben) [biz-i   viski-yi   iç-ti]
      I   we-Acc   -Acc drink-Past (no Agr)
      san-iyor-um
      believe-Pres-1sg
      I believe us to have drunk the whisky.

Trying to apply into finite Direct Complement:

(44) (ben) [(biz) viski-yi   iç-ti-k]   san-iyor-um
      I   we   -Acc   drink-Past-1PL believe-Pres-1sg
      I believe we drank the whisky.

Reflexive

Applying into finite Direct Complement:

(45) (sen$_i$) [kendi-n$_i$-i   başari-ya   ulaş-miş]
      2sg   self-your-Acc success-Dat reach-Past (no Agr)
      san-iyor-sun
      believe-Pres-2sg
      You believe yourself to have succeeded.

Trying to apply into finite Direct Complement:

(46) *(sen$_i$) [kendi-n$_i$ başari-ya   ulaş-miş-sin]
      2sg   self-your success-Dat reach-Past-2SG
      san-iyor-sun
      believe-Pres-2sg
      You believe yourself succeeded.

Trying to apply into finite Gerund:

(47) *(sen$_i$) [kendi-n$_i$-in   başari-ya   ulaş-ti**ğ-in**]-i
      2sg   self-2sg-Gen   success-Dat   reach-GER-2SG-Acc
      san-iyor-sun⁶
      believe-Pres-2sg
      You believe that yourself succeeeded.

Control in non-finite Gerunds

Gerunds in -mA also have non-finite variants, corresponding to the 'Equi' or 'Control' structures in English:

(48) a. (ben)$_i$ [PRO$_{i/*j}$ viski-yi   iç-**meğ**]-e
          I   -Acc   drink-GER-(no Agr)-Dat
          razi ol-du-m
          consent-Past-1sg
          I consented to drink the whisky.

      b. *(ben)$_i$ [PRO$_i$ viski-yi iç-**me-m**]-e
                               drink-GER-1SG-Dat
          razi ol-du-m

(49) a. (ben) sen-i$_i$ [PRO$_{i/*j}$ viski-yi
          I   you-Acc   -Acc
          iç-**meğ**]-e   zorla-di-m
          drink-GER-(no Agr)-Dat   force-Past-1sg
          I forced you to drink the whisky.

      b. *(ben) sen-i$_i$ [PRO$_i$ viski-yi iç-**me-n**]-e
                                    drink-GER-2SG-Dat
          zorla-di-m

   In this construction, the complement subject must be PRO and it must be bound to some matrix NP. Externally, these non-finite Gerunds are entirely parallel to the finite ones already discussed. We conclude that the FPC applies, as predicted, to Gerunds as well as to Direct Complements, and that the parameter relevant to finiteness in Turkish is Agreement rather than Tense.⁷

   In the foregoing we have not given an example of every rule trying to apply into every complement type. In certain cases, independent principles render a given example irrelevant to the validity of (1), and in such cases we have omitted the example in question. The resulting gaps fall into three general cases:

— Those due to the fact that the subject of a non-finite Gerund must be PRO, so Control is the only rule that could apply;

— Those due to the fact that the subject of a non-finite Direct Complement may not be PRO, so Control could not apply;

— Those due to the fact that, because of A/A, Passive and Disjoint Reference cannot apply to the subject of a Gerund, whether finite or not.

So far we have also neglected to test the accessibility of subjects of non-gerundive (lexical) NPs. And in fact an attempt to remedy this omission quickly leads us to data that seem problematic for our view. Consider for example

(50) (biz) birbir-imiz-in   tabla-**sin**-i   yika-di-k
      we   each other-1pl-Gen tray-3SG-Acc wash-Past-1pl
      We washed each other's tray.

Here the Genitive Subject of the NP *each other's tray* is bound by an element (*we*) outside of that NP, even though the NP, being marked by the suffix **si**, should be finite on our previous assumptions. Fortunately there is a neat way out of this dilemma, suggested by the fact that the only agreement marker of the Possessive paradigm (26) to misbehave like this is **si**. For just this suffix is used quite regularly outside the Possessive construction, to mark compound nouns, as in

(51) sigara   tabla-**si**
      cigarette tray-'si'
      ash tray

We propose that the Possessive -**si** is never, after all, an agreement marker in lexical NPs (in spite of our earlier glosses), but is always an instance of the same compound marker seen in (51), which is suffixed to complex nominal constituents by a completely general rule. Thus we are now claiming that the agreement paradigms for lexical and gerundive NPs, despite their superficially identical morphologies, differ at least partially in their syntactic function; specifically, the element -**si** is an agreement marker on Gerunds but not on lexical Nouns. In fact there is independent evidence for some bifurcation between these cases, in the form of (i) the use of the same morphology in certain Relative clauses and (ii) the non-occurrence of the third person plural **1-Ar** with overt genitives in lexical NPs. A full description of these points would take us beyond the scope of this paper, and anyway it would not prove the specific claim we are making about -si. Establishing the needed bifurcation does, however, defeat a possible objection to this claim.

Note that while the -si of lexical NPs is outside of the agreement system, 'aparadigmatic', the same element is apparently the third person marker in Gerunds (and, incidentally, Relatives). This is how we explain the fact that it renders the one type of NP opaque, but not the other.

To complete this section, we note that relative clauses also occur in both finite and non-finite forms.[8] Hence they constitute a further testing ground for our theory. And in fact we believe they provide us with positive evidence. To substantiate this, however, we would have to settle some tricky questions about impersonal passives, which we cannot discuss here.

4. Conclusion

The point of this paper has been to provide evidence that the 'Tensed-S' and 'Specified Subject' Conditions of Chomsky (1973) are, in slightly modified form, principles of Universal Grammar. This hypothesis would explain how certain rules of Turkish are bounded, without requiring us to decide whether the Conditions in question control directly the operation of the relevant rules, or merely filter the resulting 'logical forms'.

In particular, we have argued that the principle corresponding to the 'Tensed-S' Condition actually refers to a more general notion of 'Finiteness', rather than to 'Tensedness'; in Turkish Finiteness is demonstrably not 'Tensedness', but the presence of a *Subject Agreement marker*, where 'Subject' is understood roughly as the Nominative of a finite clause, the Genitive of a finite NP or Relative Clause, or the first Accusative of a non-finite Direct Complement.

This conclusion makes it an urgent matter to define 'Finiteness' in general, since the claim that the 'Tensed-S' Condition is in some sense universal would lose much of its empirical content if each language were free to substitute arbitrarily an idiosyncratic parameter for 'tense' in its definition of finiteness.

Of course the most obvious move from here is to replace the term 'Tense' with 'Personal Agreement' in the statement of the Tensed-S Condition; indeed, this was how we first reacted to the data we have presented, and at least one listener in each of the several groups that have heard our evidence came up with the same proposal. Even so, we are sceptical of this straightforward move, if only because it seems, like the original Tensed-S Condition, rather too concrete.

What we have in mind is a language *just like Turkish, except that the Personal Agreement markers regularly precede the Tense suffixes* in Sentences. We predict that if such a language could exist, then it would use neutralisation of Tense, not of Personal Agreement, to differentiate finite from non-finite phrases for purposes of Opacity.

This prediction is based on the observation that Tense is shown on the *first* Auxiliary element in an English clause, and Agreement on the *last* element of verbal morphology in Turkish. Given that Auxiliaries precede the Main Verb in English and follow it in Turkish, this suggests that the *verbal Specifier furthest from the Main Verb* is the key to the definition of 'finiteness'. In particular, if we supply enough internal bracketing in the series of verbal elements in any clause, we can say that a clause is opaque unless the Main Specifier, the superior Verbal Specifier governed by the Subject, is *aparadigmatic.* We take *aparadigmatic* to refer, in English, to the initial elements of Aux not showing tense or modals, in Turkish, to the elements of the final slot of verb inflection not showing person or number. If we substitute 'phrase' for 'clause' in the preceding formulation and eliminate 'verbal', we generalise our principle to distinguish finite and non-finite NPs, as well. And in general, we complete our formulations of the FPC and the SAC with the following definitions:

(52)   A phrase $X^{\urcorner}$ is *finite* if its Main Specifier Q is paradigmatic, that is, the independently motivated oppositions in Q are not neutralised;

and

(53)   The *Main Specifier* of $X^{\urcorner}$ is the superior Specifier of X governed by its Subject.

Observe that our theory supports the classical $\bar{X}$-hypothesis that S is a projection of V and that it sharpens the resemblance between the FPC and the SAC, in that we must use the notion 'Subject' in the sense of $\bar{X}$-theory to state both principles.

Our theory may have some advantage in the description of a

language which, like many Australian languages (and, apparently, some dialects of English), completely lacks overt Agreement but still distinguishes infinitives, which cannot show Tense. If we claimed that Agreement was universally the crucial element for characterising finiteness, then we would not only have to posit completely 'abstract' personal inflections for these languages, but would also have to tie their distribution to the presence of Tense. These manoeuvres are unnecessary under our more general approach.

Notes

1. See example (40) and note 5 for a discussion of examples where only the FPC is violated. There exist similar examples (involving Control cases) where only the SAC is violated and where the result is considerably better than when both SAC and FPC are violated. Thus, in contrast to (40b) in note 5, we get (40c), which is rather more acceptable:

> (40)c. ?/] yazar-lar [———— iç-meğ]-e   razi ol-du-lar
>   author-pl   drink-NOM-(no Agr)-Dat consent-Past-3pl
>   **viski-yi**
>   whisky-Acc
>   *The authors consented to drink the whisky.*

2. In accordance with general Turkological practice, we shall use archiphonemes in our representations of suffixes. The surface values for the vowels are spelled out by the well-known rules of Vowel Harmony.
3. The bracketing and labelling of the English glosses reflect our analysis of the Turkish strings; needless to say, neither of the two Complements in question is thus held to be an NP in English.
4. At first glance, (33) looks like a counter-example to our claim that Direct Complements cannot be Objects of Postpositions, since the Direct Complement is followed by the element **gibi** (*like*), which occurs elsewhere as a Postposition. However, there is independent evidence (not presented here) to the effect that **gibi** is not a Postposition in construction like (33); rather, it is adjoined to the verb **görün** to form the complex Verb **gibi görün** (*look like*). Evidence for such a restructuring is presented in Kornfilt (1976, 4).
5. This example (40) where Toppling violates only the FPC is not as bad as the comparable example where it violates both the FPC and SAC (cf. the Introduction, at note 1):

> (40)b. ??/* dinleyici-ler [yazar-lar-in   ———— iç-tiğ-in]-i
>   listener-pl   author-pl-Gen   drink-GER-3 AGR-Acc
>   san-iyor-lar   **viski-yi**
>   believe-Pres-3pl -Acc

Some speakers do not even reject (40b) in the first place. It is conceivable that there is a dialect split here, but this pattern is typical of 'derivative generation' (cf. Chomsky, 1970), by which speakers may accept certain ungrammatical sentences which are sufficiently analogous to grammatical ones; see George (1980, Ch. 6) for discussion.

6. Analogous examples constructed by using the third person reflexive **kendisi** instead of first or second person are grammatical. This is not a problem for us, however, since the **kendisi** is, on independent grounds, not a bound anaphor of sentence grammar; in particular, its antecedent may be found in a previous utterance, and, in its honorific use, need not have an antecedent at all. Hence, it is no surprise that it occurs irrespective of the Conditions. The first and second person reflexives, in contrast, are bound anaphors in the strict sense, so their distribution is constrained by Sentence Grammar conditions, as shown by the examples in the text.

7. We should also mention that the reason why Control cannot take place in finite Gerunds cannot be a morphological restriction against Control Verbs taking finite complements; as (30) shows, agreement marking under **razi olmak** (*consent*) is possible (as it is, in fact, under many other Control Verbs).

8. One point of special interest concerning Relative Clauses is the fact that those Relatives we would have to call finite (the -**Dlk**-construction) show their inaccessible Subject in the Genitive, not the Nominative. This, of course, suggests on the face of it that the NIC is insufficiently general in comparison to our FPC. Chomsky (personal communication) has claimed that this argument against the 'On Binding' approach could be defused by an analysis of the relevant subjects as abstract Nominatives that are spelled out as Genitive by a superficial 'glitch' of the morphology. This *ad hoc* manoeuvre might work here, but seems hopeless in the analogous case of Gerunds, where we would like to say that the inaccessible Subjects are Genitive for the same reason that the Subjects of lexical NPs are Genitive, so that an abstract Nominative analysis is less plausible. One might still hope to defend the NIC account by decomposing the Genitive into subfeatures including the Nominative (see Thiersch, 1978), but there are other Relative Clause facts, too complicated to present here, that may still cause trouble for the NIC.

For more information about the morphological alternation found in Turkish Relative Clauses, cf. Underhill (1972) and Hankamer and Knecht (1976).

References

Chomsky, N. (1970), 'Remarks on Nominalization' in R. Jacobs and P. Rosenbaum (eds.), *Readings in English Transformational Grammar*, Blaisdell, Waltham, Massachusetts
———— (1973), 'Conditions on Transformations', in S. Anderson and P. Kiparsky (eds.), *Festschrift for Morris Halle*, Holt, Rinehart and Winston, New York
———— (1976), 'On *Wh*-Movement' in P. Culicover, T. Wasow, and A. Akmajian (eds.), *Formal Syntax*, Academic Press, New York, 1977
———— (1980), 'On Binding', this volume, Ch. 1. Previously published in *Linguistic Inquiry* 11, 1–46
George, L. (1980), 'Analogical Generalizations of Natural Language Syntax', doctoral dissertation, MIT, Cambridge, Massachusetts
Hankamer, J. and L. Knecht (1975), 'The Role of the Subject/Non-subject Distinction in Determining the Choice of Relative Clause Participle in Turkish' in *Papers from the VI. Meeting of NELS*. Published as Vol. 6 of the *Montreal Working Papers in Linguistics*, 1976
Kornfilt, J. (1976), 'Some Aspects of Turkish "Subject Raising"', unpublished paper, Harvard University
Rizzi, L. (1978), 'Violations of the WH-Island Constraint in Italian and the Subjacency Condition' in *Montreal Working Papers in Linguistics*, 10
Underhill, R. (1972), 'Turkish Participles', *Linguistic Inquiry*, 3, 87–99

3 Nominative Marking in Italian Infinitives and the Nominative Island Constraint

Luigi Rizzi

0. In this paper I would like to discuss various infinitival constructions in Italian from which some conclusions of theoretical interest can be drawn. First of all, one of them provides straightforward evidence that the Nominative Island Constraint, recently proposed by Chomsky (1980), is empirically more adequate than its classical alternative, the Tensed-S Condition. Secondly, it can be shown that there is a certain tension between the requirements of the Nominative Island Constraint and the proper way of capturing the generalisation accounted for via the NP to VP filter in Chomsky and Lasnik (1977); in particular, a superficial review of the relevant facts seems to suggest that the maximisation of the explanatory power of the Nominative Island Constraint is incompatible with Chomsky's recent proposal to derive the NP to VP filter from independently-motivated aspects of the Case marking mechanism. In fact, it will be shown that, upon careful consideration, these two constructs turn out to be fully compatible in their optimal form, and this result will be shown to follow from independently motivated aspects of the nominative marking process in Italian.

1. Epistemic verbs and some verbs of saying can be found in Italian in the surface environments shown in (1) and (2). These verbs can take bare infinitival complements whose empty subject positions are interpreted as anaphoric to the head of the relative construction in (1) and to the *wh*-phrase in a higher COMP in (2):

(1) a. Le persone$_i$ che suppongo ——$_i$ non esser state messe al corrente delle vostre decisioni sono molte.

The persons$_i$ that I suppose ____$_i$ not to have been acquainted with your decisions are many.

b. La donna$_i$ che Mario temeva ____$_i$ aver tradito la nostra causa era Giovanna.

The woman$_i$ that Mario feared ____$_i$ to have betrayed our cause was Giovanna.

c. Gianni$_i$, che sostengo ____$_i$ aver sempre fatto il suo dovere, non meritava di essere punito.

Gianni$_i$, who I assert ____$_i$ to have always done his duty, didn't deserve to be punished.

d. La donna$_i$ che Mario affermava ____$_i$ non volerlo sposare era mia sorella.

The woman$_i$ that Mario stated ____$_i$ not to want to marry him was my sister.

(2) a. Quante persone$_i$ supponi ____$_i$ non essere state messe al corrente delle vostre decisioni?

How many people$_i$ do you suppose ____$_i$ not to have been acquainted with your decisions?

b. Non ho ancora capito quante persone$_i$ temessi ____$_i$ aver tradito la nostra causa.

I haven't yet understood how many people$_i$ you feared ____$_i$ to have betrayed our cause.

c. In questo ufficio, mi domando quale impiegato$_i$ tu possa sostenere ____$_i$ aver sempre fatto il suo dovere.

In this office, I wonder which employee$_i$ you can assert ____$_i$ to have always done his duty.

d. Non ho ancora capito quale delle due sorelle$_i$ Mario affermasse ____$_i$ non volerlo sposare.

I haven't yet understood which one of the two sisters$_i$ Mario stated ____$_i$ not to want to marry him.

Given ordinary assumptions on the transformational derivation of relative clauses and interrogative clauses, these sentences are to be derived from underlying structures of the type

(3)   ... V [$_S$ NP inf VP]

where the embedded subject NP is lexically realised as a *wh*-element. This element is transformationally moved to the matrix COMP, and then, in case of the relative construction (1), deleted under non-distinctness with the head.

Now, the interesting thing to notice is that, if *Wh* Movement does not apply, extracting the subject from the infinitival clause, then the surface structure which is derived is unacceptable: sentences (4), which correspond closely to the initial structures of (1) and (2) are not accepted by native speakers:

(4) a. *Suppongo [s quelle persone non essere state messe al corrente delle vostre decisioni]
       I suppose [s those persons not to have been acquainted with your decisions]

     b. *Mario temeva [s questa donna aver tradito la nostra causa]
       Mario feared [s this woman to have betrayed our cause]

     c. *Sostengo [s Gianni aver sempre fatto il suo dovere]
       I assert [s Gianni to have always done his duty]

     d. *Mario affermava [s questa donna non volerlo sposare]
       Mario stated [s this woman not to want to marry him]

Roughly speaking, the situation seems to be the following: an initial structure like (3) must be postulated, under ordinary assumptions, in order to derive sentences like (1) and (2). But, if the embedded subject is not extracted from the infinitival clause, the derived surface structure is ill-formed. This is the standard situation which justifies recourse to a surface filter.

For the time being, I will adopt the formulation (5), which is clearly reminiscent of Chomsky and Lasnik's NP to VP filter:

(5) *[NP inf VP], if NP lexical.[1]

2. The filtering approach predicts that an underlying structure like (3) can be rescued not only by *Wh* Movement, but by whatever transformation destroys the forbidden configuration (5). Now, there are other transformations which could, in principle, extract the embedded subject in (3): one is NP Movement in the passive or impersonal construction, another is clitic movement.[2] These transformations should operate as indicated in the following abstract structures:

(6) a. [NP e] essere V + to [s NP inf VP] (passive) construction]

     b. [NP e] si + V [s NP inf VP] (impersonal **si** construction)

     c. NP V [s[NP CL] inf VP] (clitic movement)

But this expectation is not fulfilled: if NP Movement or CL Movement apply on these structures, the derived sentences are unacceptable ((7a–b) are derived via NP Movement in passive, (7c–d) are derived via NP Movement in the impersonal construction, (8a–d) are derived via CL Movement):

(7) a. *Quelle persone erano supposte _____ non essere state messe al corrente delle vostre decisioni.
           Those people were supposed _____ not to have been acquainted with your decisions.
     b. *Questa donna era temuta _____ aver tradito la nostra causa.
           This woman was feared _____ to have betrayed our cause.
     c. *Quegli impiegati si sostengono _____ aver sempre fatto il loro dovere.
           Those employees PRO asserts _____ to have always done their duty.
     d. *Queste ragazze si affermavano _____ non volerli sposare.
           Those girls PRO stated _____ not to want to marry them.
(8) a. *Mario li suppone _____ non essere stati messi al corrente delle vostre decisioni.
           Mario them-supposes _____ not to have been acquainted with your decisions.
     b. *Gianni la temeva _____ aver tradito la nostra causa.
           Gianni her-feared _____ to have betrayed our cause.
     c. *Piero li sostiene _____ aver sempre fatto il loro dovere.
           Piero them-asserts _____ to have always done their duty.
     d. *Mario la affermava _____ non volerlo sposare.
           Mario her-stated _____ not to want to marry him.

There are some lexical variations here. With some epistemic verbs, such sentences as (7)–(8) are not fully ungrammatical, but are marginally acceptable to various degrees. I will assume here that the basic case to be explained is the full ungrammaticality of (7)–(8), and that the cases of marginal acceptability are to be treated via analogy, along lines I will discuss in the Appendix.

Let us focus on the contrast between sentences (1)–(2), which are acceptable, and (7)–(8), which are not. Now the question is: why can structure (3) be rescued by *Wh* Movement, but not by NP Movement or CL Movement?[3]

An obvious way to make the appropriate difference comes to mind immediately. Suppose that, contrary to what is currently assumed in the framework I am adopting here, the rules involved in the relative and interrogative construction on the one hand, and the rules involved in the passive, impersonal and clitic construction on the other are very different in nature, in that the first are essentially structure dependent, while the second are essentially relation dependent. In other words, suppose that NP Movement is to be stated as (9a), and CL Movement is to be stated as (9b), somewhere in the grammar:

(9) a. The object becomes the subject.
     b. The object is cliticised to V.

Now, the asymmetry (1)–(2)/(7)–(8) would follow automatically: structures like (3) could be rescued by *Wh* Movement, while the equivalents of the former NP Movement and CL Movement could not apply on such structures, since the relevant NP does not bear the appropriate grammatical relation to the main verb. Therefore, the contrast (1)–(2)/(7)–(8) seems to argue for a mixed theory of rules, such as the one advocated by some versions of relational grammar, or by Joan Bresnan's recent work on 'realistic' grammar.[4]

Instead of further investigating how the contrast in question can be treated in such frameworks, I will now pursue a different line of inquiry, and try to ask the question: how could the classical, purely structure dependent theory deal with these facts?

3. In order to give an interesting answer to this question it is now necessary to take into account other aspects of Italian syntax. In declarative sentences of modern standard Italian, a subject NP can never be positioned between the aspectual auxiliary and the past participle in compound tenses, or between the copular verb **essere** and a predicative AP:

(10) a. Mario ha accettato di aiutarci.
          Mario has accepted to help us.
      b. *Ha Mario accettato di aiutarci.

But in other types of clauses, the ordering Aux NP past part. (or **essere** NP AP) is allowed: a gerundival sentence like (11b) is acceptable, ((11a), acceptable for some speakers, is excluded for many, a fact which will be briefly discussed later on):

(11)   a.   Mario avendo accettato di aiutarci, potremo risolvere il
             problema.
             *Mario having accepted to help us, we'll be able to solve the
             problem.*
       b.   Avendo Mario accettato di aiutarci, potremo risolvere il
             problema.

In order to account for the asymmetry between (10) and (11), I will
assume, without specific argument, that the grammar of Italian has a
rule, which I will call 'Aux preposing', which moves an auxiliary (or
copula) to the left of the subject, under certain conditions to be
specified (which include gerundival Aux, and exclude Aux in
declarative sentences), and Chomsky adjoins it to S.[5]

Aux preposing, which applies quite ordinarily in gerundival
clauses, can also apply in infinitival clauses, most naturally if the
subject is a stressed pronoun:

(12)   a.   Così facendo, suppongo [aver lui voluto compiere un
             gesto di buona volontà]
             *By doing this, I suppose [to-have he/him wanted to
             accomplish an act of good will]*
       b.   Ho sempre sostenuto [non esser lui in grado di affron-
             tare una simile situazione]
             *I have always asserted [not-to-be he/him able to face such
             a situation]*

The resulting sentences are stylistically highly marked, but if the
inversion rule does not apply, these structures are unacceptable, at
any stylistic level:

(13)   a.   *Così facendo, suppongo [lui aver voluto compiere un
             gesto di buona volontà]
       b.   *Ho sempre sostenuto [lui non essere in grado di
             affrontare una simile situazione]

The contrast between (12) and (13) follows from the filtering
approach I have proposed. Given underlying structures like (13), if
the inversion rule applies, sentences (12) are derived, which are
acceptable at their peculiar stylistic level. If the inversion rule (which
I assume to be optional) does not apply, structures (13) are derived.
These are ruled out by the filter (5).[6]

In short, the contrast (12)–(13) is an interesting confirmation of the filtering approach, since it shows that not only the *wh*-extraction of the subject, but also other transformations which destroy the forbidden configuration (5) permit an acceptable outcome from an initial structure like (3). This is exactly the situation predicted by the filtering approach.

4. Before turning to the main problem, i.e., why the structures at issue cannot be rescued via NP Movement and CL Movement, it is now necessary to make a brief digression on the proper formulation of general conditions on binding. Consider the well-known contrast

(14) a.   John believes [$_\bar{S}$ himself to be very smart]
      b.   *John believes [$_\bar{S}$ that himself is very smart]

According to the approach proposed by Chomsky (1973), the ungrammaticality of (14b) is due to a violation of the Tensed-S Condition (henceforth TSC). In his recent paper 'On Binding', Chomsky (1980) proposes an alternative to TSC, that is to say, the Nominative Island Constraint (henceforth NIC):

(15)   NIC: A nominative anaphor cannot be free in $\bar{S}$.

(15) accounts for the contrast (14a–b). (14b) is excluded because the anaphor *himself*, subject of a tensed sentence, is marked nominative, and is free in the embedded $\bar{S}$, since its antecedent *John* is outside $\bar{S}$; this structure is therefore ruled out by NIC. On the other hand, (14a) is possible because the anaphor *himself* is free, as before, in the embedded $\bar{S}$, but it is not nominative (since it is assumed that only subjects of tensed Ss are marked nominative). Therefore, NIC does not apply.

Chomsky has proposed the NIC as an alternative to the TSC essentially for metatheoretical reasons, i.e., in order to avoid the redundancy of the TSC with the other binding principle, the Specified Subject Condition, or 'Opacity Condition' in the recent terminology. But it is clear that TSC and NIC make empirically distinct predictions in certain cases; it is therefore possible to construct crucial experiments. The two approaches would obviously make diverging predictions in all cases in which the notion 'subject of a tensed S' and the notion 'NP marked nominative' are not overlapping. For instance in the following situation: suppose that in some language, for some reason the subject NP of a certain type of infinitival complement is marked nominative. Suppose now that an anaphor, say a reflexive pronoun, is placed in subject position of this infinitival construction; now, the TSC approach would predict that the resulting structure is acceptable (if, of course, independent conditions on anaphora are not violated), while the NIC approach would predict it is unacceptable.

While this crucial situation does not seem to arise in English, it does arise in Italian. In Italian, the distinction between nominative and non-nominative is morphologically reflected only in the I and II person singular stressed pronouns, in the following way:

	+NOM	−NOM
I	io	me
II	tu	te

Consider now again the marked construction exemplified in (12); if we insert a I or II person singular pronoun in subject position of the infinitival complement, it has to be marked nominative:

(16) a. Hanno sempre sostenuto [$_S$, non esser $\left\{ {io \atop *me} \right\}$ in grado di
        affrontare una simile situazione]
        They have always asserted [not to be $\left\{ {I \atop *me} \right\}$ able to face
        such a situation]

      b. Così facendo, suppongo [aver $\left\{ {tu \atop *te} \right\}$ voluto compiere un
        gesto di buona volontà]
        By doing this, I suppose [to-have you + NOM wanted to
        accomplish an act of good will]

Since in this infinitival construction the subject of an untensed sentence is marked nominative, this is the crucial environment to test the respective predictions of TSC and NIC. As the following examples show, the predictions of NIC are correct:

(17) a. Mario ha sempre sostenuto [non esser lui in grado di
          affrontare una simile situazione]
          Mario has always asserted [not-to-be he able to face such
          a situation]

b. *Mario ha sempre sostenuto [non esser se stesso in grado di affrontare una simile situazione]
Mario has always asserted [not-to-be himself able to face such a situation]

In (17b) a reflexive pronoun (i.e., an anaphor) has been inserted in subject position of the infinitival complement and the resulting structure is unacceptable. In (17a) the personal pronoun **lui**, subject of the infinitival complement, can be interpreted as anaphoric to the main subject: in other words, disjoint reference does not apply.

These two facts are a problem for the TSC approach, which predicts the acceptability of (17b) and the unacceptability of (17a) in the anaphoric reading; but they are predicted by the NIC approach which therefore receives strong empirical support. Given the morphological evidence in (16) that the subject NP of this infinitival construction is marked nominative, the NIC predicts that this NP behaves under all relevant respects like the subject of a tensed clause, and so it does.

5. We are now able to give an answer to the main question raised before, i.e., why structures (3) can be rescued via *Wh* Movement, but not via NP Movement or CL Movement. Now, this pattern strikingly resembles one found elsewhere in the grammar, i.e., the behaviour of the subject of a tensed clause. It is well known that the subject of a tensed clause can be extracted by *Wh* Movement, but not by NP Movement or CL Movement. For instance, given an initial structure similar to sentence (18a), sentence (18b) can be derived, but (18c–e) cannot:

(18) a. Sostengo che i tuoi amici sono tornati.
I assert that your friends have come back.
b. Gli amici che sostengo che sono tornati sono molti.
The friends that I assert that _____ have come back are many.
c. *I tuoi amici erano sostenuti che _____ fossero tornati.
Your friends were asserted that _____ had come back.
d. *I tuoi amici si sostenevano che _____ fossero tornati.
Your friends PRO asserted that _____ had come back.
e. *Mario li sostiene che _____ sono tornati.
Mario them asserts that _____ have come back.

The grammaticality judgements remain unchanged, with one exception if we substitute an infinitival complement for the tensed complement of (18):

(19) a. *Sostengo i tuoi amici esser tornati.
           I assert your friends to have come back.
      b. Gli amici che sostengo ——— esser tornati sono molti.
           The friends that I assert ——— to have come back are many.
      c. *I tuoi amici erano sostenuti ——— esser tornati.
           Your friends were asserted ——— to have come back.
      d. *I tuoi amici si sostenevano ——— esser tornati.
           Your friends PRO asserted ——— to have come back.
      e. *Mario li sostiene ——— esser tornati.
           Mario them asserts ——— to have come back.

While the TSC approach is intrinsically incapable of accounting for the similarity, between (18) and (19) the NIC approach predicts it, if certain natural assumptions are made. Let us compare (18) and (19) in detail. First of all, let us account for the only difference between them, i.e., the grammaticality of (18a) versus the ungrammaticality of (19a). In the framework proposed here, this difference follows from the fact that filter (5) applies to (19a), while, of course, it cannot apply to (18a), since the embedded clause is tensed. If we turn to the similarities of (18) and (19), the obvious move is now to try to trace them back to the NIC.

Recall that examples (16) provide straightforward morphological evidence that the subject position of (at least) this particular infinitival construction is marked nominative.[7] I will furthermore assume that Case marking rules are obligatory (this assumption is necessary for independent reasons: see Chomsky (1980, fns. 30, 45). From these considerations, it follows that sentences (19c–e) are excluded: consider the surface structures of these sentences, which are schematically reproduced in (21):

(21) c. NP_i essere $V + to$ [$_S$ t_i inf VP]
      d. NP_i si $+ V$ [$_S$ t_i inf VP]
      e. ... $cl_i + V$ [$_S$ t_i inf VP]

Nominative marking obligatorily applies on the embedded subject traces, and these structures are ruled out by NIC, since the traces count as nominative anaphors, and are free in the embedded clauses.

But consider now the surface structure of (19b), assuming successive cyclic application of *Wh* Movement:

(22)   Gli amici$_i$ che sostengo [$_S$[COMP t$_i$] t$_i$ essere tornati ...]

The trace in subject position is marked nominative, as before, but it is not free in $\bar{S}$ (since it is bound by the trace in COMP), therefore NIC does not apply; as far as the trace in COMP is concerned, it is independently plausible that it does not receive Case at all (see Chomsky (1980), pp. 87–8 this volume for relevant discussion).[8]

In conclusion, the NIC approach correctly predicts the parallel behaviour of this infinitival construction and ordinary tensed clauses with respect to: non application of disjoint reference; non-occurrence of reflexives in subject position; extractability of the subject via *Wh* Movement; and non-extractability of the subject via NP Movement and CL Movement. This coherent clustering of properties strongly argues for the correctness of the NIC approach.

6. Let us now turn to the main difference between the infinitival construction (19) and the corresponding tensed construction (18), i.e., the contrast (18a)/(19a). I have provisionally proposed to account for this contrast by having recourse to filter (5), that is to say, essentially to Chomsky and Lasnik's NP to VP filter. But in his recent paper Chomsky (1980), following a suggestion by Jean-Roger Vergnaud, has shown that the NP to VP filter need not be stipulated for English, since its main effects follow from independent principles of case marking. Chomsky shows that the Case marking mechanism can be constructed in such a way that it does not assign Case to the subject position of untensed sentences, so that, if this position is lexically filled, it cannot receive Case, and the structure is ruled out by a different filter proposed in that paper, which rules out lexical NPs that have no Case.

But, if the analysis I have just presented is correct, it creates a serious problem for any attempt to reduce the ungrammaticality of sentences like (19a) to aspects of the case marking mechanism in a straightforward way. The reason is the following: if (19a) is ruled out because its lexical subject **i suoi amici** lacks case (in other words, if the Case assignment mechanism is constructed in such a way that the subject position of untensed sentences does not receive case), then the simple, appealing explanation of the contrast (19b)/(19c–e) in terms of NIC is lost. If my explanation is correct, then the subject position of this infinitival construction has to be marked for Case, and has to be marked nominative, which is independently supported by (16). Then (19a), and more generally the effects of the NP to VP filter cannot simply be traced back to the Case assignment mechanism. And still, it is my opinion that Vergnaud's original idea and Chomsky's elaboration on it are basically correct, in spite of the problem just mentioned; in fact, the aim of this section is to try to show that the Case marking approach not only can be rendered compatible with the preservation of the full explanatory power of NIC, but also provides an explanation for a range of facts which fall outside the scope of the analysis developed so far. The key to the problem will be shown to be the proper formulation of the nominative marking rules in Italian, a detail which was left entirely open in the preceding account.[9]

6.1   Consider the Case marking rules proposed for English by Chomsky (1980), which I will informally represent in terms of grammatical relations:

(27)   a.   The subject of a tensed S is marked nominative
       b.   The object of a verb is marked objective
       c.   The object of a preposition is marked oblique

If we now want to account for nominative marking in infinitives (i.e., in (16), etc.) two basic possibilities are available with respect to (27):
   A. the main nominative marking process of Italian differs from (27a) in that, in Italian, surface subjects are always marked nominative, irrespective of the tensed/untensed character of their clauses;
   B. the main nominative marking process is the same for English and Italian (i.e. (27a)), but the grammar of Italian has a subsidiary Case marking process which is operative (at least) in the infinitival construction at hand.
   Let us now assume that solution B is basically correct, and that the proper formulation of the subsidiary nominative marking rule crucially involves postverbal subjects, irrespective of the tensed/untensed character of their clauses, approximately as follows:[10]

(28)   A postverbal subject is marked nominative

If (27)–(28) are (some of) the Case marking rules of Italian, then the contrast (12)–(13) (repeated here as (29)) can be explained in terms of case marking, along the lines indicated in Chomsky (1980), and filter (5) need not be stipulated:

(29) a.   Ho sempre sostenuto [non esser lui in grado di ...]
     b.   *Ho sempre sostenuto [lui non essere in grado di ...]

(29b) is now excluded since the lexical NP **lui** does not receive Case, and the structure is therefore rejected by the filter which requires that all NPs be marked for Case (see below). (29a) is acceptable since the post-auxiliary subject receives nominative Case by (28).

6.2 We are now left with the problem of accounting for such paradigms as (19). Two basic questions should be given an answer:

A. If the preverbal subject position in the infinitive in (19c–e) does not receive Case (this follows from the Case marking rules (27)–(28)), how are these structures to be excluded? It is obvious that the account proposed in section 5, which makes straightforward reference to NIC, has to be qualified.

B. Whatever modification of our preceding account we introduce to solve problem A, it should at the same time preserve our previous explanation (alternatively, allow some different satisfactory account) of the fact that *wh*-extraction of the embedded subject is possible.

In order to account for A, I will now introduce a minor modification in Chomsky's system. That is to say, I will stipulate that not only lexical NPs, but also traces have to be marked for Case in surface structure. This result is achieved by the following filter[11]:

(30)   *NP, unless it is marked for Case

Consider now again for instance (19b,e), which are reproduced below as (31a,b):

(31) a.   Gli amici che sostengo _____ esser tornati.
        The friends who I assert _____ to have come back.
     b.   *Mario li sostiene _____ esser tornati.
        Mario them asserts _____ to have come back.

The respective surface structures would be:

(32) a.   Gli amici$_i$ che sostengo [$_S$[$_{COMP}$ t$_i$] t$_i$ esser tornati]

b.   Mario li$_i$ sostiene [s̄[COMP e] t$_i$ esser tornati]

Now, these structures are both excluded by filter (30), since the trace in subject position is not marked for case[12] (the trace in COMP in (32a) is irrelevant, because of free delection in COMP). This accounts for the ungrammaticality of (31b), but seems to leave unexplained the acceptability of (31a). Why is this structure not ruled out by filter (30)?

In fact, (32a,b) are not the only surface structures which our grammar associates with (31a,b); since Aux preposing can apply in the infinitival clause, the following structures are derivable, too:

(33)   a.   Gli amici$_i$ che sostengo [s̄[COMP t$_i$] esser t$_i$ tornati]
       b.   Mario li$_i$ sostiene [s̄[COMP e] esser t$_i$ tornati]

Rule (28) can apply on these structures, so that the embedded subject traces get marked nominative, and filter (30) does not apply; but now, it is NIC which becomes relevant again, and makes the appropriate distinction: (33b) is excluded since the embedded subject trace (anaphor) is marked nominative, and is free in S̄; (33a) is acceptable, since the nominative anaphor is bound by the trace in COMP (which, in turn, does not fall into the domain of NIC since it is not marked for case, nor into the domain of filter (30), since it can be deleted via free deletion in COMP).

In conclusion, our grammar correctly associates a well-formed structural representation with the acceptable sentence (31a),[13] but doesn't associate any well-formed representation with the un-acceptable sentence (31b). The two surface structures which the transformational component associates with (31b) (i.e. (32b) and (33b)) are ruled out by filter (30) and NIC respectively. With the introduction of the case marking system (27)–(28)–(30) we are able to maintain (a qualified version of) our explanation via NIC of such paradigms as (19) and, at the same time, we can preserve Chomsky's explanation of the NP to VP filter. The appropriate device seems to be filter (30), which overlooks the distinction between lexical NPs and traces, thus implying the hypothesis that phonetically-un-realised NPs which result from the application of movement rules behave like phonetically-realised NPs with respect to case marking requirements (on the case marking requirements for PRO, see below).[14]

7. A possible objection which might be raised against the preceding analysis is the following. In the new account proposed in section 6, the ungrammatical sentence (31b) is associated by the transformational component with two distinct surface structures, one of which (i.e., (32b) is excluded by filter (30), and the other (i.e., 33b)), by NIC. Now, it is well known that Italian, like many other languages, has a rule which optionally deletes subject pronouns — Subject Pronoun Drop, a rule which should not be confused with the PRO deletion convention discussed below. If we consider again the proposed explanation of the unacceptability of (31b), we can see that the existence of a Subject Pronoun Drop rule creates a problem: in fact, Subject Pronoun Drop should be able to delete the trace in subject position in (33b) (for reasons discussed in Chomsky and Lasnik (1977)) so that filter (30) could not apply, and the structure would be incorrectly generated. How can our account of the ungrammaticality of sentences like (31b) be rendered compatible with the fact that Italian is a subject pronoun drop language?

A possible solution of this problem could consist in showing that Subject Pronoun Drop is inapplicable in untensed sentences. This is rather natural on intuitive grounds: Subject Pronoun Drop is generally possible in languages with rich verbal inflection, which allows recoverability (in an intuitive sense) of the information lost in the deletion process. But in an infinitival clause this possibility does not exist, since an infinitival verb is not inflected. Therefore, the traditional 'functional' explanation of the fact that Subject Pronoun Drop only exists in languages with rich verbal inflection suggests that Subject Pronoun Drop should be inapplicable, in these languages too, in infinitival clauses.

In fact, there is straightforward evidence that this speculation is correct. Consider the following paradigm:

(34) a. Credevo che $\left\{ {loro \atop \emptyset} \right\}$ fossero disposti ad aiutarci.

I believed that $\left\{ {they \atop \emptyset} \right\}$ *were ready to help us.*

  b. Credevo esser $\left\{ {loro \atop *\emptyset} \right\}$ disposti ad aiutarci.

I believed to-be $\left\{ {they \atop \emptyset} \right\}$ *ready to help us.*

In the tensed clause (34a) the subject can freely drop, but in the corresponding infinitival clause, acceptable at its specific stylistic level, application of Subject Pronoun Drop creates an unacceptable structure: we are therefore led to conclude that Subject Pronoun Drop does not apply in infinitival clauses, so that the problem raised at the beginning of this section does not exist.

But, one might ask, what about tensed clauses? How are sentences like (18c–e) excluded? Of course, no problem arises in this case: given the derived structure

(35)   ... [s[COMP *e*] t$_i$ TENSE ...]

rule (27a) obligatorily applies, and the subject trace gets nominative Case, so that the structure is ruled out by NIC. The fact that the subject trace is optionally deleted by Subject Pronoun Drop is entirely irrelevant, since what is crucially involved in this case is a well-formedness constraint on logical form,[15] not a filter.[16]

8. In this section we will briefly review the implications of the analysis developed in section 6 for other infinitival constructions in Italian.

Consider first structures of control:[17]

(36)   a.   Mario vuole [s PRO venire con noi]
             Mario wants to come with us.
       b.   Mario spera [s PRO di venire con noi]
             Mario hopes 'of' to come with us.
       c.   Mario ha pregato Piero [s PRO di venire con noi]
             Mario asked Piero 'of' to come with us.
       d.   [s PRO venire con voi] mi è difficile.
             To come with you to-me-is difficult.
       e.   Mario non sa [s quando PRO venire con voi]
             Mario doesn't know when to come with you.

To avoid being ruled out by filter (30), the occurrences of PRO should be marked for Case; but no Case marking rule can apply on the PRO subjects in the structural positions indicated in (36). Therefore, the requirement of filter (30) to the effect that all NPs must be marked for Case seems to incorrectly exclude all kinds of control structures, so that the whole analysis seems to need revision in order to allow such grammatical structures as (36) to be generated.

In fact, Chomsky's (1980) system offers a straightforward solution for this problem. For independent reasons, concerning the interrelations of syntax and phonology, Chomsky assumes that unindexed occurrences of [$_{NP}$ e] (= PRO) are deleted in the course of the left path of the grammar of note 16, by the rule:

(37) [$_{NP}$ e] → ∅

Now, once this PRO deletion convention has applied, control structures like (36) are no longer in the domain of filter (30); so that nothing prevents their being generated. The interaction of filter (30) with convention (37) operates to make a distinction between lexical subjects and traces, on the one hand, which must be marked for Case, and PRO 'control' subjects on the other hand, which are exempted because of (37). Therefore, there is a possible derivation for the acceptable sentences corresponding to (36), and control structures are not a problem for our analysis.[18]

Less obvious, of course, is the account in our framework of 'subject raising' structures. Consider the following surface structure:

(38) Gianni$_i$ sembrava [$_S$ t$_i$ dormire]
      Gianni seemed to sleep

(where t$_i$ is, as usual, an abbreviation for [$_{NP_i}$ e]). The embedded subject trace in (38) must be marked for Case; moreover, it must be marked non-nominative, because of NIC. But no Case marking rule is available in our system to achieve this result.

There seem to be two basic possible solutions for this problem:

A. the assumption that sentences corresponding to structures like (38) are derived via subject raising ('move NP') is to be abandoned: such sentences are simply instances of control structures, to be treated on a par with (36), as proposed in Jenkins (1976), Bresnan (1978);

B. the classical derivation for (38) is maintained, but it is assumed that subject raising verbs have the marked property that they govern objective marking of the embedded subject, across the S̄ boundaries.[19]

At first glance, solution A might seem preferable, because of its conceptual simplicity; but, on the other hand, there seem to be good reasons to preserve the classical derivation for (38) (for a brief discussion of some of these reasons see Rizzi (1976)). What is more interesting is that the two hypotheses make different predictions in at least one case: under the reasonable assumption that Case marking rules (at least, the one which is relevant here) apply to surface structure, solution B predicts that, while 'control' complements should be allowed to move around with a certain freedom, subject raising complements cannot be moved to a position such that the embedded subject trace could not be marked for Case, since such structures would be ruled out by filter (30).[20] On the other hand, solution A predicts that the two kinds of complements should behave exactly alike with respect to movement.

This prediction can be tested. Control infinitival clauses can be clefted, in Italian, with slightly varying degrees of naturalness:

(39) a. E' venire con voi che Mario vuole.
          It is to come with you that Mario wants.
      b. E' di dover venire con voi che spero.
          It is to have to come with you that I hope.
      c. E' di venire con voi che l'ho pregato.
          It is to come with you that I him-asked.
      d. E' venire con voi che mi è difficile.
          It is to come with you that to-me-is difficult.
      e. E' quando venire con voi che ancora non so.
          It is when to come with you that I don't know yet.

But subject raising infinitival clauses can never be clefted:

(40) a. *E' dover partire che i nostri amici sembrano.
          It is to have to leave that our friends seem.
      b. *Era lavorare troppo che pareva.
          It was to work too much that he appeared.

Minimal pairs can be constructed: a verb like **sembrare** takes double subcategorisation in Italian, as subject raising verb, and as control verb. In the control frame, the infinitival complement is introduced by the preposition **di**, and the embedded subject position is controlled by the matrix dative (the 'experiencer'):

(41) a. Mario sembrava lavorare troppo.
          Mario seemed to-work too much.

b. Mi sembrava di lavorare troppo.
   It to-me-seemed 'of' to-work too much.

Now, only the control **sembrare** can be clefted:

(42) a. *Era lavorare troppo che Mario sembrava.
      b. Era di lavorare troppo che mi sembrava.

Notice that this difference cannot be attributed to the fact that the traces in subject position of the infinitival complement in (40) and (42a) are not *c*-commanded by their antecedents, since that would also exclude the control structures (39) and (42b) under the natural assumption that proper binding requirements are the same for traces and PROs.

Assume that cleft sentences are derived à la Vergnaud, via COMP to COMP movement of the focused constituent, and subsequent movement of it from the last COMP to the focus position. Then, the respective surface structures of, e.g., (42a,b) would be the following:

(43) a. Era [$_S$ t$_i$ lavorare troppo] che Mario$_i$ sembrava t
      b. Era [$_S$ PRO di lavorare troppo] che mi sembrava t

Given this derivational assumption (which seems plausible on independent ground: see Chomsky (1980) for discussion), hypothesis B predicts the contrast in acceptability between (42a) and (42b), (39) and (40), etc. In (43a), the embedded subject trace is not *c*-commanded by **sembrare** in surface structure, therefore it cannot receive Case, and the structure is filtered out by (30).[21] At the same time, filter (30) cannot rule out (43b), (37) having applied, so that nothing prevents the derivation of (42b).

However, if we were to assume base generation plus control for 'subject raising' structures (i.e., solution A, then nothing would prevent generation of (40) and (42a) and the contrasts (39)–(40), (42a)–(42b) would be left unexplained.

Without putting too much weight on this argument, which certainly needs to be further elaborated, I think it is fair to conclude that there seems to be some independent evidence for hypothesis B, so that our general analysis can be rendered fully compatible in a non *ad hoc* way with the classical derivational hypothesis concerning infinitival structures like (38).

9. Conclusions

The main goal of this paper was to discuss some aspects of the infinitival syntax in Italian which are relevant for the current theoretical debate. The main results arrived at can be summarised as follows:

A. There is direct empirical evidence in favour of the NIC approach, and against its classical alternative, the TSC. The evidence comes from an infinitival construction in which the (post-Aux) subject NP is marked nominative. The subject position in this construction behaves, in all relevant respects (movement and construal processes), like the subject position of a tensed clause. This generalisation, captured by NIC, is obviously missed by the TSC approach.

B. The maximisation of the explanatory power of the NIC, in spite of prima facie refuting evidence, can be fully reconciled with Chomsky's recent proposal to derive the * NP to VP filter from independently motivated aspects of the Case marking mechanism. This result can be achieved by extending Chomsky's *N filter to cover both lexical NPs and traces, essentially in the spirit of Rouveret and Vergnaud (1980).

Appendix

With the main verbs indicated in (1)–(2), (7)–(8) the contrast between *wh*-extraction and NP/CL extraction of the subject is very sharp. But with a restricted subclass of epistemic verbs, NP/CL extraction gives marginally acceptable results: compare the following examples with (7)–(8):

(44) a. ??Questa donna era reputata ____ aver tradito la nostra causa.
This woman was reputed ____ to have betrayed our cause.

b. ?Queste strade si ritengono ____ essere state costruite in tempo di guerra.
These roads PRO believes ____ to have been built during the war.

(45) a. ?Mario la riteneva ____ aver tradito la nostra causa.
Mario her-believed ____ to have betrayed our cause.

b. ?Lo giudico ———— aver sempre fatto il suo dovere.
    I him-judge ———— to have always done his duty.

This marginal acceptability is not expected, given the analysis I have proposed so far, and calls for an explanation. Notice, first of all, that the following generalisation seems to hold: the set of verbs marginally allowing NP/CL extraction of the embedded subject seems to coincide exactly with the set of the verbs of the relevant class which are also subcategorised for structures ———— NP AP:

(46) $\begin{Bmatrix} \text{Reputo} \\ \text{Ritengo} \\ \text{Giudico} \end{Bmatrix}$ tuo fratello un disgraziato.

$I \begin{Bmatrix} \textit{repute} \\ \textit{believe} \\ \textit{judge} \end{Bmatrix}$ *your brother a wretch.*

(47) * $\begin{Bmatrix} \text{Temo} \\ \text{Sostengo} \\ \text{Affermo} \end{Bmatrix}$ tuo fratello un disgraziato.

$I \begin{Bmatrix} \textit{fear} \\ \textit{assert} \\ \textit{state} \end{Bmatrix}$ *your brother a wretch.*

Notice that the object noun phrase in this peculiar construction can be freely passivised or cliticised:

(48) a. Tuo fratello era $\begin{Bmatrix} \text{reputato} \\ \text{ritenuto} \\ \text{giudicato} \end{Bmatrix}$ una brava persona.

b. Lo $\begin{Bmatrix} \text{reputato} \\ \text{ritenevo} \\ \text{Giudicavo} \end{Bmatrix}$ una brava persona.

If the generalisation is correct that the verbs marginally permitting NP/CL movement also permit sentences like (48) as fully grammatical, it seems plausible that the marginal acceptability of (44)–(45) is not to be accounted for via direct generation (plus some interacting factor which reduces acceptability), but as a derivative analogical process: sentences like (44)–(45) would be marginally accepted in analogy with the fully acceptable (48). In fact, sentences corresponding to (1)–(2), but such that the embedded subject has not been moved from its base position seem to be significantly better than (4):

(49) a. ??Reputo questa donna aver tradito la nostra causa.
    b. ?Ritengo queste strade esser state costruite in tempo di guerra.
    c. ??Giudico queste persone aver sempre fatto il loro dovere.

This fact suggests a simple account of the analogical process. Suppose that the verbs which take both the following kinds of complements:

(50) a. _____ NP AP
    b. _____ [$_S$ NP inf VP]

marginally allow a re-analysis of (50b), basically in terms of (50a), as a structure of control like the following:

(51)   _____ NP [$_S$ PRO inf VP]

Since sentences like (49) seem to be more marginal than those like (44) and (45) it is to be assumed that the re-analysis is slightly favoured when the postverbal NP has been displaced.

This analogical account has several advantages:

A. It accommodates such facts as (44)–(45) with our analysis and explains the difference in degree of acceptability between (44), (45), (49) and the corresponding sentences derived via *Wh* Movement of the subject, which are fully acceptable:

(52) a. La donna che reputavo _____ aver tradito la nostra causa.
        The woman that I reputed _____ to have betrayed our cause.
    b. Quante strade ritieni _____ esser state costruite in tempo di guerra?
        How many roads do you believe _____ to have been built during the war?
    c. Le sole persone che giudico _____ aver sempre fatto il loro dovere sono le seguenti: ...
        The only persons that I judge _____ to have always done their duty are the following: ...

B. The analogical account captures the generalisation that structures like (44)–(45) are (marginally) acceptable only with main verbs which also enter structures _____ NP AP.

C. It provides some basis for understanding the fact that such structures as (44), (45) and (49) attain the maximum degree of naturalness when the infinitival VP is of the type 'copulative verb + AP':

(53) a. ?Ritenevo Mario essere una persona onesta.
          I believed Mario to be an honest person.
      b. Mario era ritenuto _____ essere una persona onesta.
      c. Lo ritenevo _____ essere una persona onesta.

Suppose that, as proposed by Chomsky (1980), for independent reasons a surface structure like (53a) is mapped into the following partial logical form by rules of the syntax of LF:

(54) _____ NP [$_S$ PRO essere AP]

Now, it is not unnatural to assume that, *ceteris paribus*, analogical acceptability is favoured when the LF analogue of the structure in question is independently generable by structure building rules belonging to the syntax of LF. If something like this tentative assumption is correct, then the more natural status of (53) as compared to (44), (45) and (49) is accounted for.

D. There seems to be a slight semantic difference between the following two sentences:

(55) a. Ritengo non esser lui in grado di affrontare questo
          compito.
          I believe not-to-be he able to face this task.
      b. Lo ritengo non essere in grado di affrontare questo
          compito.
          I him-believe _____ not-to-be able to face this task.

Intuitively speaking, **ritengo** seems to be a diadic predicate in (55a), meaning that I have an opinion concerning a certain state of affairs (exactly the same interpretation is found when **ritenere** takes a tensed complement), while in (55b) it seems to be a triadic predicate, meaning that I have a certain opinion about a certain person in connection with a certain state of affairs. For instance, in a situation in which I do not have any first-hand knowledge of the person designated by the subject of the infinitive, (55b) seems to be less appropriate than (55a) (or the corresponding structure with a tensed complement). This intuition is reflected in the structures, if we adopt the analogical solution just proposed. The respective structures of (55a,b), after the analogical re-analysis, would be the following:

(56) a. NP V S
      b. NP V NP S

In conclusion, the re-analysis hypothesis represented in (51) seems to be fairly well motivated, and I will adopt it as a solution for the problematic cases (44)–(45).

Notes

1. Where 'lexical' means 'dominating lexical terminal material', so that an infinitive with a subject trace does not satisfy the structural description of the filter. Whether or not the NP to VP filter has to distinguish between lexical NPs and traces is discussed in Chomsky and Lasnik (1977). See also section 6 for a discussion of this problem in a slightly different framework.
2. An analysis of the impersonal **si** construction is given in Rizzi (1978a); this article also deals with the syntax of clitic pronouns in Italian, basically following Kayne (1975).
3. Notice that these verbs generally allow NP/CL Movement of their direct objects:

(i)   Mario non lo supponeva.
       Mario didn't it suppose.
(ii)   Questa donna era temuta da tutti.
       This woman was feared by everyone.
(iii) Queste opinioni si sostengono correntemente.
       These opinions PRO asserts currently.
(iv)   Lo affermo un'altra volta.
       I it state once more.

so that the unacceptability of (7)–(8) cannot simply be attributed to an idiosyncrasy of the main verb.
4. See Perlmutter and Postal (1977), Bresnan (1978).
5. This characterisation of the rule is grossly inadequate. First of all, the rule applies not only with the aspectual auxiliaries and the copula, but also with such modal verbs as **dovere** (*must*), **volere** (*want, will*) **potere** (*can, may*); moreover, if it indeed applies most naturally with these verbs, its application with other verbs gives results which could not be properly characterised as ungrammatical, but rather as marginal to a variable degree. Since a detailed discussion of the exact nature of this rule would lead us too far afield, I will provisionally assume that the rough characterisation given in the text is basically correct. Notice that, because of examples like (12b) this formulation implies that the negative element **non** can be cliticised to the auxiliary verb.

6. I am now making the provisional assumption that filter (5) makes explicit reference to the S̄ brackets, so that the application of Aux preposing suffices to destroy the forbidden configuration.

7. The morphological evidence solely concerns post-auxiliary subjects, since pre-auxiliary lexical subjects are not allowed in this construction (cf. (19a), etc.). In order to give a solution of first approximation to this problem I will now make the simplifying assumption that nominative marking applies on the subject NP of this infinitival structure irrespective of its position with respect to the auxiliary. A more adequate account is given in section 6.1.

8. A simpler solution, which does not necessarily presuppose successive cyclic application of *Wh* Movement in (22), is available if we adopt the idea, developed in Rizzi (1978b) and originally due to Noam Chomsky, that the variable substituted for the trace left behind by the first application of *Wh* Movement does not count (in Italian at least) as 'anaphor' in the relevant sense.

9. The whole argumentation presented in this section 6 is due to a suggestion by Guglielmo Cinque, who pointed out to me that, contrary to my previous opinion, the optimalisation of the explanatory power of NIC could be rendered compatible in an elegant way with Chomsky's case marking approach to the NP to VP generalisation. I would like to thank him for allowing me to emend this section in line with his important remark.

10. Rule (28) might be the same Case marking process which is operative with postverbal subjects in tensed clauses, e.g.

(i)   Viene Gianni.
       Is coming Gianni.
(ii)   Vengo io/*me.
       *Am coming I/*me.*

One might further speculate that rule (28) is restricted, in the unmarked case, to languages which have free inversion of the subject (Italian, Spanish, Old French, but not English, modern French, etc.).

Alternatively, one might propose that the nominative marking rule which is operative in this case is specific to the marked construction Aux NP ... But this alternative to the more general formulation suggested by the informal statement (28) does not seem to me satisfactory for two reasons:

A. even those speakers who do not consider the construction at hand as one of the productive constructions of their grammar, have clear intuitions of relative grammaticality about such pairs as (16); therefore, a solution in which the nominative marking process in question is contingent upon previous learning of the marked construction Aux NP ... does not seem appropriate. This problem, of course, does not arise if nominative marking in such cases falls under a more general process which is learned independently (as suggested by (28)).

B. If it is true that the only languages which can have nominative marking of postverbal subjects in infinitives are those languages which have free inversion of the subject in tensed clauses, then this generalisation is captured by (28), but it would be overlooked by a solution making use of a specific Case marking process for the construction Aux NP ...

11. This should replace Chomsky's (1980) filter (70). The implications of (30) on the whole Case marking system will be considered with some care in section 8.

Rouveret and Vergnaud (1980) propose a system in which Chomsky's filter (70), which concerns lexical NPs, is supplemented by a filter concerning lexical NPs and traces, which stars any such NPs which are not properly governed. If this approach is correct, then (30) is dispensed with, and the grammar includes Chomsky's filter (70) and Rouveret and Vergnaud's filter (125). As the reader can easily verify, the results achieved by (30) remain unchanged if the system is modified along these lines.

12. Alternatively, if the solution alluded to in note 11 is adopted, (32a,b) would be excluded because the trace in subject position is not properly governed. The full extention of this approach to our data would require some further specifications, which I will not develop here. See Rouveret and Vergnaud (1980) for relevant and detailed discussion.

13. In fact, there are reasons to believe that (33a) is not the only well-formed structural representation which is to be associated with (31a). First of all, as pointed out before, while sentences like (29a) are restricted to a very special stylistic level, sentences like (31a) are more natural on ordinary stylistic levels as well. Therefore, if the only possible derivation of (31a) were via Aux preposing, it would become impossible to attribute the marked status of (29a), etc., to the application of this rule, as seems reasonable.

The stylistic discrepancy between (31a) and (29a) has a correlate on cross-linguistic grounds, which creates a similar problem for our account. Couquaux (1978) points out that a paradigm analogous to the one discussed here exists in French:

(i)   *Jules croyait [Max pouvoir venir].

(ii)   Max, que Jules croyait [t pouvoir venir] a du rester à la maison.

(iii)   *Je les ai crues [t être sorties de l'église].

(iv)   *Cet industriel a été cru [t pouvoir payer la rançon].

This arrangement of data shows that our analysis is not sufficiently general: in fact, French does not have the 'Aux preposing' construction:

(v)   *Jules croyait [avoir lui fait son devoir].

Given the non-existence of (v), a derivation of (ii) like the one proposed for the Italian equivalent in (33a) becomes highly implausible. This suggests again that there should be possible derivations of such acceptable sentences as (31a) other than the one indicated in (33a). An interesting possibility is the one indicated in Kayne (1980b). I will not attempt here an adaptation of Kayne's system to my analysis, which would require some significant modifications of the account proposed in the text. For the time being, it is sufficient to notice that if an alternative derivation exists for (31a), this does not necessarily imply that the proposed account of the contrast (31a)–(31b) is incorrect.

14. We noticed before, in connection with (11), that as far as gerundival clauses are concerned, there is some dialectal variation. Given the following two gerundival structures:

(i)   Aux NP ...

(ii)   NP Aux ...

while (i) is acceptable for all speakers, (ii) is acceptable only for some. According to the analysis proposed in the text, we can now assume that, while (i) falls into the general case (28), some speakers may have generalised rule (27a) to gerundival clauses (perhaps under the influence of the corresponding French structures: **Jean ayant téléphoné à Pierre ...**).

Alternatively, one might propose that in (ii) the pre-Aux noun phrase is not in subject position, but in dislocated position, so that it is marked for case by the independently necessary rule(s) which account(s) for case marking of dislocated NPs.

It is unclear how this alternative hypothesis could be tested. Some evidence is provided by the fact that gerundival clauses, in general, do not take left dislocated phrases:

(iii)   Avendo parlato a Gianni, ...
        Having talked to Gianni, ...
(iv)   *A Gianni, avendogli parlato, ...
        To Gianni, having-to-him talked, ...

But the issue is, for the time being, quite unclear.

As Guglielmo Cinque points out, the solution presented in this section predicts that *wh*-extraction of the subject of an infinitival clause should be possible only when the infinitival clause satisfies the conditions in which subject-Aux inversion can apply (i.e., the verb is in the compound form Aux + Past Participle, or is the copula, or is a modal; see note 5); otherwise, subject — Aux inversion being inapplicable, the embedded subject trace could not be marked for case and the structures would be ruled out by (30). This prediction seems to be correct:

(i) a.   *?Mario, che sostengo diventare più simpatico, ...
           Mario, who I assert to become more charming, ...
     b.   Mario, che sostengo esser diventato più simpatico, ...
           Mario, who I assert to have become more charming, ...
     c.   Mario, che sostengo poter diventare più simpatico, ...
           Mario, who I assert to be able to become more charming, ...
(ii) a.   ??Gianni, che temo non apprezzare la tua scelta, ...
           Gianni, who I fear not to appreciate your choice, ...
     b.   Gianni, che temo non aver apprezzato la tua scelta, ...
           Gianni, who I fear not to have appreciated your choice, ...
     c.   Gianni, che temo non poter apprezzare la tua scelta, ...
           Gianni, who I fear not to be able to appreciate your choice, ...

But, if this result is certainly implied by the proposed account, it is unclear whether or not this fact can be taken as an independent argument for it: as Richard Kayne points out to me, similar facts seem to hold for English and French as well, where a structural solution is highly implausible. Therefore, the low acceptability of (ia), (iia) can perhaps be independently attributed to some semantic (aspectual) incompatibility, so that it cannot be taken as a cogent argument for our Case marking system.

15. Kayne (1980a) suggests that NIC might apply not on fully developed LFs, but on an earlier level, before the application of the rules which associate a 'quantifier interpretation' to *wh*-interrogatives (see Chomsky, 1975 and 1977). This possibility is fully compatible with the analysis presented in the text (but it would exclude the alternative suggested in note 8).

Kayne (1980b) argues that the distinctive property of Subject Pronoun Drop languages like Italian is that in such languages the NIC doesn't hold for null anaphora. Of course, if this hypothesis is correct, the proposed account of paradigms like (19) will have to be revised. I will not discuss here Kayne's important hypothesis (which was proposed after this paper was written). I plan to examine it in detail in a work in progress.

16. The trace in COMP is irrelevant, since it is deletable via free deletion in COMP, which prevents application of (30). The fact that the trace in COMP counts with respects to the binding principles but doesn't count with respect to filters is a consequence of the organisation of the grammar proposed in Chomsky and Lasnik (1977):

1. Base rules
2. Transformations
3a. Deletion rules   3b. Rules of the Syntax of Logical Form

4a. Filters
5a. Phonology
6a. Stylistic rules

From this organisation it follows that something which is deleted (e.g. the trace in COMP in (33a)) is invisible to filters; but counts as well as non deleted material with respect to the well-formedness conditions on LF (NIC and Opacity), since deletion rules and the syntax of LF belong to two separate and (arguably) non-interacting paths of the grammar, while filters operate after deletion rules in the same path.

17. The symbol 'PRO' is used here to represent $[_{NP}\ e]$, i.e., an occurrence of an empty noun phrase which is unindexed in surface structure (i.e., is not a trace), and is to be indexed by the construal rule(s) which determine(s) control.

18. It is interesting to notice (Guglielmo Cinque, private communication) that control structures never allow the marked construction Aux NP Past part:

(i) a.   Mario vorrebbe che tu fossi venuto con noi.
        Mario would want 'that' you had come with us.
     b.   *Mario vorrebbe esser tu venuto con noi.
        Mario would want you to have come with us.
     c.   Mario vorrebbe esser venuto con noi.
        Mario would want to have come with us.

(ii) a.   Francesca non sa a chi lui sia fedele.
        Francesca doesn't know to whom he is loyal.
     b.   *Francesca non sa a chi esser lui fedele.
        Francesca doesn't know to whom to be he loyal.
     c.   Francesca non sa a chi esser fedele.
        Francesca doesn't know to whom to be loyal.

An obvious way to account for this fact would be to stipulate obligatory control, as in Chomsky and Lasnik (1977); some more satisfactory solutions are perhaps available in the system I have proposed, but I will not further investigate this point here.

19. This implies that the obligatoriness of raising, i.e., the ungrammaticality of

(i) *Sembrava [Gianni dormire]

cannot be attributed to the fact that the embedded subject is not marked for Case. If one adopts the framework of Rouveret and Vergnaud (1980), along the lines alluded to in note 11, the statement of the text '... they govern objective marking of the embedded subject ...' should become '... they govern the embedded subject ...'. In fact, this is essentially the hypothesis adopted by Rouveret and Vergnaud for raising verbs, with the difference that, in their account, the fact that subject raising verbs govern the embedded subject traces need not be treated as a lexical idiosyncrasy, since it follows from structural properties of the raising construction.

20. I am assuming c-command to be a necessary condition for a verb to govern objective case of a NP. This condition is, of course, not sufficient. See Chomsky (1980), Rouveret and Vergnaud (1980) for detailed discussion.

21. With the natural assumption that the copular verb **essere** used in the cleft construction does not have the marked property of governing objective case across S̄ boundaries. In the analysis mentioned in note 11, the ungrammaticality of (43a) would follow from the fact that, given the following derived structure,

(i) Era $[_{\bar{S}}[_{TOP}[_{\bar{S}}$ t lavorare troppo]] $[_{\bar{S}}$ che Mario sembrava]]

the verb **essere** does not govern the embedded subject trace for structural reasons (given Rouveret and Vergnaud's (1980) definition of the relation 'govern').

References

Bresnan, J. W. (1978), 'A Realistic Transformational Grammar' in M. Halle, J. W. Bresnan, G. Miller (eds.), *Linguistic Theory and Psychological Reality*, MIT Press, Cambridge, Massachusetts

Chomsky, N. (1973), 'Conditions on Transformations' in S. R. Anderson, P. Kiparsky (eds.), *A Festschrift for Morris Halle*, Holt, Rinehart & Winston New York

———— (1976), 'Conditions on Rules of Grammar', *Linguistic Analysis*, 2

———— (1977), 'On *Wh*-Movement' in P. Culicover, T. Wasow, A. Akmajian (eds.), *Formal Syntax*, Academic Press, New York

———— (1980), 'On Binding', this volume. Previously published in *Linguistic Inquiry*, 11, 1–46

Chomsky, N. and H. Lasnik (1977), 'Filters and Control', *Linguistic Inquiry*, 8

Couquaux, D. (1978), 'On Trace Interpretation', unpublished manuscript, Université de Aix-Marseille II

Kayne, R. (1975), *French Syntax*, MIT Press, Cambridge, Massachusetts

———— (1980a), 'Binding, Clitic Placement and Leftward Quantifier Movement', this volume

———— (1980b), 'Extensions of Binding and Case Marking', *Linguistic Inquiry* 11, 75–96

Jenkins, L. (1976), 'NP Interpretation' in H. C. van Riemsdijk (ed.), *Green Ideas Blown Up*, University of Amsterdam

Perlmutter, D. and P. Postal (1977), 'Towards a Universal Characterisation of Passivisation' in *Proceedings of the Third Annual Meeting of the Berkeley Linguistics Society*, Berkeley, California

Rizzi, L. (1976), 'La "Montée du sujet", le *si* impersonnel, et une règle de restructuration dans la syntaxe italienne', *Recherches linguistiques* 4, Université de Paris VIII, Vincennes

———— (1978a), 'A Restructuring Rule in Italian Syntax' in S. J. Keyser (ed.), *Recent Transformational Studies in European Languages*, MIT Press, Cambridge, Massachusetts

———— (1978b), 'Violations of the WH Island Constraint in Italian and the Subjacency Condition' in *Montreal Working Papers in Linguistics*, 10

Rouveret, A. and J.-R. Vergnaud (1980), 'Specifying Reference to the Subject: French Causatives and Conditions on Representations', *Linguistic Inquiry* 11, 97–202

June 1978

4 Empty Subjects, Case and Agreement and the Grammar of Dutch*

Eric J. Reuland

0. Introduction

0.1 Background

In Chomsky's article 'On Binding' (Chomsky 1980), henceforth OB, a proposal is developed to account for the fact that in the unmarked case the subject position of a tenseless clause in English is nonlexical. Basically the proposal is as follows. It is assumed that every lexical NP in English must be marked for Case. This marking is abstract. It rarely has phonetic effects. There are three Cases, namely nominative Case, objective Case, and oblique Case. The Cases are assigned to all NPs (not only those which are lexical) according to the rules in (1).

(1) a. NP is oblique when governed by Prepositions and certain marked verbs
    b. NP is objective when governed by V
    c. NP is nominative when governed by Tense.

The notion of government is defined as in (2).

(2) α is governed by β if α is c-commanded by β and no major category or major category boundary appears between α and β.

Application of these rules presupposes an analysis of S, VP, and PP as in (3).

159

(3) a. S = NP Tense VP
     b. VP = V NP ...
     c. PP = P NP

The requirement that every lexical NP in English must be marked for Case is expressed by the filter (4), under the assumption that Case percolates to the head noun. Where NP is PRO, or trace, there is no N and hence the filter does not apply.

(4)   *N, where N has no Case

Case is assigned in such a manner that at the level of surface structure the conditions given in (5) hold true.

(5)   ... an NP has Case when (1) it is properly governed under (68) (= *(1)*); (2) it is in COMP and its trace is properly governed under (68); (3) it is oblique and it or its trace is properly governed under (68a) (= *(1a)*) (p. 76)

This proposal enables one to account for the ungrammaticality of sentences such as (6a), with an analysis as in (6b), in the following way.

(6) a. *They wondered what Sam to tell Bill.
     b. they wondered [s̄ what [s Sam to [vp tell Bill t]]]

The subject of the infinitival clause, *Sam*, is not assigned nominative Case within its own clause, since the construction is tenseless; it is not governed by the Tense of the matrix clause since both the S̄ and the S boundary intervene. It is separated from the verb *tell* by the VP-boundary, and from the verb *wondered* by both the S̄ and S boundaries again, so the conditions for the assignment of objective Case are not satisfied either. Since none of the conditions for Case assignment are met, it is assigned no Case at all, and filter (4) applies.

    Although the filter (4) is limited to lexical NP, the rules for Case assignment are not so limited in the framework of OB. Thus, not only lexical NP, but also PRO and trace are assigned nominative Case if they are governed by Tense. This makes it possible to account for the ungrammaticality of sentences such as those in (7) by means of the Nominative Island Constraint (NIC), given in (8).

(7) a. *I know what PRO did.
     b. *They wondered what *each other* did.
(8) a nominative anaphor cannot be free in S̄

It is assumed that the empty subject position in (7a) is occupied by the anaphor PRO. Both PRO in (7a) and *each other* in (7b) are governed by Tense, and therefore assigned nominative Case under (1c). Since both are anaphors, and free in S̄, the sentence containing them will be marked ungrammatical by NIC.

0.2 Organisation

The basic question concerning us in this paper will be in how far this account can be generalised to explain similar facts in some other Indo-European languages, such as Dutch. The analysis in OB hinges on four assumptions: (a) nominative Case is assigned by non-empty Tense only; (b) every base-generated null subject represents an anaphor; (c) Case assignment is obligatory; (d) empty NPs are marked for Case. All four of these will be shown to be in need of revision.

Our analysis will be based on the observation that in some languages there are apparently tenseless clauses with nominative subjects. We will discuss these facts in the first section. This will lead us to the assumption that the subject is assigned nominative Case in general and not only when governed by Tense as assumed in OB (see (a) above). In the resulting framework neither the explanation given above for the ungrammaticality of (6a), nor the one accounting for (7a) works any more. In the second section principles of subject/verb agreement are discussed. It is these principles which account, in the modified framework, for the ungrammaticality of (6a) and (7a): a nominative NP requires an agreeing verb form, and an infinitival form is not in the agreement class of any NP, causing constructions such as (6a) to be marked ungrammatical; a tensed verb form requires a nominative to agree with, and this condition is violated in (7a). The third section deals with null subjects, both in languages admitting them generally and in languages prohibiting them as a rule. It is shown there that on the basis of the principles of agreement developed in the second section a straightforward account can be given of these phenomena. The account does not involve deletion, and as a consequence avoids certain difficulties connected with deletion. In the fourth section it is shown that the analysis given also explains the '*that*-trace filter', showing the data it was designed to cover to be instances of a more general pattern. It is observed that the application of NIC to a supposedly nominative trace as discussed in OB yields a puzzling consequence, which can be explained as an instance of the same general pattern. The fifth section, finally, discusses a reinterpretation of subject/verb agreement as a special instance of restrictions on coreference.

0.3 Some Preliminaries about Dutch Clause Structure

One of the main reasons why the approach of OB to the question of how to account for the ungrammaticality of sentences such as (6a) and (7a), seems so attractive is its generality, suggesting that it might be easily transferred to other languages exhibiting similar phenomena. In Dutch, for instance, infinitival clauses such as the one in (6a) do not have lexical subjects either, and also Dutch equivalents to the sentences of (7) are ungrammatical. These facts would seem to be easily accounted for in principle by (1), (2), and (4). However, if this approach is to work for a given language, the grammar of that language must at least meet the requirement that at the relevant level a sufficiently rich structure is available for the subject and object NPs, and also Tense and V to ensure that the rules of (1) apply unambiguously. The same holds true for the level on which according to OB the conditions quoted in (5) must be statable, namely surface structure. Now, the analyses of Dutch presented to date do not make available any level satisfying this requirement: tense is generally treated as a feature on the verb, both in base structure and surface structure (cf. Evers (1975), Koster (1975, 1978)). Van Riemdijk (1978) discusses briefly the question whether there is a separate Aux position, but leaves the matter unresolved, while Evers explicitly analyses auxiliary verbs such as **hebben** 'have' as main verbs. Evers (1975) in contra-distinction to the other authors mentioned leaves open even the question whether there is a VP. The other authors assume there is a VP without argument. Our first task will therefore be to sketch a grammar of Dutch, which permits us in principle to apply Chomsky's proposals to the language.

For the purpose of this paper I will simply assume that there is a VP in Dutch, and also that there is a separate tense node outside the VP, though I have defended both these assumptions elsewhere.[1] Dutch is V-final underlyingly (cf. Koster (1975, 1978) and Evers (1975) for discussion) and the arguments given there hold true also for the finite verb. We will therefore take it that the equivalent of (3) for Dutch is (9).

(9) a. S = NP VP Tense
     b. VP = NP ... V

The dots in (9b) stand for material such as PPs and particles. These
are only relevant to us in that they may intervene in both base and
surface structure between the direct object and the verb. The fact
that they do, and the fact that the VP intervenes between the subject
NP and Tense motivate a change in the definition of government.
Apparently in the case of Dutch, and other languages as well, if the
notion of government is to be the significant notion for case
assignment, material such as the VP in (9a) and PPs, particles, etc. in
(9b) should not keep the relevant NP from being governed by Tense
or V. For the sake of concreteness I will replace (2) by (10), which
meets our requirements without any unattractive consequences
following.[2]

(10) α is governed by β if α is c-commanded by β and, if γ is a
       major category, no boundary of γ appears between α and β
       unless both α and β are c-commanded by γ.

In the surface structure of *root* clauses the position of the finite
verb in Dutch differs from the position indicated by (9b). In
declarative root clauses the finite verb occupies the second position
from the left. This is illustrated in (11).

(11) a. dat Piet de kaartjes gratis **krijgt** (verbaast me niet).
          that Piet the tickets free gets (surprises me not)
      b. Piet **krijgt** de kaartjes gratis.
          Piet gets the tickets free.

This difference between root clauses and subordinate clauses is
usually accounted for by assuming that the grammar of Dutch
contains a rule of *Verb-placement*, restricted to root clauses, moving
the finite verb from its clause-final position to the left. Clearly, if the
underlying structure is as indicated in (9) there must be a process
fusing the highest verb of the clause with tense in order to yield a
tensed verb. It is easily seen that if the conditions in (5) are to hold
true at the level of surface structure, and the rule of Verb-placement
is a transformation, the rule fusing Tense with the highest verb must
also be a transformation, unless one is willing to assume morphological processes moving material over an essential variable.

Finite verbs such as **krijgt** will be assumed to have been base inserted under V in the VP, and adjoined to a verbal position under Tense by the transformation *Move V*, leaving a trace in its original position. As a consequence we must modify slightly the condition contained in (5), that in order for some NP to have objective Case at the level of surface structure either it or its trace must be governed by V. This condition will now be assumed to apply where V is the *trace* of a verb.

For the sake of concreteness I give the relevant part of the expansion of T(ense) in (12), and schematic derivations of (11b) in (13), and (13′).

(12)   T → [V tense]

where [*V tense*] is a complex symbol, *tense* being possibly unrealised, yielding tenseless clauses. V defines a position in which certain auxiliaries may be base inserted, and which is a target for *Move V*. For example auxiliaries such as **heeft** will be assumed (contrary to Evers (1975)) to be base inserted under Tense (although nothing in the argument will depend on that assumption). Note that henceforth we use T for the node which most closely corresponds to Chomsky's Tense in OB; nevertheless, as we shall see, the feature *tense* performs some of the functions which Chomsky assigns to the node Tense.

(13)   a.   [$_S$ Piet [$_{VP}$ de kaartjes gratis [$_V$ krijg-]] [$_{T+V \atop +tense}$]]

      b.   [$_S$ Piet [$_{VP}$ de kaartjes gratis [$_{V_j}$ e]] [$_{T+V}^{krijgt_j} \atop +tense$]]

                                        Move V

      c.   [$_S$ Piet [$_{T_i+V}^{krijgt_j} \atop +tense$] [$_{VP}$ de kaartjes gratis [$_{V_j}$ e]] [$_{T_i}$ e]]

                                        V-placement

Provided the rule accounting for V-second in root clauses refers to *tense* (which it must do in any case), the order in which *V-placement* and *Move V* apply is immaterial, as shown in (13′).

(13′)   a.   [$_S$ Piet [$_{VP}$ de kaartjes gratis [$_V$ krijg-]] [$_{T+V \atop +tense}$]]

      b.   [$_S$ Piet [$_{T+V \atop +tense}$] [$_{VP}$ de kaartjes gratis [$_V$ krijg-]] [$_{T_i}$ e]]

                                        tense-placement

c. [s Piet [$_{T_i + V}^{krijgt_j}$] [vp de kaartjes gratis [$_{V_j}$ *e*]] [$_{T_i}$ *e*]]
   +*tense*

Move V

The rule of *V-placement* will therefore be renamed *tense-placement* — which is how we shall refer to it henceforth.

1. Nominative Subjects in Tenseless Clauses

One of the main features of the approach to subjectless infinitivals in OB warranting interest is that it seems so easily generalisable to other languages. It expresses an insight into the structure of human language *per se*.

There are, however, some facts about Dutch and some other Indo-European languages as well that appear to be at variance with the specific proposal formulated in (1). In (1c) assignment of nominative Case is made dependent on the presence of a governing Tense node. Now there are cases in Dutch where we find lexical NP with nominative Case in the subject position of a clause without Tense marking. An example is given in (14).

(14) a. (Driesje vocht met Aadje.) Hij toen snikkend naar zijn
         (*Driesje fought with Aadje.*) *He then sobbing   to   his*
         moeder lopen.
         mother run.
      b. (Driesje vocht met Aadje.) *Hem toen snikkend naar
         zijn moeder lopen.

Hij is nominative Case; **hem** is the form in oblique and objective Case. There are no specific restrictions on the choice of adverbials and verbal complements in such sentences.

The form **lopen** in (14) is an infinitive; it cannot be treated as some aberrant tensed form of the verb, since it may not appear in second, or first position: (15) is ungrammatical.

(15) *Hij lopen toen snikkend naar zijn moeder.

There is no manifestation of agreement phenomena either (cf. the next section). Another reason not to assume tense marking in these constructions is that the infinitive is compatible with future, present, and past time adverbials and contexts. Such a use of the infinitive is not restricted to Dutch.

In Latin we find a comparable use of the infinitive: the *infinitivus historicus*. This is illustrated in (16)

(16) Igitur reges populique finitumi bello temptare.
      therefore kings$_{nom}$ *people*$_{nom}$ *and neighbouring*$_{nom}$ *with war*
      try
      Therefore the neighbouring kings and people tried (the Romans) with war.

The example is taken from Sallustius (1938). There are many other examples there, as there are elsewhere in the literature.

Similarly we find, in Dutch, locutions such as (17) with an adjective instead of an infinitive.

(17) Hij vandaag blij.
      he today   glad

Such constructions, with a nominative subject, are well known from Slavonic languages, such as Russian, and also again from Latin. The relevant point is that in all these cases the form of the subject is nominative, although there is no sign of Tense. The idea that Tense has been deleted in these cases would run counter to the principle of recoverability of deletions.[3]

There are now two main options for us in order to have such sentences admitted. The first is to treat the presence of the nominative here as unmarked and change the rule of Case assignment accordingly. This change implies that the resulting theory will claim that *nominative* is *the* unmarked Case for the subject. The second option is to account for these data as resulting from an exception to the rule of Case marking. Choosing the first option we may remain very close to the principles of OB. It can be realised by simply reading Tense in (1c) as *anything in the position of Tense dominating lexical material.* For English this entails that the subject of an infinitival clause is assigned nominative Case since it is governed by the infinitive marker *to.* For Dutch we get the same result, since the rule *Move V*, applying regardless of whether *tense* is or is not null, substitutes a verb for the empty verb position under T. So, T will be nonempty even if *tense* is empty. If we apply (1c) as it stands, having Tense there refer to the node T rather than *tense*, then nominative Case will be assigned to the subject NP in both tensed and tenseless clauses indiscriminately. If we choose the second option this entails that we must assume that under the relevant conditions even empty *tense* may exceptionally assign nominative to the NP it governs, or else, that Tense in (1c) refers to *anything in the position of Tense dominating lexical material*, as under the first option, but only under the relevant exceptional conditions.[4]

There is, however, a fact that argues against the second option. The languages under consideration all exhibit to some extent the phenomenon of subject/verb agreement, i.e. the form of the verb and the subject NP must be compatible (this will be treated in more detail in the next section). However, **hij** and **lopen** in (14) are not ordinarily compatible, and neither is **temptare** in (16) ordinarily compatible with a third person plural subject. Sentences as in (14) and (16) must be treated therefore as exceptions to the rules of subject/verb agreement anyhow. So, under the second option they are exceptions to two principles: Case assignment and agreement; under the first option only to one: agreement. Under the assumption that exception statements count as complications of the grammar we conclude that a grammar modified according to the first option yields a simpler account of the phenomena at hand.[5] This gives us a prima facie reason for pursuing this route. We will see that it will also lead to interesting simplifications elsewhere in the grammar.

The proposed change in the conditions under which nominative Case is assigned has far-reaching consequences, in that it necessitates a number of modifications in Chomsky's original account. Chomsky proposed to account for the ungrammaticality of tensed declaratives without an overt subject, such as (7a), by assigning Case not only to lexical NP, but also to PRO and trace: a sentence containing a nominative anaphor free in $\bar{S}$ is marked ungrammatical by NIC. If we assume that in infinitival clauses the T position is nonempty generally (being at least filled by a verb), this means that in our modified version of the OB account nominative Case will be assigned to a PRO subject of such clauses. This, in turn, implies that both (18) and (19) will be marked ungrammatical by NIC.

(18)   ze vroegen zich af [$_{\bar{S}}$ wat$_i$ [$_S$ PRO [$_{VP}$ t$_i$ aan VN [$_{V_j}$ e]]
       they wondered   what to (the weekly) Vrij Nederland
       [$_T$ te schrijven$_j$]]]
       to write

(19)   *ze vroegen zich af [$_{\bar{S}}$ wat$_i$ [$_S$ PRO [$_{VP}$ t$_i$ aan VN [$_{V_j}$ e]]
       [$_T$ $\begin{smallmatrix}\text{schrijf}\\\text{+pres}\\\text{+1 sing}\end{smallmatrix}$]]]

Example (19) is indeed ungrammatical, showing the pattern of (7a), but (18) is grammatical. In Chomsky's analysis there is a difference between PRO in (18) and PRO in (19). The latter is marked nominative, causing NIC to apply: the former is not. In our analysis both will be marked nominative if we apply the principles of Case marking as we have revised them. We must therefore ensure that (18) is not ruled out. An interesting possibility to pursue now is that of having Case assigned to lexical NP only.[6] Provisionally, we make that assumption. If PRO in (18) has no Case, NIC cannot apply, so (18) will not be rejected. Of course, if PRO in (18) has no Case, PRO in (19) will also have no Case. Therefore NIC will not apply there either. Thus while we have succeeded in avoiding the application of NIC to (18) we have thereby made it impossible to explain the ungrammaticality of (19) by reference to NIC, since the latter now applies only to lexical anaphors, as in (7b). Given that the ungrammaticality of (19) remains unexplained, we may seem to have made little progress. However, as we shall show in the next section, this is not so.[7]

2. Subject/Verb Agreement

In many languages of various types we find subject/verb agreement. It may be roughly characterised in the following way: the set of NPs is split up into a number of subclasses, and there is a mutual dependence between the subclass of the subject NP, and the form of the verb it is the subject of: some verb forms co-occur with certain NP classes as their subjects but not with others. In English we find a remnant of the agreement system in the ungrammaticality of *John walk*, or *I walks* as compared to *John walks* or *I walk*. In Dutch the agreement system is more elaborate than in English, although, not as complex as those found in languages such as Latin or Russian.

We will take our examples from Dutch: the sentences in (20).

(20) a. Ze vragen zich af wat **hij** aan de krant schrijft.
          they wonder   what he to the newspaper writes
      b. *Ze vragen zich af wat **hij** aan de krant schrijf—
          they wonder   what he to the newspaper write
      c. Ze vragen zich af wat **ik** aan de krant schrijf—
          they wonder   what I to the newspaper write
      d. *Ze vragen zich af wat **ik** aan de krant schrijft
          they wonder   what I to the newspaper writes

Both (20b) and (20d) contain a violation of subject/verb agreement which is the sole reason for their ungrammaticality. Example (20b) can be made grammatical by replacing the first person singular form **schrijf** by the third person singular form **schrijft**, or by replacing the third person singular form **hij** by a first person singular form such as **ik**. The converse holds true for (20d). Any adequate grammar of Dutch must contain the means to express the fact that the form of the highest verb in a clause and some property of the NP in subject position are mutually dependent, i.e. they must belong to compatible classes.

Consider now the examples in (21).

(21) a. *Ze vragen zich af wat **hij** aan de krant te schrijven.
          they wonder   what he to the newspaper to write
      b. *Ze vragen zich af wat **PRO** aan de krant schrijf—
          they wonder   what   to the   write
          (1sg)   *newspaper*

Clearly (21a) would be ruled out by the same principle ruling out (20b) and (20d), unless **te schrijven** were to be specifically included in the class of verb forms compatible with a third person singular subject NP. Since, but for exceptional conditions, no infinitive will occur in the agreement class of any NP class, (21a) would remain ungrammatical under all substitutions of lexical subjects for **hij**. In (21b) there is a violation of the principles of agreement in the other direction: there is a verb form subject to agreement, but no lexical NP for it to agree with — and again this would remain true whatever agreement forms were substituted for '1sg'.

Now, (21a) is the form which is no longer covered by the Case filter (4) after the changes proposed in the previous section, and (21b) the one no longer covered by NIC. So, since any account of agreement in Dutch will rule these examples out independently, it does not lead to a loss of descriptive adequacy, but rather to the elimination of a redundancy if we assign nominative Case to the subject regardless whether the clause is tensed or not, at the same time modifying Case assignment so as to restrict NIC to *lexical* anaphors. This is an interesting result in itself. For sake of concreteness I will now formulate the rules of agreement, but in order to avoid unnecessary complications in the exposition I will give them here in a preliminary form.

The relevant configuration for agreement is given in (22).

(22) $[_S NP_j \dots [_T tense_i]]$
       where $1 \leqslant i, j \leqslant 6$

The rules of agreement check whether i belongs to f (j); j, and i being NP and tense classes. As in other Indo-European languages six NP classes are traditionally distinguished in Dutch and correspondingly six classes of finite verb forms. Given the fact that subject NPs will be marked nominative, and only these, reference to nominative NP in the formulation of agreement will suffice. The facts we have been dealing with can be accounted for by the pair of syntactic surface filters given in (23).[8]

(23)   a.   *Nominative NP_j unless governed by *tense*$_{f(j)}$
       b.   **tense*   unless governed by Nominative

Example (20b) is filtered out as ungrammatical since **schrijf** is not an element of the class *tense*$_{f(hij)}$; the nominative subject **hij** is simply not governed by an appropriate verb form. In (21a) the subject **hij** is governed by **te schrijven**, but again **te schrijven** is not in the class *tense*$_{f(hij)}$, causing a violation of (23a). Example (20a) is grammatical since on the relevant level **hij** is governed by **schrijft** which is in *tense*$_{f(hij)}$, and **schrijft** is governed by a nominative (both under the definition of government given in (10)). Finally (21b) is ungrammatical since the tensed form **schrijft** is not governed by a nominative.

Since under (23) agreement is restricted to nominative subjects, there will be no violation of agreement in English sentences such as (24).

(24)   I believe $[_{\bar{S}}[_S$ him to be a fool]]

The subject of the embedded clause *him* has objective case; as a consequence it does not need to be governed by a compatible verb form. However, we have yet to account for the possibility of *him* being objective. In the framework of OB *believe* is a specially marked verb, assigning Case to an NP through an $\bar{S}$ and an S boundary. This NP is also governed by *to*, however. So, under the proposal we are discussing it will also be assigned nominative Case. Incorporating the proposal of OB as it stands would therefore give a conflict of Case assignment. This conflict can be resolved by taking the rules of Case assignment to operate optionally. The only reason in OB why they had to be obligatory resided in the fact that sentences such as

(21b) had to be ruled out by NIC, and this could be guaranteed only by having PRO obligatorily marked nominative. The restriction of Case marking to lexical NP therefore obviates the necessity for obligatory Case assignment. Since the other rules in Core grammar such as base rules and transformations also apply optionally, we might actually expect optional rather than obligatory Case assignment. Theoretically, our proposal is preferable.[9]

We have accounted for the facts of agreement by giving in (23) two separate rules: one, (23a), representing a property of nominative NPs, the other, (23b), a property of tensed verb forms. A nominative NP must 'find' a verbal form to agree with, and for a tensed verbal form there must be a nominative NP as its subject. This is tantamount to saying that these are separable facts. This is clearly correct. Sentences such as **hij huilen**, treated in the first section, are exceptions to (23a); imperatives, on the other hand, are exceptions to (23b), but not to (23a). This is illustrated in (25).

(25) a. Wees blij.
   he glad
  b. Wees jij blij.
   be you glad
  c. *Wees hij (jullie, etc.) blij.
   be he (you, etc.) glad
  d. Weest blij.
   be$_{plur}$ *glad*
  e. Weest jullie blij.
   be you$_{plur}$ *glad*
  f. *Weest jij (hij, etc.) blij.
   be you$_{sing}$ *(he, etc.) glad*

The Dutch imperative is generally characterised by the zero formative for the singular and a /t/ for the plural. The verb **zijn** (*to be*) is somewhat special, moreover, in that it has a distinct suppletive stem **wees** for the imperative, establishing the necessity of analysing constructions such as (25b,e) as imperatives beyond doubt. Now both singular and plural forms of the imperative may occur without a subject. When they do, they constitute exceptions to (23b). When a subject is present, it must agree with the form. This is shown by the ungrammaticality of (25c), where the second person singular imperative occurs with a third person singular, or a second person plural subject; and by the ungrammaticality of (25f) for corresponding reasons.

In order to account for the fact that imperatives are exceptions to the requirement of filter (23b) that finite verb forms be governed by a nominative we will replace the latter by (26).[10]

(26)   *tense$_{-I(mperative)}$ unless governed by Nominative

Summarising, we have shown, on the basis of our rules of subject/verb agreement, that the proposal made in the first section to restrict Case assignment to lexical NP and to have nominative Case assigned also to the subject NP of a tenseless clause does not lead to a loss of descriptive adequacy, but eliminates a redundancy. Besides that, it makes it possible to treat the rules of Case assignment as optional, as are the other rules in Core grammar.

In the next section we will direct our attention to the position of empty subjects in tensed clauses in general. We will show that on the basis of the theoretical modifications proposed thus far they can be given a more satisfactory account, and certain puzzles arising in the framework of OB can be eliminated.

4. Empty Subjects in Tensed Clauses

4.1 On So-called Subject Deletion

Under the approach adopted here, the ungrammaticality of sentences such as (21b), repeated here as (27) is claimed to be due to a violation of (26), and not to a violation of NIC.

(27)   *Ze vragen zich af wat PRO aan de krant schrijf.
        they wonder   what   to the newspaper write

Although this presumably might be taken to show that (26) and NIC are related principles, the roles they play in an account of languages which admit sentences without overt subjects show that they are not notational variants, but that an approach on the basis of principles like (26) is to be preferred. The type of sentences meant, found in languages such as Spanish, Portuguese, Modern Greek, Czech, etc., is illustrated by the example (28), taken from Czech.

(28)   nevím   [š co [š t dělá]]
        (I) not know   what   does
        I do not know what he does.

Chomsky and Lasnik (1977), citing Perlmutter, assume a special rule of subject pronoun deletion to account for such phenomena. In a framework in which PRO is treated as an anaphor irrespective of its position, and in which NIC operates on empty NPs in subject position, it is necessary to account for cases like (28) in terms of a rule deleting subject pronouns prior to the level at which NIC applies. If one were to assign to (28) the surface structure

(29) [s[s PRO nevím [s̄ co [s PRO t dělá]]]]

it would be marked ungrammatical by two violations of NIC. Moreover, quite apart from NIC, it would be ungrammatical because it would be regarded as containing two free variables after translation into logical form. Notice that this could not be remedied by deleting PRO. For although surface filters apply after deletion, the translation rules apply before deletion. (I assume that the grammar is organised as in OB.)

In any case, the subject deletion approach has some rather *ad hoc* features. Not only is it necessary to have a special set of rules which perform the subject deletion, but it is also necessary to have for each such language a separate set of deletable subject pronouns. In Czech for instance these cannot be identified with the pronouns as they appear overtly in sentences. The overt pronouns in their nominative forms are used to express emphasis or contrast. One could not therefore simply derive (28) from (30) by subject deletion:

(30) já nevím   [s̄ co   [s on t   dělá]]
      I not know   *what*   *he*   *does*
      Emph   Emph

Rather one would have to derive (28) from (31).

(31) *I* nevím [s̄ co [s *he* t dělá]]

where I and he are respectively the forms of the (obligatorily) deleted Czech first person singular and third person singular non-emphatic pronouns.[11] In (28) it was still possible, as we saw, to make a guess as to the form of the 'deleted' pronoun. In the next case this is a bit more difficult: (32).

(32) tady se dobře jí   a   pije
      here self well   eats and drinks
      acc
      Here is eaten and drunk well.
      Here one eats and drinks well.

If a pronoun is inserted as a subject it will normally be interpreted as referring to the thing being eaten, so in this case it would not only be a special pronoun, subject to obligatory deletion, but it would also have a special interpretation, unlike the interpretation of any other overt NP in that position. The following picture emerges. There are tensed clauses in Czech without an overt subject, namely (28). The theory of syntactic structure *per se*, makes available tensed clauses without an overt subject, namely (29). These are ruled out as possible sources for subjectless clauses by NIC, instead a rule of subject deletion is needed, and a special class of deletable subjects, which in some cases, namely (32), are subject to an interpretation rule which is shared by no lexical NP subject. This is a rather complicated grammar for a simple fact.

In the framework developed in the preceding sections we can account for these facts by two simple assumptions. First, Czech is not subject to a filter such as (26). Thus the presence of *tense* never makes it obligatory to have a lexical subject. Secondly, the content of the subject argument of the Czech finite verb form may in effect be supplied by the form of the agreement marking on the verb itself. This makes (29) available as the source for (28). Filter (23a) will account for the ungrammaticality of sentences containing a violation of agreement, as for instance when a sentence with a structure like that of (30) contains **já nevíš**, **nevíš** being the second person singular form.

The special behaviour of sentences such as (32) can be accounted for by the assumption that the impersonal passive meaning is exclusively related to lexical representations in which the subject contents of the argument are determined by the agreement marker. If a subject is present, and the subject argument of the verb is already internally bound it will be impossible to integrate that subject semantically: we have in logical form an expression that is not well-formed, containing a predicate with more arguments than it has argument places.[12] Clearly an account based on (26) instead of NIC yields a simpler grammar.

4.2 Filters and Empty Subjects

In this section I will show that (26) in a revised form is superior to NIC for a different reason, namely that it makes it possible to overcome a problem in the explanation in OB for the fact that in certain constructions object *wh*-phrases are easier to extract from their clauses than subject *wh*-phrases. It will be shown that on the basis of (26) this fact follows from a condition on governors in COMP Position which is also reflected in the phenomena covered by the *that-trace* filter discussed in Chomsky and Lasnik (1977). Thus the *that-trace* filter can be eliminated in favour of this more general condition. Moreover, this condition does not, like the filters, lead to incorrect predictions about languages such as Icelandic and Dutch.

Chomsky notes in OB (p. 89) that the following sentences, though both ungrammatical, differ as to the degree of their ungrammaticality.

(33) a. who$_1$ [$_S$ did you wonder [$_S$ what$_2$ [$_S$ t$_1$ saw t$_2$]]]
      b. what$_1$ [$_S$ did you wonder [$_S$ who$_2$ [$_S$ t$_2$ saw t$_1$]]]

Both are blocked by subjacency, nevertheless (33a) is much worse than (33b). Chomsky proposes to attribute the difference to NIC. In (33a) t$_1$ is a nominative trace free in $\bar{S}$, whereas in (33b) the nominative trace t$_2$ is not free in $\bar{S}$, because it is bound by *who*$_2$.

This explanation is, however, problematic, since the rules and principles of OB also provide another derivation for the sentences in (33) with a different surface structure. With this surface structure the sentences are also blocked, but for a different reason. We give this surface structure in (34).

(34) a. who$_1$ [$_S$ did you wonder [$_{\bar{S}}$[COMP t$_1$[COMP what$_2$]] [$_S$ t$_1$ saw t$_2$]]]
      b. what$_1$ [$_S$ did you wonder [$_{\bar{S}}$[COMP t$_1$[COMP who$_2$]] [$_S$ t$_2$ saw t$_1$]]]

The sentences in (34) are ungrammatical because they contain a violation of the c-command condition on anaphor and antecedent. In (34a) the occurrence of t_1 in the embedded clause is properly bound by t_1 in COMP which is bound in turn by *who*$_1$. It is ungrammatical, however, because t_2 is not c-commanded by *what*$_2$. It is therefore not properly bound, a mark of ungrammaticality. In the same manner in (34b) it is t_2 which is not bound by its antecedent.

We see now that in (34b) it is a nominative trace which is not properly bound, whereas t_2 in (34a) is objective. We must therefore conclude that (34b) contains a violation of NIC. Assuming with Chomsky that NIC is in a sense an inviolable constraint, it follows that (34b) should be worse than (34a). Under different derivations for the same sentences NIC apparently makes different predictions as to their relative (un)grammaticality. This is obviously unsatisfactory. Moreover it would be much more reasonable if in structures like those given above, violations of subjacency and violations of the conditions on proper binding amounted to the same thing. Since both these derivations are possible, NIC makes inconsistent predictions. I see no sense in which one of them would be more impossible than the other.

This can be remedied only by having Case assignment limited strictly to lexical NP. In that case, the subject traces in (33) and (34) will not be assigned nominative Case, and as a consequence NIC cannot apply, and is irrelevant. Hence a different explanation must be found for the facts under consideration. Such an explanation must be based on a property shared by the derivations in (33) and (34), which makes it possible to bring the difference between (33a) and (34a) on the one hand, and (33b) and (34b) on the other, under a common denominater. In both (33a) and (34a) the subject is farther away from its original site than in (33b) and (34b): moreover in both (33a) and (34a) the COMP node adjacent to the trace of the subject contains lexical material.

This is reminiscent of a case discussed in Chomsky and Lasnik (1977). They formulate a filter, given here in (35), to describe the difference between (36) on the one hand, and (37) and (38) on the other.

(35)   *that [$_{NP}$ e] *except in the context* [$_{NP}$ NP_____ ...]
(36)   *Who do you think that t saw Bill.
(37)   Who do you think   t saw Bill.
(38)   the man that t saw Bill, ...

So the filter states that in general *that* followed by an empty NP is ungrammatical. A special exception condition is added to account for the fact that in relative clauses the filter does not apply.

Chomsky and Lasnik claim that filter (35) reflects a rather widespread property of languages. Languages which exhibit subject deletion are generally exempt from it. This property of those languages is explained under the assumption that the rule of subject deletion also deletes a trace in subject position. As a result of that deletion, at surface structure the condition for the filter to apply will not be met. So, in fact, Chomsky and Lasnik's (1977) account makes two claims: one is that for a language to be subject to filter (35) constitutes the unmarked case; the other is that only languages permitting subject deletion may be exempt from it.

The latter claim is incorrect as is argued convincingly in Maling and Zaenen (1978, 1980) on the basis of evidence from Icelandic, and Dutch. The relevant kind of example is given in (39).

(39)   Wie₁ zei je   [s dat [s t₁ ons daar gezien heeft]]?
        who said you   that   t us   there seen   has
        who did you say saw us there?

Examples like this are perfectly grammatical in Dutch, showing that the *that*-trace filter does not apply; yet Dutch does not 'drop' subject pronouns. In any case, in the account presented here there is no *deletion* of a subject in languages permitting tensed sentences without an overt subject. So that rule cannot be invoked to explain the fact that in these languages sentences parallel to (36) and (39) may be grammatical. No specific evidence has been given for the other claim, namely that it is less marked for filter (35) to apply — and indeed we will assume that it is *marked* for a language to exhibit phenomena of the sort covered by filter (35).

Recall that filter (26) embodies the requirement that a tensed verb form be governed by a nominative. Since traces may not be marked for Case, under the present proposal, this requirement is not met in clauses of which the subject has been extracted. So, the grammaticality of sentences such as (37), (39), or even (40) is not explained.

(40)   Jij   vroeg [s wieᵢ of [s tᵢ ons daar gezien heeft]].
        you asked   who COMP us there seen   has
        You asked who saw us there.

In order to accommodate such facts some conditions must be added to (26) as it stands. It is on the basis of this condition that the facts of the *that*-trace filter will be explained, and the fact that languages vary as to its applicability accounted for. It will then follow immediately that for languages allowing the subject position of tensed clauses to be empty the question of some condition being added to (26) does not arise; nor, as a consequence, does the question of the *that*-trace filter. Sentences such as (40) can be accounted for by specifically allowing a nominative in COMP to satisfy the requirement on tense expressed in (26). So, we will assume (26) to be replaced by (41).

(41)   *tense_-$_I$ unless governed by (i) nominative or
                                      (ii) trace, and nominative is
                                           in COMP

In this form the filter provides the basis for a straightforward account of the facts about English relativisation illustrated in (42).

(42) a. the man [s $\left\{ \begin{array}{l} \text{who} \\ \text{that} \\ \text{*}\underline{\hspace{1em}} \end{array} \right\}$ [s t saw Bill]]

      b. the man [s $\left\{ \begin{array}{l} \text{who} \\ \text{that} \\ \underline{\hspace{1em}} \end{array} \right\}$ [s Bill saw t]]

The result of applying free deletion to all of COMP (indicated by '_____') is ungrammatical if the subject is relativised, and not if the object is. This follows from (41) since if all lexical material in COMP is deleted there is no carrier of nominative Case there, causing the filter to be violated. Object relativisation is irrelevant to the filter. In the framework of Chomsky and Lasnik (1977) it is the fact that the structure *the man that t saw Bill* is grammatical which leads to the *ad hoc* exception condition in the formulation of filter (35). But the option in (42a) where *who* has been deleted, but not *that*, does not lead to a complication of filter (41), under the assumption that the deletion affects only the string *who*, leaving the nominative marking on COMP. So, the filter is satisfied by a non-null nominative in COMP, namely *that*.[13]

Cases such as (39) can also be analysed as covered by (41). The embedded clause is in the domain of a bridge verb, allowing the *wh*-word to be moved to the COMP position of the matrix clause. We will assume that the marked property of a verb that makes it a bridge for COMP/COMP movement has the general effect of permitting a constituent in the COMP position of its *own* clause to meet conditions to which the COMP position of its *complement* clause is subject. Applied to (39), (41) requires that the COMP of the embedded clause contain a nominative. Since this clause is in the domain of the bridge verb **zei**, this requirement is met by the nominative **wie** in the COMP of the matrix clause.

The property of a language such as English expressed by the *that*-trace filter can now be analysed as a restriction on the possibilities for (41) to be satisfied by a nominative not in the COMP of the clause it has been extracted from. Thus, for English (41) constitutes an absolute requirement, not to be overridden by a bridge verb, if COMP contains lexical material. This status of (41) in the grammar of English can be represented by adding the condition that the nominative and its trace be adjacent. We will refer to (41) with this requirement added as (41′).

The difference in grammaticality between the sentences of (43) can now be explained by (41′).

(43)   a.   Who do you think that Peter said saw Bill.
       b.   *Who do you think Peter said that saw Bill.

The relevant structures are given in (44).

(44)   a.   who do you think $[_S[_{COMP} t_1[_{COMP}$ that]] $[_S$ Peter said
            $[_S[_{COMP} t_2]$ $[_S t_3$ saw Bill]]]]
       b.   who do you think $[_S[_{COMP} t_1]$ $[_S$ Peter said
            $[_S[_{COMP} t_2[_{COMP}$ that]] $[_S t_3$ saw Bill]]]]]

The verb *said* allows a requirement on t_2 to be satisfied by t_1; *think* allows a requirement on t_1 to be met by *who*. The requirement on t_2 is that it be nominative and adjacent to t_3. In (44a) t_2 meets the requirement that it be adjacent to t_3. This leaves the requirement that it be nominative which because of the two bridge verbs is satisfied by *who*. In (44b) t_2 and t_3 are not adjacent, being separated by *that*. As a consequence (41′) will be violated. This explains the ungrammaticality of (44b). In this way the facts of the *that*-trace filter are accounted for. That filter can therefore be dispensed with.

In addition we can now solve the puzzle with which this sub-section began: Why is (33a) so much worse than (33b)? The reason now, that (33a) is worse than (33b), is that *saw* in (33a) is not governed by a nominative, and there is no nominative in COMP either, while in (33b) on the other hand the nominative *who* is in

COMP. This explanation does not change when we turn to the analyses given in (34): (34a) violates (41') since the trace in COMP and the one in subject position are separated by *what*; in (34b) the relevant items are adjacent.

The approach adopted here also provides an explanation for the following fact, noted in Chomsky and Lasnik (1977). In clauses headed by *whether* similar phenomena can be observed as in clauses headed by *that*. Therefore they propose to change filter (35) to the form given here as (45) (their 83).

(45)   * $\begin{Bmatrix} \text{that} \\ +\text{WH} \end{Bmatrix}$ t *except in the context* [$_{NP}$ NP — ...]

In their analysis it is an idiosyncratic fact about *that* and *whether* that they do, and of the complementiser *for* that it does not cause ungrammaticality when adjacent to an empty constituent. In our analysis this is precisely what is predicted, since *whether*, and *that* do, and *for* does not introduce tensed clauses. As a consequence *for* could never cause filter (41') to be violated.

We conclude that by basing the account of sentences such as (33) on (41') instead of NIC, we can solve a puzzle arising in the framework of OB; it follows from the analysis that the '*that*-trace' filter is not applicable to relative clauses, and so does the subject/object asymmetry as to free deletion in COMP; the analysis predicts the way the '*that*-trace' filter seems to generalise; since this filter is shown to cover a special instance of a more general phenomenon it can be dispensed with. Therefore the adoption of (41') enables us to simplify the grammar.

4.3 A Reformulation and Reinterpretation of Filter (41)

In extending filter (26) so as to account for the grammaticality of tensed clauses with the subject in COMP position, we complicated the original form of that filter specifically allowing the condition imposed by the filter to be met by a constituent in COMP. For ease of reference I state these filters here again.

(26)   *tense$_{-I}$ unless governed by nominative
(41)   *tense$_{-I}$ unless governed by (i) nominative or
                                     (ii) trace, and nominative is
                                          in COMP

(41′)   *tense$_{-1}$ unless governed by   (i) nominative or
                                           (ii) trace, and nominative is in
                                                COMP and adjacent to
                                                trace

This is not the only case where specific allowance has to be made for
an element in COMP. I refer to the conditions on Case assignment
holding on the level of surface structure, given in OB and quoted at
the beginning of this article. I repeat the relevant phrase here as (46).

(46)   '... an NP has Case ... when it is in COMP and its trace is
       properly governed.'

Since it is quite generally the case that a phrase moved to COMP
behaves in certain important respects as if it were in its original
position, the question arises whether this should not be stated
somewhere, in such a way that the fact need not be repeated in each
separate case. A natural place for this fact to be accommodated in is
the definition of *government* itself. The notion of government is one
of the means available to represent what is local in a language. It
captures that notion of 'nearness' of one constituent to the other
that is associated with the functor/argument structure the sentence
exhibits on the level of logical form.
   If one phrase is governed by another phrase this means that
provided some other conditions are satisfied, the governed phrase is
available as an argument to the governor. The very reason we had to
incorporate the exception condition referring to COMP in (41) is
because a nominative NP in COMP is available to occupy the subject
argument position of the tensed verb of the clause. It is of course for
precisely the same reason that an NP in COMP has Case when its
trace is properly governed in its S. The NP in COMP actually has the
Case associated with its original position. It is this idea, namely the
idea that the notion of government should capture the notion of
nearness relevant to functor/argument structure, which justifies the
move to accommodate the special position of phrases moved into
COMP in the definition of government itself.
   I will therefore replace the definition given in (10) by the one in
(47).

(47)   α is *governed* by β if
       a. α is *c*-commanded by β, and if γ is a major category, no

boundary of γ appears between α and β unless both α and β are c-commanded by γ.
or
b. α or β is in COMP and a. applies to its trace

Under this definition of government (41) can be reduced to its original form (26). Just as languages may differ as to what are bounding nodes for movement, so it is possible for them to differ as to the conditions that items in COMP position must satisfy in order to be eligible as governors of governees.

The marked property of languages such as English requiring a nominative in COMP and its trace to be adjacent we will represent by a condition added to (47) for these languages, to the effect that a governor in COMP must be adjacent to its trace. Definition (47) with this condition added will be referred to as to (47′). Thus the relevant facts of English are accounted for by (26) together with (47′).

This reduction of (41′) to (26) restores the simplicity of the original approach at least partly. Yet, (26) still contains a complication introduced by necessity: imperatives are exempt from the filter. This is expressed by the restriction to tense$_{-I}$. In languages such as Dutch, imperatives are not the only exceptions to the requirement that a tensed verb must be governed by a nominative. There are impersonal passives as well. An example is given in (48a), and a probable structure in (48b).

(48) a. In dit huis wordt gedanst.
          in this house is danced
      b. [$_S$ [$_{PP}$ in dit huis] [$_{Aux}$ wordt] [$_{VP}$[$_V$ gedanst]]]

Here it is not a matter of simply listing **wordt** as an exception to (26), since (49) is ungrammatical.

(49) *Wordt gedanst.
       is   danced

Rather **wordt** may occur as an exception to (26) only if it is governed by an adverbial of place, or time.[14] This would be awkward to incorporate in the filter. This suggests that we should consider more carefully the principles underlying the facts it covers. Such a reconsideration is the more desirable since the rule as formulated is unusual for a filter in that it expresses a requirement on **tense** that may be satisfied not only by a constituent in one of the positions specified by the rule, but also (under the conditions we specified) by a constituent in a more remote position.

We will base a reinterpretation of the facts covered by the filters (26/41) on the following consideration. By using a feature such as [−I] in order to exempt imperatives from the rule, a redundancy is introduced. A similar redundancy would be introduced if we were to account for the behaviour of impersonal passives by adding such a feature. For all such clauses with null subjects must be represented on the level of logical form without a free variable in the position of the subject. In section 4.1 we suggested that in these cases the subject variable in the lexical representation of the items concerned be internally bound. However, as long as filter (26) refers to syntactic structure, these facts cannot be linked. Yet, a tensed verb form is not subject to (26) in precisely those cases where its lexical representation is such that after translation into logical form it will not give rise to a free variable if no subject is present.[15] This generalisation is not restricted to imperatives and impersonal passives. It holds also true for languages admitting tensed clauses with null subjects generally.

A less misleading way of expressing what is the case when the lexical representation of a finite verb contains an internally-bound argument position is to say that *the translation of that verb contains an expression equivalent to the translation of a pronoun*. The difference between finite verb forms that do not and those that do require a non-null syntactic subject can be explained on this basis as analogous to the difference between pronouns and anaphors: finite verb forms *requiring* an overt subject are translated into logical form as expressions containing an *anaphor* in subject position, and not a pronoun, while finite verb forms that do *not* require an overt subject contain *pronouns* in this position. On this basis the correlations between the syntactic behaviour and the behaviour on the level of logical form of tensed verbs is made obvious. Thus, the presence versus absence of an anaphor in the translation of the verb — rather than the presence or absence of tense — is the relevant parameter for the rule accounting for the facts covered by filter (41/26). The pertinent factor is that an anaphor (but not a pronoun) in the subject position of the translation of a finite verb yields ungrammaticality unless it is governed by a nominative. If we were to incorporate this factor into some principle, it would immediately follow that this principle would not apply to any clause containing a finite verb translated in such a way that a non-anaphoric pronoun appeared in subject position. This would eliminate the redundancies noted.

This approach enables us also to take care of the problem posed by impersonal passives, namely why it is that (48) is grammatical unlike (49). Under the assumption that the third person singular form of the passive auxiliary **worden** (i.e. **wordt**) has one lexical representation available in which the position of the subject anaphor is occupied by an anaphor that can only be bound by a governing place or time designating expression, it follows that (48) is grammatical and (49) is not. This alternative to (41/26) can be formulated as (50).

(50)   *nominative anaphor *unless governed by* nominative

This nominative anaphor we may think of as being represented on the level of surface structure in the form of the personal endings, the agreement markers, of the finite verb.

For the benefit of the reader I recapitulate the relevant cases in (51).

(51)   a.   *They wondered [$_\bar{S}$ what [$_S$ PRO did t]]
       b.   *They wondered [$_\bar{S}$ what [$_S$ each other did t]]
       c.   They wondered [$_\bar{S}$ what [$_S$ he did t]]
       d.   They wondered [$_\bar{S}$ who [$_S$ t did that job]]
       e.   Who did they say [$_\bar{S}$ t [$_S$ t did that job]]
       f.   *Who did they say [$_\bar{S}$ t that [$_S$ t did that job]]

Example (51a) is ungrammatical since the verb form *did* (containing a nominative anaphor, for it is finite) is not governed by a nominative. For neither PRO, being empty, nor *what*, being objective, is nominative. Example (51b) is also ungrammatical: *each other* is an anaphor, and it is lexical; it is governed by T, and is therefore assigned nominative Case. It is not governed by a nominative, however. As a consequence (50) is violated by the nominative anaphor *each other*. In (51c) the finite verb is governed by the nominative *he*. In (51d) COMP contains the nominative *who*, which is adjacent to the trace. In these cases the finite verb is therefore properly governed. This is also the case in (51e), since the subordinate clause is in the domain of a bridge allowing the requirement on COMP that it contain a nominative to be met by the COMP of the matrix clause. In the last example, finally, the anaphor in the lexical representation of *did* violates (50), since *that* in COMP causes the condition that trace and nominative in COMP be adjacent to be violated. It is now immediately clear that (50) is almost identical to NIC: the treatment of (51b), with a lexical anaphor in the syntactic subject position, shows that it covers all cases of NIC not yet covered by (51/26).

Condition (50) can actually be identified as NIC in the form which that condition has to assume in a framework in which empty NPs do not bear Case, and are not all without exception represented as variables in Logical Form: a nominative anaphor may not be free in $\bar{S}$, and it is free unless governed, in the sense given, by a nominative.[16]

Interpreting the relation of the agreement marker of a tensed verb to its subject as the relation of an anaphor to its antecedent also gives rise to an interesting generalisation concerning agreement. For subject/verb agreement can now be taken as a special case of the conditions restricting application of Co-index. In (52a) *John* and *I* cannot be co-indexed because of person agreement, gender agreement keeps *John* and *she* from being possibly coreferential in (52b), and number agreement is responsible for the fact that *John* and *each other* cannot be co-indexed in (52c).

(52) a. *$John_i$ said that I_i wanted to come.
      b. *$John_i$ said that she_i wanted to come.
      c. *John said that he_i hated each $other_i$.

Rather, in the unmarked case the conditions on interpretation will have to be such that *John, I,* and *she* will necessarily be assigned different interpretations. Equally the violations of subject/verb agreement, in (53) will be ascribed to the fact that the personal pronoun *I* and the anaphor in *wants* have no interpretations in common, and similarly with the personal pronoun *he* and the anaphor in *want.*

(53) a. *I_i $wants_i$ to come.
      b. *He_i $want_i$ to come.

This concludes our discussion of the proper position in the grammar of the rule governing the presence of overt subjects in tensed clauses.

5. Summary and Conclusions

We have been investigating how the principles of OB can be extended to cover facts of other languages. We observed that in some cases nominative Case *must* be assigned to subjects of tenseless clauses, and we saw that the assumption that the subject has nominative Case in general, together with an independently motivated principle of subject/verb agreement enabled us to simplify the grammar in an interesting way. It is necessary in this approach to have Case assignment limited to lexical NPs. It is precisely this feature that made it possible to provide a very general account of null subjects in tensed clauses, covering both the case of languages that admit them generally and the case of languages admitting such constructions only in the periphery. The analysis explains the *that*-trace filter, showing the data it was designed to cover to be instances of a more general pattern. We have concentrated mainly on phenomena of subject/verb agreement in relation to the principles requiring the presence of a nominative NP as the subject in tensed clauses, and the absence of such NPs in tenseless clauses. We have not discussed phenomena of NP Movement, and NP-interpretation. These do not shed any new light on the facts we have been dealing with, and are fully accounted for by the principles arrived at.[17]

Principle (50), and filter (23a), together with filter (4), and the convention that empty NPs do not carry Case, and do not automatically give rise to variables on the level of logical form, account for all cases of subject/verb agreement on a principled basis, and for the facts accounted for by NIC under Chomsky's original analysis.

Notes

*The ideas on which this article is based have developed from the work I did while writing my dissertation. Many of them can be found in its first chapter, written January 1979. Other people have been working on similar problems, witness for instance Kayne (1980) and also Chomsky's Pisa lectures. Although sometimes similar in details these proposals are different in important respects, and often based on different considerations. It would have been interesting to add a detailed comparison of these approaches. However limitations of space and time prevented my doing that. I leave this to the interested reader. I am very much indebted to Frank Heny. Without his stimulating help and advice as to contents and organisation of this paper, and without his effort to eliminate my numerous mistakes in grammar and style, I could not have written it. I am also grateful to Arnold Evers and Sjaak de Mey for their comments on my previous endeavours to treat this material. Of course, I alone am responsible for the remaining mistakes.

1. Evidence for the existence of a VP in Dutch can be found in phenomena of VP-fronting, which are rather similar to those discussed for English in Akmajian, Steele, Wasow (1979). Also such VPs may not contain a tensed verb form as their highest verb, lending support to the decision to generate Tense outside the VP. Cf. Reuland (1979) for discussion, and also, in more detail, Reuland (in preparation).

2. To give an example: in (9a) NP is α, Tense is β, and VP is γ; VP is a major category and its boundaries appear between NP and Tense; however, both of them are c-commanded by VP, so it does not keep them from governing each other. The subject NP is not governed by V, since the VP boundary intervenes, and though the VP c-commands the subject NP it does not c-command V, violating the unless-part of (10). The definition of government given here seems to give similar results to the proposals developed by Chomsky in his Pisa lectures (Spring 1979). I have not compared them in any detail.

3. Intuitively one could say that in the case of Russian verbless constructions recoverability would not be violated under a deletion approach, since sentences such as (i)

(i)   On bol'shoy.
      he big

are interpreted as having present tense. However, the only way to represent this in the grammar, as far as I can see, would be by generating in the lexicon a complete set of doublets, i.e. each adjective (and each noun), not ordinarily marked for present tense, would have a doublet that is so marked. Not a very attractive proposal. In the case of Dutch infinitives even this solution is not available, since as remarked in the text, they do not behave like finite verb forms.

4. Having nominative Case assigned by a governing empty *Tense* node is undesirable for theoretical reasons, since it would imply that these cases involve an exception not so much to a rule, but rather to a fundamental principle of rule application: unindexed empty nodes are in principle not eligible as governors. Perhaps the English absolute nominative construction also deserves mention in this connection, as in (*Brindle gave Steve a warm welcome ...*) *he being a bachelor* (cf. Kruisinga and Erades (1953)). Its treatment will be postponed to another study, however.

5. See note 8 below.

6. Chomsky in his Pisa lectures formulates a proposal to exempt PRO from Case assignment. The reasons he adduces are, however, different from mine.

Koster (1978) proposes to abandon NIC altogether. In the framework of OB, NIC seems to provide the sole motivation for assigning Case to empty categories at all. So, when dropping NIC one might as well take the step of limiting Case assignment to lexical NP. We will, however, retain NIC for lexical anaphors. Koster proposes to take care of lexical anaphors such as *each other* in the subject position of tensed clauses by the assumption that they are lexically marked as [+objective]. Retaining NIC seems to provide, however, a more principled account for the fact that in a number of languages elements such as *each other* are excluded in this position. Later we will show that the remaining cases of NIC follow from a special property of nominative anaphors in general.

7. The restriction of Case assignment to lexical NP seems to constitute a reinterpretation of the notion of Case as compared with the way this notion is used in the framework of OB. Under the reinterpretation, it will be a typically morpho-syntactic category; in the framework of OB Case is a marking available for expressions in the language of logical form. However, since under the revision Case markings are available for the rules translating expressions of surface syntax into logical form, there will be no difference in those cases where a lexical NP is marked for

Case. We will see in the later sections that this restriction of Case assignment to lexical NP has independent support. Support of a descriptive as well as a theoretical nature. Moreover a curious asymmetry is removed; the set of items undergoing Case assignment has now become the same as the set of items subject to checking for Case assignment.

8. Actually (23a) is a filter schema, while (23b) is not. It is sufficient to state the dependency between the specific NP and verb classes only once; it is represented in (23a), since there may also be agreement in constructions where the subject is optional. These are not subject to (23b). (23b) does not contain the requirement that the nominative is an NP. The resulting greater generality is made use of once.

As it stands filter (23a) would rule out the tenseless clauses with nominative subject discussed in the previous section. These can be admitted by adding to filter (23a) the exception condition in (i).

(i)   or unless governed by infinitive, Adj, or (nominative) NP in root clauses.

Clearly the condition is *ad hoc*, but it is to be expected that *ad hoc* conditions may be necessary in the periphery of the grammar. (NB. Note the difference between 'peripheral' and 'marginal'.)

9. If Case assignment is optional there are the following possibilities for a structure such as (24).

(i)   I believe [$_S$[$_S$ h-   to be a fool]] (where h- stands for the third person sing.
                                          masc. pronoun without Case)
(ii)   I believe [$_S$[$_S$ he   to be a fool]]
                          +nom
(iii)   I believe [$_S$[$_S$ him to be a fool]]
                          +obj
(iv)   I believe [$_S$[$_S$ h? to be a fool]]
                          +nom
                          +obj

(i) is out by filter (4); (ii) is out because of a violation of (23a); (iv) is out because of a conflict of Case assignment; (iii) remains as the only grammatical possibility. In cases where the complementiser *for* is involved we get a similar range of options with the same result.

10. For sake of concreteness we may assume the feature *tense* of rule (12) to be expanded as in (i).

(i)   tense → [±Past, α person/number, ± I(mperative)]

where α takes the values 1 ... 6.

11. In Chomsky and Lasnik (1977) n. 57 it is suggested that in languages which admit the absence of subjects freely, an abstract feature [+pro] is base generated. This too seems a rather *ad hoc* move. [+pro] must be in all respects similar to PRO: it has a phonetic null realisation, it occupies a position where no lexical insertion has taken place; its only function is to indicate an empty subject position that does not cause a violation of NIC. If [+pro] is assigned Case, it will require some extra mechanism in order to account for the fact that it does not cause a violation of agreement. If it is not assigned Case this also requires explanation.

It does not contribute in any clear way to semantic interpretation either. Moreover it should be noted, that under this approach also the correlation between allowing 'subject deletion' and not being subject to the '*that*-trace' filter cannot be represented; cf. the discussion of this filter below.

12. See my thesis (§§ 0.2, 6.0) for a more detailed discussion of that principle.

13. Actually this amounts only to the claim that there is in English a process similar to the process in French which changes **que** to **qui** under certain conditions (cf. Kayne (1975) and (1981), Chomsky and Lasnik (1977)).

Chomsky and Lasnik (1977) account for the ungrammaticality of the option in (42a) where all of COMP has been deleted by bringing it under the filter for tensed clauses, which they give in the form of (i).

(i) *$[_\alpha$NP tense VP] unless $\alpha = \bar{S}$ and is adjacent to and in the domain of $[+F]$, *that*, or NP

Notice, however, that this causes a complication on the formulation of the filter. For it makes it necessary to resort to the variable labelling the bracket of the structural condition, and the condition $\alpha = \bar{S}$. If we were to simplify the filter as in (ii), this would cover all cases covered by (i), except precisely for the ungrammaticality of the relevant option in (42a), cf. the discussion in the article cited.

(ii) *$[_S$ NP tense VP] unless adjacent to and in the domain of $[+F]$, *that*, or NP

14. I have no explanation for the fact that it is precisely the third person singular form of the verb which has this property. It might be connected with the fact that in general this form is the least marked of the finite verb forms.

15. See note 12 above.

16. Perhaps the principle should be formulated as in (i).

(i) a. a subject anaphor may not be free in $\bar{S}$
     b. a subject anaphor is free unless it is governed by a member of a proper category

In the unmarked case a proper category could be assumed to be nominative, while in marked cases place and temporal categories could be admitted. In this way the treatment could be generalised so as to include other properties of the impersonal constructions, like those illustrated in (ii).

(ii) a. Jan zei dat in dit huis wordt gedanst.
          Jan said that in this house is danced
      b. *Jan zei dat wordt gedanst.
          Jan said that is danced
      c. Jan vroeg waar wordt gedanst.
          Jan asked where is danced
      d. Waar zei Jan dat wordt gedanst.
          where said Jan that is danced
      e. *Waar deed Jan de mededeling dat wordt gedanst.
          where did Jan make the communication that is danced

The facts of (ii) show that the required adverbial in impersonal constructions behaves like the subject in at least an important respect. Whether this really motivates a formulation as in (i) can perhaps be settled by further investigations.

17. The relevant cases are exemplified in (i) and (ii).

(i) a. PRO seems John to be ill
     b. John seems t   to be ill
     c. it seems   John to be ill
     d. PRO seems that John is ill
     e. it seems   that John is ill
     f. John seems that t   is ill

(ii) a. John asked Bill [s PRO to read the book]
      b. John asked Bill [s whether PRO read the book]

(ia) is ungrammatical since the pair (PRO, *seems*) violates (50), and (*John, to be*) (23a), or (4). (ib) is grammatical since *seems* is governed by *John*, and the trace does not cause a violation of (23a), or (4). (ic) is ungrammatical because *John* is either nominative, violating (23a), or without Case with violation of (4). (id) violates (50); (ie) is grammatical, and, finally, in (if) the nominative anaphor in the lexical representation of *is*, is governed by the trace, but not by the nominative *John*, since the latter has not left its clause by COMP; as a consequence *is* is not governed by a nominative, causing a violation of (50). The cases with NP interpretation, illustrated in (ii) are exactly parallel. (iia) is grammatical for the same reason as (ib); (iib) is ungrammatical for the same reason as (if).

References

Akmajian, A, S. Steele, and T. Wasow (1979), 'The Category Aux in Universal Grammar', *Linguistic Inquiry* 10, 1–64
Besten, H. den (1976), 'Het kiezen van lexicale delenda', *Spektator* 5–6/7, 415–32
Chomsky, N. (1965), *Aspects of the Theory of Syntax*, MIT Press, Cambridge, Massachusetts
———— (1980), 'On Binding', this volume. Previously published in *Linguistic Inquiry* 11, 1–46
Chomsky, N. and H. Lasnik (1977), 'Filters and Control', *Linguistic Inquiry* 8, 425–504
Evers, A. (1975), *The Transformational Cycle in Dutch and German*, distributed by the Indiana University Linguistics Club
Harkins, W. E. (1953), *A Modern Czech Grammar*, King's Crown Press, New York and London
Kayne, R. (1975), *French Syntax; the Transformational Cycle*, MIT Press, Cambridge, Massachusetts
———— (1980), 'Extensions of Binding and Case Marking', *Linguistic Inquiry* 11, 75–96
Koster, J. (1975), 'Dutch as a SOV Language', *Linguistic Analysis* 1, 111–36
———— (1981), 'Binding, Quantifiers, Clitics and Control', this volume
———— (1978), *Locality Principles in Syntax*, Foris Publications, Dordrecht
Kruizinga, E. and P. A. Erades (1953), *An English Grammar*, P. Noordhoff N.V. Groningen, Djakarta
Maling, J. and A. Zaenen (1980), 'Germanic Word Order and the Format of Surface Filters', this volume
Reuland, E. J. (1979), *Principles of Subordination and Construal in the Grammar of Dutch*, Doctoral dissertation, State University of Groningen, The Netherlands
———— (in preparation) *Government and the Search for Aux*
Riemsdijk, H. van (1978), *A Case Study in Syntactic Markedness: the Binding Nature of Prepositional Phrases*, Foris Publications, Dordrecht
Sallustius, C. C. (1938), *De Coniuratione et Bello Catilinae*, E. J. Brill, Leiden

5 Binding, Quantifiers, Clitics and Control*

Richard S. Kayne

1. Binding, Quantifiers and Clitics

1.1 In earlier work,[1] we proposed that the Specified Subject
Condition (SSC) is what accounts for the ungrammaticality of
French sentences such as (2), which contrast with the grammatical
sentences of (1):

(1) a. Elle voudrait le manger.
    She would like it-eat (i.e. *She would like to eat it.*)
 b. Je croyais la connaître.
    I thought to know her (i.e. *I thought that I knew her.*)
 c. Je tiens à vous revoir.
    I am anxious to see you again.
 d. Elle a laissé Jean lui offrir un livre.
    She let John give her a book.

(2) a. *Elle le voudrait manger.
 b. *Je la croyais connaître.
 c. *Je vous tiens à revoir.
 d. *Elle lui a laissé Jean offrir un livre.

In the framework of Chomsky (1980), with the SSC reformulated in
his (27) and (112) as the opacity condition, our SSC proposal can be
reformulated as follows: The relevant structure of (the first example
of) (2) is **Elle le$_i$ voudrait** [$_S$ **PRO manger** [$_{NP_i}$ *e*]]. In this structure,
[$_{NP_i}$ *e*] is an anaphor in the domain of the subject of $\bar{S}$, namely **PRO**.
Furthermore, this anaphor [$_{NP_i}$ *e*] is free in $\bar{S}$, since there is nothing
co-indexed with it in $\bar{S}$. Consequently, (2) is excluded as a violation
of the opacity condition.

   On the other hand, had Clitic Placement (Cl-Pl) applied to attach
the clitic to the embedded verb, as in (1), we would have: **Elle
voudrait** [$_S$ **PRO le$_i$ manger** [$_{NP_i}$ *e*]]. Here the anaphor [$_{NP_i}$ *e*] is still in

191

the domain of the subject of $\bar{S}$, but it is not this time free in $\bar{S}$, since it is co-indexed with an element with $\bar{S}$, namely le$_i$.[2] Consequently there is no violation.

The ungrammaticality of (2) reflects a systematic fact about French: clitics can never successfully be extracted from an embedded infinitival $\bar{S}$.[3] There is thus a minimal contrast between Cl-Pl and leftward quantifier movement (L-Tous) — the latter can successfully extract elements from certain infinitival $\bar{S}$:

(3) a. Marie a tout voulu faire.
         Mary has everything wanted to do. (i.e. *Mary has wanted to do everything.*)
     b. Elle n'aurait rien osé faire.
         She NEG would have nothing dared to do. (i.e. *She would not have dared to do anything.*)
     c. Tu vas tout devoir apprendre.
         You will have to learn everything.
     d. Vous n'avez rien pu dire.
         You were not able to say anything.
     e. Il a tout failli rater.
         He has almost missed everything.
     f. Il a tout fallu lire.
         It was necessary to read everything.

With all these matrix verbs, the facts of (2) hold for Cl-Pl:

(4) a. *Marie l'a voulu faire.
     b. *Elle ne l'aurait pas osé faire.
     c. *Tu vas les devoir apprendre.
     d. *Vous ne l'avez pas pu dire.
     e. *Il les a failli rater.
     f. *Il l'a fallu lire.

We will assume that an adequate description of French, and an adequate linguistic theory, cannot be content with simply noting this contrast.

In Kayne (1975, section 1.4), we envisaged accounting for the possibility of (3) through a rule of Equi-NP-Deletion that would delete the embedded subject prior to the application of L-Tous, in the case of matrix verbs like **vouloir**, **oser**, **devoir**, **pouvoir**, **faillir**, **falloir**. This deletion rule had the implicit effect of eliminating (3) as a potential problem for the SSC. Although the original motivation explicitly provided for this deletion rule is no longer compelling,[4] let us ask whether such a deletion rule could still help to distinguish (3) from (4).

In the framework of Chomsky (1980; his (1)), the answer would seem *a priori* to be negative, given the fact that the opacity condition applies to representations in LF (logical form), and the assumption that deletion rules are on a different track from LF, so that they cannot feed the opacity condition.[5]

This negative answer is reinforced by three significant disadvantages associated with the deletion proposal. First, such a deletion rule would now be *ad hoc*, in the sense that it would now be motivated by no consideration exterior to the problem of (3). Second, the embedded subject is essential for the opacity condition account of (4). Thus if such a deletion rule could feed the opacity condition in the case of (3), it would presumably be able to do the same in (4), but then (4) should be grammatical, too. This problem is especially acute in (5) versus (6):

(5)   Marie a tout voulu lui donner.
      Mary has wanted to give him everything.
(6)   *Marie lui a tout voulu donner.

If it is the absence of the supposedly deleted subject that allows **tout** to move into the matrix S in (5), then why can the clitic not follow?[6]

Finally, consider the contrast between (7) and (8), which we suggest is parallel to that between (3) and (4):

(7)   a.   ?Je veux tout que tu leur enlèves.
           I want you to take everything (away) from them.
      b.   ?Je ne veux rien que tu fasses (d'autre).
           I don't want you to do anything (else).
      c.   ?Il faut tout que je leur enlève.
           It's necessary that I take everything (away) from them.
      d.   ?Il ne faut rien que tu fasses.
           You mustn't do anything.
(8)   a.   *Je les veux que tu achètes.
      b.   *Il les faut que tu fasses.

With those verbs of (3) that accept tensed complements, L-Tous can, for many speakers, move **tout** or **rien** out of a tensed embedded S̄.[7]

Comparable sentences with Cl-Pl are completely impossible. The conclusion is inescapable: Whereas a deletion rule might have had some initial plausibility as a way of distinguishing (3) from (4), no such solution is feasible at all for (7) versus (8), since the embedded subject is overtly present. We conclude that the apparent ability of L-Tous to skirt the strictures of the opacity condition is not to be described in terms of a deletion rule.[8]

We propose, rather, that the difference between Cl-Pl and L-Tous with respect to the opacity condition is better stated as follows: The trace left by Cl-Pl counts as an anaphor for opacity, whereas the trace left by L-Tous does not.

This proposal is consistent with the organisation of grammar given in Chomsky (1980), since it makes reference only to transformations (Cl-Pl, L-Tous) and to properties of LF (opacity, characterisation of 'anaphor'), and so does not lead to difficulties concerning the place of deletion rules. Nor does it require any non-principled extrinsic ordering. Finally, it gives a unified account of the possibility of (3), (7) as opposed to (4), (8).

Taking (3) versus (4), we have, in the first example of each: ... **voulu** [$_S$ **PRO faire** [$_{NP_i}$ e]]. In (4), the trace of Cl-Pl, [$_{NP_i}$ e], counts as an anaphor and therefore falls in the realm of the opacity condition, which excludes it since the anaphor is free in $\bar{S}$ and in the domain of the subject PRO. In (3), [$_{NP_i}$ e] is again free in $\bar{S}$ and in the domain of the subject, but since it does not count as an anaphor, being the trace of L-Tous, it falls outside the realm of the opacity condition and there is consequently no violation.

Taking (7) versus (8) we have, in the last example of each: ... [$_{\bar{S}}$ **que tu fasses** [$_{NP_i}$ e]]. Exactly the same reasoning applies: In (8), the trace of Cl-Pl, being an anaphor, yields a violation of opacity by virtue of being free in $\bar{S}$ and in the domain of the subject **tu**. In (4), the trace is of L-Tous, hence not an anaphor, so there is no violation, despite the parallelism in structure.

The proposal that the trace of L-Tous does not count as an anaphor for the opacity condition is to be related to a suggestion of Chomsky's (1980) based on work by Rizzi (1978a), namely that the set of elements that count as anaphors for the opacity condition does not include the trace of *Wh* Movement. The following claim is now a natural one: *Wh* Movement and L-Tous form a natural class with respect to immunity from opacity because both involve the movement of quantifier-like elements (clearly so for L-Tous, and arguably so for *Wh* Movement (see Chomsky (1976))). Cl-Pl, on the other hand, does not involve quantifier-like elements, and so is strictly subject to the opacity condition, as seen in (4) and (8).

One way to express this generalisation between quantifier-like elements and the immunity of their traces from opacity is essentially given by Chomsky (1977) (1980): assume that a rule of variable insertion can apply in the construction of LF from surface structures, replacing the trace of *Wh* Movement, and now, in French, L-Tous, by a variable; i.e. $[_{NP_i} e] \rightarrow [_{NP_i} x]$, in particular in (3) and (7). The trace of Cl-Pl is not so replaced; thus in (4) and (8) we continue to have $[_{NP_i} e]$. Assume further that the opacity condition applies at this stage, i.e. subsequent to such variable insertion, and furthermore that $[_{NP_i} e]$ but not $[_{NP_i} x]$ counts as an anaphor for it. Then the desired distinction is drawn correctly.

1.2 The instances of L-Tous that we have so far considered have all involved the leftward movement of **tout** and **rien**. There also exist sentences in which **tous** appears to have moved leftward:

(9) a.   Marie a tous voulu les revoir.
          Mary has all wanted them-see again
          (i.e. *Mary has wanted to see them all again.*)
     b.   ?Il faut tous que tu les revoies.
          It is necessary that you see them all again.

Since (9) resembles (3) and (7) with respect to movement into the matrix S, **tous** must not have a trace that is an anaphor for the opacity condition. Furthermore, the presence of **tous** must not alter the opacity condition status of the trace of Cl-Pl, since (10) is ungrammatical, just as (4) and (8):

(10) a. *Marie les a tous voulu revoir.
      b. *Il les faut tous que tu revoies.

To see how these observations mesh with the framework of section 1.1, it is necessary to attack the question of **tous** more generally: **Tous** can occur to the right of a NP to which it is bound, much as with English *all*:

(11) a. Mes amis sont *tous* partis.
      b. My friends have *all* left.

There are some well-known restrictions, common to French and English:

(12) a. *La mère de mes amis est tous partie.
      b. *The mother of my friends has all left.*
(13) a. *Mes amis pensent que je suis tous parti.
      b. *My friends think that I have all left.*

These restrictions recall those found with anaphors like *each other*:

(14) *The mother of my friends likes each other.
(15) *My friends think that I like each other.

They suggest that in (12) and (13), **tous** and *all* be considered anaphors in the sense of Chomsky (1980).

The status of **tous** and *all* as anaphors allows one to assimilate (12) to (14), and thereby to the general requirement that an anaphor have an antecedent that c-commands it. In (12), **mes amis** and *my friends* fail to c-command **tous** and *all*;[9] hence the ungrammaticality of (12a,b).

Similarly, (13) is now assimilated to (15): Although **tous**, *all*, and *each other* do have a c-commanding antecedent, that antecedent is outside the S̄ containing the subject in whose domain the three anaphors are found. In other words, each is free in the domain of the subject of the embedded S̄, and hence in violation of the opacity condition.

The analysis of **tous**, and *all* as anaphors cannot, of course, be extended to (9), where *tous* lacks any c-commanding antecedent. At the same time, we want to maintain the anaphoric status of these words in (11)–(13). In essence, we want **tous** to have some status in (9), other than anaphoric, such that that new status is not transferable to, i.e. not viable in, (11)–(13).

Our proposal is this: floating **tous** and *all* both normally have the status of anaphors at the level of representation defined by the binding conditions,[10] but **tous** can alternatively have the status of 'quantifier', in the following sense: Although floating **tous** and *all* must, as anaphors, normally have a c-commanding antecedent, within the limits imposed by the opacity condition, this requirement can be suspended, in the case of **tous**, if there is some element that can itself be construed as bound by **tous** qua quantifier, i.e. some element c-commanded by **tous** and interpretable as a variable bound by **tous**.

Thus in (9) **tous** is licit, despite the absence of an appropriate antecedent, because there is some element which **tous** can be taken to bind qua quantifier, namely the trace of **les**[11]. In other words, (9) is licit with **tous** qua quantifier, although illicit with **tous** qua anaphor. Conversely, (11) is licit only with **tous** qua anaphor. Examples (12)–(13) are licit in neither way. (In essence, floating **tous**, if it is to be interpretable, must be linked to some argument position; French allows this to be done in either of two ways. Compare the discussion in Chomsky (1980) of his (5).)

Consider now the contrast between (9) and (16):

(16)　a.　*Marie a tous voulu revoir ses amis.
　　　　b.　*Il faut tous que tu revoies tes amis.

These examples show that although **tous** can bind, qua quantifier, the trace of a clitic, it cannot so bind a lexical NP.[12] Our idea is that the relation in (9) between **tous** and the trace of Cl-Pl is comparable to that holding between the quantified NP and the pronoun in sentences such as (17):

(17)　Everyone loves his children.

This phenomenon has been discussed by Chomsky (1976) and Williams (1977), both of whom (in somewhat different ways) treat it as involving the interpretation of a pronoun as a bound variable. If we assume that the rule interpreting as a bound variable a pronoun in English and French extends in French to the trace of Cl-Pl, and furthermore that that rule cannot interpret as a bound variable (i.e. cannot apply to) a non-null non-pronominal NP,[13] then (9) versus (16) is accounted for. In (16), floating **tous** is licit neither as anaphor (for lack of a *c*-commanding antecedent) nor as quantifier (for lack of an appropriate *c*-commanded NP of an appropriate 'non-lexical' type).

If this analysis is correct, then, returning to (10), we must be sure that the pronoun-as-variable rule relevant to (9) and (17) does not interfere with our proposals of section 1.1: either the pronoun-as-variable rule must not apply until after the point of application of the opacity condition, or the anaphoric character of the trace of Cl-Pl must remain unaffected by that rule.

That the pronoun-as-variable rule should turn out not to prevent the trace of Cl-Pl from counting as an anaphor for the opacity condition is actually not surprising, in the sense that the same is obviously true of reflexives, which are interpreted as variables in sentences like 'Everyone finds himself irresistible'. Despite this possibility of interpretation as a variable, (18) and (19) are equally ungrammatical:

(18)   *John wants Mary to find himself irresistible.
(19)   *Everyone wants Mary to find himself irresistible.

That is, reflexives, too, count as anaphors for the opacity condition quite independently of whether or not they are subject to interpretation as a bound variable.[14]

2. Binding, Quantifiers and Control

2.1 We return in this section to instances of L-Tous involving **tout** and **rien**, beginning with the observation that there are no grammatical sentences comparable to (7) (repeated here in part as (20)) in which the extracted **tout** or **rien** corresponds to the embedded subject:

(20)   ?Il faut tout que je leur enlève.
        It's necessary that I take everything away from them.
(21) a. *Je veux tout que leur soit enlevé.
        I want everything to be taken away from them.
      b. *Je ne veux rien que soit fait par ce type.
        I NEG want nothing to be done by that guy.
      c. *Il faut tout que soit détruit.
        It's necessary that everything be destroyed.
      d. *Il ne faut rien que tombe.
        It NEG is necessary that nothing fall.

This subject-object asymmetry is identical to that found with *Wh* Movement:

(22)   Qui veux-tu qu'elle épouse?
        Who do you want her to marry?
(23) a. *Qui veux -tu que vienne?
        Who do you want to come?

b. *Qui crois-tu que tombera?
   Who do you think will fall?

It might be thought that the ungrammaticality of (21) and (23) could be attributed to Chomsky and Lasnik's (1977) '*that — [NP *e*]' filter transposed to French. However, in the framework of Chomsky (1980), that filter can be shown with reasonable certainty to be superfluous, as we have argued in Kayne (1979/80). More specifically it seems that a filter-based analysis is inferior to one based on the Nominative Island Condition (NIC) as defined in Chomsky (1980 — see his (103) and (112)).[15]

The ungrammaticality of (21) and (23) can, consequently, be attributed to the NIC, which prohibits a nominative anaphor from being free in S̄. However, this clearly involves a paradox: our account of the grammaticality of (20) and (22) is based on the idea that the traces of L-Tous and *Wh* Movement do not count as anaphors for the opacity condition. Yet accounting for (21) and (23) via the NIC implies that those same traces do count as anaphors for it, the NIC. Why this asymmetry between the two conditions?

An answer to this question, and with it a more nearly complete solution to (21) and (23), has been provided by Chomsky (1981). We shall sketch this solution very briefly: the traces of L-Tous and *Wh* Movement will continue not to count as anaphors for the opacity condition; nor will they count as anaphors for the NIC, to the extent that that condition is merged with the opacity condition in Chomsky's new proposal. The difference between (21)/(23) on the one hand and (20)/(22) on the other will now be captured instead by a new principle which subsumes part of the NIC: the Empty Category Principle (ECP). This principle requires that any truly empty category (i.e. [e] but not PRO) be governed either by a co-indexed category or by a lexical category.[16] Given this formulation, it is irrelevant to the ECP whether traces are anaphors or not. It is rather the factor of government which separates the pairs in question. Assuming that government of the trace by a co-indexed category holds in none of (20)–(23), the contrast between (20), (22), in which the trace **e** is governed by V, and (21), (23), in which the trace **e** is governed by no lexical category, follows straightforwardly: the latter pair is in violation of the ECP.

2.2 Although L-Tous and *Wh* Movement behave alike with respect to the NIC/ECP, as indicated by (21) and (23), as well as with respect to the opacity condition, as indicated by (3), (7), (20) and (22), they differ in their behaviour with respect to the **que/qui** rule discussed by Moreau (1971) and Kayne (1976). This rule is responsible for the existence of (24), to be compared with (23):

(24) a. Qui veux-tu qui vienne?
          Who do you want that come?
          (i.e. *Who do you want to come?*)
      b. Qui crois-tu qui tombera?
          Who do you think (that) will fall?

When the embedded subject has been extracted by *Wh* Movement, the complementiser **que** can be replaced by **qui**, in which case the violation displayed in (23) is nullified. The same does not, however, hold for L-Tous. Thus (21a–d) do not become grammatical if **que** is replaced by **qui**.[17] For example:

(25) a. *Je veux tout qui leur soit enlevé.
      b. *Il faut tout qui soit détruit.

In order to understand why L-Tous and *Wh* Movement diverge just here, we must examine the **que/qui** alternation in more detail. We note at the outset that this **qui** appears in at least one non-*wh* construction, so that (25) could not be accounted for simply by restricting the **que/qui** rule to *wh*-environments.
The non-*Wh* construction we have in mind is that of (26):

(26) Je l'ai rencontré qui sortait du cinéma.
      I met him (that was) leaving the movies.

The essential argument that (26) does not involve *Wh* Movement, but rather a rule of control, is based on the observation that (26) has no counterpart in which it is the embedded object that is missing from its normal position:[18]

(27) *Je l'ai rencontré que Marie embrassait.
      I met him that Mary was kissing.

This asymmetry is precisely that found in (28) versus (29) (and in control constructions in general):

(28)   Je l'ai rencontré sortant du cinéma.
         I met him coming out of the movies.

(29)   *Je l'ai rencontré Jean emmenant au cinéma.
         I met him John taking to the movies.

Our hypothesis is that (26) and (28) have representations such as: **Je l$_i$'ai rencontré [$_{NP_i}$ e] [$_S$[$_{COMP}$ que] PRO sortait du cinéma], Je l$_i$'ai rencontré [$_{NP_i}$ e] [$_S$[$_{COMP}$ e] PRO sortant du cinéma]**. A rule of control co-indexes the embedded subject PRO with the matrix object [$_{NP_i}$ e]. Since the embedded PRO in question is itself the subject of the embedded $\bar{S}$, the opacity condition is clearly irrelevant, as desired.

The comparable representations for (27) and (29) would be: **Je l$_i$'ai rencontré [$_{NP_i}$ e] [$_S$[$_{COMP}$ que] Marie embrassait PRO]** and **Je l$_i$'ai rencontré [$_{NP_i}$ e] [$_S$[$_{COMP}$ e] Jean emmenant PRO au cinéma]**. But here the embedded PRO is in the domain of the embedded subject and free within the embedded $\bar{S}$ (whether co-indexed with the matrix [$_{NP_i}$ e] or not). Thus (27) and (29) are excluded as violations of the opacity condition.[19]

Although the opacity condition correctly distinguishes (26) from (27) under the assumption that what is involved is control, (26) itself appears to pose a problem for the NIC, since it appears to involve a nominative anaphor PRO free in its $\bar{S}$ (since bound by an element (the matrix object [$_{NP_i}$ e]) lying outside that $\bar{S}$). However, this problem was already implicit in the contrast between (23) and (24). If the former is in violation of the NIC, and if the two differ only in the form of the complementiser, how is it that the latter is not in violation of the NIC?[20] We shall adopt a suggestion of Pesetsky's (1979), to the effect that the requisite antecedent for the embedded subject trace in (24) is **qui** itself, and not the intermediate trace in COMP. Thus the embedded $\bar{S}$ in (24) has the representation: [$_{\bar{S}}$[$_{COMP}$[$_{NP_i}$ e] qui$_i$] [$_S$[$_{NP_i}$ e] ...]][21]. Similarly, according to Pesetsky, the requisite antecedent for the subject trace in simple relatives such as (30) is the indexed complementiser **qui**:

(30)   la fille qui viendra demain
         the girl that will come tomorrow

It is now natural for us to claim that a more accurate representation for (26) is **Je l$_i$'ai rencontré [$_{NP_i}$ e] [$_S$[$_{COMP}$ qui$_i$] PRO sortait du cinéma]**. A rule of control co-indexes the embedded PRO with the matrix [$_{NP_i}$ e]. But the embedded PRO is then bound in $\bar{S}$, by qui$_i$, whence the absence of any NIC violation, as desired.[22]

The availability of an indexed complementiser **qui**$_i$ to permit control of a nominative PRO is of course extremely limited. Thus, there is no tensed **qui** counterpart to the infinitival control examples of (31):

(31)   Marie veut partir.
         Mary wants to leave.
         J'ai dit à Marie de partir.
(32)   *Marie veut qui parte.
         *J'ai dit à Marie qui parte.

If we compare (31) with (28), which does have a tensed **qui** counterpart, namely (26), we notice a correlation between the existence of a **qui**-counterpart and the non-extractibility of an object from the embedded S̄:

(33)   a.   Quel garçon Marie veut-elle embrasser?
               Which boy does Mary want to kiss?
         b.   Quel garçon as-tu dit à Marie d'embrasser?
(34)   *Quelle fille l'as-tu rencontré embrassant?
                                             (Kayne (1975, Ch. 2, note 75))

This suggests that, although both involve control, (31) and (28) differ significantly in structure, and more specifically, that whereas the embedded S̄ of (31) is a complement of V, that of (28) is not. Furthermore, (26) is hypothesised to involve control too, and is like (28) in other ways (v. note 18), especially in not allowing the extraction of an embedded object, as seen in (35):

(35)   *Quelle fille l'as-tu rencontré qui embrassait?

Thus (26) too should have an S̄ complement not dependent on V.

Our proposal is that (26) and (28) have representations congruent to those of relative clauses, except for the *Wh* Movement vs. control difference: **Je l$_i$'ai rencontré [$_{NP}$[$_{NP_i}$ *e*] [$_S$[$_{COMP}$ qui$_i$] [PRO sortait du cinéma]]]** and **Je l$_i$'ai rencontré [$_{NP}$[$_{NP_i}$ *e*] [$_S$[$_{COMP}$ *e*] [PRO sortant du cinéma]]]**. (PRO is ultimately co-indexed with [$_{NP_i}$ *e*].)

The ungrammaticality of (34) and (35) thus reduces to Ross's (1967) Complex NP Constraint, or, more deeply, to Chomsky's (1973) subjacency principle.

Moreover, the appearance of **qui**$_i$ in (26) and (30), as opposed to

(32), is now seen to depend on the existence of a common [$_{NP}$ NP $\bar{S}$] structure. If the assignment of an index to the complementiser **que** is a necessary condition for the change from **que** to **qui**, then (32) follows from the assumption that an index can be assigned from a NP to a complementiser across $\bar{S}$ only in the [$_{NP}$ NP $\bar{S}$] configuration.[23]

We are supposing here that in (30) the source of the index for the complementiser is the head NP **la fille**, rather than the null phrase in COMP. On the other hand, the **qui**$_i$ of (24) presumably does receive its index from the null phrase that is in the lower COMP as a result of the successive cyclic application of *Wh* Movement. This difference in source may correlate with the 'recherché' character of (24) noted by Milner (1979, p. 111) (neither (26) nor (30) is 'recherché'). Thus we might speculate that index assignment from a (null) NP in COMP to a complementiser is 'marked',[24] noting that English would then be 'unmarked' in so far as there is no English equivalent to (24):

(36)   *Who do you think that left?

Our [$_{NP}$ NP $\bar{S}$] proposal for (26) and (28) recalls Akmajian (1977). However, his [$_{NP}$ NP VP] structure is clearly inappropriate for (26) (and so presumably for (28)). This is so despite the fact that in standard French (26) cannot have a non-PRO subject:[25]

(37)   *Je l'ai rencontré que tu sortais du cinéma.

Thus (26) is a case of seemingly obligatory control within a Tensed $\bar{S}$ containing a complementiser. None the less, there is another way of accounting for the ungrammaticality of (37), given the attribution to (26) (and (28)) of a NP-$\bar{S}$ structure; these examples share a non-trivial property with relative clauses:[26]

(38)   The man that went to Paris is named Bill.
(39)   *The man that Mary went to Paris is named Bill.

In other words, we can account for (37), along with (39), through the requirement that in any [$_{NP}$ NP $\bar{S}$] structure, the $\bar{S}$ must contain a position bound by the head NP.[27]

Let us return now to the question of (25). We are assuming (optional) index assignment to **que** in the environment:

[$_{NP}$ **NP**$_i$[$_{\bar{S}}$[$_{COMP}$ **que**] ...]] (COMP may also contain a null *wh*-phrase, as in (30)), and 'marked' index assignment in the environment: [$_{COMP}$ **NP$_i$ que**]. Index assignment is, furthermore, a necessary condition for the appearance of complementiser **qui**.

In (25), *Il faut tout qui soit détruit, L-Tous moves **tout** from the embedded $\bar{S}$ into the matrix. The question, then, is whether the derived structure of (25) corresponds to either of the environments that permit index assignment to the complementiser. We note first that it is not clear that moved **tout** is a NP. But even if it were, there would still be good reason to think that the structure of (25) matches neither of the index-assigning environments. This is so, since to produce one of the required environments, L-Tous would have to either place **tout** in COMP or left-adjoin it to $\bar{S}$.[28] Presumably, if L-Tous could have such an effect in (25), it could do the same in simple sentences. Yet (40a) is ungrammatical — as opposed to (40b):

(40) a. *Tout elle comprend.
      b. Elle comprend tout.
          She understands everything.

Essentially, **tout** can be moved only into adverbial positions (Kayne, 1975, sect. 1.3). Similarly, (42) is impossible, alongside (41):

(41) Qu'elle comprenne tout, cela va de soi.
      That she understands everything, that's self-evident.
(42) *Tout qu'elle comprenne, cela va de soi.

Tout in (42) contrasts also with the preposed *wh*-phrase of (43):

(43) Quoi qu'elle fasse, Jean sera contre.
      Whatever she does, John will be against (it).

(In the same way, (40) contrasts with simple *wh*-interrogatives, e.g. **Où elle va?** (*Where is she going?*).) We conclude from such examples that L-Tous can neither place **tout** in COMP nor adjoin it to $\bar{S}$.[29] Consequently, the application of L-Tous to **Il faut que tout soit détruit** cannot produce a structure meeting the conditions for index assignment.[30] Whence the ungrammaticality of (25), and the desired distinction, with respect to **que/qui**, between L-Tous and *Wh* Movement, i.e. between (25) and (24).

Notes

* We are grateful to Guglielmo Cinque, Joseph Emonds, Frank Heny, Jean-Yves Pollock, Knut Tarald Taraldsen and Jean-Roger Vergnaud for their helpful comments. Section 1.1 of the present article is essentially the same as section 1 of Kayne (1978).

1. Kayne (1975, *passim*, e.g. 272, 286–7, 328n, 414–15). The relevance of the SSC to clitic placement in Portuguese and Italian has since been argued for by Quicoli (1976a) and Rizzi (1978b) respectively. The presentation of the SSC in Kayne (1975) was in pre-trace theory terms, although it was obliquely indicated there (pp. 293n, 309n) that the essential SSC ideas could be transposed straightforwardly into trace theory. (Quicoli (1976a) and Rizzi (1978b) are explicitly in terms of trace theory).

2. Given Chomsky's (1980) definition of 'free' (in his (111)) it should also be the case that le_i c-commands the anaphor (i.e. its trace). Since the first branching category α_1 dominating le_i is V: ... [$_V$ **le manger**] NP ... (see Kayne, 1975, sect. 2.5), we must allow for c-command as in Reinhart (1976, p. 148). That is, we must allow the possibility of counting for the determination of c-command α_2, the category immediately dominating α_1, where α_2 is of the same category type as α_1. If there exist cases such as: [$_V$[$_V$[$_V$ clitic$_i$ V] ...] [$_{\beta_i}$ e]], e.g. locatives or extrapositions, then we would want c-command to allow a(ny) number of α_i of the same category type.

3. Apart from the causative construction. There too, the SSC/opacity condition provides a revealing account (see Kayne, 1975 and Rouveret and Vergnaud, 1980).

4. That motivation had to do with the structural description of L-Tous and the (then assumed, but no longer valid) terminal character of the *to* be deleted subject (see Pollock, 1978 and Chomsky, 1977).

5. With the consequence that the grammaticality of the Portuguese, Italian, and Spanish equivalents of (4) cannot be attributed to a deletion rule either, as had been proposed by Quicoli (1976a). (Certain difficulties with Quicoli's specific proposal are discussed by Radford, 1977.) A more likely correct approach would seem to be that of Rizzi (1976, 1978b) and/or Zubizarreta (1978).

For example, Rizzi argues that the grammar of Italian contains a 'restructuring rule', the application of which is a prerequisite to the generation of (the equivalent of) (4). From this point of view, we can say that French differs from Italian precisely in lacking such a rule. (This rule would have to be learned from the data, if children learning French did not spontaneously utter (4). This would be of interest for the (statistical) interpretation of markedness, if most languages with clitic placement were like Italian.) This way of localising the difference between French and Italian is supported by the absence in French of **Je suis **voulu partir**, with the auxiliary switch argued by Rizzi to be correlated with restructuring. Note especially that that construction did exist in French before the seventeenth century (see Gougenheim (1971, p. 172)), as of course did (4). Thus these two changes can likely be reduced to one, namely the loss of the restructuring rule.

The application of that rule in Italian, Spanish, and Portuguese requires a controlled subject, whence the impossibility even in those languages of the equivalent of (8).

6. The ordering account given in Kayne (1975, pp. 24, 272, 309) depended on the SSC being a condition on rule application (as in Chomsky (1973)). The opacity condition, since it applies at LF, is incompatible with such an ordering account. In any case, the particular extrinsic ordering that we used (the deletion rule was extrinsically ordered after Cl-Pl, but not L-Tous) did not follow from any more general principle(s), so that little light was shed on the question of why (3) and (4) differ.

7. It seems clear that **tout** and **rien** are really in the matrix in (7): ?**Il a tout fallu que je leur enlève, ?Il n'a rien fallu que je fasse**.

For the speakers in question, (7) is perfectly acceptable. The '?' indicates that for others, (7) is unacceptable, probably for reasons related to ?**Je ne veux que tu voies personne** versus **Je ne veux voir personne** (*I NEG want to see no one*), though we won't pursue this similarity here; see Kayne (forthcoming, Note 1) for relevant discussion.

8. Contrary to Quicoli (1976b, sect. 2.5). We are in agreement here with Pollock (1978, p. 108). Pollock's (p. 110n) proposal is, modulo the difference in framework, fairly similar to our own below. On the fact that (7) and (3) share a certain sensitivity to the choice of matrix verb (supporting the decision to treat them uniformly) see Pollock (sect. 3) and Kayne (1978, appendix).

9. A definition of c-command is given in Chomsky (1980) in the text above his (17); see also note 2 to the present paper.

10. Non-floating **tous** and *all*, that is **tous** and *all* within a larger NP in subject or object position, as in *All of my friends have left*, seem clearly not to be anaphors. Compare our parenthesised remark below that, in essence, the anaphoricity of **tous** is simply one way of linking **tous** to an argument position.

11. Rather than the clitic itself, since it seems more natural to have **tous** bind an argument position, and since we want to bring out the parallelism with **ces garçons, que mon ami a tous voulu revoir** (see Kayne, 1975, sect. 1.2), and with ?**Marie a tous voté pour** (*Mary has voted for all (of them)*); in the latter, noted by Ruwet (1978, p. 204), we assume a null NP object of **pour**, presumably PRO, as in **Marie a voté pour**.

12. There exist sentences like **Elle a tout mangé le(s) gâteau(x)**; we assume, as in Kayne (1975, sect. 1.5), that these (and perhaps the example of note 40 there) involve an adverbial (i.e. neither anaphor nor quantifier) **tout**.

Although anaphoric 'tous' can be excluded in (16) because **tous** there is not *c*-commanded by **ses/tes amis**, the same does not hold for ****Marie a promis de revoir tous bientôt ses amis**, ****Marie a voulu revoir ses amis tous**. These may indicate that '*c*-command' is not a sufficiently restrictive necessary condition for antecedent-anaphor configurations (see Kayne (in preparation)).

13. In standard French, non-null pronominal NP's pattern here with (16), not with (9): ****Marie s'est tous présentée à eux**. (I. Haïk has pointed out the non-standard (third person) ??**J'ai tous voté pour eux**.)

Dissymmetry between (trace of) clitic and non-clitic pronoun also occurs with 'disjoint reference': **Jean$_i$ a parlé de lui$_i$** versus ****Jean$_i$ lui$_i$ parle**. This perhaps suggests a different approach to (16), excludable if non-null non-pronominal NPs have to be free not only with respect to *c*-commanding arguments, but also with respect to c-commanding floating **tous**. Disjoint reference for (traces of) clitics in French would then have to be blind to the latter, to allow (9). Compare the insufficiency of **tous** as a binder for the clitic trace in ****Marie les voudrait avoir tous lus d'ici un an**. Similarly disjoint reference would be blind to **tous** for *wh*-traces and PRO, given note 11.

A disjoint reference approach to (16) would have something in common with that of Fauconnier (1971, Chs. III–2, V–1), Baltin (1978), and especially Milner (1973, pp. 137–40); all note, explicitly or implicitly, the consequence that the directionality of **tous** movement need not be stipulated (unlike the approach to (16) of Kayne (1975, sect. 1.10) — cf. note 4 above); ideally, we would like to subsume L-Tous under 'Move α' (Chomsky (1980). Compare Chomsky (1977, p. 77).)

14. Thus reflexives and pronouns are different from *wh*-traces and the traces of **tout** and **rien** insofar as these traces derive their status as non-anaphors precisely from their being bound variables (or phrases containing bound variables — see Chomsky, 1977, pp. 83–4). The crucial difference thus seems to be between 'being' and 'being (derivatively) interpreted as'; cf. also Higginbotham (1978/9).

15. For example, the NIC, but not the filter, approach can give a reasonable account of the contrast between (23) and **Que veux-tu que fasse Marie?** (*What do you want Mary to do?*).

16. The ECP applies to all **e**, independently of questions of anaphoricity. In Kayne

(1981a), we suggest a modification of the ECP which introduces the notion of co-indexing, i.e. of binding, into the 'lexical category' part of the ECP; this makes the ECP uniformly sensitive to the notion of binding, and so emphasises a certain continuity between the NIC and the ECP (for example, our 1979/80 NIC proposal transposes fairly straightforwardly into the ECP framework).

17. **Il ne faut rien qui tombe** is possible but only with **qui tombe** a relative on **rien**.

18. Other arguments are given in Kayne (1975, 2.10). For a study of some perhaps related constructions, see Rothenberg (1971).

19. The same idea was available within the SSC framework — see Kayne (1976, note 20) and Williams (1975). The reading of (28) in which PRO is controlled by the matrix subject lies outside the scope of this article.

20. For ease of exposition, we shall speak of the trace of *Wh* Movement as being subject to the NIC, as in Chomsky (1980), rather than to the ECP. Since both these principles in effect require that the trace in subject position have an antecedent within S̄, the distinction can be overlooked for this discussion of the **que/qui** rule.

21. Actually, Pesetsky proposes that the trace in COMP is deleted; we shall assume, rather, that it is present and that it is not a proper antecedent for the subject trace because the non-null **qui** prevents it from *c*-commanding the subject trace (v. Kayne, 1981a). Treating this **qui** as a complementiser allows one to maintain the phonological generalisation discussed by Tranel (1978, sect. 4.3.2) (the analysis considered in Kayne (1978, sect. 2) of **qui** did not). Indexed complementisers are also proposed in Borer (1979). Bresnan and Grimshaw's (1978, sect. 7) indexed COMP nodes may exist, if the percolating index leaves a copy on the node COMP, but we would not expect a COMP$_i$ to be a possible antecedent for an empty category or for an anaphor (nor to be relevant to Kayne and Pollock's (1978) 'stylistic inversion', although indexed complementisers might be).

22. In the framework of Chomsky (1981, forthcoming), this analysis of (26) implies either that it is S̄ rather than S that is the minimal governing category for subject NPs, or that the PRO following **qui**$_i$ is ungoverned. The introduction of indexing means that to exclude (27), the opacity condition would have to require an antecedent within S, not S̄ (cf. Freidin and Lasnik (1979)); in Chomsky's 'Pisa' framework, it emphasises that the minimal governing category of an NP governed by V is S, not S̄.

23. On this configuration, compare Koster (1978, p. 105). In essence, the question is when S̄ can fail to act as a barrier to government. In Kayne (1981a), it is suggested that certain such instances must involve the assignment of a government index (in the sense of Rouveret and Vergnaud, 1980) from V to S̄. From this viewpoint, we should probably say that a complementiser can receive an index from a NP outside S̄ only via percolation down from the S̄ node, with S̄ able to receive an index from NP only in the configuration at hand.

24. If so, then in **C'est Jean qui est là** (*It's John who's there*), the source of the index must be **Jean**. This suggests that the environment for index assignment should be generalised to [$_\alpha$ NP S̄], or perhaps to [$_\alpha$ X̄ S̄]; cf. the notion of 'predication' in the reference of note 27.

The absence of **Marie a la possibilité qui$_i$ parte* is straightforward. That of **J'ai convaincu Marie qui parte* follows from the fact that the NP-S̄ sequence there is not a constituent.

25. Gross (1968, p. 124) notes that the embedded S̄ in (the equivalent of) (26) cannot have an auxiliary: **Je le vois qui a travaillé*. This recalls Akmajian's (1977, p. 431) **I heard Mary having played my song*, while vitiating his argument, given the Tensed S̄ in French (cf. Gee (1977, p. 463)). M.-R. Manzini tells us that similar tense and auxiliary restrictions are found in an Italian construction which does not impose 'obligatory control', **L'ho visto che pioveva** (*I saw him that it was raining*).

26. Pursuing this parallelism between (26), (28) and relative clause structures, we note the existence of the -ant form in relative-like **Tout homme ayant plus de six**

enfants ... (*Any man having more than six children* ...), as well as the need to analyse **Elle était là qui pleurait comme une Madeleine** as congruent to relative clause extraposition. The apparent obligatoriness of extraposition here recalls Rouveret (1978, sect. 2.2) and perhaps Chomsky and Lasnik (1977, pp. 464ff.), in which case *a man to fix the sink* might be control rather than *Wh* Movement. It is possible that (26), (28) also involve extraposition.

Both (26) and (28) may be incompatible with the absolute version of the A/A principle. However, it may be possible to duplicate the results obtained by that principle for PPs in Kayne (1975, sects. 2.7, 2.8) by means of the more general ECP (see Kayne, 1981a); that the ECP would provide a deeper account is strongly suggested by the fact that the A/A had to be limited to extractions (Kayne (1975, Ch. 2, pp. 183ff. and fn 76; and Ch. 5, pp. 55ff.)), in effect to empty categories.

The ungrammaticality of *Je le connais, qui est intelligent may be related to the fact that relative clauses cannot have anaphoric heads: *John believes himself, who I find intolerable, to be quite pleasant. Perhaps the anaphoric status of the head is transmitted to the *wh*-phrase, whose governing category is that of its trace.

Returning to the -*ant* form, we note that it does not occur as widely as English -*ing*: *I thought about leaving* versus *J'ai pensé à partant*; *Leaving is no fun* versus *Partant n'est pas drôle*. This wider distribution for -*ing* suggests that English *I heard John leaving* could be V-S̄ (cf. Kayne, forthcoming, Note II), perhaps in addition to V-[$_{NP}$ NP S̄]. This would allow *the woman who I heard John praising*, which contrasts with (34). [$_{NP}$ NP S̄] may be appropriate for ??*the woman who I've often watched him imitating* (cf. Gee, 1975, p. 368).

The [$_{NP}$ NP S̄] analysis reduces **avec son mari buvant/qui boit comme un trou** (with her husband drinking like a fish) (Ruwet (1978)) from P NP S̄ to P NP, and makes **Ce que j'ai vu, c'est ton frère qui courait à toute vitesse** (Ruwet, 1978, note 12) look like a normal pseudo-cleft.

27. Cf. Chomsky (1977, pp. 81, 92) on relatives, dislocation and topicalisation. *Je l$_i$'ai rencontré qu'elle$_i$ sortait du cinéma is like *la fille$_i$ que tu lui$_i$ as parle, in standard French.

The [$_{NP}$ NP S̄] analysis of (26), (28) accounts straightforwardly for the uniform optionality of that S̄ (Kayne (1975, Ch. 2, fn. 75)), and perhaps, too, for the absence of any corresponding construction with a dative clitic (by relating it to the lack of non-null, non-clitic prepositionless datives in French).

28. Left-adjunction would yield [$_S$ **tout** S̄], a relevant possibility, given note 24.

29. There might be adjunction to S̄ in (43) (see Ruwet, 1975/6, sect. 2,I and Fradin, 1977).

This property of L-Tous should be compared to the absence of any systematic syntactic counterpart to May's (1977) QR.

The assumption that successive cyclic movement through COMP is limited to phrases of a type that can normally appear in COMP also plays a role in the relative extractability of **combien** and **beaucoup** (see Kayne, 1981a).

30. Recall that index assignment is a necessary condition for the appearance of complementiser **qui**, not a sufficient one. For two approaches to specifying when (in our terms) an indexed complementiser is to be spelled as **qui**, see Milner (1979, p. 110) and Taraldsen (1978). (When the sufficient condition holds, the indexed complementiser can then not appear as **que**, as seen in (23), *Je l'ai rencontré que sortait du cinéma and *la fille que viendra demain. All three constitute NIC/ECP violations if the indexing rule is not applied.) (The optimal sufficient condition will insure that **qui** cannot appear in **les choses que dira Jean** (*the things that John will say*): *les choses qui dira Jean.)

References

Akmajian, A. (1977), 'The Complement Structure of Perception Verbs in an Autonomous Syntax Framework' in P. W. Culicover, T. Wasow, A. Akmajian (eds.), *Formal Syntax*, Academic Press, New York, 427–60

Baltin, M. R. (1978), *Toward a Theory of Movement Rules*, Doctoral dissertation, Massachusetts Institute of Technology, Cambridge, Massachusetts

Borer, H. (1979), 'Restrictive Relative Clauses in Modern Hebrew', unpublished paper, Massachusetts Institute of Technology

Bresnan, J. and J. Grimshaw (1978), 'The Syntax of Free Relatives in English', *Linguistic Inquiry* 9, 331–91

Chomsky, N. (1973), 'Conditions on Transformations' in S. Anderson and P. Kiparsky (eds.), *A Festschrift for Morris Halle*, Holt, Reinhart & Winston, New York, 232–86

——— (1976), 'Conditions on Rules of Grammar', *Linguistic Analysis* 2, 303–51

——— (1977), 'On Wh Movement' in P. W. Culicover, T. Wasow and A. Akmajian (eds.), *Formal Syntax*, Academic Press, NY, 71–132

——— (1980), 'On Binding', this volume. Previously published in *Linguistic Inquiry* 11, 1–46

——— (forthcoming-a), 'Markedness and Core Grammar' in A. Belletti, L. Brandi, G. Nencioni and L. Rizzi (eds.), *Theory of Markedness in Generative Grammar — Proceedings of the III GLOW Conference*

——— (1981), *Lectures on Government and Binding*, Foris, Dordrecht

Chomsky, N. and H. Lasnik (1977), 'Filters and Control', *Linguistic Inquiry* 8, 425–504

Fauconnier, G. (1971), *Theoretical Implications of Some Global Phenomena in Syntax*, Doctoral dissertation, University of California, San Diego. Published by Garland, New York, 1979

Fradin, B. (1977), *Les concessives extensionnelles en français moderne*, Thèse de doctorat de troisième cycle, Université de Paris VIII, Vincennes

Freidin, R. and H. Lasnik (1979), 'Disjoint Reference and Core Grammar', unpublished paper

Gee, J. P. (1975), *Perception, Intentionality, and Naked Infinitives: A Study in Linguistics and Philosophy*, Doctoral dissertation, Stanford University, Palo Alto, California

——— (1977), 'Comments on the Paper by Akmajian' in P. W. Culicover, T. Wasow, and A. Akmajian (eds.), *Formal Syntax*, Academic Press, New York, 461–81

Gougenheim, G. (1971), *Etudes sur les périphrases verbales de la langue française*, Nizet, Paris

Gross, M. (1968), *Grammaire transformationnelle du français: syntaxe du verbe*, Larousse, Paris

Higginbotham, J. (1978/9), 'Pronouns and Bound Variables', *CUNYForum* 5–6 (NELS 9), 304–27

Kayne, R. S. (1975), *French Syntax*, MIT Press, Cambridge, Massachusetts

——— (1976), 'French relative "que"' in F. Hensey and M. Luján (eds.), *Current Studies in Romance Linguistics*, Georgetown University Press, Washington, DC, 255–99

——— (1978), 'Le condizioni sul legamento, il Collocamento dei clitici e lo Spostamento a sinistra dei quantificatori', *Rivista di Grammatica Generativa* 3, 147–71

——— (1979/80), 'Extensions du liage et du marquage du cas', *Lingvisticae Investigationes* 3, 29–55; 'Extensions of Binding and Case-Marking', *Linguistic Inquiry* 11, 75–96

————— (1981a), ECP, *Extensions, Linguistic Inquiries*, 12, 93–133

————— (1981b), 'Unambiguous Paths' in J. Koster and R. May (eds.), *Levels of Syntactic Representation*, Foris, Dordrecht

————— (forthcoming), 'Two Notes on the NIC' in A. Belletti, L. Brandi, G. Nencioni and L. Rizzi (eds.), *Theory of Markedness in Generative Grammar — Proceedings of the III GLOW Conference*

Kayne, R. S. and J.-Y. Pollock (1978), 'Stylistic Inversion, Successive Cyclicity, and Move NP in French', *Linguistic Inquiry* 9, 595–621

Koster, J. (1978), *Locality Principles in Syntax*, Foris, Dordrecht

May, R. (1977), *The Grammar of Quantification*, Doctoral dissertation, Massachusetts Institute of Technology, Cambridge, Massachusetts

Milner, J.-C. (1973), *Arguments linguistiques*, Mame, Tours

————— (1979), 'La redondance fonctionnelle', *Lingvisticae Investigationes* 3, 87–145

Moreau, M.-L. (1971), 'L'homme que je crois qui est venu; qui, que: relatifs et conjonctions', *Langue Française* 11, 77–90

Pesetsky, D. (1979), 'Complementizer-Trace Phenomena and the Nominative Island Condition', unpublished paper, Massachusetts Institute of Technology, Cambridge, Massachusetts

Pollock, J.-Y. (1978), 'Trace Theory and French Syntax' in S. J. Keyser (ed.), *Recent Transformational Studies in European Languages*, MIT Press, Cambridge, Massachusetts, 65–112

Quicoli, A. C. (1976a), 'Conditions on Clitic Movement in Portuguese', *Linguistic Analysis* 2, 199–223

————— (1976b), 'Conditions on Quantifier Movement in French', *Linguistic Inquiry* 7, 583–607

Radford, A. (1977), 'La teoria della traccia, la condizione del soggetto specificato e la salita dei pronomi clitici nelle lingue romanze', *Rivista di Grammatica Generativa* 2, 241–315

Reinhart, T. (1976), *The Syntactic Domain of Anaphora*, Doctoral dissertation, Massachusetts Institute of Technology, Cambridge, Massachusetts

Rizzi, L. (1976), 'Ristrutturazione', *Rivista di Grammatica Generativa* 1, 1–54

————— (1978a), 'Violations of the *Wh* Island Constraint in Italian and the Subjacency Condition' in *Montreal Working Papers Linguistics*, 10

————— (1978b), 'A Restructuring Rule in Italian Syntax' in S. J. Keyser (ed.), *Recent Transformational Studies in European Languages*, MIT Press, Cambridge, Massachusetts, 113–58

Ross, J. R. (1967), *Constraints on Variables in Syntax*, Doctoral dissertation, Massachusetts Institute of Technology, Cambridge, Massachusetts

Rothenberg, M. (1971), 'Les propositions relatives à antécédent explicite introduites par des présentatifs', *Etudes de Linguistique Appliquée*, nouvelle série, no. 2, 102–17

Rouveret, A. (1978), 'Result Clauses and Conditions on Rules' in S. J. Keyser (ed.), *Recent Transformational Studies in European Languages*, MIT Press, Cambridge, Massachusetts, 159–87

Rouveret, A. and J.-R. Vergnaud (1980), 'Specifying Reference to the Subject: French Causatives and Conditions on Representations', *Linguistic Inquiry* 11, 97–102

Ruwet, N. (1975/6), 'Montée du sujet et extraposition', *Le Français Moderne* 43, 97–134; 'Subject Raising and Extraposition' in F. Hensey and M. Luján (eds.), *Current Studies in Romance Linguistics*, Georgetown University Press, Washington, DC

————— (1978), 'Une construction absolue en français', *Lingvisticae Investigationes* 2, 165–210

Taraldsen, K. T. (1978), 'On the NIC, Vacuous Application and the That-Trace Filter', unpublished paper

Tranel, B. (1978), 'On the Elision of [i] in French *qui*', *Studies in French Linguistics* 1, 53–74

Williams, E. S. (1975), 'Small Clauses in English' in J. Kimball (ed.), *Syntax and Semantics* 4, Seminar Press, New York

———— (1977), 'Discourse and Logical Form', *Linguistic Inquiry* 8, 101–39

Zubizarreta, M.-L. (1978), 'Pour une restructuration sémantique', Mémoire de Maîtrise, Université de Paris VIII, Vincennes

6 Government and Relativisation in Celtic

Stephen Harlow

0. Introduction: Conditions on Relative Deletion

In this paper I shall be discussing the syntax of relative clauses and related constructions in literary Welsh. These constructions present a number of complex descriptive problems and I will try to show how, although a number of details remain to be worked out, some recent proposals of Chomsky's (1980 and forthcoming a and forthcoming b) lead to a more explanatory account than earlier work (cf. Awbery 1977). Relative clauses in Welsh are syntactically similar in many respects to the corresponding constructions in a related language, Irish, studied by McCloskey (1978) and I will borrow heavily from McCloskey's work in the discussion which follows. I will not be primarily concerned with Irish, but I think that the analysis that I will propose here for Welsh does in fact carry over to Irish in essential respects and I shall draw frequent comparisons with Irish, although any conclusions I come to about Irish should be treated as somewhat more tentative.

Welsh relative clauses show the following characteristics: when the position relativised on is a subject or a direct object of a finite clause, the relative clause contains a 'gap' and the complementiser of the relative clause is **a**:[1]

(1) *Subject*
y dyn [ₛ a werthodd _____ y byd]
the man COMP sold the world
the man who sold the world

(2) *Object*
y llong [ₛ a werthodd y dyn _____]
the boat COMP sold the man
the boat that the man sold

213

When the position relativised on is the object of a preposition or is in a possessive NP a resumptive pronoun occurs in the relativisation site and the complementiser is **y/yr**:

(3) *Object of preposition*
    y   dyn [s y   siaradasoch chwi ag   **ef**]
    the man COMP talked   you with him
    the man that you talked with
(4) *Possessive NP*
    y   dyn [s yr   oedd **ei** fam   gartref]
    the man COMP was   his mother at-home
    the man whose mother was at home

These data are reminiscent of the examples from Irish discussed by McCloskey (1978), in which we find a pattern of relativisation parallel to (1)–(4) (taken from McCloskey, 1978: Ch. 2):

(5) *Irish*
  a. *Subject*
    an fear [s aL   dhíol ____ an domhan]
    the man COMP sold   the world
    the man who sold the world
  b. *Object*
    an bád [s aL   dhíol an fear ____][2]
    the boat COMP sold the man
    the boat that the man sold
  c. *Object of preposition*
    an fear [s aN   dtabharann tú   an t-airgead **dó**]
    the man COMP give   you the money   to-him
    the man that you gave the money to
  d. *Possessive NP*
    an fear [s aN   bhfuil **a**   mháthair sa bhaile]
    the man COMP is   his mother   at home
    the man whose mother is at home

The one difference so far between Welsh and Irish is that a 'gap' is the only possibility in affirmative relative clauses in Welsh when a direct object is relativised (cf. 2). Irish, however, allows an alternative to (6a), in which a resumptive pronoun occurs in the relativisation site and the complementiser is aN, (6b):

(6) *Irish*

    a. an scríbhneoir [$_S$ aL   mholann na mic-léinn _____]
       the writer   COMP praise   the students

    b. an scríbhneoir [$_S$ aN   molann na mic-léinn é]
       the writer   COMP praise   the students
       the writer who the students praise

A resumptive *subject* pronoun, however, in either (1) or (5a), is ungrammatical:

(7) a. *Welsh* *y dyn [$_S$ y   gwerthodd **ef** y byd
           the man COMP sold   he the world

    b. *Irish* *an fear [$_S$ a   ddiolan **sé** an domhan]
           the man COMP sells   he the world
           the man who sold the world

In view of these similarities between Welsh and Irish we can focus on the descriptive problems presented by these constructions by adopting initially the analysis proposed by McCloskey for the Irish examples. McCloskey argues that relative clauses in Irish do not involve *Wh* Movement and proposes a rule of Relative Deletion which deletes a pronoun co-indexed with the head NP, under certain conditions (McCloskey 1978: 50f):

(8) *Relative Deletion*

SD	X	NP$_j$	[Y	NP	Z]	W
				[+PRO]$_k$		
	1	2	3	4	5	6

SC	1	2	3	∅	5	6

Conditions: i   j=k
               ii. obligatory if term 4 is subject of its clause
               iii. optional if term 4 is direct object of its clause
               iv. blocks if term 4 is neither subject nor object of its clause

Accepting that Relative Deletion is also responsible for the corresponding Welsh data, we only need to change the conditions in (8) to:

(9) Conditions (for Welsh):
 i.   j=k (=8i)
 ii. obligatory if term 4 is subject or direct object of its clause
 iii. blocks if term 4 is neither subject nor object of its clause (=8iv)

McCloskey (1978: 127), discussing the Irish version of Relative Deletion, concedes that the conditions in (8) are 'not pretty' and suggests that 'in the best case we would like the facts that they were designed to handle to fall out as consequences of the interaction of the deletion rule with other, independently motivated, principles — either general principles belonging in the grammar of modern Irish or principles of Universal Grammar.'

In this paper, working with data drawn principally from Welsh, but drawing on McCloskey's examples in Irish, I will try to show how the proposals of Chomsky referred to above make it possible to dispense with the conditions on Relative Deletion in (8) and (9). The patterns of complementiser alternation and gap versus resumptive pronoun are a result of the interaction between a general principle of Welsh — and Irish — agreement — and a principle of Universal Grammar — the Empty Category Principle.

1. The Empty Category Principle

In 'On Binding' (p. 89, this volume) Chomsky (1980) points out that there is a difference in degree of unacceptability between (10) and (11):

(10)   *Who$_2$ [did you wonder [$_\bar{s}$ what$_1$ [t$_2$ saw t$_1$]]]
(11)   ?What$_1$ [did you wonder [$_\bar{s}$ who$_2$ [t$_2$ saw t$_1$]]]

Observing that (10) is noticeably worse than (11), Chomsky suggests in effect that the ungrammaticality of (10) is exacerbated by a violation that is on a par with that of (12):

(12)   *John seems [$_\bar{s}$ t will go]

That is, both (10) and (12) involve a violation of the Nominative Island Condition (NIC):

(13)   a nominative anaphor cannot be free in $\bar{S}$.

The subject traces in (10) and (12) are both free in $\bar{S}$ and hence violate the NIC. In (11), on the other hand, t_2 is bound by *who*$_2$ in S.

Other factors, however, motivate a reconsideration of (10) as an NIC violation, as Chomsky (forthcoming) points out. Firstly, there are languages, in which sentences like (10) are fully grammatical, while the analogue of (12) is still ungrammatical. Secondly, languages which permit sentences like (10) display a cluster of properties (which Chomsky terms the Residue of the NIC (RESNIC)) which languages not permitting (10) do not, such as 'long' *Wh* Movement, as in (10), free 'stylistic inversion', 'missing' subjects in simple finite clauses and violations of the '*that*-trace filter' (cf. Chomsky and Lasnik, 1977: 451). These facts lead Chomsky to propose that (12) is indeed a violation of NIC, but that (10) is the consequence of the violation of an independent principle of Universal Grammar, the Empty Category Principle (ECP):

(14) $[_{NP}\ e]$ must be governed

Government is defined in 15:[3]

(15) α governs β iff α minimally c-commands β and
        a. $\alpha = N, V, A, P$ ($=$ Lexical Government)
   OR   b. α is co-indexed with β

(Minimally c-commands $=_{def}$ α c-commands β and there is no γ such that α c-commands γ and γ c-commands β and γ does not c-command α.

In English, the ECP has the effect of restricting *Move NP* to positions in which an NP is governed under (15). If predicates such as *seem* are assigned the lexical property of deleting $\bar{S}$ (as proposed by Chomsky, 1981) the structure (16) resulting from *Move NP* is well formed because $[_{NP}\ e]$ is lexically governed by the verb *seem*:

(16)   There$_i$ seems $[_S [_{NP_i}\ e]$ to be a problem]

Predicates such as *want*, on the other hand, which do not permit $\bar{S}$ deletion, do not allow comparable structures resulting from *Move NP* because $[_{NP}\ e]$ is not governed by *wants* in 17 (since $\bar{S}$ intervenes):

(17)   *There$_i$ wants $[_S [_S [_{NP_i}\ e]$ to be a problem]]

Sentence (10) is excluded by the ECP since t_2 is not properly governed under (15b) by a co-indexed governor (i.e. trace or *wh*-word in COMP). In (11), however, t_2 *is* governed by *who*$_2$, so (11) is not a violation of the ECP.

The grammaticality of structures like (10) in Italian and the other RESNIC properties follow from (15b) and Chomsky's (1981) proposals about Agreement. Chomsky suggests that the basic expansion of S in Italian is (18):

(18) S   → NP INFL VP
      INFL → [±TENSE], AG

AG is an abbreviation for the features for Gender, Number and Person. NPs are divided into five types: i. full lexical NP; ii. [$_{NP}$ *e*]; iii. anaphors (i.e. NPs lexically stipulated as requiring an antecedent, such as *each other*); iv. Pronouns; v. PRO. Pronouns and PRO form the class of Pronominals, defined as NPs containing features for Gender, Number and Person (i.e. AG); Pronouns also contain a phonetic matrix; PRO does not.[4]

AG in (18) strictly sub-categorises a pronominal argument (i.e. Pronoun or PRO). In addition, AG may be indexed. The indexing of AG is, however, a parametric property of UG: Italian has indexed AG, French and English do not. 'Missing subjects' (one of the RESNIC phenomena) are the consequences of selecting PRO rather than Pronoun in the base, and the application of the (universal) rule of Delete PRO, which deletes the Case and Gender, Number and Person features of an indexed NP without a phonetic matrix (i.e. [$_{NP_i}$ AG[→[$_{NP_i}$ *e*]). The index assigned to PRO is however retained, giving the following derivation for Italian:[5]

(19) a. [$_S$ PRO[$_{INFL}$ AG] VP] (base)
      b. [$_S$ PRO$_i$ [$_{INFL}$ AG$_i$] VP] (indexing)
      c. [$_S$[$_{NP_i}$ *e*] [$_{INFL}$ AG$_i$] VP] (PRO-deletion)

[$_{NP_i}$ *e*] in (19c) is governed by the co-indexed AG, and thus does not violate the ECP (by 15b). Italian consequently permits 'missing subjects' without violation of the ECP because it allows indexing of AG. French and English, in contrast, do not permit indexing of AG in (19), so deletion of a PRO subject would be a violation of the ECP, since the resulting [$_{NP}$ *e*] would not be properly governed.

Chomsky extends this theory of agreement to object clitics (e.g. in

French and Italian), arguing that these are of the form:

(20) [$_V$ AG V]   (AG=Clitic)

The 'missing' pronominal object in a sentence such as (21a) is the consequence of strict subcategorisation for PRO, indexing and PRO deletion; the derivation of (21a) being (21b–d):

(21) a. Je le voyais
      b. Je [$_V$ le voyais] PRO
      c. Je [$_V$ le$_i$ voyais] PRO$_i$ (indexing)
      d. Je [$_V$ le$_i$ voyais] [$_{NP_i}$ e] (PRO-deletion)

In (21d), [$_{NP}$ e] is properly governed by the co-indexed AG **le**, in accordance with the ECP (15b).

2. Agreement in Welsh

In this section I shall show that co-indexing of AG, PRO-deletion and the ECP correctly account for 'missing subjects' and for a number of other cases of 'missing NPs' in Welsh. Welsh shows subject-verb agreement in simple finite clauses (22) and also freely allows null subject-pronouns in such sentences:

(22) a. Darllen-ais i y   llyfr[6]
          read   -1S I the book
      b. Darllen-ais y   llyfr
          read   -1S the book
          I read the book

The possibility of (22b) is predicted under the theory outlined above if it is assigned the structure (23), giving (23b) after indexing and PRO-deletion:

(23) a. [$_S$ darllen [$_{INFL}$ AG] PRO y llyfr]
      b. [$_S$ darllen [$_{INFL}$ AG$_i$] [$_{NP_i}$ e] y llyfr]

[$_{NP}$ e] in (23b) is properly governed by the co-indexed AG, in accordance with the ECP. A pronominal object in sentences like (22) is not governed by AG and the ECP correctly predicts that [$_{NP}$ e] cannot appear in such a position:

(24) a. darllen-ais i ef
          read   -1S I it (masc)
      b. *darllen-ais i [NP *e*]
          I read it

Like French and Italian, Welsh also has object clitics (with non-finite verbs only). Again assuming the structure (20), indexing and PRO deletion, the ECP correctly predicts a missing pronominal object only when the governing clitic is present (cf. (25b) and (25c)):

(25) a. yr   oedd-wn i [VP yn ei   ddarllen ef]^7
          COMP was -1S I prt   AG3MS read   it (masc)
      b. yr oedd-wn i[VP yn [V ei$_i$ ddarllen] [NP$_i$ *e*]]
      c. *yr oedd-wn i [VP yn [V darllen] [NP *e*]]
          I was reading it

Welsh has an additional agreement context in which the predictions of the ECP can be tested directly: prepositions can agree with their pronominal objects, but in this case agreement is a lexically determined property — there are some prepositions which do not have agreement forms. **Am** (about), for example, agrees with its pronominal objects. Compare (26a) where **am** does not agree with its 'full' NP object with (26b) where it carries the 3MS suffix -**o**:

(26) a. soniais i am   y   dyn
          talked I about the man
          I talked about the man
      b. soniais i amdan-o   ef^8
          talked I about-3MS him
          I talked about him

As we have seen above, the ECP predicts that the presence of the 3MS AG in (26b) allows a null pronoun in (26), and such is in fact the case:

(27) soniais i [PP[P[P amdan-] o$_i$]] [NP$_i$ *e*]]
                              AG

In contrast, the preposition **â** (with) does not have an agreement form. Compare (28a) and (28b):

(28) a. euthum i â   Mair i'r   sinema
          went   I with Mary to the cinema
          I took Mary to the movies
      b. euthum i â   hi i'r   sinema
          went   I with her to the cinema
          I took her to the movies

In (28b) â with a pronominal object has the same form as in (28a) where the object is a full NP (cf. (26a) and (26b)). Sentence (28b) consequently allows no null pronoun after â:

(29) *euthum i â [$_{NP}$ e] i'r sinema

since [$_{NP}$ e] is not governed by a co-indexed AG and violates the ECP.

There is one further situation in which agreement occurs: possessive NPs in Welsh take the following form, in which the 'possessor' NP follows the head:

(30) [$_{NP}$ Mab [$_{NP}$ y   dyn]]
          son   the man
      the man's son

If the possessor NP is pronominal, an agreeing clitic appears in the determiner position of the outer NP:

(31) [$_{NP}$[$_{DET}$ ei] fab ef][9]
      AG3MS   son he
      his son

In (31), as expected, the pronoun **ef** is optional:

(32) [$_{NP}$[$_{DET}$ ei$_i$] fab [$_{NP_i}$ e]]

The ECP is satisfied in (32) if **ei** and [$_{NP}$ e] are co-indexed and the governor in (32) is **ei**. We only need to allow DET in Welsh to subcategorise a pronominal complement.

To sum up so far, the theory outlined above (the ECP, indexed AG and PRO deletion) correctly predicts the optionality of pronouns in a large variety of constructions in Welsh in a unified way. The only language particular stipulations that are necessary are the lexical properties of INFL, verbs, prepositions and determiners.

3. Relative Clauses and Related Constructions

I shall argue below that the agreement properties discussed above are all that is needed to account for the facts covered by McCloskey's conditions on Relative Deletion in both Welsh and Irish, but first it is necessary to state some basic assumptions about the analysis of Relative Clauses and *wh*-questions in Welsh. Slightly modifying McCloskey's analysis and notation, I am assuming that the grammar of Welsh contains the Phrase Structure Rules in (33):

(33) a. $\bar{\bar{S}} \rightarrow \bar{X}\ \bar{S}$ (Where $\bar{X}$ = NP, PP, VP, AP)[10]
     b. $\bar{S} \rightarrow$ COMP S
     c. $S \rightarrow$ INFL NP VP
     d. VP $\rightarrow$ V (NP) (PP)
     e. NP $\rightarrow$ NP $(\bar{S})$
     f. INFL $\rightarrow$ {TENSE, AG}

Rule (33c) together with the local transformation (34) ('local' in the sense of Emonds, 1976), accounts for the difference in word order between tensed and non-tensed clauses:

(34)   TENSE NP V $\Rightarrow$ 3 + 1 2 $\emptyset$[11]

Rule (34) preposes a verb immediately to the right of the subject NP into initial position in a tensed sentence, giving the subordinate clause word order contrast in (35a) and (35b):

(35) a. disgwyliais i [$_S$ yr ennillai   John]
       expected   I that would-win John
       I expected that John would win.
     b. disgwyliais i [$_S$ i John ennill]
       expected   I for John win
       I expected John to win.

Example (35b) exhibits the base order defined by (33), in which the subject of the lower clause **John** precedes the non-finite verb **ennill**; (35a) is the result of the application of verb preposing (34):

(36)   ... [$_S$ yr [$_S$ [$_{INFL}$-ai] John [$_{VP}$ ennill]]

Rule (34) is optional; if it does not apply, a grammatical formative

gwneud (in the sense of Emonds, (1979: 27)) is inserted to the left of INFL. In (37a) the rule has applied; in (37b) **gwneud** has been inserted.

(37) a. ennill-odd John

won-PAST John
John won
  b. gwnaeth John ennill
      'did'   *John win*

I will not embark on a detailed justification of the Phrase Structures rules in (33) but will restrict myself to pointing out some of the consequences. The analysis provided by (33) makes it possible to capture the generalisation that relative clauses exhibit identical properties to *wh*-questions and 'cleft' sentences, when the constituent in 'pre-COMP' position is an NP. When the 'extraction' site is in subject or direct object position in these constructions, we find the characteristic patterning of the direct relatives (1) and (2): a gap in the extraction site and the presence of complementiser **a**.

(38) *Subject*
  a. Relative clause
      ... [$_{NP}$[$_{NP}$ y dyn] [$_S$ a   [$_S$ ddarllenodd ———— y   llyfr
           the man COMP read   the book
      ar y trên]]]
      on the train
      the man who read the book on the train
  b. *Wh*-question
      [$_S$[$_{NP}$ pa ddyn] [$_S$ a   [$_S$ ddarllenodd ———— y   llyfr
        which man   COMP read   the book
      ar y trên]]]
      on the train
      Which man read the book on the train?
  c. Cleft
      [$_S$[$_{NP}$ y dyn] [$_S$ a   [$_S$ ddarllenodd ———— y   llyfr
        the man COMP read   the book
      ar y trên]]]
      on the train
      (It was) the man who read the book on the train.

(39)   *Direct Object*
    a. Relative Clause
          ... [$_{NP}$[$_{NP}$ y   llyfr] [$_S$ a   [$_S$ ddarllenodd y dyn
                  the book COMP   read   the man
                  ——— ar y   trên]]]
                  on the train
          the book that the man read on the train
    b. *Wh*-question
          [$_{\bar{S}}$[$_{NP}$ pa   llyfr] [$_S$ a   [$_S$ ddarllenodd y dyn
                which book COMP   read   the man
                ——— ar y   trên]]]
                on the train
          Which book did the man read on the train?
    c. Cleft
          [$_{\bar{S}}$[$_{NP}$ y   llyfr] [$_S$ a   [$_S$ ddarllenodd y dyn
                the book COMP   read   the man
                ——— ar y   trên]]]
                on the train
          (It was) the book that the man read on the train.

If the 'extraction' site is the object of a preposition or in a possessive NP, all three constructions exhibit the properties of the indirect relatives (3) and (4): a resumptive pronoun in the extraction site and the complementiser **y**:

  (40)   *Prepositional Object*
      a. Relative Clause
          [$_{NP}$[$_{NP}$ y trên] [$_S$ y   [$_S$ darllenodd y dyn
                the train COMP   read   the man
          y   llyfr arno]]]
          the book on-it
          the train that the man read the book on
      b. *Wh*-question
          [$_{\bar{S}}$[$_{NP}$ pa   trên] [$_S$ y   [$_S$ darllenodd y dyn
                which train COMP   read   the man
          y   llfyr arno]]]
          the book on-it
          Which train did the man read the book on?
      c. Cleft
          [$_{\bar{S}}$[$_{NP}$ y trên] [$_S$ y   [$_S$ darllenodd y dyn
                the train COMP   read   the man

y llyfr arno]]]
the book on-it
(It was) the train that the man read the book on.

(41) *Possessive NP*

   a. Relative Clause
      [$_{NP}$[$_{NP}$ y dyn] [$_S$ y [$_S$ gwelais i ei fab]]]
         the man COMP saw I AG3MS son
      the man whose son I saw

   b. *Wh*-question
      [$_S$[$_{NP}$ pwy] [$_S$ y [$_S$ gwelais i ei fab]]]
         who COMP saw I AG3MS son
      Whose son did I see?

   c. Cleft
      [$_S$[$_{NP}$ y dyn] [$_S$ y [$_S$ gwelais i ei fab]]]
         the man COMP saw I AG3MS son
      (It was) the man whose son I saw.

However, since $\bar{\bar{S}}$ allows pre-COMP expansions of phrasal categories other than NP, *wh*-questions and clefts show additional possibilities not available in relative clauses. If $\bar{\bar{S}}$ is expanded as PP, we get (preferred) variants of (40b and c):

(42) a. *Wh*-question
      [$_S$[$_{PP}$ ar ba trên] [$_S$ y [$_S$ darllenodd y dyn
         on which train COMP read the man
      y llyfr ——]]]
      the book
      On which train did the man read the book?

   b. Cleft
      [$_S$[$_{PP}$ ar y trên] [$_S$ y [$_S$ darllenodd y
         on the train COMP read the
      dyn y llyfr ——]]]
      man the book
      (It was) on the train that the man read the book.

The sentences of (42) give the effect of pied-piping, but the base-generated analysis provided by (33) accounts automatically for the absence of any pied-piping possibility in relative clauses; that is, for the fact that there is no alternative to (40a) comparable to English *the train on which the man read the book*. A similar distinction in the case of possessive NPs is also accounted for

automatically by the base structures of (33). If the pre-COMP NP in
S̄ is a possessive NP, we again get the effects of pied-piping.

(43) a. *Wh*-question
    [$_\bar{S}$[$_{NP}$ mab pwy] [$_S$ a   [$_S$ welais i ——]]]
    son who COMP saw I
    Whose son did I see?
   b. Cleft
    [$_\bar{S}$[$_{NP}$ mab y dyn] [$_S$ a   [$_S$ welais i ——]]]
    son the man COMP saw I
    (It was) the man's son that I saw

I shall have nothing further to say here about clefts and *wh*-
questions with phrasal categories other than NP in pre-COMP
position and will concentrate, as a single phenomenon, on those
constructions which involve Relative Deletion, that is, constructions
with NP in pre-COMP position (whether they be relative clauses,
wh-questions or clefts).

4. Relative Deletion and Agreement

4.1 Indirect Relatives

McCloskey (1978) treats sentences such as (5c) (repeated here as (44))
as containing a resumptive pronoun, i.e. as cases where Relative
Deletion is blocked:

(44) *Irish*
    an fear [$_S$ aN dtabhrann tú an t-airgead dó]
    the man COMP give you the money to-him
    the man you give the money to

Superficially, relativisation on the objects of prepositions in Welsh
seems to show the same phenomenon (cf. 3, repeated here as (45)):

(45) y dyn [$_S$ y siaradasoch chwi ag *(ef)]
    the man COMP talked you with him
    the man that you talked with

However, the discussion of agreement above prompts a reconsideration of this interpretation of examples like (45). Recall that

there are two categories of preposition in Welsh: those which agree with their pronominal objects and those which do not. Both categories of preposition may be followed by a phonologically realised pronominal object:

(46) a. Non-agreeing
          siaradais i ag   ef
          spoke   I with him
          I spoke with him
      b. Agreeing
          soniais i amdan-o   ef
          talked I about-3MS him
          I talked about him

PRO-deletion was shown to be possible, in accordance with the ECP, in sentences with agreeing prepositions such as (46b), but not in sentences with non-agreeing prepositions, such as (46a) (cf. (28)–(31)). As (45) shows, Relative Deletion may not delete the pronoun **ef**. Relativisation on the prepositional object in (46b), however, produces a different result:

(47) y   dyn [s y   soniais i amdan-o (*ef)]
      the man COMP talked I about-3MS
      the man that I talked about

As (47) demonstrates, Relative Deletion does apply *when its output is properly governed under the ECP* (cf. (26) and (27)). It is apparent that the assumption that Relative Deletion in Welsh is subject to almost identical conditions on its application as those proposed by McCloskey for Irish (cf. (8) and (9)) is not as straightforward as the initial examples (1) through (5) would suggest. A direct application of the Irish conditions on Relative Deletion to Welsh would follow only if we were to interpret the agreeing preposition **amdano** in (47) as containing the pronoun analysed as term 4 of Relative Deletion (8), which is what McCloskey does for Irish. In Welsh, however, this interpretation of the victim of Relative Deletion is clearly inadequate: agreeing prepositions allow both the pronominal AG suffix (**-o** in the case of **amdano**) and a separate pronominal object (**ef** in (46b)). In non-relativisation contexts such as (46b), the pronominal object is optional (cf. the discussion of PRO-deletion above). In relativisation contexts however, such as (47), the pronominal object is impossible. If we continue with the assumption that Relative Deletion is responsible for the 'gaps' in relative clauses we have a straightforward account of the impossibility of a pronominal object in (47) — provided we take the 'missing' pronominal object and not the agreement suffix as satisfying term 4 of Relative Deletion. This discussion of relativisation on the objects of prepositions leads, then, to the following conclusion: Relative Deletion is obligatory, provided that its output does not violate the ECP. In other words, Relative Deletion is subject to exactly the same conditions as Delete-PRO, but is obligatory.

I will now show that this result, derived from a consideration of PPs, applies also to the objects of non-finite verbs and to possessive NPs (30) through (32)). Recall that the pronominal objects of non-finite verbs are subcategorised by a pro-clitic and that, in consequence, PRO-deletion may apply to give a 'null-pronoun' (cf. 25):

(48) a. yr   oeddwn i [$_{VP}$ yn darllen y   llyfr]
         COMP was   I   prt read   the book
         I was reading the book.

     b. yr   oeddwn i [$_{VP}$ yn ei$_i$ ddarllen ef$_i$]
         COMP was   I   prt AG3MS read   it (masc)
         I was reading it.

     c. yr   oeddwn i [$_{VP}$ yn ei$_i$ ddarllen [$_{NP_i}$ e]]
         COMP was   I   prt AG3MS read
         =48b

Taking the post-verbal pronominal NP as satisfying term 4 of Relative Deletion (and not the agreement clitic), we predict that relativisation on the object of the verb **darllen** in (48) should give a gap (=[$_{NP}$ e]) governed by a pro-clitic agreement element. Such is in fact the case as (49) shows:

(49) y   llyfr [$_S$ yr   oeddwn i yn *(ei) ddarllen _____]^{12}
      the book COMP was   I prt AG read
      the book that I was reading

A parallel situation holds in possessive NPs. Possessor NPs follow the head noun in a possessive phrase. If the possessor is pronominal an agreement clitic appears in determiner position of the dominating NP and PRO deletion is consequently possible (cf. 30–32):

(50) a. gwelais i [NP fab y   dyn]
          saw   I   con the man
          I saw the man's son.
      b. gwelais i [NP ei$_i$ fab ef$_i$]
          saw   I AG3MS son he
          I saw his son.
      c. gwelais i [NP ei$_i$ fab [NP$_i$ *e*]]
          = 50b

Again, Relative Deletion gives the same result as Delete-PRO (i.e. (50c)), with a gap and the agreement clitic:

(51) y   dyn [$_S$ y   gwelais i [NP *(ei) fab _____]]
      the man COMP saw   I   AG son
      the man whose son I saw

These examples argue that the assumption I made at the beginning of the paper, that the analysis proposed by McCloskey for Irish could be transferred to Welsh was wrong. Given the analysis of agreement that I have proposed, we do not need any language specific conditions on Relative Deletion at all, only a single (universal) condition on the distribution of [NP *e*], which accounts also for a class of facts independent of relativisation — the general optionality in Welsh of pronouns governed by agreement elements.

I have shown so far that the ECP with obligatory Relative Deletion wherever possible provides a better account of the applicability of Relative Deletion in Welsh that the stipulated conditions of (9), but it might reasonably be suggested that this has no implications for Irish and that we still need McCloskey's conditions in (8) to account for the effects of Relative Deletion in that language. I suggest, however, that there is in fact evidence that the same arguments that I have deployed for Welsh apply to Irish. The clearest instance comes from possessive NPs, which are syntactically very similar to those of Welsh. In both languages, the possessor NP follows the head:

(52) a. *Welsh* mab [NP y dyn]
                   son the   man
                   the man's son
      b. *Irish* mac [NP an fhir]
                   son the   man (gen)
                   the man's son

In both languages also, the head noun is preceded by what appears to be a pronominal possessor:

(53) a. *Welsh*   ei   fab
                    '*his*' *son*
      b. *Irish*   a   mhac
                    '*his*' *son*

I have argued that **ei** in (53a) is in fact an agreement clitic which sub-categorises a pronominal possessor NP, which is base-generated in the same post-head position as the full NP, **y dyn**, in (52a) and can be phonologically realised, as in (54):

(54) ei$_i$ fab ef$_i$
      AG son he
      = 53a

Thus, form (53a) is the consequence of selecting PRO rather than a pronoun and subsequent PRO-deletion and has in fact the structure (cf. (30)–(32)):

(55) ei$_i$ fab [$_{NP_i}$ *e*]
      AG son

McCloskey argues (1978: 49f) that, in Irish, possessor NPs are base-generated in pre-head position under DET and that non-pronominal NPs are obligatorily post-posed to the right of the head. This analysis fails to take into account the fact that there are in Irish constructions parallel to the Welsh (54):

(56) a mhac-sa   =*his son*

In (56) the head is followed by an 'emphatic particle' **sa**, and (56) thus has the contrastive reading '*his* son'). **Sa** is part of the following paradigm:

(57)   Singular   Plural
      1   -sa, -se   -na, -ne
      2   -sa, -se   -sa, -se
      3   -san, -sean (M)   -san, -sean
          -sa, -se (F)

These 'emphatic particles' have a distribution exactly parallel to that of pronouns in Welsh. They not only occur in the possessor NP position in possessive NPs like (56) but also occur in the position of prepositional objects (see (58)) and in subject position following finite verbs:

(58)

	Irish ó (from)		Welsh o (from)	
	Sing	Plural	Sing	Plural
1	uaim (se)	uain (ne)	ohonof (i)	ohonom (ni)
2	uait (se)	uaibh (se)	ohonot (ti)	ohonoch (chwi)
3	uaidh (sean) (M)	uathu (san)	ohono (ef)	ohonynt (hwy)
	uaithi (se) (F)		ohoni (hi)	

The principal difference between Irish and Welsh is that the 'emphatic particles' of Irish are phonetically different from the 'independent pronouns' (with which they are in complementary distribution). It does not seem unreasonable to suggest the same analysis for Irish as I have proposed for Welsh: that the 'emphatic particles' are in fact pronouns, governed by agreement elements which determine their phonetic form. By extension of the argument from Welsh it is these pronouns which satisfy the target predicate of Relative Deletion (incidentally accounting for their non-occurrence in relativisation sites). If this rather brief discussion in on the right lines, it is reasonable to suggest that Relative Deletion in Irish is also subject to the ECP.

4.2 Direct Relatives

In the cases considered thus far I have shown that the well-formedness conditions on [$_{NP}$ e] resulting from PRO-deletion and Relative Deletion are identical. This is at first glance not true of direct relatives. It was pointed out above that PRO-deletion cannot apply to direct object NPs in simple tensed sentences because the resulting [$_{NP}$ e] is not governed by co-indexed AG, in violation of ECP (cf. (24), repeated here as (59)):

(59) a. darllenais i ef
          read   I it(masc)
          I read it.
      b. *darllenais i [$_{NP}$ e]

In relative clauses and *wh*-questions on the other hand, deletion is not only possible, in Welsh it is obligatory. Relativising on (59) consequently gives (60):

(60) a. y llyfr [s a   [s ddarllenais i [NP *e*]]]
        the book COMP read   I
    b. *y llyfr [s a   [s ddarllenais i ef]]
        the book COMP read   I it(masc)
        the book that I read

It looks, from the contrast between (59) and (60), as if the hypothesis that PRO-deletion and Relative Deletion are constrained by the same principle (the ECP) is wrong. I shall show below that this conclusion is premature and that the data in (59) and (60) do in fact follow from the ECP.

McCloskey (1978a: Chs. 2 and 7) points out that relative clauses and related constructions in Irish display a complex pattern of complementiser alternations. Simple relative clauses are introduced either by **aL** or by **aN**. In McCloskey's analysis, the selection of **aL** or **aN** is determined by whether Relative Deletion leaves a pronoun or not. In (61a (=6b)), where there is a pronoun é in the relativisation site, the complementiser is **aN**; in (61b (=6a)), where deletion has taken place, the complementiser is **aL**:

(61) *Irish*
    a. an scríbhneoir [s aN   [s molann na mic -léinn é]]
        the writer   COMP   praise the students him
    b. an scríbhneoir [s aL [s mholann na mic-léinn ____]]
                          COMP
        the writer who the students praise (him)

The general pattern is (62) (cf. McCloskey, 1978: 9):

(62) a. NP [s aN [s ... Pronoun ...]]
    b. NP [s aL [s ... _____ ...]]

Since McCloskey treats the agreement forms which occur in possessive NPs and PPs as cases of retained pronouns, (62) covers sentences like (63a (=5d)) and (63b (=5c)):

(63) *Irish*
   a. an fear [$_S$ aN [$_S$ bhfuil a   mháthair
       the man COMP is   his(=AG) mother
       sa bhaile]]
       at home
       the man whose mother is at home
   b. an fear [$_S$ aN [$_S$ dtabharann tú an t-airgead
       the man COMP   give   you the money
       dó]]
       to-him
       the man that you give the money to

Welsh has a similar pattern of complementiser alternation, **a** when
the position relativised on is subject or direct object in a VSO
sentence; **y/yr** otherwise:

(64) a. y dyn [$_S$ a   [$_S$ werthodd ____ y byd]]   (=1)
          the man COMP   sold   the world
          the man who sold the world
      b. y llong [$_S$ a   [$_S$ werthodd y dyn ____]]   (=2)
          the boat COMP   sold   the man
          the boat that the man sold
      c. y dyn [$_S$ yr [$_S$ oedd ei fam ____ gartref]] (=4)
          the man COMP   is   AG mother   at-home
          the man whose mother was at home
      d. y dyn [$_S$ y   [$_S$ siaradasoch chwi ag ef]]   (=3)
          the man COMP   talked   you with him
          the man who you talked with

Above I argued that **ei** in (64c) is not in fact an instance of
pronoun retention, but rather AG governing the post-head [$_{NP}$ *e*]
resulting from Relative Deletion. The preposition **â** (**ag** before
vowels) which occurs in (64d), as was pointed out above, happens
not to have an agreement form. If we choose an agreeing preposition
the pronoun **ef** in (64d) disappears:

(65) y dyn [$_S$ y   [$_S$ dywedais i yr hanes wrth-o ____]]
      the man COMP   said   I the story to-AG
      the man that I told the story to

The alternation of **y** and **a** cannot be attributed to the presence or absence of a resumptive pronoun in the relative clause, since in (64c) and (65) there is no resumptive pronoun under the analysis of indirect relatives proposed above. A first approximation to the conditions on the appearance of **y** would be that it occurs when

    i. the [NP e] resulting from Relative Deletion is properly governed

OR ii. when there is a resumptive pronoun.

Such a formulation (which holds also for **aN** in Irish), correctly accounts for the non-occurrence of **y**/**aN** with [NP *e*] in direct object position (since [NP *e*] in that position is not properly governed (cf. the discussion of (24)) but it fails to explain why [NP *e*] is possible there at all. An explanation *is* possible, however, if we approach the problem the other way round and, instead of trying to determine the choice of complementiser from the structure of the relative clause, use the complementisers to determine when deletion is possible.

In English the only NP position governed by COMP is the subject:

(66)

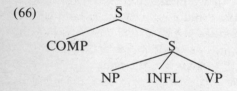

In Welsh, however, COMP in a VSO sentence governs both subject and object NPs:

(67)

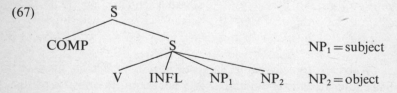

The possibility, demonstrated in (64b), of [NP *e*] in the position of NP_2 in (67) is permitted under the ECP if it is properly governed by a co-indexed element in COMP. In other words (64b) is accounted for if **a** is the governor of the empty object NP.

Let us try the following analysis, and explore the consequences:

i.   the expansion of COMP in finite clauses in Welsh is (68):

    (68)   COMP → NP **(y)**

ii.   NP in COMP may be lexically filled by **a**.[13]

If **a** is co-indexed with a PRO object in a VSO clause, PRO deletion will leave an [NP e] which is properly governed by the co-indexed **a** in COMP to give (69 (=64b)):

(69) y   llong [s a_i [s werthodd y   dyn [NP$_i$ e]]]
      the boat COMP sold   the man
      the boat that the man sold

PRO deletion is not possible in simple finite clauses such as (59) because there is no **a** to govern [NP e].

Sentences such as (69) are the result of verb pre-posing, rule (34) applying within the relative clause to give VSO order. As was pointed out above, verb pre-posing is optional. If it applies the VP is pruned (cf. note 11). If it does not the grammatical formative **gwneud** may be inserted to the left of INFL, but if this happens the VP generated by the base rules (33) remains and an object NP in VP is not in a position where it is governed by COMP. If government and the ECP are in fact involved in (69), it should be the case that PRO deletion is not possible within a VP, even with co-indexed **a** in COMP; (70) is thus correctly predicted to be ungrammatical:

(70) *y llong [s a_i [s wnaeth y   dyn [VP werthu [NP$_i$ e]]]
      the boat COMP 'did'   the man   sell

Sentences like (70) are only possible if [NP e] is properly governed by clitic AG inside VP:

(71) y   llong [s y   [s gwnaeth y dyn [VP ei$_i$ werthu [NP$_i$ e]]]]
      the boat COMP 'did'   the man   AG sell

Since verb pre-posing is only possible in finite clauses we also predict that clitic government will be required in non-finite clauses, as in (72):

(72) gwn i [s beth [s i [s PRO [VP 'w$_i$ darllen [NP$_i$ e]]]]]
      know I   what COMP   AG read
      I know what to read.

COMP in (67) does, however, govern the subject (NP$_1$) and **a** does indeed occur when the subject NP is relativised (64a). This is curious, since, as I have shown above (cf. (22)–(23)), PRO deletion is possible in simple tensed clauses because subject [$_{NP}$ e] is properly governed by INFL. We seem, in (64a), to have a situation of double government, by **a** in COMP and by AG in INFL. A more detailed investigation of subject relativisation and agreement shows that this is not in fact the case.

In simple finite clauses, verbs agree with their pronominal subjects in number and person, a distinction which is preserved under PRO-deletion. Thus as well as (73a), we find (73b):

(73) a. darllen-odd$_i$ ef$_i$ y   llyfr
          read AG(3S) he the book
      b. darllen-odd$_i$ [$_{NP_i}$ e] y llyfr
          AG3S
          He read the book.

Likewise, the PRO-deletion form corresponding to (74a) is (74b):

(74) a. darllenas-ant$_i$ hwy$_i$ y   llyfr
          read   AG(3P) they the book
      b. darllenas-ant$_i$ [$_{NP_i}$ e] y llyfr
          read   AG(3P)

A plural pronominal subject requires a plural agreement form in (74). If the head of a relative clause is plural, it normally requires that the [$_{NP}$ e] resulting from Relative Deletion is governed by a plural AG:

(75) a. y   llong [$_{\bar{S}}$ y   [$_S$ gwnaeth John [$_{VP}$ ei$_i$ werthu [$_{NP_i}$ e]]]]
          the boat COMP 'did'   John   3S sell
          the boat that John sold
      b. y   llongau [$_{\bar{S}}$ y   [$_S$ gwnaeth John [$_{VP}$ eu$_i$
          the boats COMP 'did'   John   3P
          gwerthu [$_{NP_i}$ e]]]]
          sell
          the boats that John sold

In (75a) the agreement clitic is singular **ei**; in (75b) it is plural **eu**. Number agreement is also obligatory in PPs and Possessive NPs.

Relativisation on subject NPs produces a totally different pattern:

(76) a. y   dyn [$_S$ a   [$_S$ ddarllenodd [$_{NP}$ *e*] y   llyfr]]
          the man COMP   read   the book
          the man who read the book
      b. y   dynion [$_S$ a   [$_S$ ddarllenodd [$_{NP}$ *e*] y   llyfr]]
          the men   COMP   read   the book
          the men who read the book

In (76b) the head NP **y dynion** is plural, but the verb **darllenodd** is singular. Using the expected plural verb **darllenasant** (cf. (74)) produces an ungrammatical result. The explanation for this unexpected form of agreement is straightforward if we treat subject and object relativisation in the same way: they both involve government by **a** in COMP. The correct analysis of (76) is (77), not (78):

(77) a. y dyn [$_S$ a$_i$ [$_S$ ddarllenodd [$_{NP_i}$ *e*] y llyfr]]
      b. y dynion [$_S$ a$_i$ [$_S$ ddarllenodd [$_{NP_i}$ *e*] y llyfr]]
(78) a. y dyn [$_S$ a [$_S$ darllen-odd$_i$ [$_{NP_i}$ *e*] y llyfr]]
      b. y dynion [$_S$ a [$_S$ darllen-odd$_i$ [$_{NP_i}$ *e*] y llyfr]]

By this analysis **darllenodd** in (76) is not in fact an agreement form at all. The **-odd** suffix here represents TENSE only (recall that INFL = TENSE and AG). This interpretation is supported by the fact, mentioned above, that 'full' NPs fail to trigger agreement. With prepositions, for example, we have the following contrast, where the singular and plural NPs in (79a and b) trigger no agreement, but the singular and plural **pronouns** do:

(79) a. am   y   dyn
          about the man
      b. am   y   dynion
          about the men
      c. amdano   ef
          about AG(3MS) him
      d. amdanynt   hwy
          about AG(3P) them

Finite verbs behave in the same way with respect to NP vs pronominal agreement:

(80) a. darllen**odd** y   dyn
          read   the man

b. darllen**odd** y dynion
   read   the men
c. darllen**odd** ef
   read   3S he
d. darllen**asant** hwy
   read   3P   they

The parallelism between (79) and (80) suggests that just as **am** in (79a/b) is a non-agreeing form of the preposition, so -**odd** in (80a/b) is the non-agreeing form of TENSE.

Traditionally opinion on the status of Welsh **a** is divided. For example, Morris-Jones (1931) takes the view that it is a pronoun, Richards (1938) that it is a 'relative particle'.[14] McCloskey (1978: 10–12) claims explicitly that **aL** in Irish is not a pronoun. He points out that **aL** (like **a** in Welsh) lacks any indication of the typical characteristics of pronouns in the Celtic languages, i.e. Case, animateness, number or gender. This argument is, however, not an overwhelming one. In many languages (such as Chinese) pronouns lack all of these typically pronominal characteristics. Even in English (which McCloskey cites in support of his contention) relative pronouns show neutralisation of the number and gender distinctions of the rest of the pronominal system (i.e. *who* versus *he, she, they*). For many speakers of English the Case distinctions of the pronominal system (*he/him, she/her,* etc.) are also neutralised, with *who* used throughout. In many varieties of English even the animate/inanimate distinction (*who/which*) is neutralised, giving *what* (e.g. *the man what I was talking to, the book what I was reading*). There is, it seems to me, no reason to accept McCloskey's line of argument against pronominal status of Irish **aL** or Welsh **a**.

In Welsh there is some phonological evidence in favour of pronominal status for **a**. Like all the Celtic languages, Welsh manifests a complex set of phonological processes affecting initial consonants, traditionally called 'mutation'. Many cases of mutation are triggered by particular lexical items, but there is a form of mutation which is triggered by a syntactic environment. Initial consonants undergo 'soft' mutation when immediately preceded by an NP, i.e.:[15]

(81) NP ——

Examples are:

(82) darllenodd [_{NP} John] lyfr   (<llyfr)
      read   John book
      John read a book.

In (82) **llyfr** mutates following the NP **John**.[16] However, if the
negative particle **dim** occurs between **John** and **llyfr**, as in (83), it is
dim that mutates (>**ddim**), not **llyfr**:

(83) ni ddarllenodd [_{NP} John] ddim llyfr
      not read   John no   book
      John didn't read a book.

In the Welsh counterpart of *There* Insertion, the subject NP of a
tensed clause mutates. Compare (84a), in which **tŷ** is unmutated,
with (84b) where the mutated form **dŷ** occurs:

(84) a. y   mae tŷ   yn y pentref
          COMP is house in the village
          A house is in the village
      b. y   mae [_{NP} yna] dŷ   yn y pentref[17]
          COMP is   there house in the village
          There is a house in the village.

The following examples show the same phenomenon:

(85) a. y   mae [_{NP} digon o ddewis] [_{PP} yn [_{NP} y
          COMP is   enough of choice   in   the
          farchnad]]
          market
      b. y   mae [_{PP} yn [_{NP} y farchnad]] [_{NP} ddigon
          COMP is   in   the market   enough
          o ddewis]
          of choice
          (There) is plenty of choice in the market.

In (85a) **digon** follows a verb and is unmutated; in (85b), however,
where the subject NP has been moved round the PP, **digon** is
mutated to **ddigon**, following the NP **y farchnad**.[18]

It is significant that **a** triggers in the initial consonant of the
following verb precisely this pattern of mutation, in contrast to the
complementisers **y** and **na**. The form **y** is not a mutation trigger at all

and **na** triggers a more complex pattern: soft mutation of **g, b, d, m, ll** and **rh**, but 'aspirate' mutation of **c, p** and **t**. Thus this appears to provide positive evidence for the NP status of **a**.

McCloskey puts forward another argument against pronominal status for **aL** in Irish. He points out that complementisers shows the following systematic alternations, determined by the tense of the verb of their clause (cf. McCloskey, 1978: 11):

(86) *Irish*

	Non-past	Past
go		
Affirmative	goN	gurL
Negative	nachN	nárL
aN		
Affirmative	aN	arL
Negative	nachN	nárL
aL		
Affirmative	aL	aL
Negative	nachL	nárL

(N and L indicate the mutation type triggered by the complementiser)

A past tense pronoun would indeed be an embarrassment for the analysis I am proposing, but the interesting thing about (86), which McCloskey does not point out, is that in fact **aL** is unique among the complementisers in *not* showing a past/non-past alternation. In fact, far from supporting McCloskey's claim that **aL** is a complementiser, (86) tends to demonstrate the contrary.[19] If **aL** is a pronoun, the absence of a tense distinction requires no explanation.

5. The Distribution of y and a

Taking **a** as a pronominal makes possible a unified account of the distribution of empty NPs, subsuming both relativisation and Delete-PRO under a single generalisation: the Empty Category Principle.[20] It also makes possible a non-*ad hoc* account of why **a** cannot occur in COMP in indirect relatives. We need only assume that in Welsh it is *pronouns* which are translated as variables in Logical Form.

This works straightforwardly in sentences like (87) where Relative Deletion does not apply, and where there is a pronoun (**ef**):

(87) y   dyn [s y   [s siaradasoch chwi ag   ef]]
      the man COMP   spoke   you with him
      the man that you spoke with

In sentences like (88) on the other hand, to which Relative Deletion has applied, there is no pronoun object:

(88) y   dyn [s y   [s soniasoch chwi amdan-o$_i$ [NP$_i$ e]]]
      the man COMP   talked   you about-AG
      the man that you talked about

There *is* a pronoun in (88), however, — the agreement suffix -**o**. Assume that this suffix, and agreement elements in general, translate as bound variables in LF which are assigned the argument position of the [NP e] with which they are co-indexed. A requirement, along the lines of Freidin's Principle of Functional Relatedness (1978: 537), that there be a one-to-one relationship between lexical NPs and argument positions, now gives an explanation for the absence of **a** in indirect relatives. In (89), if **a** is co-indexed with the empty object NP, it is assigned an argument position in LF. If it is not co-indexed, (89) is bad for two reasons: i. **a** is a free argument in LF and ii. [NP e] is not governed, in violation of the ECP:

(89) y   dyn [s a   [s welais i [NP e]]]
      the man COMP saw   I
      the man that I saw

If **a** is co-indexed with [NP e] in (90), on the other hand, we have an ill-formed LF representation because two pronouns are assigned the same argument position in LF. If the agreement pronominal is not co-indexed with [NP e], **a** is assigned an argument position, but [NP e] is not properly governed and the agreement pronominal is a free argument:

(90) a. *y dyn [s a   [s welais i ei   fab [NP e]]]
         the man COMP saw   I AG son
         the man whose son I saw
      b. *y dyn [s a   [s soniais i amdan-o [NP e]]]
         the man COMP talked   I about   AG
         the man I talked about

One further point requires to be dealt with: why does **a** occur in the COMP of relative constructions at all? The principle proposed above accounts for the non-occurrence of **a** in COMP in indirect relatives but is merely permissive with respect to its occurrence in direct relatives. The ECP requires that [$_{NP}$ e] be governed, but does not stipulate that the governor must be **a**. To be specific, recall that the subject of a simple finite clause can be [$_{NP}$ e], because INFL contains AG (cf. (22) and (23)):

(91)   a.   darllenas-ant$_i$ hwy$_i$ y   llyfr
            read   AG3P they the book
            They read the book.
      b.   darllenas-ant$_i$ [$_{NP_i}$ e] y llyfr
            =91a

Given the discussion so far, it ought to be possible to have (ungrammatical) (92a) as an alternative to the grammatical (92b) (cf. the discussion of (74)):

(92)   a.   *y dynion [$_{\bar{S}}$ y   [$_S$ darllenas-ant$_i$ [$_{NP_i}$ e] y   llyfr]]
            the men   COMP   read   AG3P   the book
      b.   y   dynion [$_{\bar{S}}$ a$_i$ [$_S$ ddarllenodd [$_{NP_i}$ e] y   llyfr]]
            the men   AG   read   the book
            the men who read the book

In (93a), [$_{NP}$ e] is properly governed, there is a pronominal **-ant** available for translation into a variable in LF and there is no **a** in COMP. What then is wrong with (92a)? Let us approach an answer to this question by observing first that $\bar{S}$ structures like that in (92a) can in fact occur in relative clauses, provided that the $\bar{S}$ containing the extraction site is not adjacent to the head NP:

(93)   y   dynion$_i$ [$_{\bar{S}}$ y   [$_S$ dywedodd John [$_{\bar{S}}$ y
       the men   COMP   said   John COMP
       [$_S$ darllenas-ant$_i$ [$_{NP_i}$ e] y   llyfr]]]]
       read   -AG   the book
       the men that John said (that) read the book

The crucial property of (92) is that it involves the highest COMP. It would appear that the head of a relative construction must bind an NP in the adjacent COMP. This conclusion is reinforced by sentences like (94):

(94) ??y dynion$_i$ [$_S$ na [$_S$ wn i ddim [$_S$ pa wragedd$_j$ [$_S$ a$_j$
the men   NEG know I not   which women   AG
[$_S$ welas-ant$_i$ [$_{NP_i}$ *e*] [$_{NP_j}$ *e*]]]]]]
saw AG3P
the men who I don't know saw which women

Such sentences are marginal, but what is relevant is that (94) can only have the interpretation indicated by the indices given. Awkward though (94) is, it cannot possibly have the interpretation shown in (95):

(95) *y dynion$_j$ [$_S$ na [$_S$ wn i ddim [$_S$ pa wragedd$_i$ [$_S$ a$_j$
the men   NEG know I not· which women   AG .
[$_S$ welas-ant$_i$ [$_{NP_i}$ *e*] [$_{NP_j}$ *e*]]]]]]
saw AG3P
the men who I don't know which women saw

The **a** in (94) can only be interpreted as **pa wragedd** (which women), the NP adjacent to the COMP in which **a** occurs and not as **y dynion** (the men).

There is interesting evidence from Irish which is relevant to this question and which supports this analysis. In simple relative constructions the distribution of **aL** and **aN** in Irish is parallel to that of **a** and **y** in Welsh (cf. (5)). Taking **aL** as a pronoun and **aN** as a complementiser gives the same results for Irish as the analysis above gives for Welsh. Relativisation into a sentential complement in Irish however gives possibilities not generally available in Welsh. If the NP relativised on is a subject or direct object (i.e. in direct relatives) **aL** occurs in the COMP of the sentential complement, and also in each higher COMP giving the pattern in (96):

(96) NP [$_S$ aL ... [$_S$ aL ... [$_S$ aL [$_S$ ... [$_{NP}$ *e*] ...]]]]

For example, relativising on the object of S$_2$ in (97a) gives (97b) (cf. McCloskey, 1978: 20):

(97) *Irish*
a. deir siad [$_{S_1}$ go [$_S$ síleann an t-athair [$_{S_2}$ go
say they COMP thinks   the father   COMP
[$_S$ bposfaidh Síle   é]]]]
will-marry Sheila him
They say that the father thinks that Sheila will marry him.

b. an fear [$_{\bar{S}_0}$ aL   [$_S$ deir siad [$_{\bar{S}_1}$ aL   [$_S$ shíleann an
    the man COMP say   they COMP thinks   the
    t-athair [$_{\bar{S}_2}$ aL   [$_S$ phosfaidh Síle [$_{NP}$ e]]]]]]]
    father   COMP will-marry Sheila
    the man that they say that the father thinks that Sheila
    will marry

$\bar{S}_2$ has the structure of a simple relative clause with an empty NP
governed by **aL** in COMP, which is repeated in $\bar{S}_1$ and $\bar{S}_0$. Indirect
relatives show two possibilities. One takes the following form:

(98)   NP [$_{\bar{S}}$ aL ... [$_{\bar{S}}$ aL ... [$_{\bar{S}}$ aN [$_S$ ... pronoun ...]]]]

For example, relativisation on the object of the preposition **i** (in) in
(99a) gives (99b):

(99) a. deir siad [$_{\bar{S}_1}$ go   [$_S$ measann sibh   [$_{\bar{S}_2}$ go
          say they COMP   think   you(pl) COMP
          [$_S$ bhfuil an eochair insa   doras]]]]
          is   the key   in-the door
          They say that you think that the key is in the door.
     b. an doras [$_{\bar{S}_0}$ aL   [$_S$ deir siad [$_{\bar{S}_1}$ aL   [$_S$ mheasann
          the door COMP say   they COMP think
          sibh [$_{\bar{S}_2}$ aN   [$_S$ bhfuil an eochair ann$_i$ [$_{NP_i}$ e]]]]]]]
          you COMP is   the key   inAG
          the door that they say that you think that the key is in

Since $\bar{S}_2$ in (99b) contains a pronoun (in the agreeing preposition
ann) the analysis proposed above correctly predicts that the pronoun
aL cannot occur in COMP of $\bar{S}_2$. Note that **aN** is not the
complementiser that occurs in $\bar{S}_2$ in the non-relative (99a).

The second possibility in indirect relatives retains the declarative
complementiser **go**, except in the highest COMP, giving the patterns
in (100) as an alternative to (98):

(100)   NP [$_{\bar{S}}$ aN ... [$_{\bar{S}}$ go ... [$_{\bar{S}}$ go [$_S$ ... pronoun ...]]]]

An explanation for these facts is available within the theory of
binding proposed by Bresnan and Grimshaw (1978), in which
binding is subject to subjacency (cf. Chomsky, 1973: 247). If the
highest COMP contains an NP with a phonetic matrix (i.e. **aL**),

Bresnan and Grimshaw's conditions on binding give (101 (=96, 97b)) as a well-formed structure, with S as a binding node.

(101)   NP [$_S$ aL$_i$ [$_S$ ... [$_S$ aL$_i$ [$_S$ ... [$_S$ aL$_i$ [$_S$ ... [$_{NP_i}$ e] ...]]]]]]

Structure (102) is also well formed according to Bresnan and Grimshaw's binding conditions, but is blocked because **aL** in the lowest COMP is a free argument in LF:

(102)   *NP [$_S$ aL$_i$ [$_S$ ... [$_S$ aL$_i$ [$_S$ ... [$_S$ aL$_i$ [$_S$ ... pronoun$_i$ ...]]]]]]

However, an alternative to (102) which satisfies both conditions is (103 (−98, 99b)), where the NP in the lowest COMP is not lexical:

(103)   NP [$_S$ aL$_i$ [$_S$ ... [$_S$ aL$_i$ [$_S$ ... [$_S$[$_{NP_i}$ e] [$_S$ ... pronoun$_i$ ...]]]]]]

aN appears to be the form of the declarative complementiser (otherwise **go**) when COMP contains [$_{NP}$ e]. Note that in (100) **aN** appears in the highest COMP, which suggests that it has the structure (104)

(104)   NP [$_S$[$_{NP_i}$ e] aN [$_S$ ... [$_S$ go [$_S$ ... [$_S$ go [$_S$ ... pronoun$_i$ ...]]]]]]

That is, the subjacency condition on binding is optional in Irish and applies when NP in the highest COMP is phonetically realised.[21]

This approach to (96)–(100) gives a simple account of the distribution of **aN**. If we interpret the occurrence of **aN** in the highest COMP of (100) and the COMP of indirect relatives as I propose, we have evidence for the obligatory presence of NP in the highest COMP. It is straightforward to go from this to an explanation for the ungrammaticality of (92a). If the highest COMP in a relative clause *must* contain a co-indexed NP, in the direct relative cases, this NP will also *govern* a subject or object. We have seen from the discussion of (74)–(78) that, when two alternative governors are available, (COMP or INFL), only one is permitted. Given that the NP in the highest COMP must be co-indexed with an NP in S, this effectively dictates the choice of governor in (92), namely **a**. For (105a) is starred because [$_{NP}$ e] is doubly governed, while (105b) is starred because NP in COMP must be indexed with an NP in S. Only (105c) satisfies both binding and government. In (105c), NP$_i$ is in fact **a**:

(105)   a.   *y dynion [$_S$ NP$_i$ [$_S$ ddarllenas-ant$_i$ [$_{NP_i}$ e] ...
                  the men   read   AG3P

    b. *y dynion [s NP [s ddarllenas-ant$_i$ [$_{NP_i}$ e] ...
    c. y dynion [s NP$_i$ [s ddarllen-odd [$_{NP_i}$ e]

The case of object NPs is slightly different, since they do not involve double government. In a configuration like (106), the object pronoun is only governed by NP in COMP, which sanctions Relative Deletion, but, if Relative Deletion does not apply, (106) is well formed provided that NP in COMP is not lexical.

(106) ... [s NP$_i$ [s V INFL NP Pronoun$_i$]]

Both possibilities are realised in Irish:[22]

(107) *Irish*
    a. an scríbhneoir [s aL$_i$ [s mholann na mic-léinn
        the writer   COMP   praise   the students
        [$_{NP_i}$ e]]]   (=6a)
        him
    b. an scríbhneoir [s[$_{NP_i}$ e] aN [s molann na mic-léinn
        the writer   COMP   praise   the students
        é$_i$]]]   (=6b)
        him
        the writer who the students praise

I hope that I have succeeded in demonstrating the validity of the claim that I made at the beginning of this article: that the conditions on the deletion of NPs in relative constructions in Welsh, and, as far as I can judge, in Irish too, reduce to a single local condition — the Empty Category Principle.[23] I have restricted the discussion to those constructions putatively involving McCloskey's rule of Relative Deletion. A more comprehensive study is needed before the applicability of the approach which I have outlined here to cases of extraction involving constituents other than NP can be evaluated.

In conclusion, I would like to show how the analysis proposed here extends naturally to negative relative clauses in Welsh and provides an explanatory account of the differences between positive and negative relative clauses with respect to deletion and agreement. Consider the following data:

Subject Relativisation

(108) a. (positive) y   dynion a   ddarllenodd ____
                    the men   AG read(3S)

              y   llyfr
              the book
              the men who read the book

  b. (negative) y   dynion na   ddarllenasant ———
              the men   NEG read(3P)
              y   llyfr
              the book
              the men who didn't read the book

Object Relativisation

(109) a. (positive) y   llyfr a   ddarllenais i ———
               the book AG read   I
               the book which I read
      b. (negative) y   llyfr na   ddarllenais i ef
               the book NEG read   I it(M)
               the book which I didn't read

(108a) shows the absence of 'subject-verb' agreement discussed above (cf. 76–7), whereas in its negative counterpart (108b) the plural verb form **ddarllenasant** is required. In (109a) a resumptive object pronoun is not permitted, whereas in the negative example (109b) it is. In other words, the distribution of subject-verb agreement and empty object NPs versus resumptive pronouns found in positive relative clauses is reversed in negative ones. Note that this reversal is restricted to the subject and object positions, the agreement and deletion possibilities for other NP positions are unaffected by negation. This is, however, precisely what we should expect, given that negation is expressed in these examples by a negative complementiser (**na**, the negative counterpart to **y**). The *c*-command condition on government means that in these examples, in which the COMP node has the structure shown in (110),

(110)

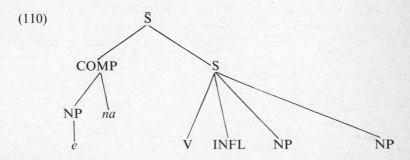

since the NP in COMP does not *c*-command the subject of object NPs it does not govern them either and Welsh must revert to the same patterns of deletion as are available in non-relativisation contexts. Because the subject and object of (110) are the only ones which can be affected by changes in the structure of COMP under the analysis proposed here we correctly predict that other NP positions are unaffected by negation.

Notes

    * I would like to thank Connie Cullen, Frank Heny, Nigel Vincent and Anthony Warner for their readiness to help me sort out my ideas and Dwyryd Jones for his patience in answering my endless questions.
    1. I shall argue below that **a** is not in fact a complementiser, but will continue to use the term until the distinction between **a** and **y** is discussed in detail.
    2. The complementisers (cf. n 1) **aL** and **aN** are homophonous. They are, however, phonologically distinct in that they trigger different sets of initial consonant changes ('mutations') in the immediately following word. **aL** triggers 'Lenition', **aN** 'Nasalisation', hence the notation (taken from McCloskey 1978: 9).
    3. This definition of government is taken from Chomsky (1981) and differs slightly from that given in Chomsky (1980, p. 75, this volume).
    4. Note that $[_{NP} e] \neq$ PRO. Although both lack a phonetic matrix, PRO is not 'empty' since it contains AG.
    5. The theory of indexing proposed in Chomsky (1981) is simply free indexing, constrained by the theory of binding:

A.   If α is an anaphor or has no phonetic matrix then
     1.   it is a variable
     2.   it is bound in every governing category
B.   If NP is case-marked then
     1.   it is an anaphor
     or
     2.   it is free in every governing category
C.   If α is pronominal it is free in every minimal governing category. (α is a governing category for β = there is some γ such that γ governs β and α contains γ. α is a minimal governing category for β = α is a governing category which properly contains no governing category and α = S or NP.)

    6. The full paradigm for the past tense of **darllen** (read) is

	Singular	Plural
1	darllenais (i)	darllenasom (ni)
2	darllenaist (ti)	darllenasoch (chwi)
3	darllenodd (hi)(fem)	darllenasant (hwy)
	(ef)(masc)	

    7. Note that, unlike French and Italian, Welsh allows 'doubling' of clitic AG and object pronoun as in (25a). The full paradigm for VP structures like (25) is

	Singular	Plural
1	fy V (i)	ein V (ni)
2	dy V (di)	eich V (chwi)

3   ei V (ef)(masc)   eu V (hwy)
         (hi)(fem)

    8. **amdano** also contains the stem augment **-dan-**. The complete paradigm for **am** is:

	Singular	Plural
1	amdanaf (i)	amdanom (ni)
2	amdanat (ti)	amdanoch (chwi)
3	amdano (ef)(masc)	amdanynt (hwy)
	amdani (hi)(fem)	

    9. **mab** in (31) has undergone an initial consonant change, triggered by the 3MS clitic **ei**, which is not relevant to the discussion here. I assume the following structure for possessive NPs in Welsh:

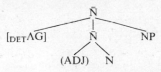

    10. I am using $\bar{S}$ to subsume clefts and *wh*-questions (McCloskey's (1978) Q). I assume that the feature structure of $\bar{S}$ distinguishes these two constructions.
    11. See Emonds (1979) for a proposal that local transformations contain a maximum of three terms. I will assume that the VP node in (33c) is pruned as a result of the application of (34). See also Jones and Thomas (1977) for an analysis of Welsh along the same lines.
    12. Notice that the base generation of pronominals in relative clauses (as opposed to a movement analysis) accounts also for the difference between Welsh and French with respect to clitic retention in relative clauses and questions. Both Welsh and French have clitic pronouns in non-relative sentences:

i.   yr   wyf i [$_{VP}$ yn ei$_i$ weld [$_{NP_i}$ e]]
    COMP am I Prt   AG see
                      3MS
    I am seeing him.
ii. je le$_i$ vois [$_{NP_i}$ e]
    I see him

In relative clauses Welsh retains the clitic, whereas French does not:

iii. y   dyn [$_S$ yr   wyf i [$_{VP}$ yn *(ei$_i$) weld [$_{NP_i}$ e]]]
    the man COMP am I Prt   AG   see
    the man who I am seeing
iv. l'homme que je (*le) vois [$_{NP}$ e]

In French an NP is moved from the position of [$_{NP}$ e] by *Wh* Movement and the resulting trace is properly governed by the verb **vois**. In Welsh on the other hand Relative Deletion is defined over pronominals, which are subcategorised by the clitic. The structural description of RD is not met unless Term 4 is pronominal, and the subcategorisation properties of clitics require that if a pronominal occurs in iii. it will be governed by a clitic.
    13. **a** and **y** cannot occur in COMP simultaneously. One way of dealing with this would be to adopt the Doubly Filled COMP Filter of Chomsky and Lasnik (1977: 435). There are constructions in Welsh, however, which apparently permit a doubly filled COMP:

i. y   tŷ   [$_S$ lle   yr   [$_S$ ywf i   yn   byw_____]]
    the house where that am   I   Prt live
    the house where I live

I will not attempt to formulate the conditions excluding [$_{COMP}$ **a y**] sequences here.

According to the definition of government given in (15), COMP in (67) does not minimally *c*-command NP$_1$ or NP$_2$ because of the presence of V. The question of how government operates in languages which have sentences lacking a VP is an open one at present. In what follows in the text I shall show that the assumption that NP$_1$ and NP$_2$ are governed by elements in COMP and not by V leads to a number of correct generalisations about relativisation in Celtic. A possible revision of government which would permit the correct empirical results would be to define lexical government over minimal projections of phrasal categories, excluding V in (67) if S ≠ V^{max}. I shall assume this revision in what follows.

14. Awbery (1977) treats **a** as a pronoun and proposes a split analysis of relative clauses: movement in the **a** cases and deletion in the **y** cases.

15. Soft mutation is represented orthographically as

p → b   b → f   m → f
t → d   d → dd   ll → l
c → g   g → ∅   rh → r

See Awbery (1975) for exemplification and discussion or Bowen and Rhys Jones (1960) and Rhys Jones (1977) for exemplification. There are interesting questions involved in determining which NPs 'count' in 81. Roughly speaking the NPs which trigger soft mutation are those which occur in 'case-marked' positions (in the sense of Chomsky, 1980). Lexical subjects of finite clauses trigger mutation (dyn > ddyn):

i.   gwelodd [$_{NP}$ ef] ddyn
     saw   he   man
     We saw a man.

and so does [$_{NP}$ e] in the same position:

ii. gwelodd$_i$ [$_{NP_i}$ e] ddyn
     He saw a man.

Lexical subjects of non-finite clauses trigger mutation of the initial consonant of the following verb (gweld > weld)

iii. yr   wyf   i   yn   disgwyl [$_S$ i [$_{NP}$ John] weld y   dyn
      COMP   am   I   Prt expect   for   John   see   the   man
      I expect John to see the man.

PRO subjects however do not:

iv   yr   wyf   i   yn   disgwyl [$_S$ PRO gweld y   dyn]
     COMP   am   I   Prt expect   see   the   man
     I expect to see the man.

I will not pursue the implications of this distinction further here.

16. It is not the object status of **llyfr** in (82) which is responsible for the mutation. If a direct object does not follow an NP position (in a sentence with a periphrastic verb, for example) no mutation occurs:

i.   yr   oedd John   yn   darllen llyfr
     COMP   was   John   Prt read   book
     John was reading a book.

17. **yna** passes the standard tests for NP status for *there* in English. It can, for

example, be 'raised', cf. i. and ii.

i.   y   mae'r tŷ   yn   debyg   o   fod   yn   y   pentref
     COMP is the house   Prt likely of be   in   the   village
     The house is likely to be in the village.
ii. y   mae yna   yn   debyg   o   fod   tŷ   yn   y   pentref
     COMP is 'there'   Prt likely of be   house   in   the   village
     There is likely to be a house in the village.

18. It may be that the mutation of **digon** is in fact not an instance of (81) but of a more general phenomenon of which (81) is a special case, namely mutation in the environment:

i.   X̄—— (where X̄ = NP, AP, VP, PP)

This generalisation, if correct, does not affect the point being made in the text.

19. There is another peculiarity about the arrangement of 'complementisers' in (86), i.e. that each affirmative complementiser has a corresponding negative one. (This interpretation is presumably what leads McCloskey to make the claim that all complementisers show past/non-past alternants. The 'negative counterpart' of **aL** in (86) does alternate, although **aL** itself doesn't). However, closer inspection shows that there is in fact only one negative complementiser: **nachL/nárL**. A less misleading presentation of the facts about the complementiser system would be:

	Non-Past	Past
Affirmative	goN	gurL
	aN	arL
Negative	nachL	nárL

The factors determining the selection of **goN** versus **aN** will be discussed below. McCloskey (1978: 13–18) discusses a number of cases of **aL** introducing clauses which do not contain extraction gaps. The proposal in the text that **aL** is a pronoun does not preclude the possibility that there may also be a homophonous complementiser.

20. The only difference between Relative Deletion and PRO-deletion is that the former is obligatory (in the sense that it must apply whenever its output is well formed under the ECP) whereas the latter is optional. Given that the two rules are in all other respects identical, it is open to question whether Relative Deletion exists as a distinct rule. The discussion which follows in the text assumes that the semantic interpretation of relative constructions is defined over the output of Relative Deletion. A possible approach to the apparent obligatoriness of Relative Deletion would be to seek general principles which preclude taking the **boldface** pronoun in i. as an LF variable

i.   *y dyn y   soniais i amdan-o$_i$ **fe**$_i$
     the man COMP talked I about AG him

Examples like i. are reminiscent of sentences like ii. in English where t cannot be taken as anaphoric to **he** (cf. iii)

ii. who$_i$ did he say t$_i$ saw John
iii. He$_i$ said that he$_i$ saw John

If the explanation of 'strong crossover' cases like ii. (see Chomsky (1981) for discussion) can be generalised to i., then Relative Deletion can be subsumed under PRO-deletion. This suggestion may not be viable, however, because there are a number of other cases in Welsh which require [$_{NP}$ e] in agreement contexts, but which do not involve *wh*-quantification, such as personal passives:

iv. mae John$_i$ wedi cael ei$_i$ ladd [$_{NP_i}$ e]
     is   John   after get AG   kill
     John has been killed

See Awbery (1976: 76–88) for discussion of constructions involving this phenomenon.

21. There are in effect two 'routes' from a variable to the highest COMP: (a) if the variable is in S, it may be bound directly by NP in the highest COMP ($=104$); (b) binding may be through successive COMPs ($=103$) and if the variable is itself in COMP (i.e. the direct relatives) this is the only possibility ($=101$). In finite clauses Welsh only allows option (a) and option (b) may be involved in non-finite clauses like i. (cf. Richards, 1938: 86f) and Morris-Jones, 1931: 91):

i.   y   pethau a   orchmynnodd yr   Arglwydd eu   gwneuthur
     the things   ordered   the Lord   AG3P   do
     the things that the Lord ordered to do ($=$Exodus 25.1)

i. follows from the proposals in the text if it has the structure ii:

ii. y pethau [$_S$ a$_i$ [$_S$ orchmynodd yr Arglwydd [$_S$[$_{NP_i}$ e]
     [$_S$ PRO eu$_i$ gwneuthur [$_{NP_i}$ e]]]]]

If ii. is correct, the possibility of [$_{NP}$ e] in COMP of non-finite clauses may be the explanation for sentences like iii:

iii. beth   yr ydych chwi yn ei   ddisgwyl i mi ei   wneud
     what (masc) COMP are you Prt AG3MS expect   to me AG3MS do
     What do you expect me to do?

The peculiarity of iii. is that it not only has an agreement clitic in the expected place (i.e. preceding the lower verb **gwneud**), but also before the main clause verb **disgwyl**. It may be that iii. is another instance of [$_{NP}$ e] in the COMP of a non-finite clause, governed by the proclitic in the higher verb, i.e.:

iv. beth [$_S$ yr   [$_S$ ydych chwi [$_{VP}$ yn ei$_i$ ddisgwyl [$_S$[$_{NP_i}$ e]
     what   COMP   are   you   Prt   AG   expect
     [$_S$ i   mi ei$_i$ wneud [$_{NP_i}$ e]]]]]]
     to   me AG   do

Although examples like iii. are attested in writing I have not yet found an informant who confesses to having reliable judgements about them, so these remarks must be taken as purely speculative.

22. The ungrammaticality of the Welsh equivalent of (107b) must be stipulated. In this context see the discussion of negative relative clauses below.

23. McCloskey's analysis of these constructions runs up against a number of problems. He takes the existence of (98) with a 'resumptive pronoun' as demonstrating the inadequacy of successive cyclic *Wh* Movement (1978: 22–26) but proceeds from this to assume that COMP to COMP processes are not involved at all. Since he treats **aL, aN** and **go** as complementisers, his solution to the alternations discussed above is to take **aL** as the highest complementiser and **go** as the base generated complementiser in lower COMPs (as in the non-relatives (97) and (99)). Subsequent to Relative Deletion, an optional transformation converts **go** to **aL** (1978: 208) to give (96):

i.   W$_1$ $\bar{X}_j$ W$_2$ [goN W$_3$ [$\bar{x}_j$ e] W$_4$] W$_5$
     1   2   3   4   5   6   7   8
     1   2   3   **aL**   5   6   7   8

The successive cyclic effects of (i) are guaranteed by the following condition (1978: 211)

ii. 'Any sentence which can be analysed as below:
     W$_1$ $\bar{X}_j$ W$_2$ [$_S$ **go**N W$_3$ [$\bar{x}_j$ e] W$_4$] W$_5$
     is ungrammatical'

There are two things wrong with this. Firstly, note that ii. simply recapitulates the structural description of i. which is an unpleasant redundancy. Secondly, (i) is in effect an unbounded filter. Here is McCloskey on filters (1978: 145): 'If we had to give filters the power of unboundedness, the attractiveness of this approach to accounting for the obligatoriness of deletion in subject position would be much diminished.' I concur. Examples (98) and (100) are derived by revising i. so that it applies to clauses containing a co-indexed pronoun; a second (obligatory) transformation converts **aL** to **aN** (1978: 217)

iii. W_1 np_j W_2 **aL** W_3 NP W_4
                          $[+PRO]_j$
    1   2   3   4   5   6   7
    1   2   3   **aN**   5   6   7
If W_3 contains no occurrence of a relative complementiser which
c-commands term 6

i., ii. and iii. are not sufficient to guarantee (98), since the filter ii. specifies a gap, not a pronoun, so McCloskey proposes another unbounded filter (1978: 220):

iv. $*W_0$ np_j W_1 **aL** W_2 **goN** W_3 NP W_4
                                      $[+Pro]_k$
    1   2   3   4   5   6   7   8   9
    if j = k; if 4 and 6 c-command 8

I leave it to the reader to decide the relative merits of these approaches.

References

Awbery, G. M. (1975), 'Welsh Mutations: Syntax or Phonology?' *Archivum Linguisticum* VI (new series)
――― (1976), *The Syntax of Welsh: a Transformational Study of the Passive*, Cambridge University Press, Cambridge
――― (1977), 'A Transformational View of Welsh Relative Clauses', Bulletin of the Board of Celtic Studies XXVII, University of Wales
Bowen, J. T. and T. J. Rhys Jones (1960), *Teach Yourself Welsh*, Teach Yourself Books, English Universities Press, London
Bresnan, J. and J. Grimshaw (1978), 'The Syntax of Free Relatives in English', *Linguistic Inquiry* 9
Chomsky, N. (1973), 'Conditions on Transformations', in S. Anderson and P. Kiparsky (eds.), *A Festschrift for Morris Halle*, Holt, Rinehart & Winston, New York
――― (1980), 'On Binding', this volume. Previously published in *Linguistic Inquiry* 11, 1–46
――― (1981), *Lectures on Government and Binding*, Foris, Dordrecht
――― (forthcoming), 'Principles and Parameters in Syntactic Theory' in D. Lightfoot and N. Hornstein (eds.), *Explanation in Linguistics*, Longmans, London
Chomsky, N. and H. Lasnik (1977), 'Filters and Control', *Linguistic Inquiry* 8
Emonds, J. E. (1976), *A Transformational Approach to English Syntax*, Academic Press, New York
――― (1979), 'Generalized NP-Inversion: Hallmark of English', unpublished manuscript
Freidin, R. (1978), 'Cyclicity and the Theory of Grammar', *Lingusitic Inquiry* 9

Jones, M. and A. R. Thomas (1977), *The Welsh Language: Studies in its Syntax and Semantics*, University of Wales Press, Cardiff

McCloskey, M. J. (1978), *A Fragment of a Grammar of Modern Irish*, Texas Linguistic Forum No. 12, University of Texas, Austin

Morris Jones, J. (1931), *Welsh Syntax*, University of Wales Press, Cardiff

Rhys Jones, T. J. (1977), *Living Welsh*, Teach Yourself Books, Hodder and Stoughton, London

Richards, M. (1938), *Cystrawen y Frawddeg Cymraeg*, University of Wales Press, Cardiff

7 Germanic Word Order and the Format of Surface Filters*

Joan Maling and Annie Zaenen

One of the most familiar features of Germanic languages is the position of the finite verb:

The finite verb must be the second immediate constituent of the S in which it occurs.

We will call this the Verb-second Constraint (V/2).[1] V/2 is perhaps most familiar as a characteristic of main clauses in German and Dutch. It also applies to embedded tensed clauses as well as main clauses in Icelandic and Yiddish. With some minor qualifications concerning the placement of adverbs, this is also true of other Scandinavian languages; however we have not investigated the syntax of these languages deeply enough to know if the V/2 position is basic and the adverb preposed, or vice versa. Only in English has V/2 been lost, leaving only traces, for example, in the inversion of subject and auxiliary required after fronted negative adverbs[2] (but not in direct *wh*-questions, according to our hypothesis). We believe that V/2 is an important typological characteristic of the Germanic languages. Our preliminary study of this constraint has led to a variety of theoretically interesting questions which we will illustrate here with reference to Icelandic. The proper formulation of V/2 in Icelandic has implications for the theory of filters in syntax in two ways: first, it provides evidence on the proposed format of filters, and secondly, it provides counter-evidence to a proposed universal filter.

This paper is organised as follows: we will first motivate the need for V/2 in the grammar of Icelandic and discuss briefly our account of (1) direct *wh*-questions, (2) Left Dislocation and (3) embedded sentences with extracted subjects. In the second half, we turn to the question of how this constraint should be stated and its implications for the theory of filters.

1. The V/2 Constraint and Its Consequences in Icelandic

In Icelandic, the unmarked word order in tensed declarative clauses is SVO, as illustrated in (1). The finite verbs are in bold type.

(1) Hún **sagði** mér að hún **hefði** unnið að brúarsmíði í sumar.
     She said [to] me that she had worked at bridge building summers.

Icelandic also allows Topicalisation[3] to occur freely in embedded clauses, as illustrated in (2).

(2) a. *Hún* **sagði** að í sumar **hefði** hún unnið að brúarsmíði.
     b. Ég **held** að smalann **muni** tröll taka a morgun.
         I think that the-shepherd-[acc] will trolls take tomorrow.

When Topicalisation applies in embedded clauses, the subject and finite verb must be inverted; if no inversion occurs, the sentences are ungrammatical, as shown in (2'):

(2') a. *Hún **sagði** að í sumar hún **hefði** unnið að brúarsmíði.
      b. *Ég **held** að smalann tröll **muni** taka á morgun.

The same is true, of course, in main clauses. This fact is easily accounted for by assuming that the same principle (V/2) governs word order in *both* main and embedded clauses. This assumption has interesting consequences for the syntactic analysis of Germanic languages, and for linguistic theory as well; these consequences are discussed below, as we turn to our account of two constructions which fall outside the V/2 principle: *wh*-questions and Left Dislocation.

1.1 Wh-*fronting*

While Topicalisation in embedded clauses triggers inversion, *wh*-fronting in embedded clauses does not, as shown by the contrast in the word order of embedded clauses between (2) and (3):

(3) a. Hann **spurði** hvenær hún **hefði** unnið brúarsmíði.
   He asked when she had worked at bridge building.
   b. Hann **spurði** hvern tröll **myndu** taka á morgun.
   [acc]
   He asked who trolls would take tomorrow.

If SVI applies in the embedded clauses, then the sentences are ungrammatical as illustrated in (3′):

(3′) a. *Hann **spurði** hvenær **hefði** hún unnið að brúarsmíði.
    He asked when had she worked at bridge building.
   b. *Hann **spurði** hvern **myndu** tröll taka á morgun.
    He asked who would trolls take tomorrow.

We can account for this difference by assuming that the derived structure of indirect questions and embedded Topicalisations are as shown in the diagrams in (4):

(4) a.   *Wh*-fronting   b.   Topicalisation

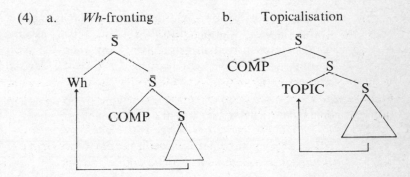

The facts then follow if S (and not S̄) is the domain of the V/2 Constraint. We assume that *wh*-fronting involves Chomsky-adjunction of the *wh*-word to S̄ as shown in (4a). Support for this comes from the fact that in all Germanic languages which allow *wh*-words to co-occur with the complementiser, this is the observed order. This is possible in OE and ME, OIce, in Swedish, and in some dialects of Dutch. Not only can the *wh*-words occur together with *that* in these languages, but the *that*-clause following the fronted *wh*-word behaves as one constituent as shown by the Dutch and Swedish examples in (5):

(5) a. Piet heeft gevraagd **wanneer** en Marie heeft gezegd **waar dat** we elkander gaan zien.

> *Pete has asked **when** and Mary has said **where that** we will see each other*
b. Pelle frågade **var**, och Eva frågade **när**, **som** vi träffades.
   *Pelle asked **where** and Eva asked **when** **COMP** we met.*

(The Dutch example is in standard spelling but the word choice and grammar is in the dialect of South Brabant.) One of the better supported constraints on movement rules is that only constituents can be moved. If we assume that this principle is respected by Right Node Raising, as argued by Bresnan (1974), the examples in (5) show that the *that*-clauses are constituents.[4] Note that in all of these examples the Topicalised constituent always *follows* rather than precedes the complementiser. Note also that we are not assuming a *Wh* Movement analysis of Topicalisation, since it is inconsistent with the word order facts. We will return to this below.

1.2 Direct Wh-*questions in Icelandic*

Direct questions do not exhibit the same word order as indirect questions. If the *wh*-word is adjoined to the S̄ node, and we assume that main clauses are derived in parallel fashion, then the non-embedded counterparts to the sentences in (3) have the derived structures shown in (6):

(6) a. [s̄ Hvenær [s **hefur** hún unnið að brúarsmíði]]?
         When has she worked at bridge building?
     b. [s̄ Hvern [s **munu** tröll taka á morgun]]?
         Who will trolls take tomorrow?

Then the verb will be the first constituent in direct *wh*-questions at the level of S, apparently violating V/2.

1.2.1 Word Order in Direct Questions. In Dutch and German, where V/2 applies to main clauses only, it has generally been assumed that the V/2 Constraint accounts for the surface positions of the verb in direct *wh*-questions as well as in declaratives, including Topicalisations, as shown in (7):

(7) a. Wie **zag** zij gisteren?
         Who saw she yesterday?
         Wanneer **zag** zij Jan?
         When saw she John?

b. Jan **zag** zij gisteren.
   John saw she yesterday.
   Gisteren **zag** zij Jan.
   Yesterday saw she John.

This indicates that the word order in declaratives and *wh*-questions reflects a single generalisation, and implies that the V/2 Constraint applies at the S̄ level in order to include the fronted *wh*-word in its domain.

But our analysis of Icelandic accounts for V/2 in embedded clauses by assigning different derived structure to *wh*-questions and Topicalisations, such that the fronted *wh*-phrase is outside S while the Topicalised constituent remains under S.

(8) a. Ég spurði hvenær [s hún **hefði** séð Jón].
         I asked when [s she had seen John].
     b. Ég held að [s í gær **hafi** hún séð Jón].
         I think that [s yesterday has she seen John].

Assume that main clauses are derived in parallel fashion; then the non-embedded counterparts to the sentences in (8) have the derived structures shown in (9):

(9) a.   *Wh*-question   b.   Topicalisation

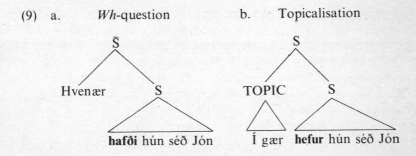

Then direct *wh*-questions (but not Topicalisations) are an exception to the V/2 Constraint since they are verb-initial at the level of S. (Remember that there is no Subject-Verb Inversion in indirect questions.)

However another generalisation about the position of the tensed verb will capture all the facts quite naturally: V/2 order applied to declaratives (and embedded clauses) but V/1 order applied to *all* direct questions, both *wh*-questions and yes-no questions. The domain of both word order constraints is S and not S̄, and the same Subject-Verb Inversion rule applies in both *wh-* and yes-no questions, putting the verb in S-initial position.

This generalisation has several interesting consequences. First, the difference in word order between *wh*-questions and Topicalised sentences in English is explained by the fact that English does not have a V/2 Constraint, but does have a Subject-Aux Inversion rule. Secondly, the fact that Topicalisation and direct questions cannot co-occur in the same S is explained by the conflict in word order frames. Topicalisation would make it impossible to respect the V/1 frame for direct questions.

(10)   *[$_S$ John [$_S$ saw she yesterday]]?

Assuming that the domain of the word order frames is the topmost S in an S-over-S derived structure, then V/2 and V/1 cannot both be satisfied simultaneously.

Our analysis claims that the word order in *wh*-questions and yes-no questions reflects a single generalisation, whereas the word order in declaratives and *wh*-questions does not. We predict that the word order in declaratives will change independently of the word order in *wh*-questions. This prediction is supported by the diachronic evidence from within Germanic, since this is exactly what happened in English. While V/2 was not an absolute rule in OE, the tendency was for the finite verb to be in second position in main clauses. This tendency was lost for declaratives as illustrated in (11a). In *wh*-questions, however, the verb still directly follows the *wh*-phrase in what has traditionally been considered second position.[5]

(11)   a.   John she *saw* yesterday.
        b.   Who *did* she see yesterday?

But as we have suggested, this can also be considered 'first position' at the level of S. The word order for questions in Germanic has always been V/1 at the level of S (this includes *wh*-questions in our analysis), whatever the position of the verb in declarative main clauses (see e.g., Behaghel, 1932). In fact, in the very oldest records the verb tended to be clause-final (or at least later than second position) in declaratives, but not in *wh*-questions.

1.3 Topicalisation and Left Dislocation

Let us now return to the derived constituent structure of Topicalised sentences. Many analyses of fronting rules in the recent literature, e.g. Emonds (1976), Bowers (1976), Löwenstamm (1977), attempt to collapse *wh*-fronting with Topicalisation as two instances of COMP-substitution. But such analyses cannot account for the word order facts in Icelandic without completely *ad hoc* restrictions on SVI or surface filters having the effect of preventing SVI from applying in embedded clauses just in case COMP contains a *wh*-phrase. This will not only be true for Icelandic, but also of Yiddish, where V/2 applies to embedded clauses.

The word order facts also bear on another proposal concerning the structure of Topicalisation. Chomsky (1977) 'On *Wh* Movement', gives the same derived constituent structure to Topicalisation and Left Dislocation as shown in (12), and distinguishes them only by the fact that *Wh* Movement has applied in the case of Topicalisation, moving a *wh*-pronoun into COMP-position, and subsequently deleting it there. For this *Wh* Movement analysis of Topicalisation there is no direct evidence, but it is supposed to explain the fact that Topicalisation obeys island constraints, whereas Left Dislocation does not, as observed by Ross.

(12)

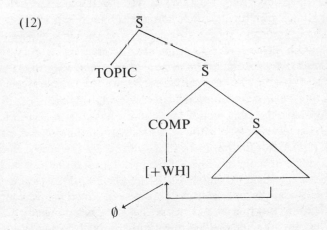

In Chomsky's current framework, all constructions that obey island constraints are analysed as instances of *Wh* Movement.

An example of Left Dislocation in Icelandic is given in (13).

(13)   Smalinn[i], ég **held** að tröll **muni** taka hann[i] á morgun
       Shepherd-the [nom], *I think that trolls will take him*
       tomorrow.

We see that the Left Dislocated constituent does not count for the
Verb-Second Constraint. This is also true of German and Dutch, as
was pointed out by van Riemsdijk and Zwarts (1974). Our analysis
for Left Dislocation in Icelandic is exactly the same as for those
languages: namely, the Left Dislocated constituent is not a part of
the S, but instead is base-generated under some loosely connected
node[6] as shown in (14), where $\bar{S}$ is a root S.

(14)   Left Dislocation:

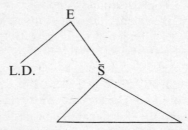

This structure predicts that in a declarative, inversion after Left
Dislocation is ungrammatical, which is the case, as shown in (15):

(15)   *Smalinn[i] **held** ég að tröll muni taka hann[i] á morgun.
       The shepherd think I that trolls will take him tomorrow.

When, as in Chomsky's analysis, Left Dislocation and
Topicalisation have the same structure, it is not possible to account
for the difference in word order: for Left Dislocation the domain of
the Verb-second Constraint has to be the S-node in (12), whereas for
Topicalisation, the domain must be $\bar{\bar{S}}$. One might attempt to link the
difference to the presence of some feature $[\pm wh]$, since this is, under
Chomsky's analysis, the only distinction between Left Dislocation
and Topicalisation. But this use of features gives the wrong result, as
can be seen by looking at embedded questions. Embedded questions
must have the feature $[+wh]$, but there is no inversion inside S; that
same feature $[+wh]$ would have to trigger inversion in the case of
Topicalisation.

There are many systematic differences between Topicalisation and
Left Dislocation in Icelandic which argue against collapsing them.

For example, Topicalisation is common in embedded clauses, but Left Dislocation is impossible. The many differences noted by van Riemsdijk and Zwarts (1974) for Dutch are true of Icelandic as well. However since this question is not directly relevant to the theory of filters, we simply summarise the differences in table (16). The only criterion which needs explanation is the restriction on dummy það. Since dummy það occurs only in S-initial position in Icelandic, it is incompatible with Topicalisation, but of course, can occur as the initial constituent after the Left Dislocated element in the structure shown in figure (14).

(16)	Topicalisation	LD
Can occur in embedded S?	yes	no
Contains a resumptive pronoun?[7]	no	yes
Initial C followed by complete S?	no	yes
Initial C counts for V/2?	yes	no
Case of initial NP?	varies	nominative
Can initial C be any nontensed C?	yes	no
Can initial C be indefinite?	yes	no[8]
Can initial C be part of an idiom?	yes	no
Can initial C be reflexive/reciprocal?	yes	no
Can dummy það occur?	no	yes
Initial C followed by interrogative?	no	yes
Can initial C be followed by imperative?	no	yes
Obeys island constraints?	yes	no

1.4 Embedded Clauses with Extracted Subjects

We have argued that V/2 is a constraint on all tensed declarative clauses in Icelandic, that *wh*-questions as well as yes-no questions have V/1 word order, and that Left Dislocation is accounted for by analysing it as shown in (14). There remains one clause type to be accounted for: the case of embedded clauses whose subjects are extracted in a later cycle. In the examples shown in (17), the finite verb appears as the first constituent in the embedded S.

(17) a. Hver heldur þú að [s ⎯⎯⎯ sé kominn til Reykjavíkur]?
          Who think you that ⎯⎯⎯ was come to Reykjavik?
      b. þetta er maðurinn, sem þeir segja að [s ⎯⎯⎯ hafi framið glæpinn].
          This is the-man that they say that ⎯⎯⎯ has committed the-crime.
      c. þetta sverð heldur konungurinn að [s ⎯⎯⎯ sé galdrasverð].
          This sword thinks the-king that ⎯⎯⎯ is a-magic-sword.

We have argued elsewhere (Maling and Zaenen, 1977, 1978) that such sentences can be explained by counting the trace left by *Wh* Movement or other extraction rules as the first constituent for the V/2 Constraint. Note that this explanation implies a distinction between the traces left by 'extraction rules' and those left by NP Movement rules, since the latter do not count for V/2, as we have shown in Maling and Zaenen (1978). The distinction between these two rules classes goes back at least as early as Ross. Bresnan's (1976) framework of Realistic Grammar makes exactly this prediction for trace theory. Another point of interest in sentences like those in (17) lies in the observation that Icelandic lacks the 'Fixed Subject Constraint', even though personal pronoun subjects are obligatory. Hence Icelandic provides a counter-example to the surface filter shown in (18), which Chomsky and Lasnik (1977) proposed as a linguistic universal.

(18) *[s that [NP *e*] ...] unless $\bar{S}$ or its trace is in the context:
      [NP NP ⎯⎯⎯ ...]
      (=C&L (68))

Chomsky and Lasnik restate as shown in (19) a cross-linguistic correlation originally proposed by Perlmutter (1971):[9]

(19) The filter (68) is valid for all languages that do not have a rule of Subject-Pronoun Deletion, and only these.
      (=C&L (71))

They claim that trace theory thus explains the cross-linguistic correlation. The crucial assumption here is that an independently motivated rule of Subject-Pronoun Deletion will apply to the structure referred to in filter (18), converting (20a) into (20b):

(20) a.   b.

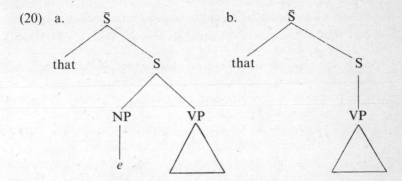

thus erasing the trace left by any rule which has extracted the subject, and leaving filter (18) with nothing to reject. Their assumption is that '... deletion removes a category and its contents', (p. 453) whereas movement rules leave a category and a trace behind.

Now in Icelandic, *wh*-questions, relative clauses, clefts and Topicalisations all allow extraction of subject NPs immediately adjacent to the COMP **að** 'that'; in fact, deletion of **að** is only marginally possible and is certainly no better in the case of extracted subjects. But since personal pronoun subjects are obligatory in Icelandic, there is no independently motivated Pro-drop rule which can be used to account for the grammaticality of subject extraction. Moreover, Icelandic is not the only Germanic language which lacks the Fixed Subject Constraint. So does Old English (as noted by Allen 1977), as well as most dialects of Dutch and Norwegian; on the other hand, English, Danish and Swedish all obey the Fixed Subject Constraint. In Maling and Zaenen (1978) we suggest that the correct cross-linguistic correlation is between violations of the FSC and having *dummy* subjects which are not always present in surface structure. But we also show that violations of the FSC cannot be attributed to the application of an independently motivated Dummy Pro-drop rule in the manner suggested by Chomsky and Lasnik, since the dummy subject is not present at any stage in the derivation of such sentences. We show furthermore, that postulating an *ad hoc* trace deletion rule will not work in Icelandic. Presumably such a trace-deletion rule would be postulated under analogy with a rule deleting dummy subjects (for if there are no constraints on postulating trace-deletion rules, then filter (18) has no explanatory value whatsoever). We argue that the existence of such a dummy-subject-deletion rule in Icelandic is dubious; but assuming that it could be motivated, then a trace-deletion rule will quietly remove the offending trace in (20a) without going through an intermediate stage with dummy subject. However, this will not work. Note that those clauses with extracted subjects in (17) also violate the V/2 Constraint, since the embedded clauses are verb-initial rather than V/2. Yet these are clauses where one would expect V/2 order. If a nonsubject NP is extracted from an embedded clause, then V/2 is the only grammatical order, as illustrated in (21):

(21) a.   Hverjum heldur þú að [s Ólafur **hafi** hjálpað ____]?
           who-dat. *do you think that Olaf has helped*
      b.   *Hverjum heldur þú að [s **hafi** Ólafur hjálpað ____]?

Only in the case of extracted subjects is the verb in clause-initial position. The explanation is, we think, clear: the trace of the extracted subject must count as filling first position in the embedded clause. If the traces left by extraction rules are visible to surface filters, then these clauses will not violate V/2, and we can maintain V/2 as a generalisation about Icelandic word order in tensed clauses. This solution leads to a contradiction for anyone who wants to maintain the universality of filter (18): deleting subject traces will not work because the very traces which violate filter (18) are needed to satisfy the V/2 filter. Clearly the grammar of Icelandic cannot contain *both* surface filters simultaneously. Since V/2 is so much more intuitive and simple, surely it is the filter of choice. For a more complete discussion of the role of V/2 in Icelandic, see Maling and Zaenen (1978).

The picture, as we see it, is thus as follows: Icelandic declarative sentences have the tensed verb in second position, whereas direct questions have the verb in first position. The difference is linked to the 'direct speech act' that the sentence is supposed to perform: statements are V/2; requests for information are V/1, as are orders (i.e., imperatives), which we have not discussed here.[10] Indirect questions are, of course, not requests for information.

2. The discussion above demonstrates clearly that V/2 is a real generalisation about Icelandic word order, and that any apparent counter-examples can be accounted for in a straightforward and insightful way. We now turn to the problem of how the grammar will effect V/2.

2.1 V/2 can be achieved in different ways; we will discuss two possibilities. First, that V/2 is a syntactic 'conspiracy' and second, that it is a surface filter. According to the conspiracy view, V/2 is not really a part of the grammar, but rather some kind of meta-statement. The verb ends up in second position because the rules 'conspire' to get it there when they apply in the right way. To make this conspiracy work, it is obviously necessary to make use of rule conditions: obligatoriness, contextual dependencies and rule ordering. The main rules to be considered in this regard are Topicalisation, SVI and það-insertion. Let's assume the usual formulations of Topicalisation and SVI, and assume that það-insertion inserts a dummy það in sentence-initial position if nothing precedes the verb. The relevant fact about Icelandic is that dummy það does not undergo SVI; this is illustrated by the sentences in (22):

(22) a. það var mikill snjór á jörðinni.
          There was much snow on the-ground.
      b. Í gær var (*það) mikill snjór á jörðinni.
          Yesterday was (there) much snow on the-ground.
      c. Var (*það) mikill snjór á jörðinni?
          Was (there) much snow on the-ground?
      d. Hvað var (*það) á jörðinni?
          What was (there) on the-ground?

Consider first the interaction of Topicalisation and SVI: it is clear that the application of just one of these two rules will give ungrammatical declarative Ss; either both rules must apply, or neither. Therefore we need to impose both rule ordering and obligatoriness. Since dummy það occurs only in sentence-initial position, Topicalisation cannot apply if það-insertion has applied. It will not do to simply prevent SVI from applying twice in a given clause, because impersonal passives are generated with empty subject nodes, and hence það must be inserted in such sentences even though SVI has not applied.

It is clear that there are several ways of stating and ordering these three rules to obtain the right results, but they all require extensive use of rule conditions.

As observed in Williams (1977, 1980) this type of complexity in the transformational component can be avoided by associating word order templates directly with utterance types. A straightforward way to do so, is the use of positive surface filters. The most important of these is V/2 formulated in (23). (See note 13 below.)

(23) [$_S$ C V ...] where C is any constituent, and V is the finite verb.

Then the three transformations above can be stated simply, can apply optionally and in any order. Any output which doesn't meet the canonical form given in (23) above will be filtered out. We assume that the relevant S node in a Topicalised structure such as (4b) will be picked out according to some version of the A-over-A Principle, defined in terms of immediate dominance (cf. Sag (1976)), or other notion that will correctly choose the highest S if Topicalisation is formulated in terms of Chomsky-adjunction to a base-generated S-node. The ungrammatical strings shown in (24) will of course be generated by the grammar but will be filtered out.

(24)   a. [$_S$ V ...]   b.   [$_S$ C C V ...]

(24a) will be generated if only SVI applies; we assume that it is also the base-generated structure for impersonal passives, and either Topicalisation or það-insertion must apply in order to produce a grammatical sentence. (24b) will be generated if Topicalisation applies but SVI doesn't, or else if both það-insertion and Topicalisation apply. A further interpretive rule will throw out the case of það-insertion plus a definite NP ([það V NP$_{[+def]}$ ...]); this rule will be needed in any case.

The only problem is that not all rule conditions can be eliminated with this approach: það-insertion still has to apply at the end of the cycle, to prevent it from feeding SVI, and thus generating the sentences in (22b,d), which are ungrammatical even though they satisfy the V/2 filter (23).

2.2 There are three ways to avoid this use of ordering. The first is to assume that það is not inserted to fill the subject node, so that SVI will not apply to it; það might instead be inserted as a sister to the subject node. Note that in our framework það does not function to cover improperly-bound subject traces since we assume that cyclic NP Movement rules do not leave traces.

The second alternative: extrinsic ordering of SVI with respect to það-insertion in Icelandic could also be avoided by assuming that Icelandic is VSO in underlying structure, because under this assumption there is no need for a rule of SVI, and hence no ordering problem. If both það-insertion and Topicalisation apply, the resulting sentence will be filtered out by the V/2 filter. There are two problems with the VSO analysis of Icelandic: first, it makes the implausible claim that the underlying order is that of questions rather than declaratives, and secondly, the Topicalisation of subject NPs will not create an island, whereas the Topicalisation of any nonsubject NP docs.

(25)   Hvar heldur þú að Egill   **hafi** séð Ólaf?
                            (nom.)
        *Hvar heldur þú að Ólaf **hafi** Egill séð?
                            (acc.)
        Where think you that Egil has seen Olaf?

Note that the VSO analysis of Icelandic docs not solve the problem of filter (12) that we discussed above. If V/2 is a surface constraint, it needs the trace between the COMP-node and the V; in other words, the order has to be V/2 at the end of the embedded cycle.

The third way to avoid extrinsic rule ordering is to investigate the possibility of making a principled distinction between transformations that move a constituent, and rules which insert specified lexical items. We suggest that the theory of grammar order such insertion rules after all movement rules. Then the fact that það-insertion applies after SVI will be a consequence of the theory rather than an extrinsic ordering condition. This seems to us to be the most plausible approach to avoiding extrinsic rule ordering in the grammar; however, one needs to see how this suggestion generalises to languages such as English, where dummy *there* is a good input to some movement transformations. It may be that in such languages dummy-insertion is simply a node-filling operation. It has been proposed that empty nodes can be moved around by transformations just as easily as filled ones (cf. for instance Breckenridge, 1975b). Then at the end of the cycle a kind of adjustment rule applies that can insert dummies in empty subject nodes.[11] The kind of adjustment that needs to be made is *language-specific*: in Icelandic, the surface structure must be adjusted to the canonical form of tensed clauses, namely [C V ...]. In English the requirement is that there be an overt subject in *that*-clauses (and most but not all tensed clauses; cf. Bresnan, 1972). Hence the adjustment rule for English will insert a dummy *there* into empty NP nodes directly dominated by S (i.e. subject nodes). Such adjustment rules precede the application of surface filters, and have the effect of saving a certain number of otherwise legitimate derivations whose only problem is not having produced an acceptable surface configuration for that language.

We conclude that stating V/2 as a surface filter greatly simplifies the transformational component of the grammar, by allowing rule conditions to be eliminated. Moreover, it has the advantage of capturing this generalisation about word order directly, whereas the conspiracy approach has to relegate it to a meta-level. Since the V/2 Constraint is an important part of the linguistic knowledge of the native speaker, it seems preferable to state it directly.

3. However, the addition of surface structure constraints to linguistic theory raises the problem of how to constrain the constraints themselves. As is well known from discussions in the literature, from Jonathan Swift (*Gulliver's Travels*, Part III, Ch. V) to David Perlmutter (1971), and most recently in Chomsky and Lasnik (1977), filters are a very powerful grammatical device. It is necessary to constrain them in some way, to prevent them from being able to do everything, and hence explain nothing.

Chomsky and Lasnik have taken up the interesting line of research first suggested by Perlmutter (1971); they have shown that surface filters can be used to restrict the power of grammars in other ways, specifically by eliminating rule conditions altogether. They also make a first attempt to restrict the possible format of filters. They tentatively propose (pp. 488–9) two characteristics of surface filters which we believe to be untenable (although we agree that filters should be 'local'):

1. that filters deal only with properties of the complementiser system;
2. that filters are stated negatively rather than positively.

We shall consider each of these in turn. It is not clear what it means to be 'a property of the COMP system'. The strong interpretation of it would be that filters only apply to items actually *in* COMP position, or at least adjacent to COMP position. While many proposed filters do meet this characterisation, the V/2 constraint does not. It can, of course, be reformulated so as to mention COMP, for example as shown in (26):

(26)   [s COMP [s C V ...]]

where a COMP node is assumed to be present in root declaratives when the filter applies. But this seem to be a weakening of the notion 'property of the COMP system'. Other candidates for syntactic surface filters are not so easily reformulated. Consider the filters for the order of clitic pronouns in Romance languages, in particular the version proposed by Perlmutter for Spanish. Reformulated to mention COMP, it would look as shown in (27):

(27)   COMP [s NP se II I III ...]

Obviously the internal ordering of the clitic pronouns with respect to each other is not a property of the COMP system; nor is it clear that the position of the clitic sequence within the sentence should be so considered.

We suspect that there are word order constraints which are good candidates for surface filter analysis and which have nothing to do with the COMP, e.g., obligatory pied-piping could be accounted for by a surface filter *[P t].

The second characteristic of filters that Chomsky and Lasnik propose is that they be stated negatively rather than positively. All of the filters they considered were of the format

(28)   *[$_\alpha$ φ_1 ... φ_n], unless C, where:
         a. α is either a category or is left unspecified
         b. φ_i is either a category or a terminal symbol
         c.   C is some condition on (α, φ_1, ... φ_n)
              (=C&L (184))

Unfortunately, as far as the distinction between positive and negative filters goes, this format is emptied of all possible empirical content by allowing *unless*-conditions on filters. If *unless*-conditions are allowed, then every positive filter can be reformulated into a negative filter. For example, we stated V/2 as a positive filter in (23).

Without *unless*-conditions, the alternative to a positive filter is a possibly infinite set of negative filters as shown in (29):

(29) $\begin{cases} *[_S \text{ V X}] \\ *[_S \text{ C}^n \text{ V X}] \quad \text{for } n \geqslant 2 \end{cases}$

The number of negative filters necessary will depend on assumptions about such questions as (i) when rules are to be collapsed (e.g. are PP-fronting and NP-Topicalisation two rules or one?), (ii) whether a fronting rule can apply more than once per cycle, and (iii) whether certain adverbs can be base-generated in S-initial position (as has been argued by Kuno, 1971). Whatever the answers to these questions, it is likely that sequences of at least three preverbal constituents can be generated in Icelandic, obviously two can be. By comparing the negative format in (29) to the positive one in (23), it is clear that the set of negative filters is less economical than a single positive filter. Moreover, it simply misses the generalisation.

If, however, *unless*-conditions are allowed, then the positive V/2 filter can be reformulated as a single negative constraint as shown in (30):[12]

(30) $* \begin{matrix} \text{V} \\ [+\text{finite}] \end{matrix}$, unless in the context $[_S \text{ C} \_\_\_\_\_ ...]$

From this example, we see that certain syntactic generalisations can best be captured by positive filters. Moreover, the positive filter allows the generalisation to be stated without the use of *unless*-conditions. So on empirical grounds, we would like to propose that it is better to allow for positive filters; but as is clear from the previous discussion, the issue does not have any real empirical content as long as the theory does not exclude or at least severely restrict the use of *unless*-conditions and other devices that allow the reformulation of positive filters into negative ones (or vice versa). For example, V/2 could be stated in a double negative form as in (31):

(31) $*[_S \text{ C} \quad \text{C} ...]$
$$- \begin{bmatrix} +\text{V} \\ -\text{N} \\ +\text{tns} \end{bmatrix}$$

where (31) presupposes that there is only one tensed verb per clause.

Unless such devices are well-motivated on independent grounds, they contribute nothing to our understanding of the role of filters in grammar. For similar reasons, it is necessary to exclude devices that allow reformulation of non-local phenomena into local ones.

Let us assume that the theory can be constrained such that there is an empirical difference between positive and negative filters. Is it in that case desirable to limit the format of filters in such a way that only negative filters are allowed, forcing a reanalysis of the data presented above so that either no filters are used, or else the infinite set in (29)? Our initial answer is no; a transformational account of V/2 may well be possible, but as is clear from our discussion, we think that the word order constraint presented here is a good candidate for a syntactic filter. However, it is conceivable that some meta-theoretical principle(s) would point to a different answer. The most common of these principles to be invoked is based on the probable mechanisms of language acquisition. Since very little is known in this area, only very tentative remarks can be made. We would, however, like to point out the following, which also points to a negative answer to our question about the format of filters. It is known that the manipulation of negations presents complications in almost all learning processes. With respect to the problem at hand, we can ask two questions:

1. Will the child, when presented with linguistic evidence of the type we have described, come up with a positive or a negative rule (filter)?
2. Will a negative rule, or a positive rule be easier to handle, i.e., will it be easier to judge whether a sentence is grammatical or not when it must be checked against a positive or a negative rule?

A random selection from the voluminous literature on the subject (see e.g. Johnson-Laird and Wason, 1977, for information) reveals the following studies. A paper by Donaldson (1959) describes the behaviour both of teenagers and adults when asked to construct rules to match objects. The task could be performed with logically equivalent sets of positive rules, negative rules or mixtures of both, but the subjects were explicitly told that the use of a positive rule 'cost more' than the use of a negative one. In spite of this instruction, the subjects did not eliminate positive rules; and when they used negative rules, they tended to construct redundant rule systems.

Another study (Evans, 1972) shows that when conditional rules are given, and subjects have to draw inferences from them, the score on valid inferences drops dramatically when the antecedent is negative (i.e., rules of the form 'if not p, then ...'). This seems to point to the conclusion that negative rules are more difficult to work with. While it is not clear how these findings and many others of a similar kind carry over into linguistics and the learning of language, it is implausible that our 'unconscious' intellectual manipulations are diametrically opposed in this respect from the conscious ones. This suggests that research strategies that try to restrict the format of filters (or any type of linguistic rule) to negative statements without being absolutely forced to do so by the data and/or important theoretical considerations, are methodologically mistaken. It would force us to translate linguistic generalisations into a form that makes it *a priori* difficult to explain their acquisition.

4. We have shown that the format of filters proposed in C&L (1977) is not well motivated on either theoretical or empirical grounds. More positively we would like to suggest that one use of filters in syntax is linked to word order frames associated with direct speech acts.[13] For Germanic languages, we have suggested that a V/1 filter is associated with requests for information and that a V/2 filter is associated with declaratives. In the case of German and Dutch, this V/2 filter is restricted to main clauses.

Notes

* We are indebted to Joan Bresnan, Ellen Prince and Henk van Riemsdijk for comments and discussion, and especially to Höskuldur Thráinsson for the Icelandic data and discussion thereof. An earlier version of this paper was read at the Amsterdam Colloquium on 7 April 1978; this paper remains essentially as written in 1978, and has not been revised in light of more recent developments in syntactic theory e.g. in Chomsky's paper in this volume. Preparation of this paper was supported in part by NSF Grant BNS 78-16522 to Brandeis University.

1. The precise formulation of V/2 depends on certain assumptions about the nodes AUX and VP, assumptions which determine whether the finite verb will itself be an immediate constituent of S. If there is no VP-node, then the finite verb will be the second immediate constituent of S. However, if there is a VP-node, then V will not be an immediate constituent of S unless it is raised into AUX. Alternatively, V/2 could be reformulated to require that the finite verb directly follow the first immediate constituent of S.

2. These remnants of V/2 need further study.

3. We will use the term 'Topicalisation' to refer to the fronting of any major sentence constituent (except *wh*-phrases) which does not leave behind a pronominal copy; we leave open the question of whether such fronting processes are one rule or

more than one. Maling (1980) shows that in addition to Topicalisation there is a minor fronting rule which fronts past participles, predicate adjectives and certain adverbials including verbal particles. This type of 'Stylistic Inversion' is characteristic of Icelandic and Faroese as opposed to the other Scandinavian languages. Unlike Topicalisation, it is clause-bounded, extremely common in embedded clauses, and restricted to subjectless clauses of various kinds. See Maling (1980) for a fuller characterisation of the difference between these two fronting rules.

4. For another view on Right Node Raising and constituent structures, see Abbott (1976).

5. The complication of *do*-support is irrelevant to the position of the finite verb.

6. We adopt Ann Banfield's (1973) notation E for the nonrecursive initial node (E for 'expression').

7. At first glance, sentences like (i) pose a problem for the extension of this analysis to English, because they appear to be cases of Topicalisation out of direct *wh*-questions.

(i)   Yesterday, who did you visit first?

However, we think that such sentences are best analysed as cases of Left Dislocation with deleted resumptive pronoun. Note that the Dutch and Icelandic translations of such sentences have an obligatory pronoun *then*:

(ii) a.   Gisteren, wie heb je **toen** eerst bezocht?
     b.   Í gær, hvern heimsottirðu fyrst **þá**?
           *Yesterday, who did you visit **then**?*
(iii) a.   *Gisteren, wie heb je eerst bezocht?
     b.   *Í gær, hvern heimsottirðu fyrst?

The same is true of sentences with initial locative phrases:

(iv) a.   In Parijs, wie heb je **daar** bezocht?
     b.   I París, hvern heimsottirðu **þar**?
           *In Paris, who did you visit **there**?*
(v)   a.   *In Parijs, wie heb je bezocht?
     b.   *Í París, hvern heimsottirðu?

If our analysis of such sentences is correct, then it is clear that the appearance of the resumptive pronoun is not the defining characteristic of the difference between LD and Topicalisation in English. That the presence or absence of a pronoun is not universally linked to the difference between LD and Topicalisation is clear from the discussion of the Italian cases in Cinque (1977).

These examples show that the Left-Dislocated element need not be a NP; a variety of phrasal categories, including certain clauses and at least locative and temporal PPs are possible. Our initial hypothesis is that the LD element must be pronominalisable by a one-word proform in the accompanying S.

(vi) a.   *To John, I gave the book *to him*.
     b.   John, I gave *him* the book.

This requirement would explain why locative and temporal PPs are possible LD elements: precisely because they have suitable proforms, *there* and *then*.

8. This is not totally true in English, as was pointed out to us by Ellen Prince. Her corpus from Terkel's *Working* includes the following examples:

(i)   An old preacher down there, they augured under the grave where his wife was buried. (Studs Terkel (1974), *Working*, p. 44)

(ii)   One woman I had called early in the morning, she had just gotten out of the hospital. (Ibid, p. 41)

See E. Prince (1978, 1979) for further details. It is not clear that the observation carries over to Icelandic and Dutch. We have been unable to find convincing examples, but the question deserves further study.

9. Perlmutter pointed out that Dutch is a counter-example to (19); therefore he proposed only a one-way implication: languages with subject-pronoun-deletion allow the sequence '*that* V ...' See Maling and Zaenen (1978) for a discussion of Dutch and the proposed correlation.

10. In fact, the notion 'direct speech act' is not totally adequate. Searle would consider the following sentence to be a non-declarative direct speech act:

(i)   I request that you leave immediately.

But the syntactic form is that of a declarative in the languages under consideration. We are tempted to see this as an inadequacy in the distinctions made in theory of speech acts. How this theory has to be articulated is not our concern here. It suffices to observe that indirect speech acts are not relevant for the distinction that we want to make, and that our distinction comes close to the notion of direct speech act as it is made on independent grounds; see e.g. Searle (1975).

11. It may not be possible to order dummy-insertion rules at a uniform point in the grammar for all languages. In English, *there*-insertion appears to be cyclic, since subject gaps created by extraction rules cannot be filled by *there*; moreover, if the rule of Subject-to-Object Raising exists, then *there*-insertion must apply at the end of the cycle, when the empty node is still subject, in order to account for sentences like (i):

(i)   I expect there to be a problem.

(Dummy subjects occur in other nontensed clauses as well, e.g. *There being a problem* ...) In Icelandic, if there is no rule of Subject-to-Object Raising, then **það**-insertion could either be cyclic or just optional at the end of the transformational component. The picture is more complicated in Danish, in that some but not all subject gaps created by extraction rules may be filled by the dummy **der**:

(ii)   Jeg kan ikke forestille mig, hvem (**der**) kan lide den slags musik!
       I can't imagine who (there) could like that kind of music!

(iii) Her er de digte, som laereren spurgte os, hvem vi troede, (**der**) havde skrevet dem.
       Here *are the poems that the teacher asked us who we thought had written them.*

(iv)   Hvem tror politiet, (**der**) begik forbrydelsen?
       Who do the police think committed the crime?

(v)   Flere mennesker kører Volvo end $\left\{ \begin{matrix} der \\ *\varnothing \end{matrix} \right\}$ kører Porsche.

       More people drive Volvos than drive Porsches.

(vi)   En mand som (**?der**) ikke drikker ...
       A man that (who) doesn't drink ...

This use of **der** varies somewhat from dialect to dialect, but appears to be extending. All dialects accept (and even prefer) **der** in sentences (i)–(iv), and reject comparatives with unfilled subject gap as in (v). Only nonstandard dialects accept the sequence **som** der in relative clauses as in (vi), but this does suggest that in some languages, dummy insertion may have to apply at the end of the transformational component rather than cyclically. (We are grateful to Wera Hildebrand for discussion of the Dutch facts.)

12. This possibility was pointed out to us by Henk van Riemsdijk and Joan Bresnan.

13. This idea was presented orally by Williams in a talk at Harvard in the autumn of 1977 during the period our paper was being written. The written version of Williams paper (Williams, 1980) only became known to us two years after our paper was finished. As the interested reader can verify for himself there are important differences between the way Williams (1980) uses utterance types in English and our positive surface filter for Icelandic. One basic idea however, is common to both approaches, namely that such templates can be used to eliminate rule ordering and the necessity for obligatory rules.

References

Abbott, B. (1976), 'Right-Node Raising as a Test of Constituenthood', *Linguistic Inquiry* 4, 639–42

Allen, C. (1977), *Topics in English Diachronic Syntax*, Unpublished PhD dissertation, University of Massachusetts, Amherst

Banfield, Ann (1973), 'Narrative Style and the Grammar of Direct and Indirect Speech', *Foundations of Language* 10, 1–39

Behaghel, O. (1932), *Deutsche Syntax: eine geschichtliche darstellung*, IV, Carl Winters Universitätsbuchhandlung, Heidelberg

Bowers, J. (1976), 'On Surface Structure, Grammatical Relations, and the Structure-Preserving Hypothesis', *Linguistic Analysis* 2.3, 225–42

Breckenridge, J. (1975a), 'The Post-Cyclicity of *es*-insertion in German', CLS 11, 81–91

——— (1975b), 'Rules that *Nothing* Undergoes', Unpublished senior thesis, Harvard University

Bresnan, J. (1972), *Theory of Complementation in English Syntax*, Unpublished PhD dissertation, Massachusetts Institute of Technology

——— (1974), 'The Position of Certain Clause-Particles in Phrase Structure', *Linguistic Inquiry* 5, 614–19

——— (1976), 'Towards a Realistic Model of Transformational Grammar' in Morris Halle, Joan Bresnan and George A. Miller (eds.), *Linguistic Theory and Psychological Reality*, MIT Press, Cambridge

Chomsky, N. (1976), 'On *Wh*-movement' in Peter Culicover, T. Wasow and A. Akmajian (eds.), *Formal Syntax*, Academic Press, New York

Chomsky, N. and H. Lasnik (1977), 'Filters and Control', *Linguistic Inquiry* 8.3, 425–504

Cinque, G. (1977), 'The Movement Nature of Left Dislocation', *Linguistic Inquiry* 8.2, 398–412

Donaldson, M. (1959), 'Positive and Negative Information in Matching Problems', *British Journal of Psychology* 50

Emonds, J. (1976), *A Transformational Approach to English Syntax*, Academic Press, New York

Evans, J. St. B. T. (1972), 'Reasoning with Negatives', *British Journal of Psychology* 63

Johnson-Laird, P. N. and P. C. Wason (1977), *Thinking*, Cambridge University Press, Cambridge

Kuno, S. (1971), 'The Position of Locatives in Existential Sentences', *Linguistic Inquiry* 2.3, 333–78

Lowenstamm, J. (1977), 'Relative Clauses in Yiddish: A Case for Movement', *Linguistic Analysis* 3.3, 197–216

Maling, J. (1976), 'Old Icelandic Relative Clauses: an Unbounded Deletion Rule', Proceedings of the VII meeting of the North Eastern Linguistic Society, Cambridge, Massachusetts

————— (1980), 'Inversion in Embedded Clauses in Modern Icelandic', *Islenskt mál og almenn málfrœði*, 2, 175–98

Maling, J. and A. Zaenen (1977), 'Filters and Traces in Icelandic', paper read at VIII meeting of the North Eastern Linguistic Society, Amherst, Massachusetts

————— (1978), 'The Nonuniversality of a Surface Filter', *Linguistic Inquiry* 9.3, 475–97

Perlmutter, D. (1971), *Deep and Surface Structure Constraints in Syntax*, Holt, Rinehart & Winston, New York

Prince, E. (1978), 'Left Dislocation, It Makes Life Easier', paper presented at the LSA Winter Meeting

————— (1979), 'Left Dislocation: A Functional Analysis', unpublished paper, University of Pennsylvania

van Riemsdijk, H. and F. Zwarts (1974), 'Left Dislocation and the Status of Copying Rules', unpublished paper, Massachusetts Institute of Technology/University of Amsterdam

Sag, I. (1976), 'Maximization of Recoverability of Deletion', paper read at the winter meeting of the Linguistic Society of America, Philadelphia, Pennsylvania

Searle, J. (1975), 'Indirect Speech Acts' in Cole and Morgan (eds.), *Speech Acts*, Academic Press, New York

Williams, E. (1977), 'Abstract Triggers', talk given at Harvard University

————— (1980), 'Abstract Triggers', *Journal of Linguistic Research*, 1.1

8 Quechua Word Structure*

Pieter Muysken

0. Introduction

This paper will try to sketch a coherent account of Quechua word structure, clearly separating it from phrase structure. As such it will try to contribute to answering the traditional question of defining the border between syntax and morphology, a question which has particularly vexed students of Amerindian languages. Kenneth Pike, in a 1949 paper, claimed that the border cannot be defined, on the basis of an analysis of Mixteco morphology. In fact, he proposed:

> For the description of some languages it is not accurate or helpful to postulate a sharp morphology-syntax dichotomy. (Pike, 1949)

Here I would like to argue in detail that it is both accurate and helpful to postulate that dichotomy. I will do this by presenting a lexicalist analysis of Quechua verbal morphology, arguing that it is generated by word formation rules of the familiar type (cf. Aronoff, 1976).

To illustrate the kind of problems that we will have to deal with, consider a form such as (1):

(1) maqa-ra- yki
     hit   past 2s
     You hit.

In the model developed in Chomsky (1965) and Chomsky and Halle (1968), with the additional refinements imposed on it in Selkirk (1972), there are at least two ways in which this form could be presented in phrase structure:

(2) a.

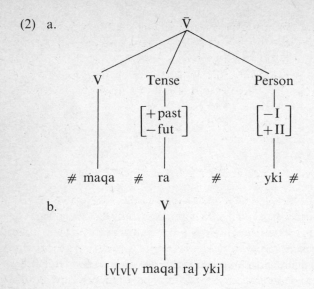

b.   V
                     |
                     |
                     |
        [v[v[v maqa] ra] yki]

In (2a) the occurrence of the stem, the tense marker, and the person marker are accounted for by phrase structure rules, in (2b) by some morphological process such as word formation rules. I will argue here for an analysis of Quechua verbal morphology such as (2b), by investigating the properties of Quechua words, and showing that these properties do not hold for Quechua phrases in the same way.

In this way, this paper will contribute to a theory of morphology. Only an explicit and sufficiently elaborate theory of syntax and morphology can provide the basis for making a clear-cut division between the two. The development of generative theory, and particularly of lexicalist syntax, has made analyses possible which were not available to Pike (1949), given the rather minimal theoretical framework existing at that time.

Once a reasonably clear separation of morphology and syntax has been accomplished, it is necessary to explore the consequences of an autonomous morphology. What properties does Quechua word structure have? How does morphology interact with syntax and semantics? These questions cannot be answered here in full. This paper does no more than discuss some of the issues involved in an exploratory fashion. I intend to demonstrate, however, that systematic study of the word structure of a morphologically complex language such as Quechua in a generative framework can yield a rich and autonomous morphological component. This paper is based almost entirely on the careful descriptive work on a Peruvian

Quechua dialect, Tarma Quechua, by Willem Adelaar (1977).

Before concluding this introductory section, an informal account needs to be given of Quechua verbal morphology, the topic mostly dealt with here, and the structure of the paper needs to be sketched.

Within the Quechua verb form, we can distinguish the following categories:

$$(3)\ \ \text{ROOT} - (\text{MODAL}) \ \dots \ (\text{MODAL}) - \left(\begin{Bmatrix} \text{MA} \\ \text{SHU} \end{Bmatrix}\right) - \left(\begin{Bmatrix} \text{TENSE} \\ \text{TAXIS} \end{Bmatrix}\right) - \text{PERSON} - \text{INDEPENDENT}$$

The category 'independent' refers to a number of class-free suffixes of negation, emphasis, etc. The category 'person' refers to a small set of person markers, to be discussed in detail later in this study. 'Tense' and 'taxis' refer to an elaborate system of tense and subordinating markers. The suffixes /-ma-/ and /-shu-/ refer to a personal object of the verb, in conjunction with the person markers. Here the term 'modal' is used in a very loose sense, to refer to a wide variety of suffixes indicating plural, aspect, reflexive, reciprocal, causative, directionality, etc.

The examples in (4) may illustrate (3) a little:

(4) a. mancha-ku- rka- n-chu
          fear   RE PL 3 NEG
          They are (not) afraid.

     b. wila-ma- nki
          tell lob 2s
          You must tell me.

     c. usha-ya-   chi- n
          end DUR CAU 3
          He makes it end.

     d. chari-pa- naku- ya- q
          hold DIR REC DUR AG
          grasping out towards each other

     e. aywa-ru- ra- y (ki)
          go   PER PA 2s
          You went.

These are the types of data that a theory of Quechua word structure will have to explain. Additional examples will appear throughout this paper. The meaning of the abbreviations used in the glosses is given in an appendix.

This paper is organised as follows:

In section 1 a general theory of word formation in Quechua is sketched, a theory which leads to a number of criteria which can be used to distinguish elements of phrase structure from elements of word structure.

Section 2 treats of a number of class-free 'independent' suffixes. It is argued that they are not generated by word formation rules, but by phrase structure rules, and then cliticised to the element on their left. Here use is made of the criteria developed in section 1.

In sections 3, 4, and 5 we turn to a number of typical properties of morphological phenomena in Quechua which should characterise the behaviour of the suffixes (other than the independent suffixes discussed in section 2) if the distribution of these elements is controlled by WFRs rather than PSRs.

Section 3 discusses the relevance for Quechua morphology of the subjacency condition (Siegel, 1977), arguing that WFRs and output filters are constrained by subjacency but also providing some potential counter-examples.

In 4 I try to show that morphological readjustment rules, such as allomorphy and truncation rules, are constrained by *c*-command: the conditioning element must *c*-command the affected element.

Section 5 briefly sketches some consequences for semantic interpretation of the theory of morphology adopted in this paper. I argue that interpretation of Quechua complex words proceeds cyclically, starting from the base. Again, examples are given of some potential difficulties for cyclical interpretation.

In 2 it was argued that one set of Quechua suffixes, the independent suffixes, are generated by PSRs; in section 6 I try to provide arguments that the suffixes constituting the Quechua verbal paradigm; person, number, and tense, are generated by WFRs. The argument, which is rather complex, draws upon the theory of morphology developed in sections 1, 3, 4, and 5.

In 7, the final section, the arguments presented so far are summed up, and some alternative solutions to the problems noted are briefly discussed.

1. The General Properties of Quechua Words

Setting apart the independent suffixes, this paper makes the claim that the major part of Quechua morphology is generated by word formation rules of the type described by Aronoff (1976) and Siegel (1978):

(5) $[_X] \Rightarrow [_Y[_X]\,p]$
     Here a base, $[_X]$, is embedded in $[_Y]$ by the addition of a suffix *p*. The affixation of *p* is conditioned by a number of properties of the base.

It is argued that (2b), repeated here in a slightly modified form as (6), is indeed the correct structure for the verb form /maqa-ya-yki/ (*you hit* (past)). There is a separate level of word structure, and every terminal node of the phrase tree dominates a word tree. The morphological tree is independent of the phonological trees as described in Halle & Vergnaud (1978). Note, for instance, that in Quechua the word tree and the stress tree are generally mirror images of each other:

(6)

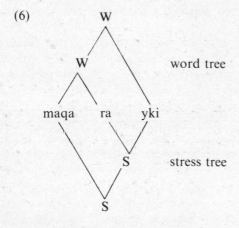

W   word tree

maqa   ra   yki

S   stress tree

In the sections 3, 4, and 5 a number of claims are made regarding Quechua word structure. These claims are logically independent, perhaps, of the general implications of a conception of word structure as outlined here.

1.1 Different Branching Properties

The main differences between trees in morphology and trees in syntax are due to the ways in which they are formed. Syntactic trees are unconstrained as to the number and type of branchings involved, while in morphology we find two conditions constraining branchings, conditions which are due to the definition of WFRs:

(7) a. at any given node, only three branchings or less can occur;

b. of any given set of sister nodes, only one can be branching;

c. of any three sister nodes, only the middle one can be branching.

It is easy to see how this follows from the definition of word formation rules. Their general format is:

(8) $[_X ...] \rightarrow [_Y \alpha [_X ...] \beta]$
where α or β or both may be null.

In the case that α and β are not null in any of the WFRs which has applied, we get a structure of the type:

(9)

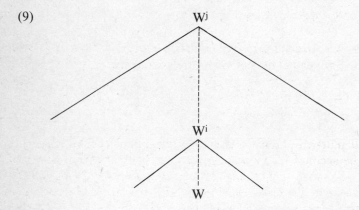

Any less complex tree results from leaving out some of the branchings.

In a structure of this general type, any more exterior suffix c-commands any more interior suffix, where exterior and interior are defined in terms of brackets. Likewise, every branching node W^j is superior in (9) to a branching node W^i. The subjacency condition, which will be discussed in the next section, is relevant for the relationship between any two nodes in the tree. The general properties of morphological trees, it is argued in this paper, are the same as those of phrase structure trees, but since word trees are of a more restricted type, the locality principles have a slightly different effect. The principles of c-command (discussed in (4)), subjacency (discussed in (3)), and cyclicity (discussed briefly in (5)) may be general principles of hierarchical structure in language, rather than being limited to syntax and morphology.

1.2 No $\bar{W}$ Convention

One similarity between PS-rules and WF-rules may be that word-internal elements may show the same kind of ordering restrictions as those to which words are subject, and which in the case of constraints on PS-rules are commonly referred to as the $\bar{X}$ convention. Note, for instance, that there is no obvious way in Aronoff's theory to account for the fact that in a language such as Quechua all WF processes are suffixation processes, and that, with one possible minor exception, prefixing does not occur.

It is tempting to formulate a kind of morphological $\bar{X}$ convention, which may be called $\bar{W}$ convention:

(10) $\quad \bar{W} \rightarrow [[X +]_W \text{ suffix*}]_{\bar{W}}$

For English presumably a convention such as (11) would hold, following the general framework of Siegel and Aronoff:

(11) $\quad \bar{W} \rightarrow [[\text{prefix*} [\# X \#]_W \text{ suffix*}]_{\bar{W}}$
$\qquad \bar{W} \rightarrow [[\text{prefix*} [+ X +]_W \text{ suffix*}]_{\bar{W}}$

General patterns of infixation, etc. occurring in particular languages could be accounted for in the same way. Note that the success of conventions such as (10) and (11) depends, as does the $\bar{X}$ convention in syntax, on the ease with which the structures existing in a particular language may be generalised into a single pattern across categories.

There are several reasons for wanting to exclude the $\bar{W}$ convention from a theory of morphology, however. First of all, the information that a language such as Quechua only has suffixes needs to be independently stipulated in the list of suffixes in the morphological lexicon. The generalisation could be made as a redundancy rule on affixes, and thus no generalisation is lost by abandoning the $\bar{W}$ convention. In the second place, making WFRs similar to PS rules by adopting a $\bar{W}$ convention has the consequence of giving morphological theory a power that it does not appear to have. Thus PS rules such as (12) specify that in a given language two NP positions are available in the VP:

(12)   VP → V NP NP ...

I know of no case where similar restrictions hold for the number of prefixes that a word may have; if we assume that rules similar to phrase structure rules operate, we could find languages with only two suffix positions available. For this reason we want to distinguish between the process of word formation, in which a single suffix is added to a base, and the process of phrase structure generation, in which a string of elements may be formed. In the third place, the subjacency condition which will be outlined in subsequent sections of this paper can be formulated more simply in a theory in which complex words are formed by the successive application of WFRs, than in one using PS rules, which define the order of strings of elements. We will return to this point later.

1.3 All Word Formation Rules Are Optional

One of the distinctions which could be made in Quechua verbal morphology is that between *obligatory* elements in the verbal form and *optional* elements. Thus, in subordinate clauses, the subordination marker is obligatory, and in all clauses but /-r/, /-y/, and /-q/ clauses, person marking is obligatory. On the other hand, suffixes such as /-la-/ (delimitative) or /-ĉa:ri-/ (experimental action) cannot be called obligatory, in that there are many verb forms without them. Note, however, that in both cases of obligatoriness, subordinate markers and person markers, we can appeal to independently motivated conditions of well-formedness on sentences (or alternatively, interpretive person and taxis agreement rules) to assure them being present in the verb form. Thus we can maintain that all word formation rules are optional.

Explaining the obligatoriness of subordination and person markers as a syntactic, not a morphological matter, removes the lack of parallelism between nominal and verbal inflection. In many languages, verbal stems cannot appear by themselves, while nouns often can. By claiming that the obligatoriness of certain suffixes is a function of the input to the agreement rules, the difference between nominal and verbal morphology is explained, since verbs enter into structures of obligatory agreement more often than nouns. In fact, in certain complex NP structures in Quechua, nominal agreement is also obligatory. However, nouns can also occur by themselves. There is in fact one case in which the verb appears without any inflection, by itself. This is the case of a 'serial' comparative construction which exists in Ecuadorian Quechua. A verb *surpass* appears in a VP complement inside another VP, but only the matrix verb is inflected, since it appears in the right configuration:

(13)   [ñuka [[kan-da   yalli]$_{VP}$ puri- ni]$_{VP}$]
       I   you AC exceed   walk   1s
       I walk faster than you.

Thus, rather than being an anomaly, the case of Ecuadorian Quechua (13) shows that the obligatoriness of person marking on the verb is not a morphological fact, but rather a syntactic or semantic one.

The foregoing discussion has made Aronoff's claim that the base of a WFR is always an independently occurring word rather meaningless, since the definition of 'independently occurring word' has been made dependent upon syntactic considerations. I assume that the definition of word can be expanded to include the type of stems that has been described and will leave the matter rest.

1.4 The Unitary Base Hypothesis

One of the possible criteria which can be used for deciding on the possible status of a given suffix derives from adopting the unitary base hypothesis (Aronoff, 1976), which claims that the base for a morphological operation can always be specified coherently with one set of features. Thus, processes which operate either on adjectives or on transitive verbs are excluded, since presumably these two categories cannot be specified coherently together with one set of features.

Thus we could argue that suffixes which can be attached to any kind of constituent cannot be derived by WFR.

1.5 The Major Category Restriction

Typically, word formation processes operate on major categories, such as nouns or verbs, not on pronouns or particles (Aronoff, 1976). This generalisation has been formalised as the Major Category Restriction, which can be stated as follows:

(14)   The Major Category Restriction:
       Only elements dominated by the categories N, A, V can serve as the base in a WFR.

On the basis of this principle we can argue, then, that suffixes attached to minor categories are not generated by WFRs.

1.6 Non-transferable Categorisation

Word formation rules take an element of a given category as their base, and result in elements of a specific category as well, which may or may not be identical to the category of the base. We assume the categories of the base and the derived form to be constants, and do not allow the category of the derived form to be a function of the category of the base. Specifically, transferable categorisation is ruled out.

Suffixes which apply to several base categories and for which the category of the base is transferred to that of the output can therefore not be derived by WFR. On the other hand, cliticised elements generated by PSR are typically dominated by the same category as the element to which they are cliticised. Often, for instance, Romance clitics are represented as dominated by $\bar{V}$, while the element to which they are cliticised is dominated by V:

(15)

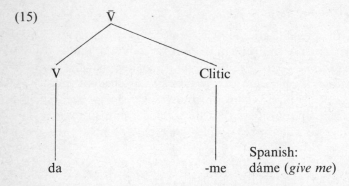

$\bar{V}$

V   Clitic

da   -me

Spanish:
dáme (*give me*)

If these clitics were generated by WFR, the rule involved would need to have the characteristic of transferable categorisation.

1.7 Summary

To sum up at this point, a theory of word structure is assumed here which has the following features:
  (a) morphological structure is created by word formation rules of a well-defined type. For this reason word trees have more restricted branching properties than phrase trees (cf. 1.1);
  (b) there is no equivalent of the $\bar{X}$ convention constraining the

operation of morphological rules. Generalisations about
suffix order will have to be stated elsewhere (cf. 1.2);
(c) all word formation rules are optional (cf. 1.3);
(d) the category of the base of a word formation rule must be
specified in a unitary way (cf. 1.4);
(e) the base functioning as the input to a word formation rule
must be of a major category, i.e. N, A, or V (cf. 1.5);
(f) the category of the output of a word formation rule must be
independent from the category of the base (cf. 1.6).

2. The Independent Suffixes

In Quechua, the independent suffixes mentioned in (6) can occur
with all types of constituents:

(16) a. ali- **m**   A
     good AF
     (It is) good.
   b. nanay-wan- **mi**   P
     pain with AF
     with pain
   c. wayna-:- **mi**   N
     lover 1s AF
     my lover
   d. puri- :- **mi**   V
     walk 1s AF
     I walk.

Their semantics relates to the phrase as a whole in which they
appear, and not to the particular word to which they are attached:
they express negation, contrast, conviction, hearsay, conjecture,
emphasis, inclusion, motivation of statement, or condition for
realisation.

I will argue here that they should be generated by phrase structure
rules, of the following kind:

(17) $\bar{\bar{X}} \to \ldots \bar{X}$ IND

where IND stands for the particular independent suffix involved.
Note that here the generalisation that the last element within a

given phrase is its head is presented with a counter-example, and we should see whether any evidence for phrase structure generation of the independent suffixes can be found. This can be done using some of the criteria developed in section 1, and we can see that they all suggest that a phrase structure rule such as (17) is part of the grammar of Quechua.

2.1 The Unitary Base Hypothesis

The Unitary Base Hypothesis would predict that the base for a word formation rule affixing the independent suffix would need to be specified in a unified way. In fact, the data given in (16) suggest that it cannot be so specified. Consequently, we can argue that the independent suffixes cannot be generated by word formation rule, and must have a syntactic source.

2.2 The Major Category Restriction

If we assume that derivational processes can only involve the major category nodes N, A, and V, then we can exclude from the inventory of derivational affixes a number of suffixes which occur with words of minor categories as well as with words from the major ones.

Not surprisingly, only independent suffixes can occur with words belonging to a minor category:

(18) a.   kay- **chu-**
           this Q
           This one
      b.   na:-   **mi**
           already AF
           Already!
      c.   ama-**m**
           not AF
           Don't (exhortative)'

Thus the 'major category restriction' provides additional evidence for the 'unitary base hypothesis' in that both lead to the same result in excluding the independent suffixes from the category of elements derived by word formation rules.

One would still have to show, of course, that the lexical elements used as examples in (18) belong to a minor category. This question is all the more relevant since most of the categories referred to as minor in the Western European languages are part of morphology in

Quechua, and the specific phonological processes which Selkirk (1972) describes for minor categories are found with the independent suffixes such as /-mi/, and not with words like those in (18), which I have assigned to minor categories.

An argument for saying that /kay/ (*this*) belongs to a minor category is the existence of a related lexical item /chay/ (*that*), if one accepts the argument presented in Emonds (1978) that only items belonging to minor categories can be affected by suppletion. One could say that /kay/ (*this*) and /chay/ (*that*) form a small paradigm in which partial suppletion occurs.

Similarly, /ama/ (*not* (exhortative)) alternates with /mana/ (*not* (indicative)), and some kind of semantic rule has to filter out specific sequences:

(19) *mana   V
        [+neg]   [+neg]
        [+ind]   [+exh]
       *ama   V
        [+neg]   [+neg]
        [+exh]   [+ind]

One could plausibly argue that only lexical items belonging to a minor category can be inherently specified for features that participate in agreement rules of the type presented in (19).

2.3 Non-transferable Categorisation

In section 1.6 it was noted that the category created by a WFR should be logically independent of the category of the base forming the input to that WFR. We may wonder what kinds of brackets the independent suffixes would confer on their base, if they were derived by WFR. To insure proper lexical insertion, we would have to assume that they are label-preserving for all features characterising the base.

A typical WFR, the one for /-mi/ (affirmative) would be:

(20) $[X]_{\alpha F1} \Rightarrow [[X]_{\alpha F1} \text{ mi}]_{\alpha F1}$
          $_{\beta F2}$ $_{\beta F2}$ $_{\beta F2}$

where F1, F2 stand for syntactic features such as $\pm N$, $\pm V$, etc.

This type of WFR, introducing variables, would considerably expand the power of the word formation component. For word formation processes in languages other than Quechua, it has not been necessary so far to use these rules as a descriptive device. If we reject rules of type (20) we have a principled basis for excluding the independent suffixes from the word formation component.

This result coincides with that of applying the Unitary Base Hypothesis and the Major Category Restriction to the derivation of the independent suffixes: following all three criteria the independent suffixes must be generated by the PSRs.

2.4 A Potential Problem

The phonetic shape of some of the independent suffixes is conditioned by the elements preceding them. This could constitute a problem for the analysis of the independent suffixes as generated by PSRs, if the phonetic conditioning would turn out to be morphological or morpho-phonological in nature. It would be plausible to limit morphologically or morpho-phonologically conditioned sound alternatiòns to the domain of the output of the word formation component.

When we consider the independent suffixes /-mi/ (affirmative), /-shi/ (hearsay), and /-chi/ (conjecture), it appears on first sight that their phonetic shape is not purely phonologically conditioned. We find that these suffixes have two forms:

(21)   a.   [mi] after (i)   long vowels;
                        (ii)   after consonants;
                        (iii) after /pi/ (*who*);
                        (iv) after short vowels but not word-finally.
         b.   [m] after short vowels word-finally.

Similarly for /-shi/ and /-chi/.

With a few minor exceptions, there are no other cases of final vowel deletions in Quechua, either in stems or in suffixes:

(22)   a.   *wayi-mi
                 house AF
         b.   wayi-m
                 house AF
(23)   a.   wayi-ta
                 house AC
         b.   *wayi-t
                 house AC

(24)   *way
       house

This would suggest that the alternation is limited to a specific class of suffixes, /-mi/, /-shi/, and /-chi/, and that would be a problem for the analysis proposed here for these suffixes as being separately generated by PSRs hence not subject to morphologically conditioned alternations.

I will argue here, however, that the rule causing the alternation is not morphologically conditioned, but determined by Quechua stress patterns. In Quechua the penultimate syllable is stressed, unless the final syllable is long in which case the latter is stressed. Thus we have:

(25) a. wayi   [wáyi]
      b. wayi-:   [wayi:]
              1s
      c. wayi-n   [wáyiŋ]
              3

Assume that stress assignment takes place initially in the domain of the output of the word formation component, as in (25a–c), and assume a final vowel deletion rule as in (26):

(26)   i → Ø/[-stress] # C ——— # #

This rule will have the following result in the different types of environments:

(27) a. wayí-:-mi   [wayí:mi]   (=(21ai))
      b. wáyi-n-mi   [wayínmi]   (=(21aii))
      c. pí-mi   [pími]   (=(21aiii))
      d. wáyi-mi- qa   [wayimíqa]   (=(21aiv))
              AF TOP
      e. wáyi-m   [wáyim]   (=(21b))

In the first column in (27) the stress is indicated before /-mi/ has been affixed. In the second column the final result.

If one interprets rule (26) as specifying that the unstressed syllable in the left environment must be open, then it yields the right results. If one assumes the number of consonants closing the unstressed syllable to have been left unspecified, (27b) is the wrong result. There the final vowel should have been deleted, since it is preceded by an unstressed syllable. There is an independently motivated restriction, however, on word final consonant sequences:

(28) $*C_2^n$ # #

This restriction will block the application of deletion rule (26), which should be formulated without reference to consonant sequences, after a closed syllable.

In the case where /-mi/ is followed by /-qa/, a topic marker, the deletion rule cannot apply because the right context is lacking. Stress is shifted to /-mi/ in these cases:

(29)   aywá-nki-mi-qa → [aywankimíqa]   (cf. (21d))
        You go

If a way can be found to describe stress reassignment coherently, the final vowel deletion rule (26) can be maintained. Since it is clearly phonological in nature, the hypothesis that /-mi/ etc. are not generated by WFR but rather by PSR can be maintained. In fact, the adoption of the hypothesis that /-mi/ etc. are not generated by WFR leads to a new formulation of the final vowel deletion rule, not in terms of morphological constraints but in terms of stress patterns.

3. The Subjacency Condition

After sketching a general theory of morphology in section 1, and setting apart the independent suffixes from the suffixes derived by WFR in section 2, we now turn to some additional constraints that might be imposed on morphological processes in Quechua. In this section I discuss subjacency.

In Siegel (1977) a version of the subjacency condition is proposed and argued to be applicable to morphology. It can be stated as follows:

(30)   In a structure of the type:
        x $]_V$ ...$]_W$ y   or
        x $[_V$ ...$[_W$ y
        no WFR may refer to both *x* and *y*, where *x* and *y* are properties of affixes, and *V* and *W* are cyclic nodes within the word.

I claim here that all word formation processes in Quechua are subject to the subjacency condition. Immediately a host of counter-examples appears, although some positive evidence can be found as well. I will argue that these types of counter-examples can be independently motivated as being ruled out by independently needed constraints on semantic interpretation. First of all, some evidence for the subjacency condition.

We find a striking example in Quechua of this limitation on co-occurrence restrictions in the case of the delimitative nominal suffix /-la-/ (*just, only*). In nouns, it precedes the person marker:

(31)   wayi- **la** -:
        house   1s
        my house only

and follows the plural marker:

(32)   pay-kuna-**la**
        he PL
        only them

Since the plural follows the person marker, a combination of the three suffixes would lead to an ordering paradox.

What we find is that /-la-/ can both precede person and follow plural or appear in either position, when the three are combined:

(33)   kiki-**la**-n-kuna
        self   3 PL
        kiki-n-kuna-**la**
        kiki-**la**-n-kuna-**la**
        just themselves

In the latter case, the double /-la-/ is interpreted as one /-la-/. Notice that the meaning of /-la-/ is so indefinite that this presents no problem. The three alternatives in (33) show that the presence of one /-la-/ cannot 'control' the presence or absence of another one, since they are separated by two cyclic nodes. The same phenomenon occurs when certain postpositions are combined, so that it is not a specific property of the plural and person markers.

3.1 Problem I: Causatives

That semantics plays a significant role in this respect is shown by the interaction of the causative and reciprocal markers in verbal morphology. Causative can both follow and precede reciprocal:

(34)   maqa-**naku**- ya-   **chi**- n
      beat   REC DUR CAU 3
      He is causing them to beat each other.

(35)   maqa-**chi**-   **naku**- rka- n
      beat   CAU REC PL 3
      They let each other be beaten.

Disregarding the semantic interpretation for a moment, to which we will return in section 5, we can state that /-chi-/ and /-naku-/ can occur in either order. Presumably, this fact can be stated in our theoretical framework by not including /-chi-/ in the environments in which /-naku-/ cannot occur, and by not including /-naku-/ in the environments in which /-chi-/ cannot occur.

But now a major problem arises: how can we exclude the following types of sequences?:

(36)   ... -chi-naku-chi-naku- ...

These are clearly out, but not ruled out by the morphological theory presented here.

We will follow the 'overgeneration' strategy sketched in Hale *et al.* (1977), and assume that the rules of semantic interpretation operating on words are so restrictive as to exclude double combinations of causatives, reciprocals, reflexives, etc. (but not double delimitatives; cf. (33)). This assumption is by no means implausible, and there is some support for it from double causatives in Ecuadorian Quechua.

While in most Quechua dialects sequences of the form:

(37)   ... -chi-chi- ...

are ruled out, in Ecuadorian Quechua we do find double causatives, but only in some circumstances, as the following forms show:

(38)   wañu-chi-chi-
      die
      to have someone kill
      ?riku-chi-chi-
      see
      to make someone show
      ??apa-chi-chi-
      take
      to make someone load

*awa-chi-chi-
weave
to make someone make someone else weave

While it is possible that the difference in acceptability between these four forms is due to the degree of lexicalisation of the leftmost /-chi-/, there are no stress or other phenomena which would lend independent support to the differential lexicalisation hypothesis (with the exception of the contraction of /wañu-chi-/ to /wañ-chi-/ in certain dialects). Therefore we will assume that the difference in acceptability between the forms of (38) is due to the ease with which the action resulting from the combination of the root and the leftmost /-chi-/ can be conceived of as a coherent whole, subject itself to being 'caused'.

The overgeneration strategy followed here will have to find support when a more precise theory of semantic interpretation for causatives is sketched; we will return to it then.

3.2 Problem II: Plurals

A more serious problem for the subjacency hypothesis in morphology can be found with respect to plural marking in Quechua. There are three plural suffixes /-rka-/, /-paːku/ and /-ri-/; their distribution is determined by their morphological environment. In most cases, only the immediate environment is relevant, so that for the most part plural marking offers no problem for the subjacency constraint. There is one case, however, which involves more than the immediate environment.

The suffix /-rpu-/ is in most circumstances followed only by /-paːku-/. After the suffixes /-rku-/ (which has several different meanings) and /-yu-/ (inward direction) and (special attention), we find alternatively /-ri-/ and /-paːku-/. When /-rku-/, /-yu-/ and /-rpu-/ (downward direction) are preceded by a suffix which ends in /-...ku-/, only /-ri-/ is allowed. Schematically:

(39) a. / rpu ____ → paːku

b. / $\begin{Bmatrix} \text{rku} \\ \text{yu} \end{Bmatrix}$ ____ → $\begin{Bmatrix} \text{paːku} \\ \text{ri} \end{Bmatrix}$

c. / ... ku + $\begin{Bmatrix} \text{rku} \\ \text{rpu} \\ \text{yu} \end{Bmatrix}$ ____ → ri

Thus the obligatory occurrence of /-ri-/ is dependent, in (39c), on a morphological specification involving two cyclic nodes.

There are two conceivable solutions to this problem, both of them rather unsatisfactory. First of all, one might want to claim that the element /-...ku-/ is a part of the following suffix, or somehow forms a lexicalised combination with it. This is highly implausible because both /-rku-/ and /-yu-/ have several specific meanings, and worse yet, /-...ku-/ can be part of several different suffixes, none of which can be combined very easily in a lexicalised combination with /-rku-/, /-rpu-/ and /-ri-/. Secondly, we might wish to argue that the impossibility of /-pa:ku-/ in the last context follows independently from a constraint on double /-ku-/ within one word. While historically this may be the explanation for the impossibility of /-pa:ku-/ here, there are several problems with this explanation. It does not explain why we cannot have /-ri-/ after /-rpu-/ when it is not preceded by /-...ku-/. Also, the constraint on double /-ku-/ would also have to be formulated across two cyclic nodes, which leaves us with the same problem for the theory. Thus the problem of plural marking remains for the time being as a potential counter-example to the subjacency condition.

3.3 Problem III: The Suffix /-rku-/

A further problem with the subjacency condition involves the sequential suffix /-rku-/. /-rku-/ is very restricted in its use, in that it only occurs with the subordinating suffix /-r/, which indicates adverbial clauses:

(40)   maki- n-ta   kutu-**rku**- r
       hand 3 AC cut   SEQ SUB
       after cutting off her hand

The suffix /-rku-/ is used 'for indicating a close temporal relationship between the events referred to by a subordinate verb and the verb to which it is subordinated, the former being shortly prior to the latter'. (Adelaar, 1977)

The problem for the subjacency condition arises because /-rku-/ and /-r/ need not be adjacent:

(41)   muyu-**rku**- chi- r
       turn   SEQ CAU SUB
       after making it turn

Given the subjacency condition, the presence of /-rku-/ cannot control the formation of /-r/ verbs.

In this case, the violation of the subjacency condition may not be so serious, because the close semantic relationship between /-rku-/ and /-r/ makes it possible that a semantic constraint on /-rku-/ interpretation is involved: it can only occur meaningfully in the context of /-r/.

3.4 Problem IV: The Past Potential Marker

Yet another possible counter-example to the subjacency condition is the potential marker in Quechua, which is part of verbal morphology. We find:

(42) aywa-nki-**man**
      go   2s POT
      you would go

In Quechua tense markers appear between the verb and the person markers, as in:

(43) aywa-**ra**- yki
      go   PA 2s
      You went.

Now the past form of the potential, which is interpreted as an irrealis mood, is not:

(44) *aywa-**ra**-yki-**man**
       you would have gone

combining the preterite marker and the potential marker, but rather a complex form involving the auxiliary /ka-/:

(45) aywa-nki-**man** ka-**ra**- n
      go   2s POT   be PA 3
      you would have gone

We need to claim that (44) is out, not for morphological reasons, but for semantic ones. Otherwise the ungrammaticality of (44) would be a direct counter-example to the subjacency condition defended here. Given the fact that there is a separate preterite form of the potential mood with the auxiliary /ka-/, the needed semantic motivation is less than straightforward.

3.5 Why Then Subjacency?

In sections 3.1–3.4 I showed some of the potential counter-evidence that one could adduce against the subjacency condition in the word formation component, and I tried to argue that in many cases one can invoke independent semantic conditions to deal with apparent violations, conditions which would not be part of word formation themselves. Still, a few difficult cases remain.

Why then was the subjacency condition argued for in the first place? First of all, the majority of the conditions on word formation processes in Quechua can be stated in terms of subjacent elements. Secondly, the adoption of the subjacency condition limits the power of the word formation component considerably. I will return to the problem of subjacency in the last section of this paper.

4. Readjustment Rules and *C*-Command

There are several instances in Quechua morphology where the affixation of a suffix causes elements in the base of the word formation rule of which it is part to undergo a change. Generally these changes can be represented as follows:

(46) $X \, a \, Y \, b \, Z \Rightarrow X \, a' \, Y \, b \, Z$

These readjustment rules are not bound by subjacency: note the intervening variable between the element affected by the change, *a*, and the element triggering the change, *b*.

They are constrained, however, by the notion of *c*-command or *c*-superiority: the affected element, *a*, is always in the *c*-domain of the triggering element, *b*:

(47)

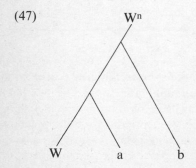

This result is trivial within the theory of word formation sketched here, since b, being added by a WFR, is always attached to a higher node than element in the base, and hence c-commands all elements in the base.

Suppose, on the other hand, that we adopted a theory of morphology in which the word contained different complex nodes, such as an inflectional node dominating tense, person, etc. Consider a tree configuration as in (48):

(48)

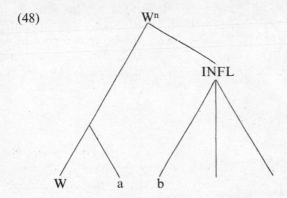

Here the c-command assumption would predict that the affixation of b could not trigger the change affecting a.

Here first a few examples will be given of readjustment rules, in sections 4.1 and 4.2. Section 4.3 explores the implications of the c-command condition for the independent suffixes, and section 4.4 describes a potential counter-example.

4.1 /-ku-/ Deletion

The first example of a readjustment rule involves cases of /-ku-/ deletion. There are several suffixes in Quechua which include this syllable:

(49)
ku	characteristic action
ku	characteristic quality
ku	reflexive
naku	reciprocal
paku	mutual benefit
ĉaku	multiple object

(Only those suffixes where /-ku-/ appears alone or as the second syllable are listed here; those where /-ku-/ is preceded by a consonant are not, since they do not appear to be involved in the process.)

The double /-ku-/ constraint is manifested in the following ways:

(a) Sequences of double /-ku-/, e.g. /-naku-ku-/ (reciprocal +characteristic action), are possible but avoided:

   naku   naku
(b) /-ĉaku-/+ra+ku ⇒ /-ĉa+ra+ku/
   paku   paku

Examples are:

(50) rika-ĉaku- *to wake up, to look around*
   rika-**ĉa-paku**-mu-n
   He woke up with a start.
(51) qapa-ĉaku- *to shout*
   qapa-**ĉa-ra**-ku-n
   He shouts continuously.
(52) rika-ĉaku- *to look around*
   rika-**ĉa-naku**-rka-ya-n
   They are looking around for each other.

Although the situation is not entirely clear, at first sight it appears that there is a /-ku-/ deletion rule in operation, which could be stated roughly as follows:

(53) CVku+CV(+)ku ⇒ 1 ∅ 3 4

Presumably, the deletion affects /-ĉaku-/ in the context _____ /CVku-/, but not in the context _____ /-ku-/, because in the latter case no trace would be left of the deletion. Also, following the same reasoning, the suffix /-ku-/ would not be affected since no trace would be left of it after deletion.

In any case, the deletion rule (53) cannot be stated locally, since the conditioning /-ku-/ appears to be two cyclic nodes away from the deleted /-ku-/. Again, one might suppose that /-ra-ku-/ in (51) is really one suffix, similar to /-pa-ku-/ and /-naku-/. This supposition is made implausible by the fact that /-ra-/ undergoes the normal process of lengthening of a suffix-final vowel, while the /a/ in /-naku-/ and /-paku-/ does not. The /-ku-/ deletion rule is constrained, of course, by the *c*-command configuration.

4.2 Vowel Lowering

A second example of a non-local readjustment rule is exhibited in the rule of /u/ → [a] affecting certain verbal suffixes. Roughly the rule can be stated as follows:

(54)　X　　$[_q$ ... V　　]　Y　$[_p$ suffix]　　Z
　　　　　　　　$\begin{bmatrix} +\text{high} \\ +\text{back} \end{bmatrix}$
　　　1　　　　2　　　3　　4　　　　5
　　　1　　　　2　　　3　　4　　　　5　⇒
　　　　　　　[−high]

The suffix labelled $[_p$] here belongs to a designated set of controlling verbal suffixes. The suffix $[_q$] stands for a number of derivational suffixes ending in /u/.

I have represented the process here as a rule of allomorphy rather than in terms of optional insertion combined with a negative filter of the following type:

(55)　*X　　$[_q$　V　]　Y　$[_p$]　　Z
　　　　　　　[+high]

The latter type of solution is undesirable because when the [p] suffix is not present, only the [+high] vowel can appear. We would need a supplementary filter:

(56)　*X　　$[_q$　V　]　Y　~$[_p$]　　Z
　　　　　　　[-high]

This filter would introduce the powerful device of a negative context specification.

Whatever formulation is given for the process, note the crucial intervening variable Y, boldface in the following example:

(57)　piča-rkU-**la:-ma:**-nqa → [pičarkala:manqa]
　　　　He will clean me a little.

More suffixes than one within a word can be affected by the change:

(58)　mayla-čakU-rU-:ri-n → [maylačakara:rin]

Here /-:ri-/ *c*-commands both /-cakU-/ and /-rU-/, of course.

In (58), the triggering suffix is the 1st person object marker /-ma-/. Its membership in the group of [$_p$] suffixes, coupled with the c-command requirement, provides an argument against structures of the type (48) at least for object marking. If /-ma-/ were part of an inflectional subtree of the word, it would not c-command the suffixes undergoing the vowel change.

4.3 The Independent Suffixes

The *c*-command requirement makes the correct prediction that the independent suffixes discussed in section 2 can never trigger a change or deletion in a more interior suffix. Since they are dominated by a separate phrase structure node, they never *c*-command word-internal suffixes of the word they are attached to.

The converse implication does not hold, of course. No prediction is made that any suffix *c*-commanding another one necessarily causes it to change. Allomorphy and deletion rules are relatively rare in Quechua.

4.4 A Problem with the C-command Condition

A potential counter-example to the claim that truncation and allomorphy rules are constrained by *c*-command configurations, in which the triggering element *c*-commands the element undergoing the deletion or change, is constituted by the past tense paradigm.

The past tense paradigm is identical to the present tense paradigm in its person marking, except in the third person:

(59) *present tense*   *past tense*
    1 V-:   v-rqa-:
    2 V-nki   V-rqa-nki
    3 V-n   V-rqa-∅   *V-rqa-n
    4 V-nchi   V-rqa-nchi

The /-n/ 3rd person marker cannot co-occur with the past tense marker. To ensure the correct results, we either formulate a filter prohibiting /-n/ affixation in the context of /-rqa-/, as in (60), or we need a deletion rule, as in (61):

(60) *-rqa-n-
(61) -n- → ∅ / rqa- ____

The first option has the undesirable consequence that, when /-n/

has not been affixed at all, person cannot be interpreted. The second option is more plausible, but it violates the condition that a triggering domain *c*-command the element undergoing the deletion or change:

(62)

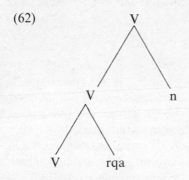

At this point, no more can be said about this problem. In Muysken (1977: 46–7) some of the historical causes of the anomaly in question are discussed.

5. Do the Rules of Semantic Interpretation Apply Cyclically?

We may assume that given the structures generated by the WFRs, the rules of semantic interpretation apply cyclically. In many cases, they appear to do so. Consider the examples of the interaction between reciprocal and causative, repeated here as (63) and (64):

(63) maqa-**chi**]-**naku**]-rka- n
      beat   CAU] REC] PL 3
      They let each other be beaten.

(64) maqa-**naku**]-ya- **chi**]-n
      beat   REC] DUR CAU] 3
      He is causing them to beat each other.

In (63) the causative interpretation rule operates first, followed by the reciprocal interpretation rule. In (64), reciprocal applies before causative. The cyclic ordering of the two interpretation rules explains the difference in meaning between (63) and (64), and therefore the interaction of causative and reciprocal constitutes an argument for the theory of word formation sketched so far.

A similar case is presented by the interaction of causative and reflexive:

(65) maqa-**chi** ⎤-**ku**⎤-n
      beat   CAU⌋ RE⌋ 3
      He lets himself be beaten.

(66) maqa-**ku**⎤-ya-   **chi** ⎤-n
      beat   RE⌋ DUR CAU⌋ 3
      He$_i$ is causing him$_j$ to beat himself$_j$.

In (65) the causative interpretation rule precedes reflexive, in (66) the reverse is the case. Here again, the principle of cyclical application of semantic interpretation rules makes the correct predictions. (I am using cases in which causative interacts with some other process because there the order of interpretation makes a crucial difference. In other cases, the semantics is much less transparent.)

The interaction of causative and aspect causes serious difficulties for the hypothesis that semantic interpretation operates in a cyclical fashion. Compare the pairs (a) and (b) of the following examples:

(67) a. muyu-**rku**- r
          turn   SEQ SUB
          after turning
      b. muyu-**rku**- **chi**- r
          turn   SEQ CAU SUB
          after making it turn, ≠ after causing it to have turned

(68) a. wañu-**ru**- n
          die   PER 3
          he has died.
      b. wañu-**ru**- **chi**- n
          die   PER CAU 3
          He has killed, ≠ He causes him to have died.

(69) a. maqa-naku-**ya**-   n
          beat   REC DUR 3
          They are beating each other.
      b. maqa-naku-**ya**-   **chi**- n
          beat   REC DUR CAU 3
          He is causing them to beat each other. ≠ He causes them to be beating each other.

In the (a) cases, which do not contain the causative marker /-chi-/, the sequential, perfective and durative markers modify the verb root, or in the last case, the derived form, preceding it. In the (b) cases, the same would be the case, if semantic interpretation were to apply cyclically. Instead, the aspect marker modifies the causative, which follows it.

A similar problem, albeit a more complicated one, involves person marking and the causative. When the causative verb contains an object marker, that marker can refer either to the underlying object, or to the matrix object:

(70) a. ñuqa-wan Mañuku-ta maqa-**chi-** **ma-** n
          I   INST Manuel AC beat   CAU 1ob 3
          He causes me to beat Manuel.
      b. Mañuku-wan ñuqa-ta maqa-**chi-** **ma-** n
          Manuel INST I   AC beat   CAU 1ob 3
          He causes Manuel to beat me.

Apparently, arguments are assigned to the subordinate predicate on the cycle after causative has applied, and the object marker in the above examples serves only to relate the first person pronoun in the VP to the verb.

A much more detailed analysis of the interaction of causatives, reflexives, object markers and reciprocals appears in Muysken (1979).

6. Inflectional Morphology

Recall the outline of the Quechua verb form given in (3), repeated here as (71):

(71) ROOT — (MODAL) ... (MODAL) — $\left(\begin{Bmatrix} \text{MA} \\ \text{SHU} \end{Bmatrix}\right)$ —

$\left(\begin{Bmatrix} \text{TENSE} \\ \text{TAXIS} \end{Bmatrix}\right)$ — PERSON — INDEPENDENT

The category 'independent' has been shown to fall outside the domain of the word formation component, but what about all the other positions exterior to what is here called 'modal': the object markers /-ma-/ and /-shu-/, the tense markers, and the subject markers? Derivation-like suffixes tend to cluster more closely around the verbal root, while inflection-like suffixes are affixed more towards the exterior of the verb form. Also, derivation-like suffixes tend to form meanings together with the verbal root in some cases, while the inflectional suffixes only rarely form a lexical combination together with the root. It is not clear whether these differences are not due to pragmatic considerations, and to the way the lexicon is stored in the brain. In any case, the two differences are never more than gradual ones, and it is not possible to divide the Quechua suffixes unambiguously into two classes. Rather, we find a continuum (cf. Muysken, 1977).

If we consider other criteria commonly used to distinguish between inflection and derivation, they hardly prove conclusively that such a distinction should be made for Quechua. One claim often made in the literature is that derivational morphology always changes the lexical category of the word, and inflection never does (Reece Allen, 1978). While in English this generalisation holds for a good number of cases, in Quechua it has no validity.

We find derivational morphology, e.g.

(72) [$_V$ punu]   *sleep*
      [$_V$[$_V$ punu] yu]   *sleep for a while*

which does not affect the lexical category, while there are also derivations which do:

(73) [$_N$ čakwas]   *old woman*
      [$_V$[$_N$ čakwas] ya]   *to grow old* (said of women)

Similarly there are inflectional processes, such as:

(74) [$_V$ punu]   *sleep*
      [$_V$[$_V$ punu] n]   *he sleeps*

which don't affect lexical categorisation, and inflectional processes which do:

(75) [$_V$ punu]   *sleep*
      [$_N$[$_V$ punu] na]   *that ... will sleep*

In the last example, the nominalising suffix /-na-/ is part of the tense/taxis paradigm, and would traditionally be classified as inflectional.

When we consider other formal distinguishing criteria, such as stress assignment or phonological behaviour, no differences between derivation and inflection emerge. While the independent suffixes were found to fall outside the domain of primary stress assignment (section 2.4), the inflectional suffixes do not. While the person and tense/taxis suffixes do not trigger allomorphy changes, the object suffix /-ma-/ does, alongside with a number of modal suffixes (section 4.2).

In this section I will try to argue that not only are there no formal differences between inflection and derivation in Quechua, which would tend to make a distinction between the two unnatural, but also that it is theoretically and empirically preferable to analyse the object, tense/taxis and person markers in exactly the same way as the derivational suffixes: as generated by word formation rules, and subject to all the conditions enumerated so far in this paper.

6.1 The Two Models

In the following sections, we will explicitly contrast the two approaches sketched in (2a) and (2b), with respect to object, tense/taxis, and person marking. They are repeated here as (76a) and (76b), and will be referred to as the abstract morpheme framework, and the word formation framework, respectively:

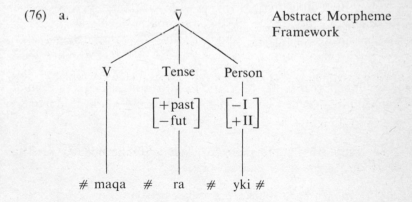

(76) a.   V̄   Abstract Morpheme
                                                Framework

            V   Tense   Person

                     $\begin{bmatrix} +\text{past} \\ -\text{fut} \end{bmatrix}$ $\begin{bmatrix} -\text{I} \\ +\text{II} \end{bmatrix}$

         # maqa #   ra   #   yki #

In the abstract morpheme framework, (a), the agreement rule has as its output a feature matrix. The actual form of the verb is determined by rules that spell out abstract feature configurations as suffixes. In this approach, the following types of rules are needed:

–a phrase structure rule expanding the verb node;
–filters to constrain the output of the agreement transformation;
–spelling out rules to map the features onto suffixes, and possibly
  readjustment rules to derive the right surface forms;
–an agreement transformation.

(76) b.   V   Word Formation
                                                  Framework

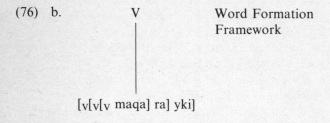

      [ᵥ[ᵥ[ᵥ maqa] ra] yki]

  In the word formation framework the actual verb form is
interpreted by an interpretive algorithm to create the feature matrix
which functions in the agreement rule. The following types of rules
are needed:
    –word formation rules;
    –constraints on suffix order;
    –interpretive algorithms and conditions on their operation;
    –filters on interpretations;
    –an agreement rule filtering out all but matching feature
    specifications.
  After presenting the present tense part of the Quechua verbal
paradigm (section 6.2), the two approaches will be presented
systematically, compared, and evaluated (sections 6.3 and 6.4).
Finally some additional evidence will be presented for the word
formation approach, regarding person marking in agentive and
gerundial clauses (6.5), the future tense paradigm (6.6), and plural
marking (6.7). A few concluding remarks are given in section 6.8.

6.2 The Paradigm

The present tense paradigm in Quechua consists of nine forms. The
relevant distinctions are those between:

(77)   first person subject   first person object
       second person subject   second person object
       third person subject
       first inclusive subject   first inclusive object

Given these four persons, it is convenient and plausible to categorise them with the features [αI], [βII], and [obj]. Thus the categories above can be represented as follows, where subject is [-obj].

(78)   −obj   +obj

$$\begin{bmatrix} +I \\ -II \end{bmatrix} \quad \begin{bmatrix} +I \\ -II \end{bmatrix}$$

$$\begin{bmatrix} -I \\ +II \end{bmatrix} \quad \begin{bmatrix} -I \\ +II \end{bmatrix}$$

$$\begin{bmatrix} -I \\ -II \end{bmatrix}$$

$$\begin{bmatrix} +I \\ +II \end{bmatrix} \quad \begin{bmatrix} +I \\ +II \end{bmatrix}$$

Since the object marker occurs to the left of the subject marker, we will represent the forms in the paradigm as follows:

(79)   maqa-ma- nki
    hit   1ob 2s
    You hit me.

$$\begin{bmatrix} +obj & -obj \\ I & -I \\ -II & +II \end{bmatrix} \text{ or } \begin{bmatrix} + & - \\ - & + \end{bmatrix}$$

Using this last abbreviatory convention, we can represent the occurring verb forms as follows:

(80)   maqa-: $\begin{bmatrix} - & + \\ - & - \end{bmatrix}$ subject 1

    maqa-nki $\begin{bmatrix} - & - \\ - & + \end{bmatrix}$ subject 2

    maqa-n $\begin{bmatrix} - & - \\ - & - \end{bmatrix}$ subject 3

    maqa-nchi $\begin{bmatrix} - & + \\ - & + \end{bmatrix}$ subject 4 (first person inclusive)

    maqa-q $\begin{bmatrix} - & + \\ + & - \end{bmatrix}$ object 2, subject 1

    maqa-shu-nki $\begin{bmatrix} - & - \\ + & - \end{bmatrix}$ object 2, subject 3

    maqa-ma-nki $\begin{bmatrix} + & - \\ - & + \end{bmatrix}$ object 1, subject 2

    maqa-ma-n $\begin{bmatrix} + & - \\ - & - \end{bmatrix}$ object 1, subject 3

    maqa-ma-nchi $\begin{bmatrix} + & - \\ + & - \end{bmatrix}$ object 4, subject 3

The paradigm for the past and the sudden discovery tenses, and for all the subordinate forms, are constructed by inserting a tense/taxis marker between the object/person suffixes. (The future tense will be discussed separately, in 6.6.) The most extensive discussion of agreement phenomena in any Quechua dialect is presented in Lefebvre and Dubuisson (1978).

6.3 The Abstract Morpheme Approach

(a) Phrase Structure. Since we find forms such as (81), where suffixes and features can be matched one-to-one, a fair phrase structure rule for the tense and person paradigm would be (82):

(81)   maqa-ma- ra- yki
        hit   1ob PA 2su
        You hit me. (past)

(82) $V \rightarrow V_{root}$ [+obj] [tense] [−obj]

Both the + and the − objective morphemes would then include $\begin{bmatrix} \alpha I \\ \beta II \end{bmatrix}$.

(b) Agreement. A preliminary version of the agreement transformation involved may be:

(83) $[v] \rightarrow \begin{bmatrix} \alpha obj \\ \beta I \\ \gamma II \end{bmatrix} / \begin{bmatrix} \alpha obj \\ \beta I \\ \gamma II \end{bmatrix}$ _____

In the formulation of this agreement rule, which collapses subject and object agreement, the case feature of the noun phrase, ±objective, is related to the feature of the abstract morpheme inside of the verb form. The [+obj] position in the verb is sensitive to the [+obj] NPs (i.e. those NPs occurring in the domain of the verb), and the [−obj] position is sensitive to the [−obj] case of the subject.

(c) Filters. A number of feature specifications which might have been transformationally derived have to be ruled out. The most important filter is the one on reflexivity. Any positive specification for either person in both positions is ruled out:

(84) $*[+F_i]$ [tense] $[+F_i]$

This filter rules out all but the nine admissible feature combinations given before.

(d) Spelling-out Rules and Readjustment Rules. Every feature matrix has its own spelling out rule. We may fairly assume the following cases:

(85)

$$\begin{bmatrix} -\text{obj} \\ +\text{I} \\ -\text{II} \end{bmatrix} \rightarrow \text{-:} \qquad \begin{bmatrix} +\text{obj} \\ +\text{I} \\ -\text{II} \end{bmatrix} \rightarrow \text{-ma-}$$

$$\begin{bmatrix} -\text{obj} \\ -\text{I} \\ +\text{II} \end{bmatrix} \rightarrow \text{-nki} \qquad \begin{bmatrix} +\text{obj} \\ -\text{I} \\ +\text{II} \end{bmatrix} \rightarrow \text{-shu-}$$

$$\begin{bmatrix} -\text{obj} \\ -\text{I} \\ -\text{II} \end{bmatrix} \rightarrow \text{-n} \qquad \begin{bmatrix} +\text{obj} \\ -\text{I} \\ -\text{II} \end{bmatrix} \rightarrow \text{-}\emptyset\text{-}$$

$$\begin{bmatrix} -\text{obj} \\ +\text{I} \\ +\text{II} \end{bmatrix} \rightarrow \text{-nchi} \qquad \begin{bmatrix} +\text{obj} \\ +\text{I} \\ +\text{II} \end{bmatrix} \rightarrow \text{-nchi}$$

A combination of these suffixes in the way specified by phrase structure rule (82) yields, disregarding the tense suffix, the following combinations:

(86)   *Predicted:*
    $\emptyset$-:
    $\emptyset$-nki
    $\emptyset$-n
    $\emptyset$-nchi
    ma-nki
    ma-n
    *nchi-n   Correct: ma-nchi
    *shu-:   q
    *shu-n   shu-nki

In the three last cases, the combination of spelling out rules leads to incorrect results. Worse is, however, that there is no principled basis for a conversion rule giving the proper results on the right. After some analysis it becomes obvious that the forms in the right column have to be independently stipulated, being irregular. The question is precisely how, since we are dealing with a non-local environment here, in which the tense markers can intervene.

Note that adopting an approach which allows for context-sensitive spelling out rules does not improve matters a great deal, since the context which would have to be specified would still be a non-local one. To account for the last form, for instance, to take the simplest case, we could formulate the spelling out rules as follows:

(87)
$$\begin{bmatrix} -\text{obj} \\ -\text{I} \\ -\text{II} \end{bmatrix} \rightarrow \text{nki/shu X} \underline{\quad\quad} \left(\text{or / shu} \begin{Bmatrix} \text{tense} \\ \text{taxis} \end{Bmatrix} \underline{\quad\quad}\right)$$

$$\begin{bmatrix} -\text{obj} \\ -\text{I} \\ -\text{II} \end{bmatrix} \rightarrow \text{n, elsewhere.}$$

We would still have to specify a variable or the intervening tense/taxis position in the rule. An additional disadvantage is that the rule is entirely arbitrary. The relation between /-shu-/ in the context and the choice of /-nki-/ has to be postulated. The other two cases of misgeneration would be even more complicated to handle, but they would not need any additional apparatus.

6.4 The Word Formation Rule Approach

(a) Word Formation Rules and Interpretive Algorithms. We need a series of word formation rules, applying individually to the verbal base, and a series of associated interpretive rules, applying cyclically. The relevant sets of rules can be stated as follows:

(88) a. $[_V \text{ X}] \rightarrow [_V[_V \text{ X}] \text{ -:}]$
interpretation: the subject of the verb in the domain of
/-:/ has the features $[+\text{I}, -\text{II}]$

b. $[_V \text{ X}] \rightarrow [_V[_V \text{ X}] \text{ -nki}]$
interpretation: the subject of the verb in the domain of
/-nki/ has the features $[-\text{I}, +\text{II}]$

c. $[_V \text{ X}] \rightarrow [_V[_V \text{ X}] \text{ -n}]$
interpretation: the subject of the verb in the domain of
/-n/ has the features $[-\text{I}, -\text{II}]$

d. $[_V \text{ X}] \rightarrow [_V[_V \text{ X}] \text{ -nchi}]$
interpretation: the subject of the verb in the domain of
/-nchi/ has the features $[+\text{I}, +\text{II}]$

e. $[_V \text{ X}] \rightarrow [_V[_V \text{ X}] \text{ -ma-}]$
interpretation: the object of the verb in the domain of
/-ma-/ has the feature $[\text{aI}]$

f. $[_V X] \rightarrow [_V[_V X]$ -shu-]

interpretation: the object of the verb in the domain of /-shu-/ has the features $[-I, +II]$

g. $[_V X] \rightarrow [_V[_V X]$ -q]

interpretation: the subject of the verb in the domain of /-q/ has the features $[+I, -II]$, and the object of the verb has the features $[-I, +II]$

These seven word formation rules and interpretive rules provide most of the information needed in the paradigm. At this point, no constraints on their application have been formulated, however.

(b) Constraints on Suffix Order. To ensure the right output, we need several negative output filters. Here the feature $[+F_m]$ will stand for the suffixes $\{/$-ma-$/$, /-shu-/$\}$, the feature $[+F_n]$ for the suffixes relating to tense, and the feature $[+F_o]$ for the suffixes $\{/$-:/, /-nki/, /-n/, /-nchi/, /-q/$\}$. These features can be thought of as morphological features specifying classes of suffixes, similar to the feature assigned to all suffixes which trigger vowel lowering in section 4.2. Given the features, we need a number of filters:

(89) a. $*[+F_n]$ $[+F_m]$

b. $*[+F_o]$ $[+F_n]$

c. $*[+F_o]$ $[+F_m]$

d. $*[+F_i]$ $[+F_i]$, where i ranges over $\{m, n, o\}$

Filter d. would be local, as formulated here, since a. through c. would filter out non-local configurations of two identically marked suffixes.

The critical reader might remark that a. through c. are together the notational variant of a positive output filter similar to phrase structure rule (82), i.e.:

(90) $[+F_m]$ $[+F_n]$ $[+F_o]$

Note, however, that we would be dealing with a positive output constraint specifying the order among optional elements. Moreover, the status of positive output constraints in generative grammar is not quite clear. I will let the matter rest here since it does not bear crucially upon the argument.

(c) Filters on Interpretations. Even given these filters, the model as presented so far overgenerates considerably, specifically, the following forms are generated:

(91) a. *-∅-∅
      b. -∅-:
      c. -∅-nki
      d. -∅-n
      e. -∅-nchik
      f. -∅-q
      g. *-ma-∅
      h. *-ma-:
      i. -ma-nki
      j. -ma-n
      k. -ma-nchi
      l. *-ma-q
      m. *-shu-∅
      n. *-shu-:
      o. -shu-nki
      p. *-shu-n
      q. *-shu-nchi
      r. *-shu-q

Of these 18 forms, only nine actually occur. Furthermore, a simple additive model of semantic interpretation would not make the right predictions. Consider, for instance, k., /V-ma-nchi/. This should be interpreted as [+I, −II object, +I, +II subject]. It actually means [+I, +II object, −I, −II subject]. How do we arrive at these results?

First of all, we need a filter ruling out forms without subject marking. I argue in Muysken (1979) that this rule may be a specific instance of the Nominative Island Condition, but that is not relevant here. We would like to make the generalisation:

(92) Verbs without subject marking are ill-formed.

This filter rules out a., g., and m.

Then we need a filter which rules out a positive specification for a person feature for both subject and object, comparable to filter (89d). The major difference between the earlier filter and this one is that (84) was formulated as a filter on base configurations, and was not local in the strict sense, while this filter will be formulated as a condition on Logical Form, where different locality principles hold.

In any case, this filter would rule out, at least in the present formulation of the interpretive rules, h., k., l., o., q., and r. which would only partially be the right result. How then can we formulate the interpretive rules to ensure the right result?

Two assumptions are needed:

(a) the interpretive rules for subject marking do not refer to subject explicitly;

(b) the two suffixes /-ma-/ and /-shu-/ carry an idiosyncratic feature [+collapse].

Consider the first assumption. It would involve reformulating the interpretive rules (88a-d). I will only give the example of the first one, (88a); the others would be similar:

(93)   interpretation: an argument of the verb in the domain of /-:/ has the features [+I, −II]

Now this seemingly has the wrong results. Consider:

(94)   maqa-:
       hit 1s

This only means *I hit x*, and not *y hits me*. Thus (93) would make too wide predictions. Note, however, that the second interpretation of (94) is independently filtered out by the filter prohibiting verbs without subject marking. Thus the reformulation of the interpretive rules does not have undesirable results in the case of simple subject marking. (We do face the problem that subjects are defined here as potential arguments of a verb.)

The second assumption relates to the feature 'collapse', which characterises the suffixes /-ma-/ and /-shu-/. Consider the cases (91k) and (91o):

(91)   k.   V-ma-nchi $\begin{bmatrix} + & - \\ + & - \end{bmatrix}$ object 4, subject 3

       o.   V-shu-nki $\begin{bmatrix} - & - \\ + & - \end{bmatrix}$ object 2, subject 3

Here the subject marking is interpreted as object marking, which has been made possible by assumption (a) above.

The collapsing rule, triggered by /-ma-/ and /-shu-/, collapses the features of the subject marking onto the object marking, leaving the subject specified negatively as [−I, −II]:

(95) [+obj] tense [−obj]   1   2   3
      αI   αI   →   αI   −I
      βII   βII   βII −II
      where the [+obj] position need only be specified for either
      ±I or ±II or both.

Rule (95) has the following effect on (91k):

V-ma-nchi

cycle 1   ——————   V-$\begin{bmatrix} +\text{obj} \\ +\text{I} \end{bmatrix}$

cycle 2   ——————   V-$\begin{bmatrix} +\text{obj} \\ +\text{I} \end{bmatrix}$ $\begin{bmatrix} -\text{obj} \\ +\text{I} \\ +\text{II} \end{bmatrix}$

collapse   ——————   V-$\begin{bmatrix} +\text{obj} \\ +\text{I} \\ +\text{II} \end{bmatrix}$ $\begin{bmatrix} -\text{obj} \\ -\text{I} \\ -\text{II} \end{bmatrix}$

Here the features of /-nchi-/ are collapsed with those of /-ma-/. Note that the collapsing rule needs to be formulated in such a way that the output is not ruled out by the constraint on uninterpreted subjects: when the feature specifications of the two sets of suffixes are collapsed, by convention the subject becomes [−I, −II].

Quite similarly, in (91o), the features of /-nki-/ are collapsed with those of /-shu-/. Collapsing is only possible if the suffixes involved do not have a non-identical interpretation.

In the case of /-shu-/, this means that it can only be combined with /-nki/, since that form has the identical person features. Thus the ungrammaticality of n., p., and q. is explained. With /-ma-/, the impossibility of collapsing does not lead to ungrammaticality, but to 'uncollapsed', separate interpretation. Thus we could say that with /-ma-/ collapsing is optional, and with /-shu-/ it is obligatory.

The only two cases which have not been explained yet are h. and r. h. should be collapsible, but is ungrammatical. I have no explanation for this fact. Quite possibly, r. can be ruled out independently, in that the collapsing rule cannot operate on the feature complex belonging to /-q/.

The word formation approach is superior to the abstract morpheme approach on several counts. First of all, by relying on general conditions of interpretation a great deal of economy is achieved. Second, the arbitrary context specifications in the context sensitive spelling rules or in the readjustment rules have been replaced by a general collapsing convention subject to several independent conditions. Third, it is possible to formulate collapsing convention (95) as operating on the level of Logical Form, where the intervening tense/taxis variable is irrelevant to locality conditions.

In the sections 6.5, 6.6, and 6.7 additional arguments will be given for the analysis of inflectional suffixes as generated by word formation rules.

6.5 Person Marking in Agentive and Gerundial Clauses

Person marking in agentive and gerundial clauses provides independent evidence for the reformulation of person interpretation rules as sketched in the previous section. We find the following paradigms:

(96)   **GERUNDIAL**

maqa-shu-r-(ni)-yki	'subject 3, object 2'
maqa ma -r-(ni)-yki	'subject 2, object 1'
maqa-ma -r-(ni)-nchi	'subject 3, object 4'
maqa-ma -r } maqa-ma -r-(ni)-: }	'subject X, object 1'
maqa- -r-(ni)-**yki**	'subject X, object 2'
maqa- -r-(ni)-**n**	'subject X, object 3'
maqa- -r-(ni)-**nchi**	'subject X, object 4'

(97)   *ι*   **AGENTIVE**

maqa-shu-q-(ni)-yki	'subject 3, object 2'
maqa-ma -q-(ni)-nchi	'subject 3, object 4'
maqa-ma -q } maqa-ma -q-(ni)-: } maqa- -q-(ni)-: }	'subject X, object 1'
maqa- -q-(ni)-**yki**	'subject X, object 2'
maqa- -q-(ni)-**n**	'subject X, object 3'
maqa- -q-(ni)-**nchi**	'subject X, object 4'

The forms which are not boldface correspond more or less to parts of the non-subordinate paradigm given above. The boldface ones show a different pattern however. Let us consider the paradigms more closely. The suffix presented in parentheses is a euphonic suffix irrelevant here. The suffixes /-q/ and /-r/ mark subordination, and their peculiarity is that the subject of the clause marked by them can be inferred from the arguments of the main clause. In the case of /-r/, subjects of main and subordinate clauses need to be identical, and in the case of /-q/ a more complicated set of inference relations hold.

The effect of both markers is then that overt subject marking of the subordinate verb (marked with /-q/ or /-r/) is optional. This is precisely the situation in which we would expect 'subject' marking (i.e. the class of suffixes {-:, -nki, -n, -nchi}) to refer to objects, since subject can be specified independently of the person markers (in the above paradigm by X). Indeed the boldface forms in (96) and (97) show that 'subject' marking can refer to objects, in those situations where the subject is specified independently.

6.6 *The Future Tense Paradigm*

While the past tense and the sudden discovery tense are relatively regular, the future tense paradigm is highly irregular, in that tense and person are collapsed; the present tense is repeated here on the right:

(98) maqa-sha(q)   'subject 1'   maqa-:
      maqa-nki   'subject 2'   maqa-nki
      maqa-nqa   'subject 3'   maqa-n
      maqa-shun   'subject 4'   maqa-nchi
      maqa-sha-yki   'subject 1, object 2'   maqa-q
      maqa-shu-nki   'subject 3, object 2'   maqa-shu-nki
      maqa-ma-nki   'subject 2, object 1'   maqa-ma-nki
      maqa-ma-nqa   'subject 3, object 1'   maqa-ma-n
      maqa-ma:-shun   'subject 3, object 4'   maqa-ma-nchi

In part this paradigm parallels the present tense paradigm discussed earlier, particularly as far as the distribution of /-ma-/ and /-shu-/ is concerned.

Most of the differences appear in the forms unmarked for object. We notice that the future person suffixes include both the tense and the person specification. In the abstract morpheme framework this fact would have to be expressed through a complex collapsing rule of the following type:

(99) Tense   Person   suffix$_q$

$$[\alpha F] \quad \begin{bmatrix} \beta I \\ \gamma II \end{bmatrix} \quad \rightarrow \quad \begin{bmatrix} \alpha F \\ \beta I \\ \gamma II \end{bmatrix}$$

Presumably in the case of the 2nd person, the future tense feature would be neutralised.

In the word formation framework, we would need interpretive rules of the following type (exemplified here with the 1st person suffix /-sha(q)/):

(100) $[_V X] \Rightarrow [_V[_V X] \text{sha(q)}]$

         Interpret the verb as $[_V \begin{bmatrix} \alpha F \\ +I \\ -II \end{bmatrix}]$

In some sense, of course, (99) and (100) constitute mirror-images of each other. Note, however, that in the word formation framework no claims are made about the underlying linear order of the features. Their order in the past and sudden discovery paradigms between object and subject marker would only be a particular morphological fact.

Consider now the 4th person subject and object marker, /-shun/. Again, we find that the 4th person transfers to object marking in the context of /-ma-/, independently of whether the suffix involved is /-nchi/, as in the present tense paradigm, or /-shun/, as in the future tense paradigm. Thus we find another argument for a word formation analysis involving interpretive rules which collapse feature configurations at the level of Logical Form.

6.7 Plural Marking

An example of a process which can be handled easily by a theory of WFR, but not by a theory involving grammatical morphemes, is plural formation. There are three suffixes, which occur in morphologically specified environments, to which I will return later:

(101)   -pa:ku-

         -ri-

         -rka-

One of them is selected within a given context, but they do not occur in the same position in the string of suffixes. /-ri-/, for instance, follows the aspect marker /-ru-/, while /-rka-/ precedes the aspect marker /-ya-/. In other respects the aspect markers among themselves show a similar distribution.

Therefore it is not possible without later shifting rules to generate plural as one category, either preceding or following aspect:

(102) $?\bar{V} \rightarrow V$ plural   aspect   tense   person
         ?   aspect   plural

The WFR theory, which just affixes the plural markers in (101) in given contexts, and assigns the feature [plural] to the resulting form, encounters none of these difficulties. At the same time it is able to handle the distribution of the aspect markers by involving the feature [aspect] in the context specifications of the relevant WFRs.

Thus we see that the WFR theory is able to handle all the facts adequately without sacrificing the possibility to make the same generalisations that a PS theory with grammatical morphemes can make.

6.8 Conclusion

By allowing a very general rule of person interpretation, which does not make reference to subjects, to interact with two general interpretative conditions, one prohibiting uninterpreted subjects (Nominative Island Condition?), and one prohibiting an identical positive feature specification for both subjects and objects (Disjoint Reference Condition?), we have provided a coherent account of Quechua inflectional processes. While the abstract morpheme framework can only provide *ad hoc* solutions for the irregular cases in (87), and for the gerundial and agentive paradigms in (96)–(97), the word formation and interpretive model as sketched can give general solutions. Also, the locality principle of strict subjacency can be partially maintained even for person marking, since the constraints formulated under the interpretive model operate on the level of Logical Form (cf. Muysken, 1979) where different locality principles hold.

7. The Internal Structure of the Lexicon and the Position of the Lexicon in the Grammar

The account given above of Quechua word structure has made it quite clear that the lexicon is organised in a way quite similar to syntax; we must distinguish:

(a)   word formation rules, the application of which is constrained by local filters, and which create hierarchical structure;

(b) readjustment rules of various sorts, the application of which
     is constrained by the *c*-command configuration;

(c) interpretive rules, which operate cyclically on the output of
     the word formation rules.

I would like to argue that the readjustment rules operate independently of the interpretive rules, so that we find the following
picture:

(103)   **WORD FORMATION**

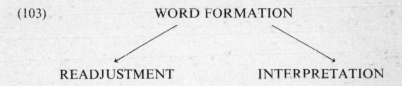

READJUSTMENT   INTERPRETATION

An argument for having the morphological readjustment rules
(truncation, allomorphy, etc.) apply independently of the semantic
interpretation of the verb form is provided by the interaction of
medial and causative in Ecuadorian Quechua. There we find /-ri-/
(medial) and /-chi-/ (causative) in forms such as:

(104) a.   riku-n
            see 3
            He sees.
       b.   riku-**ri**-n
            He is seen./He appears.
       c.   riku-**chi**-n
            He causes to see./He causes to appear.
       d.   *riku-**ri**-**chi**-n
       e.   *riku-**chi**-**ri**-n

The ungrammaticality of d. and e., combined with the ambiguity
of c., which includes the meaning which d. would have had following
the normal rules of semantic interpretation, we may postulate a rule
of /-ri-/ deletion in a specific morphological context:

(105) ri]$_V$ chi]$_V$ $\Rightarrow \emptyset$ 2

Rule (105) would apply to the already interpreted form. The surface
form (c) would have two underlying sources: the causative of both a.
and b., and would hence be ambiguous.

Quite similar is the case discussed in section 4.4, where a rule deleting the 3rd person marker in the context of the past tense marker is formulated. The interpretation of the past tense paradigm proceeds independently of this deletion rule.

In Muysken (1979) the relationship between lexical interpretive rules and the syntactic interpretive rules is discussed. I have nothing to say here about the interaction between morphological readjustment rules and various types of phonological rules. Neither will I enter into the debate about deep versus surface lexical insertion, since the outcome of that depends crucially upon the theoretical assumptions one wants to make. It may be a trivial question.

The central role that word structure plays in the grammar of Quechua appears in the extent to which there is interaction between syntactic and morphological interpretive rules. In this paper I have sketched a strong lexicalist account of verbal morphology in Quechua, arguing that only in the case of the independent suffixes is there evidence for phrase structure generation, and that all other suffixes should be derived by WFRs. It was argued that word formation is subject to a substantial number of restrictions and is tightly organised, following a set of general principles. The principles governing word structure are the same ones that govern phrase structure, and presumably, other types of hierarchical linguistic structure. The particular way in which word structure is created, however, differs from the way in which phrase structure is created, and this difference shows up in the way that the general principles of linguistic structure apply.

While in the generative study of syntax it was possible quite early to distinguish a number of central phenomena (such as *Wh* Movement) from peripheral ones, the same type of distinction is much harder to draw in the study of morphology. This is probably the reason why the generative study of word structure has barely started on a serious basis. It seems that the basic outlines of word structure, such as have been sketched in this paper and in the work cited, are obscured by at least two factors: lexicalisation and paradigmatisation.

Lexicalisation, the incorporation of affixes into roots, tends to be destructive of hierarchical structure, in the sense that cyclic boundaries disappear. Often, the lexicalised combination assumes an idiosyncratic meaning and shows erratic phonological behaviour. Since morphology is so intimately tied to the lexicon, lexicalisation is quite frequent, to the extent that in some languages most morphological structures are lexicalised. The importance of the study of

Quechua word structure on the other hand, and of the morphology of languages comparable to Quechua, is that is not the case for Quechua. We do find a great many cases of idiosyncratic lexicalisation, but also many processes which do not seem to be determined by the characteristics of individual words.

Similarly, the formation of inflectional paradigms tends to be destructive of hierarchical word structure. We have noticed that the cases where the subjacency and c-command conditions are violated most frequently involve the morphological categories of tense/taxis, person, and number. From the morphological point of view, these categories form a widely disparate set:

(106)

PLURAL	OBJECT	TENSE	PERSON
-pa:ku-			-:
-rka- ...	-ma-	-ra-	-nki
-ri-	-shu-		-n
			-nchi

From the point of view of performance, of speech production and perception, however, they form a coherent class, in that, together, they form the Quechua paradigm, in the widest sense of the word.

From the point of view of the morphological system, which mostly functions to relate individual lexical items to each other, the paradigm constitutes the marked case: a whole set of words is related to each other at once, and therefore subjacency is violated. A number of suffixes tend to be viewed as grouped together, rather than as the product of individual affixation processes. This constitutes a powerful argument for the psychological, though not morphological, reality of the paradigm in Quechua. While most cases of lexicalised and paradigmatised morphology continue to be constrained by general principles of word structure, it is here that we can expect to find most counter-examples.

Note

* Whenever Quechua examples are given in this paper without further specification, they are from Adelaar (1977). A first discussion of some of the issues raised can be found in my thesis (1977), chapter V. I am grateful for profitable discussion of the ideas raised here with Willem Adelaar, Hans den Besten, G. N. Clements, and the members of the seminar on Quechua grammar in the spring of 1979, and particularly grateful to Frank Heny for his extensive comments on several drafts.

References

Adelaar, W. F. H. (1977), *Tarma Quechua. Grammar, Texts, Dictionary*, The Peter de Ridder Press, Lisse, The Netherlands

Aronoff, M. (1976), *Word Formation in Generative Grammar*, (*Linguistic Inquiry Monographs I.*) MIT Press, Cambridge, Massachusetts

Chomsky, N. (1965), *Aspects of the Theory of Syntax*, MIT Press, Cambridge, Massachusetts

Chomsky, N. and M. Halle (1968), *The Sound Pattern of English*, Holt, Rinehart & Winston, New York

Emonds, J. (1978), 'Grammatical Formative Insertion in Minimal Post-Transformational Domains', presented at the GLOW Conference on Local Processes, Amsterdam

Halle, M. and J. R. Vergnaud (1978), 'Stress Patterns, Local Conditions on Metrical Trees, and Universal Grammar', presented at the GLOW Conference on Local Processes, Amsterdam

Lefebvre, C. and C. Dubuisson (1978), 'Les règles d'accord dans la théorie transformationelle', presented at the GLOW Conference on Local Processes, Amsterdam. A later version in English is 'The Status of Agreement Rules in a Generative Grammar', Unpublished paper

Muysken, P. C. (1977), *Syntactic Developments in the Verb Phrase of Ecuadorian Quechua*, Foris Publications, Dordrecht

—— (1979), 'Quechua Causatives and Logical Form. A Case Study in Markedness', presented at the GLOW Conference on Markedness, Pisa

Pike, K. (1949), 'A Problem in Morphology-Syntax Division', *Acta Linguistica Hafniensia* 5, 125–36

Reece Allen, M. (1978), *Morphological Investigations*, Doctoral dissertation, University of Connecticut at Storrs, Connecticut

Selkirk, L. (1972), *The Phrase Phonology of English and French*, Doctoral dissertation, MIT, Cambridge, Massachusetts

Siegel, D. (1978), 'The Adjacency Constraint and the Theory of Morphology', presented at the VIIIth NELS Conference, Amherst, Massachusetts

Appendix: List of Symbols and Abbreviations Used in The Glosses

1	first person
2	second person
3	third person
4	first person plural inclusive
$\pm$I	$\pm$ speaker
$\pm$II	$\pm$ listener
AC	accusative
AF	affirmative
AG	agentive
CAU	causative
DIR	directional
DUR	durative

INST	instrumental
NEG	negation
PA	past tense
PER	perfective
PL	plural
POT	potential
Q	question
RE	reflexive
REC	reciprocal
SEQ	sequential
SUB	subordinate
TOP	topic

With person markings:

ob	object
su	subject
s	singular

Notes on Contributors

Noam Chomsky: Professor of Linguistics, Department of Linguistics and Philosophy, Massachusetts Institute of Technology, Cambridge, Massachusetts.

Leland George: completed his PhD dissertation at Massachusetts Institute of Technology in 1980.

Jaklin Kornfilt: Graduate student in the Department of Linguistics, Harvard University, Cambridge, Massachusetts.

Luigi Rizzi: Lecturer in the Department of Linguistics, University of Calabria, Italy.

Eric J. Reuland: Senior Lecturer in the Institute for General Linguistics, Groningen University, The Netherlands.

Richard S. Kayne: Professor of Linguistics, University of Paris, Vincennes.

Stephen Harlow: Lecturer in the Department of Language, University of York, England.

Joan Maling: Associate Professor in the Linguistics Program, Brandeis University, Waltham, Massachusetts.

Annie Zaenen: Post-doctoral Fellow in the Center for Cognitive Science, Massachusetts Institute of Technology.

Pieter Muysken: Lecturer in the Institute for General Linguistics, University of Amsterdam.

General Index

Agreement: AG and indexing 218; anaphoric versus pronominal 183; as anaphor 38; co-index subsumes 185; Dutch 168–72; finiteness and 34–5, 105, 119–27; NIC replaces for PRO 171; RESNIC and 218; Turkish 105, 115–17; Welsh 219–21, indexed 41, optional pronouns and 219–21, possessives 221, prepositions 220–1

anaphor 6, 57; Agreement as 38, 183; broad sense 6; narrow sense 11; trace of L-Tous excluded 194; trace of *Wh* Movement excluded 30, 63, 153, 194, 199; trace of *Wh* Movement possibly included 29, 89

A-over-A 50; and ECP 208; restricting infinitival relatives 68

AUX Preposing 134, 154

Binding ix, 4–18; by co-arguments 33; theory 4, and compositionality 17, Pisa revision of 32

Case: assignment 19, 159–60 adjectives excluded 80–1, applied to obligatory control 78–87, at S-structure 22, by empty Tense 161, defined 75–6, exceptional 24, government and 23, in infinitive subjects 23, Move NP and 21, 36, 142, 161, 176, Nominative 23, 75, 136, 140, post-verbal subjects 140, 153, prepositional adjective objects 99, Tense and 23, to lexical NP only 161, 176, PRO 99, to *Wh* Movement and 23, 89; Turkish 108–12

c-command 11, 57; French, definition for 205; government defined by 23; morphology and 43, 325, 282; re-adjustment rules and 300–5; restricting *Wh* Movement 51

clitics: French 192–4, 206, 219; Italian 131–3, 137–8, 219; Welsh 219–20, 228–9

Co-index 56, 248; *see also* indexing

COMP *see* complementisers

complementisers: escape hatch 62; *for* as complementiser/preposition 82; French **que-qui** 200–4, 208; indexed 201–3, 207; Irish **aL** and **aN** 243–6; Irish negative 251; Welsh and 'doubly-filled-COMP' filter 249; $\emptyset$ 68, 78; Welsh y and **a** 240–8

compositionality: and Binding theory 13–18; and Opacity conditions 17

conditions: on anaphora 57; on LF 20, 28–31

construal 56; as co-index 56; Binding conditions and 30; rules 20, 27, 53

Control 30; indexing determines 94–6; obligatory 53, 67–72, Case assignment analysis 78–87, filter analysis 54, in French **que-qui** construction 200–3, not predicted by opacity 54; rule 85; Turkish 122–3

core grammar 49

deletion 52; conditions on 97; in COMP 100; in OB framework 20, 27; 'obligatory' 71–2, 228–9, in relatives explains Welsh-French contrast 249

dependent terms 6–10

disjoint reference 90–6; morphological counterpart 322; Turkish 121

domain 11, 57

ECP *see* Empty Category Principle

Empty Category Principle 39, 216–19; A-over-A and 208; definition 217; French clitics and 199; French object clitics and 219; NIC compared with 216–17; PRO deletion and 218; **que-qui** alternation explained by 200–4; Welsh y and **a** explained by 240–8

331

Selective Author Index

335

Language Index